A
DICTIONARY

OF

FOREIGN MUSICAL TERMS

AND

HANDBOOK

OF

ORCHESTRAL INSTRUMENTS

BY

TOM S. WOTTON

LEIPZIG

BREITKOPF & HÄRTEL

1907

Published April 1907.
Privilege of copyright in the United States
reserved under the Act approved March 3,
1905, by BREITKOPF & HÄRTEL, Leipzig.

PREFACE.

In these days of inexpensive full-scores, when almost everyone, with any pretence to be considered musical, possesses copies of their favourite works in the original orchestral form, some such dictionary as the present seems necessary. The previous dictionaries of musical terms were published before the cult of the "miniature" score began, and before the employment of musical directions in the composer's own language became so universal, and thus, many orchestral terms were omitted, as not being of sufficient general interest, and the explanation of many German indications (now in everyday use) was considered unnecessary. Even in Italian (the musician's language until recent years), alterations have taken place, which existing dictionaries have not noted, and hence while *Clarino*, for example, is explained as being a name for a trumpet, nothing is said as to the word being now employed in modern Italian scores as equivalent to *Clarinetto*, and terms such as *Clarone* are not mentioned at all.

The original idea of the present work was to include simply orchestral terms and instruments, but as it was obvious that for the proper understanding of a full-score, translations of indications of *tempo* and expression were necessary, these were added: thus the book, it is to be hoped, will prove as serviceable to the pianist and vocalist as to the reader of full-scores, or the player on some orchestral instrument. Obsolete terms are not given as a rule, although in many cases they have been introduced, either the better to explain their modern meaning, or because, although obsolete in general use, they are to be found in scores, which are still living. That every term employed in modern music is included, can scarcely be expected: many composers, fearful lest their ideas should be misunderstood, mark some fresh indication every few bars, and so, even if the number of musical works were less than it is, the number of musical expressions would still be enormous.

Owing to various reasons, the chief of which being perhaps the translation of foreign musical works into English by persons ignorant of musical technicalities, certain errors of nomenclature have crept into even our standard English treatises, and therefore occasional divergences may be discovered between the explanations given in the following pages and those found in one or other of these standard works. It is almost needless to state, that these variations from consecrated meanings have been given only after due consideration, and a careful collation of the various authorities, with an ultimate appeal to the scores themselves.

I here take the opportunity of tendering my best thanks to my friends Ad. Schloesser and Walter F. H. Blandford not only for many helpful suggestions, but for having been good enough to undertake the ungrateful task of overlooking the proofs.

London, 1907.

TOM S. WOTTON.

BIBLIOGRAPHY
OF THE PRINCIPAL WORKS OF REFERENCE CONSULTED.

Works in the English Language.

BERLIOZ, H.	*Treatise on Orchestration (translated by Mary Cowden Clarke; revised by Joseph Bennett).*
CORDER, F.	*The Orchestra.*
DAY, C. R.	*Catalogue of the Musical Instruments in the Royal Military Exhibition, London, 1890.*
GROVE, G.	*Dictionary of Music (1st edition); ditto (2nd edition, edited by J. A. Fuller-Maitland).*
HILES, J.	*Catechism of the Organ.*
	Dictionary of Musical Terms.
HOPKINS, E. J.	*The Organ.*
KAPPEY, J. A.	*Military Music.*
MACFARREN, SIR G. A.	*Six Lectures on Harmony.*
NIECKS, F.	*A concise Dictionary of Musical Terms.*
PROUT, E.	*Harmony, Counterpoint, Fugue, &. (separate volumes).*
	The Orchestra.
SCHUBERTH, J.	*Musical Handbook.*
STAINER, J. & BARRETT, W. A.	*Dictionary of Musical Terms.*
	Encyclopædia Britannica (10th edition).
	Standard English Dictionary (Funk & Wagnalls).

Works in the French Language.

BERLIOZ, H.	*Traité d'Instrumentation et d'Orchestration.*
DELVEDEZ, E. M. E.	*Curiosités Musicales.*
GEVAERT, F. A.	*Nouveau Traité d'Instrumentation.*
	Cours Méthodique d'Orchestration.
GUIRAUD, E.	*Traité pratique d'Instrumentation.*
JACQUOT, A.	*Dictionnaire des Instruments de Musique.*
KASTNER, G.	*Manuel général de Musique Militaire.*

LAVIGNAC, A.   *La Musique et les Musiciens.*
LAVOIX, H.   *Histoire de l'Instrumentation.*
                         Histoire de la Musique.
LUSSY, M.   *Traité de l'Expression Musicale.*
MAHILLON, V. C.   *Catalogue descriptif et analytique du Musée Instrumental du Conservatoire Royal de Musique de Bruxelles.*
                         Eléments d'Acoustique.
PARÈS, G.   *Traité d'Instrumentation et d'Orchestration à l'usage de Musiques Militaires.*
ROUGNON, P.   *Dictionnaire Musical des Locutions étrangères.*
WIDOR, C. M.   *Technique de l'Orchestre Moderne.*

Works in the German Language.

BERLIOZ, H.   *Instrumentationslehre (herausgegeben von F. Weingartner); dieselbe (ergänzt und revidiert von R. Strauss).*
BREMER, F.   *Handlexikon der Musik.*
HOFMANN, R.   *Praktische Instrumentationslehre.*
                         Katechismus der Musikinstrumente.
KOCH, H. C.   *Musikalisches Lexikon.*
LOBE, J. C.   *Lehrbuch der musikalischen Komposition: Instrumentation.*
MARX, A. B.   *Musikalische Kompositionslehre.*
RICHTER, E. F.   *Katechismus der Orgel.*
RIEMANN, H.   *Musik-Lexikon.*
WITTING, C.   *Wörterbuch der in der Musik gebräuchlichen Ausdrücke.*
                         Encyklopädisches Deutsch-Englisches Wörterbuch (Muret-Sanders).

Works in the Italian Language.

GALLI, A.   *Manuale del Capo-Musica.*
LICHTENTHAL, P.   *Dizionario e Bibliografia della Musica.*
PROUT, E.   *Strumentazione (versione italiana di Ricci).*
SANDI, F.   *Trattato di Strumentazione Pratica.*
                         Italian-English Dictionary (Millhouse & Bracciforti).

The Catalogues of the principal English, French, German and Italian makers of Musical Instruments have also been consulted, as have numerous articles in English and foreign musical magazines.

LIST OF ABBREVIATIONS USED IN THIS WORK.

Abbr.	*Abbreviation.*	Lat.	*Latin.*
adj.	*adjective.*	masc.	*masculine.*
adv.	*adverb.*	past part.	*past participle.*
dat.	*dative.*	plur.	*plural.*
Eng.	*English.*	pron.	*pronoun.*
fem.	*feminine.*	Rem.	*Remark.*
Fr.	*French.*	sing.	*singular.*
Ger.	*German.*	Sp.	*Spanish.*
Gk.	*Greek.*	subs.	*substantive.*
It.	*Italian.*	Sup.	*Superlative.*

GENERAL REMARKS.

1. The part of the verb usually given is that which is ordinarily met with in scores, although often it has been deemed advisable to give the infinitive also. It is to be noted, that in many languages the infinitive is at times used in the sense of the imperative, as:- *prendre la flûte* instead of *prenez la flûte*.

2. Both in Italian and German (and more especially in the latter), the spelling has been so altered within recent years that it is impossible to give all the forms of certain words. Where feasible, the letters which are now usually omitted are placed between brackets, thus:- *get(h)eilt*; in other cases, the two spellings are placed in their alphabetical order, and occasionally, when in spite of differences (*e. g. Controfagotto* for *Contrafagotto*), the resemblance is such as to lead to no misunderstanding, the altered spelling is omitted.

3. In modern German, Roman type is so often used that its employment throughout this dictionary needs no apology. The sign for the double *s* (*ß*) has been frequently introduced, although at the present time its use cannot be considered as universal.

4. Since in a work of this description it is impossible to enter into the differences that are found in similar instruments of various makers, it must not be taken that these differences do not exist or that they are of necessity unimportant. Because a *Heckelphon* is described as a baritone oboe, it must not be supposed that Heckel's invention is identical with the *Hautbois baryton* of the French maker, Lorée; and because a *Pelittone* is described as a saxhorn, that therefore Pelitti's instrument is precisely the same as that of Sax.

5. As it is often convenient to represent the pitch of notes other than by music type, it is as well to give here the method adopted in the following pages, adding in brackets some other methods of designating the notes of any particular octave.

C_2 to B_2. (32ft octave; CCC to BBB.)

to

8va bassa...

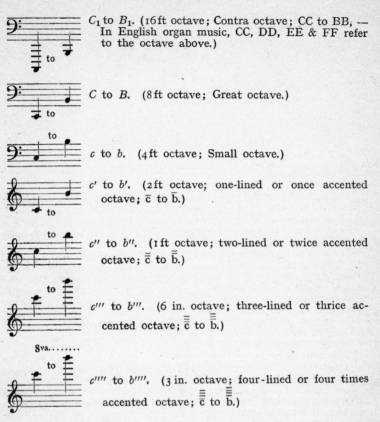

C_1 to B_1. (16 ft octave; Contra octave; CC to BB, — In English organ music, CC, DD, EE & FF refer to the octave above.)

C to B. (8 ft octave; Great octave.)

c to b. (4 ft octave; Small octave.)

c' to b'. (2 ft octave; one-lined or once accented octave; $\bar{c}$ to $\bar{b}$.)

c'' to b''. (1 ft octave; two-lined or twice accented octave; $\bar{\bar{c}}$ to $\bar{\bar{b}}$.)

c''' to b'''. (6 in. octave; three-lined or thrice accented octave; $\bar{\bar{\bar{c}}}$ to $\bar{\bar{\bar{b}}}$.)

c'''' to b''''. (3 in. octave; four-lined or four times accented octave; $\bar{\bar{\bar{\bar{c}}}}$ to $\bar{\bar{\bar{\bar{b}}}}$.)

Note. Expressions not found under the initial word of the sentence will often be found under one or other of the principal words of the phrase.

A

A. The 6th note of the normal scale of C major; in Fr. and It. it is called *la*. The highest string of the violoncello and viola, and 2nd string of the violin.

    AA. Sometimes found for A_1.

    AAA. Sometimes found for A_2.

A (Fr.). To, at, in, with, etc.

    A chaque accord. With every chord; direction for using the damper pedal in piano playing.

    A cylindres. With cylinders. *v.* Valves.

    A défaut de. In the absence of. *A défaut de clarinette basse*, in the absence of a bass clarinet.

    A demi jeu.
    A demi voix. } With half the power of the voice or instrument.

    A deux, à 2. In two parts. More often used in the contrary sense, and meaning that 2 instruments of a kind (2 flutes, 2 bassoons, etc.) are to play the same part.

    A deux cordes. On two strings.

    A deux huit. In $^2/_8$ time.

    A deux mains. For two hands.

    A deux quatre. In $^2/_4$ time.

    A deux temps. In $^2/_2$ time, or, generally, in any binary rhythm.

    A grande orchestre. For full orchestra.

    A la, à l'. To the, etc: often meaning "in the style of".

    A l'écossaise. In the Scotch style.

    A la corde. The bow kept well on the strings; *legato*.

    A la dernière mesure. At the last bar.

    A la fin. At the end.

    A la mesure. In time.

    A la pointe d'archet. With the point of the bow.

    A la polonaise. In the Polish style; in the style of a polonaise.

    A livre ouvert. (Playing) at sight.

    A mesure (battue). In strict time.

    A peine entendu. Scarcely heard.

    A pistons. With pistons. *v.* Valves.

    A première vue. At first sight.

    A quatre mains. For four hands.

    A six temps. In 6 time.

    A un quart de voix. Sung as softly as possible. *v.* Quart.

    A un temps. In one beat.

    A voix sombre. In a gloomy voice.

    A volonté. At will, at one's pleasure; *ad libitum*

A (Ger.). The note A. A♯ is *Ais*; A♭ is *As*.
    A dur. A major.
    A moll. A minor.
    A-Saite. The A string.
A (It.). To, at, with, etc.
    A ballata. In the ballad style.
    A battuta. In strict time.
    A bene placito. At pleasure, *ad libitum*.
    A cappella, a capella. (1) In the style of church music. (2) Compositions are so designated, which are either for voices alone, or in which the instrumental accompaniment is in unison or octaves with the voices. (3) A term sometimes used for *alla breve*.
    A capriccio. At pleasure, capriciously.
    A cinque. In five parts.
    A due, a 2. In two parts. More often used in a contrary sense, and meaning that two instruments play the same part. *cf*. A deux.
    A due corde. On two strings.
    A due mani. For two hands.
    A due voci. For two voices.
    A man(o) dritta. For the right hand.
    A man(o) manca. ⎱ For the left hand.
    A man(o) sinistra. ⎰
    A mezza forza. With half the power of the voice or instrument.
    A mezza voce. With half the power of the voice or instrument, but more soft than loud.
    A mezzo manico. In the middle of the fingerboard.
    A piacere. ⎱ At pleasure, *ad libitum*.
    A piacimento. ⎰
    A poco a poco. Little by little.
    A prima vista. At first sight.
    A primo tempo. In the first (original) tempo.
    A punta d'arco. With the point of the bow.
    A quattro mani. For four hands.
    A quattro parti. For (in) four parts.
    A quattro voci. For four voices.
    A rigore del tempo. In strictest time.
    A scelta del cantante. At the discretion of the singer.
    A sola voce. With the voice alone, *i. e.* without an instrumental accompaniment.
    A suo arbitrio. ⎞
    A suo beneplacimento. ⎟ At one's pleasure, *ad libitum*.
    A suo beneplacito. ⎠
    A suo com(m)odo. At one's convenience.
    a t., a tem. Abbr. of *a tempo*.
    A tempo. In time.
    A tempo com(m)odo. In a convenient time, at a leisurely pace.
    A tempo di gavotta, di minuetto, etc. In the time of a gavotte, minuet, etc.
    A tempo giusto. In exact time.
    A tempo, ma un poco più lento. In time (*i. e.* in the main time of the movement), but a little more slowly.

A tempo ordinario. In ordinary time, *i. e.* in moderate time, neither too fast nor too slow.

A tempo primo. In the first (initial) time.

A tempo rubato. Lit. "in robbed time", *i. e.* time in which, while every bar is of its proper time value, one portion of it may be played faster or slower at the expense of the remaining portion, so that, if the first half be somewhat slackened, the second half is somewhat quickened, and *vice versa.* With indifferent performers, this indication is too often confounded with some expression signifying *ad libitum.*

A tre, a 3. In three parts; or that 3 instruments should play the same part. *cf.* A due.

A tre corde. For three strings. In piano music, contradicting the use of the soft pedal, *una corda.*

A tre mani. For three hands.

A tre parti. In three parts.

A tre voci. For three voices.

A una corda. For one string, and on the piano, indicating the use of the soft pedal.

A vista. At sight.

A voce sola. For voice alone.

Ab initio (Lat.). From the beginning.

Abbandonatamente (It.). } Unrestrainedly; with abandon.
Abbandonevolmente (It.). }

Abbandono (It.). Abandonment; abandon.

Abbassamento (It.). Lowering (subs.).

  Abbassamento di mano. Lowering of the hand.

  Abbassamento di voce. Lowering of the voice.

Abbassando (It.). Lowering, diminishing the sound.

Abbassare (It.). To lower. *I Contrabassi abbasseranno d'un mezzo tono la corda La*, the double-basses must lower the A string a semitone.

Abbellimenti (It.). Embellishments, ornaments.

Abbreviations. (Abbreviations of ordinary words and terms will be found in their alphabetical order. The signs used in modern music will be found under "Signs".)

To save the trouble of writing in full a passage which is immediately repeated, it is often placed between double bars ||: :||, or

bis—written above it. In MS. music and in old engraved scores, bars which occur later are often numbered, and on their repetition, the numbers are alone written in the empty bars, with *come sopra* (as above) sometimes added. The ordinary abbreviations will be understood from the following examples: —

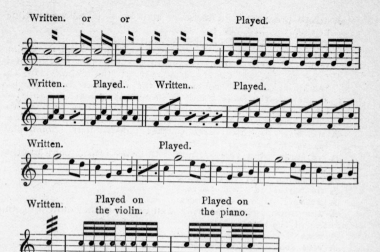

Abbreviaturen (Ger.). Abbreviations.

Abdämpfen (Ger.). To damp, mute.

Abend (Ger.). Evening.

Abendgesang. Evening hymn.

Abendgottesdienst. Evening service; vespers.

Abendlied. An evening song.

Abendmusik. A serenade.

Aber (Ger.). But, at the same time. *p. aber gut markiert,* p. but well accentuated.

Aber bestimmt. But with decision.

Aber deutlich. But distinct.

Aber immer noch Halbe. But still (beating) minims.

Aber immer noch nicht so schnell wie zu Anfang. But still not so fast as at the commencement.

Abflöten (Ger.). To play upon the flute.

Abgerundetes Spiel (Ger.). Finished execution.

Abgesang (Ger.). The last portion of a song.

Abgestoßen (Ger.). Staccato.

Abkürzungen (Ger.). Abbreviations.

Ablösen (Ger.). To detach, separate; in piano playing, to take off a finger.

Abnehmend (Ger.). Decreasing, *diminuendo.*

Abreißen (Ger.). To break off.

Abreißung (Ger.). A sudden pause.

Absatz (Ger.). An interval, a pause; a section, phrase

Abschnitt (Ger.). A section, period.

Absetzen (Ger.). To detach, to play staccato; in piano playing, to raise the finger.

Abspielen (Ger.). To play off. *Vom Blatt abspielen,* to play at sight.

Abstoßen (Ger.). To play a note in a sharp distinct manner; to play staccato.

Abt(h)eilung (Ger.). Division, part, section.

Abwärtsschreiten (Ger.). To descend (a note or an interval).

Abwechselnd (Ger.). Alternating, interchanging; changing (fingers): alternate. *In abwechselnden Chören*, antiphonally; *mit abwechselnden Manualen*, with alternate manuals; *mit Althoboe abwechselnd*, alternating with cor anglais; *mit Kl. Flöte abwechselnd*, interchanging with piccolo.

Abwechselung (Ger.). Alternation, change, modulation.

Abziehen (Ger.). To unstring a violin, etc. The opposite to *aufziehen*.

Acc. Abbr. of accompaniment.

Accablement (Fr.). Dejection, depression.

Accarezzevole (It.). Fond, caressing, flattering.

Accarezzevolmente (It.). Caressingly.

Accel. Abbr. of *accelerando*.

Accelerare (It.). To quicken, accelerate.

Accelerando (It.). Quickening, accelerating (the tempo).
   Accelerando bis . . . . . fest in gewonnenem, lebhaftem Zeitmaß. Quickening until the fast tempo is firmly established.
   Accelerando sin'al fino. Accelerating until the end.

Acceleratemente (It.). Quickly, in haste.

Accelerato (It.). Quickened.

Accentato (It.). Accented.

Accento (It.). Accent.

Accentuare, accentare (It.). To accentuate, lay a stress upon.

Accent(u)ato (It.). ⎫
Accentué (Fr.). ⎬ Accented.

Accentui(e)ren (Ger.). To accentuate.

Acciaccato (It.). Literally "crushed", and applied to a note, which is to be played as an *acciaccatura* (*q. v.*). The term is sometimes used to signify that the notes of a chord on the piano are to be played in rapid succession (considerably faster than an ordinary *arpeggio*) for the sake of greater resonance: it is an effect which is often abused.

Acciaccatura (It.). A term now used for a short *appoggiatura* (*q. v.*), a note rapidly "crushed" into the principal note. Formerly it meant a grace-note, which was played at the same time as the melody note above, but which was instantly released after being struck.

Accidentalen (Ger.). ⎫
Accidenti (It.). ⎪
Accidentien (Ger.). ⎬ Accidentals.
Accidents (Fr.). ⎭

Accolade (Fr.). A brace connecting two or more staves.

Accom., accomp. Abbr. of accompaniment, *accompagnamento*, &c.

Accompagnamento (It.). Accompaniment.

Accompagnare (It.). To accompany.

Accompagnateur (Fr.). An accompanist.

Accompagnato (It.). Accompanied.

Accompagnatore, -trice (It.). An accompanist.

Accompagnement (Fr.). Accompaniment.

Accompagner (Fr.). To accompany.

Accoppiamento (It.). The act of coupling; coupling.

> **Accoppiamento dell' O. C. (organo corale) all' O. E. (organo espressivo).** Choir coupled to swell.

Accoppiato (It.). Coupled.

Accord (Fr.). (1) A chord. (2) Method of tuning an instrument. (3) Agreement in pitch. *Tenir l'accord*, to keep the pitch: *cet instrument est d'accord*, this instrument is in tune.

> **Accord à l'ouvert.** Chord on open strings.
>
> **Accord arpégé, brisé,** *or* **figuré.** A broken chord.
>
> **Accord de septième.** Chord of the seventh.
>
> **Accord de violon.** The notes to which the strings of a violin are tuned.
>
> **Accord parfait.** A common chord.

Accordamento, Accordanza (It.). Agreement in pitch, consonance.

Accordando (It.). Tuning.

Accordante (It.). Harmonising, accordant.

Accordare (It.). To tune.

Accordato (It.). Tuned.

> **Accordati per quinta.** Tuned to the fifth. (A direction sometimes found in Timpani parts, where, when the notes are B♭—F, or C—F, some doubt might exist as to whether F were the lower or higher note.)

Accordatura (It.). Same as the Fr. *accord*.

Accordéon (Fr.). An accordion.

Accorder (Fr.). To tune.

Accordion. A free reed instrument of oblong form, with bellows worked by the left hand, with from 10 to 20 keys (or even more), and with stops for producing "effects" or chords of several notes.

Accordo (It.). A chord.

> **Accordo consono.** Consonant chord.
>
> **Accordo dissono.** Dissonant chord.

Accouplé (Fr.). Coupled. *Tous les claviers accouplés*, all the manuals coupled.

Accouplement (Fr.). Coupling.

Accrescendo (It.). Increasing, augmenting (the sound).

Accrescimento (It.). Augmentation.

Accresciuto (It.). Augmented. ("Augmented" when applied to intervals is *eccedente*.)

Accuratezza (It.). Accuracy, care, attention.

Acht (Ger.). Eight.

Achte (Ger.). Eighth. Sometimes used for *Oktave*, an octave.

Achtel (Ger.). An eighth part. Usually employed for *Achtelnote*, a quaver (the eighth part of a semibreve).

> **Achtelnote.** An eighth note, a quaver.
>
> **Achtelpause.** A quaver rest.
>
> **Achtelschlag.** A quaver beat.
>
> **Die Achtel als vorher die Viertel.** The quavers like the previous crotchets.
>
> **Die Achtel bedeutend ruhiger als soeben die Viertel.** The quavers considerably more tranquil than the previous crotchets.

Die Achtel der Triolen etwas schneller als soeben die gewöhnlichen Achtel. The quavers of the triplets somewhat faster than the preceding ordinary quavers.

Die Achtel etwas langsamer als soeben. The quavers somewhat slower than before.

Die Achtel etwas langsamer als vorher die Halben. The quavers somewhat slower than the previous minims.

Die Achtel viel gemessener als soeben die Viertel. The quavers much more measured (slower) than the previous crotchets.

Die Achtelschläge etwas langsamer als vorher die Halben. The quaver beats somewhat slower than the previous minims.

Act (Ger.). Act. *v.* Akt. *Aufzug* is perhaps now the more ordinary word.

Acte (Fr.). Act.

Acte de cadence. The two chords forming the cadence.

Acteur (Fr.). An actor.

Action musicale (Fr.). Term used by d'Indy for his later operas and corresponding to the Ger. *Handlung* (*q. v.*).

Actrice (Fr.). An actress.

Acutezza (It.). Acuteness; degree of elevation of a sound.

Acuto, -a (It.). Acute, elevated. *Voce acuta*, a high voice.

Ad lib. Abbr. of *ad libitum*.

Ad libitum (Lat.). At the will or pleasure of the executant.

Adagio (It.). adj. Slow. Less slow than *Largo* and slower than *Andante*. Used also as a subs., as "an Adagio" of Mozart.

Adagio assai. Very slow.

Adagio con molt' espressione. Slow with great expression.

Adagio di molto. Very slow.

Adagio molto semplice e cantabile. Slow and in a very simple singing style.

Adagio non troppo lento. Slow, but not too slow.

Adagio pesante. Slow and heavy.

Adagissimo (It.). Very slow: sup. of *Adagio*.

Additional accompaniments. Instrumental parts added to a score by someone other than the composer, either for the filling-in of the figured bass, or for merely "thickening" the accompaniment in accordance with modern ideas, or for the simplification of certain parts such as the extremely high trumpet parts of Handel and Bach, or as substitution for parts written for obsolete instruments. Although the result may be sometimes questioned, the term is usually held to imply an artistic desire to fit an ancient score to the requirements of modern days, and does not include the introduction of extra brass instruments into a score of (say) Mozart by a conductor suffering from "orchestral deafness".

Addolcendo (It.). Softening; gradually becoming quieter.

Addolorato (It.). Dolorous, sad, agonised.

Adirato (It.). Irritated, angry.

Ado. Abbr. of *Adagio*.

Adornamento (It.). Ornament.

Aehnlich, Aengstlich, etc. *v.* Ähnlich, Ängstlich, etc.

Æolian Harp. An oblong box, serving as a sound-board, on which are stretched cat-gut strings tuned in unison. The sounds are produced by the action of the wind vibrating the strings in harmonics.

AEVIA. The vowels in Alleluia, used as an abbreviation.

Affabile (It.). Affable, courteous, kindly.

Affanato (It.). Agitated, anxious.

Affanosamente (It.). In a painful, sad manner.

Affanoso (It.). Stifling, sultry; distressing, sad.

Affektvoll (Ger.). Same as *mit Affekt*, — with passion, fervour.

Affettato (It.). Affected, artificial.

Affetto (It.). Affection, tenderness.

Affettso. Abbr. of *affettuoso*.

Affettuosamente (It.). Affectionately, tenderly, with emotion.

Affettuoso (It.). Affectionate, tender. Occasionally used as an indication of tempo, and meaning a speed somewhere between adagio and andante.

Afflitto (It.). Sad, melancholy.

Afflizione (It.). Affliction, sorrow.

Affrettando (It.). Hastening, hurrying.

Affrettatamente (It.). Hastily.

Affrettdo. Abbr. of *affrettando*.

Affrettuoso (It.). *v.* Affrettando.

Agevole (It.). Easy, without effort; implying a light, facile execution.

Agevolezza (It.). Facility, ease.

Agg. Abbr. of *aggiungi*, add.

　　Agg. Contrabasso 16 e **Basso** 8. Add diapasons 16 and 8 ft.

　　Agg. Ripieno. Add Mixture.

Aggiungi (It.). Add; from *aggiugnere*, or *aggiungere*.

Aggiustamento (It.). Adjustment, agreement.

Aggiustatamente (It.). With justness, regularity; strictly in time.

Aggradevole (It.). Agreeable, pleasing.

Aggrappando (It.). Grappling, hooking. In harp music, hitching a pedal into one of the notches in the pedestal, to raise the pitch of the instrument.

Agilità (It.) ⎫
Agilité (Fr.) ⎬ Agility, lightness, nimbleness.

Agilmente (It.). Nimbly.

Agitamento (It.). Agitation.

Agitatamente (It.). With agitation.

Agitato (It.). Agitated, troubled, excited.

　　Agitato con passione. Agitated with passion.

　　Agitato con pianto. Agitated with grief.

　　Agitato molto *or* **assai.** Very much agitated.

Agitazione (It.). Agitation.

Agiti(e)rt (Ger.). Agitated.

Agito. Abbr. of *agitato*.

Agnus Dei (Lat.). "Lamb of God". One of the parts of the Mass. Used as a subs., as "the Agnus Dei" of Weber's Mass.

Agréments (Fr.). Grace notes, embellishments.

Agreste (Fr.). Rural, sylvan, rustic. *Dans un sentiment de gaîté agreste*, with a feeling of rustic gaiety.

Ähnlich (Ger.). Similar, like.

Ai (It.). To the (masc. plur.).

Aigu, -guë (Fr.). Sharp, shrill, acute. *Petite trompette aiguë en mi ♭,* or *petite trompette en mi ♭ aigu,* small trumpet in high E ♭.

Air (Fr.). Air, aria, song.

Ais (Ger.). A-sharp, A♯.
    Ais dur. A-sharp major.
    Ais moll. A-sharp minor.

Aj. Abbr. of *ajoutez,* or *ajouter,* add. (*v.* Remark I.).
    aj. Fl. 4 P. au Récit. Add flute 4ft to swell.

Ajouter (Fr.). To add.

Akademie (Ger.). Academy, college.

Akkompagnement (Ger.). Accompaniment. (Usual word *Begleitung.*)

Akkompagni(e)ren (Ger.). To accompany. (Usual word *Begleiten.*)

Akkord (Ger.). A chord. *Dissonierender Akkord,* discord.
    Akkord in Dur. Major chord.
    Akkord in Moll. Minor chord.
    Die Akkorde möglichst gebunden. The chords as smoothly as possible.

Akt (Ger.). Act. *cf.* Aufzug.

Al (It.). A compound of *a* and *il,* at the, to the, etc. (masc. sing.).
    Al fine. To the end.
    Al loco. At the place; used after *8va* or *8va bassa,* and meaning that the notes are to be played in the octave written. *cf.* Loco.
    Al meno. To the least, *i. e.* becoming as soft as possible.
    Al piacere. At the pleasure (of the performer).
    Al rigore di tempo. In strict time.
    Al rovescio, al riverso. By contrary motion.
    Al seg. Abbr. of *al segno.*
    Al segno ✳. To the sign ✳; meaning that the performer has to return to the sign, and then play on till he reaches the word *fine,* or a double bar with a pause above it.

Alberti bass. A bass consisting of broken chords, so-called after Domenico Alberti (*circa* 1717—1740).

Albumblatt (Ger.). "An album leaf", a short composition ostensibly intended for the pages of an album, and therefore partaking of the nature of an impromptu.

Alerte (Fr.). Alert, active, nimble.

Aliquot tones. Overtones, upper partials. *v.* Harmonics.

Aliquottöne (Ger.). Aliquot tones.

All (Ger.). All, every; plur. *alle* (*q. v.*).

Alla, all' (It.). Compound of *a* and *la,* to the, at the, etc. (fem. sing.). Like the Fr. *à la, alla* often means "in the style of".
    All' antico. In the ancient style.
    Alla ballata. In the ballad style.
    Alla breve. In a modern sense, $^2/_2$ time, often written as 𝄵; a tempo of two beats to a bar.
    Alla breve taktieren (Ger.). Beat *alla breve.*
    Alla burla, ma pomposo. In a burlesque style, but pompously.
    Alla caccia. In the hunting style.
    Alla camera. In the style of chamber music.
    Alla cappella. In the style of church music. *cf.* A cappella.
    Alla coda. (Go) to the coda, *i. e.* the concluding portion of the piece.

Alla francese. In the French style.
All' inglese. In the English style.
All' italiana. In the Italian style.
Alla màrcia. In march style.
Alla mente. (1) A barbarous-form of counterpoint in 3rds and 5ths, in use in the 14th and 15th centuries. (2) Extemporaneous.
All' ongarese. In the Hungarian style.
All' ottava bassa. In the lower octave.
Alla Palestrina. (1) In the style of Palestrina. (2) Same as *a cappella*.
Alla polacca. In the style of a polonaise.
Alla scozzese. In the Scotch style.
Alla tedesca. In the German style.
All' unisono. In the unison.
Alla zampogna. In the manner of a bagpipe.
Alla zingara. In the gipsy style.
Alla zoppa. In a halting manner; in a syncopated rhythm.
Allargando (It.). Enlarging, broadening; gradually slackening the tempo.
Allargando al fine. Slackening until the end.
Alle (Ger.). All, every (plur.). Used in scores after "Solo" or "*ein allein*" to signify that all the instruments (violins, violas, etc.) are to be employed.
Alle ersten. All the first (violins, etc.).
Alle Hörner mit höchster Kraftentfaltung. All the horns with the utmost vigour.
Alle mit — bezeichneten Noten sollen während ihrer ganzen Dauer gleichmäßig stark ausgehalten werden. All the notes marked — must be held with equal strength throughout their whole duration.
Alle Saiten. All the strings; in piano music, *tre corde*.
Alle zweiten. All the second (violins, etc.).
Allegramente (It.).
Allègrement (Fr.). } Gaily, joyously.
Allegrettino (It.). Not so fast as *allegretto*. Sometimes used for a short composition marked *allegretto*.
Allegretto (It.). Diminutive of *allegro*. A tempo, which is somewhat animated, but not so fast as *allegro*.
Allegretto grazioso. Moderately fast with a graceful execution.
Allegretto, quasi andantino. A slow allegretto; one which is almost an *andantino*.
Allegretto scherzando. Moderately animated and playfully.
Allegretto tranquillo. Tranquilly without being dragged.
Allegretto un poco agitato. Moderately fast and somewhat agitated.
Allegretto villereccio. Moderately fast, in a rural style.
Allegrezza (It.).
Allegria (It.). } Mirth, gladness, joyousness.
Allegrissimo (It.). Sup. of *allegro*; very fast, but not so fast as *presto*.
Allegro (It.). Literally, joyous, gay, cheerful, mirthful. In music, the word is used to express a tempo between *moderato* and *presto*, and perhaps covers a greater range of metronomic value than any

other tempo indication, in *Tannhäuser* for instance the ⎮ in *Allegro* ¢ time varying from 69 to 108. It is greatly modified by the adjective or words with which it is associated, but always indicates a brilliant, animated execution. The term has been incorporated into other languages, and is also used as a subs., *e. g. un allegro très rhythmé*, a very rhythmical allegro.

Allegro agitato. Quick and agitated.

Allegro agitato e appassionato assai. With restless animation and very impassioned.

Allegro allegro. An intensified form of *allegro*.

Allegro assai. Very fast.

Allegro assai moderato. Very moderate *allegro*.

Allegro assai quasi presto. Very fast, almost *presto*.

Allegro assai vivo. Very quick *allegro*.

Allegro ben moderato. Fast, but very moderately so.

Allegro brillante. Fast and with brilliant execution.

Allegro brioso. Quick and with spirit.

Allegro comodo. Conveniently fast. *cf.* Comodo.

Allegro con allegrezza. Quick and with joyousness.

Allegro con brio. Fast and with vivacity.

Allegro con fuoco. Fast and with fire.

Allegro con moltissimo moto. Fast and with the greatest movement (animation).

Allegro con moto. Fast and with animation.

Allegro con spirito. Fast and spirited.

Allegro deciso. Quick and in a decided manner, *i. e.* with a well marked rhythm.

Allegro di bravura. A brilliant *allegro*, full of warmth and virtuosity.

Allegro di molto. Very fast.

Allegro di moto. Fast, with animation.

Allegro feroce. Quick and with ferocity.

Allegro fiero. Fast and proudly.

Allegro frenetico. Fast and with frenzy.

Allegro fuocoso. Fast and with fire.

Allegro gaio. Animated and gaily.

Allegro giusto. Fast and in strict time.

Allegro impetuoso. With impetuous speed.

Allegro ma non presto. Fast without being too fast.

Allegro ma non troppo. Fast, but not too much so.

Allegro maestoso. Quick, but stately.

Allegro marziale. Quick and in a martial style.

Allegro moderato. Moderately fast.

Allegro molto e con brio. Very fast and with verve.

Allegro mosso. Fast and animated. *v.* Mosso.

Allegro non tanto. Not too fast.

Allegro piacevole. Agreeably fast, *i. e.* neither too fast nor too slow.

Allegro risoluto. Fast and with decision.

Allegro sciolto. Fast and with a free, nimble execution.

Allegro sostenuto. Fast but sustained.

Allegro spirituoso. Quick and with spirit

Allegro tranquillo. Tranquilly but with a certain amount of animation.

Allegro veloce. Fast and rapidly.

Allegro vivace. Faster than *allegro*; quick and brisk.

Allegro vivo. Faster than *allegro*; quick and lively, very quick.

Allegro vivo e leggiero. Very quickly and lightly.

Allein (Ger.). Alone, solo. *Eine Violine allein*, one violin alone.

Allemand, -nde (Fr.). German. *Allemande.* (1) a dance; (2) one of the movements of a suite.

Allentamento (It.). A slackening, relaxation.

Allentando (It.). Slackening.

Allmählich, allmälig (Ger.). Gradually, little by little, by degrees.

Allmählich belebend. Gradually becoming animated.

Allmählich bewegter. Gradually with more motion.

Allmählich ein wenig zurückhaltend. By degrees somewhat slackening.

Allmählich etwas beruhigter. Gradually a little more tranquilly.

Allmählich etwas fließender. Gradually somewhat more flowing, *i. e.* faster.

Allmählich etwas mäßiger in Zeitmaß. By degrees in rather more moderate tempo.

Allmählich etwas zurückhaltend. Gradually somewhat slackening.

Allmählich immer belebter, auch im Zeitmaß. With growing animation, but in tempo.

Allmählich immer gedehnter. Constantly more drawn-out (slackened).

Allmählich immer ruhiger. With growing tranquillity.

Allmählich lebhafter. Gradually faster.

Allmählich nachlassend. Slackening little by little.

Allmählich sich beruhigend. Becoming calmer by degrees.

Allmählich wieder bewegter. Gradually again with more motion.

Allmählich wieder etwas langsamer. Again gradually somewhat slower.

Allmählich wieder mäßiger. Gradually again more moderately.

Allmählich wieder zurückhaltend. Gradually again slackening.

Allo. Abbr. of *allegro*.

Allongez (Fr.). Draw-out; slacken the time.

Allora (It.). Then; at that time.

Alltto. Abbr. of *allegretto*.

Allure (Fr.). Manner, way. *Avec une allure gaie*, in a gay manner, gaily.

Allzu (Ger.). Too, rather too, much too. Mostly used in combination.

Allzugleich. ⎫ Altogether.
Allzumal. ⎬
Allzusehr. Much, very much.

Allzuviel. Too much, overmuch.

Alphorn, Alpenhorn (Ger.). A wooden trumpet-like instrument, from 3 to 8 feet long, used in Switzerland for the *Ranz des Vaches* (*q. v.*). Only the Natural Scale (*v.* Harmonics) can be produced on it, the notes which are out of tune, according to the modern

scale, being particularly characteristic. There is a smaller variety
made out of a horn.

Als (Ger.). As, like; than; but; when.

Also (Ger.). Thus, so, in this way; therefore, consequently.

    Also nicht weniger geschwind. Consequently not less quick
    (*i. e.* as quick as before).

Alt. The notes from *g''* to *f'''* are said to be "in alt" (*alto*).

Alt (Ger.). (1) Old. *Im alten Menuettempo*, in old minuet time.
(2) Alto, contralto. (Many of the following compound words are
sometimes written as two words, often joined by a hyphen.)

    Alt-Clarinette. *v.* Altklarinette.

    Alt-Cornett. *v.* Altkornett.

    Altflöte. Alto flute, practically the same as what is called the
    Bass Flute in English. It goes down to *g*, and has been used
    by Weingartner in *Das Gefilde der Seligen.*

    Altflügelhorn. *v.* Althorn.

    Altgeige. The viola.

    Althoboe. The *Englische Horn*, the cor anglais.

    Althorn. An instrument corresponding to the Fr. *Saxhorn alto
    en mi♭*, usually called in English, Tenor horn. *v.* Saxhorn.

    Altklarinette. The alto clarinet.

    Altkornett. Another name for the *Althorn.*

    Altophikleid. The alto ophicleide.

    Altposaune. The alto trombone.

    Altsarrusophon. The alto sarrusophone.

    Altschlüssel. The alto clef.

    Altstimme. The alto or contralto voice.

    Alttrompete. The alto trumpet (in B♮ or A♭), an instrument
    used in German and Austrian cavalry bands. The notes sound
    a minor 7th or minor 6th above the written ones.

    Altviole. The *Viola da braccio.*

    Altzeichen. The C clef on the 3rd line.

Alta (It.). Fem. of *alto*, high. *Ottava alta*, an octave higher.

Altération (Fr.). ⎰ The alteration in the pitch of a note by raising
Alteration (Ger.). ⎱ or lowering it a semitone.

Altéré (Fr.). (1) Altered. (2) Weakened. *D'une voix altérée*, with
weakened voice.

Alternativo (It.). Alternate; by turns.

Alternato (It.). Altered (in pitch); alternate.

Altieramente (It.). Proudly.

Altissimo (It.). Sup. of *alto*, high. The octave from *g'''* to *f''''* is
called "in altissimo".

Altist (Ger.). A male alto.

Altista (It.). An alto singer.

Altistin (Ger.). A contralto.

Alto. The highest male voice, the counter-tenor, having a compass
from about *g* to *c''*. The alto part is as a rule taken by a bass
voice singing in falsetto, and the female voice of similar range is
usually designated a contralto. The term "alto" is applied to
a number of instruments taking a position in the harmony corresponding to the alto voice, but unfortunately the various nations
differ as to what is that position, the French for example calling

a viola an *"alto"*, while we call it a "tenor", still however writing for it in the alto clef. Amongst the multitude of Brass Instruments (*q. v.*) this inconsistent nomenclature is especially confusing.

Alto Clarinet. An instrument of the same compass as the ordinary clarinet, but sounding a 5th or 6th lower according as to whether it is in F or E♭.

Alto clef. The C clef on the 3rd line.

Alto Sarrusophone. A member of the sarrusophone (*q. v.*) family, but practically never employed.

Alto Saxophone. (in E♭ or F.) In many respects the most satisfactory member of the saxophone (*q. v.*) family, and the one usually employed for solos in the symphonic orchestra into which it has been introduced by many French composers (Bizet, Charpentier, Massenet, etc.).

Alto-tenor Clarinet. Same as alto clarinet.

Alto Trombone. Often called the "Trombone in E♭" (its fundamental note), and now seldom found in the orchestra. *v.* Trombone.

Alto (Fr.). adj. Alto. subs. The viola in the symphonic orchestra; the *saxhorn-alto en mi♭* in the military band.

Alto, -ta (It.) adj. High. (The instruments specified as "alto" in Eng. and Fr., and *Alt* in Ger., are called "contralto" in It.) subs. The alto voice.

Altri (It.). Plur. of *altro*; the others, the rest.

Altro, -a (It.). Other, different, another. *Una meta legato e l'altra meta pizz.*, one half legato and the other half pizzicato.

    Altra gran cassa. Another bass drum.

    Altro lampo. Another flash of lightning.

Alzamente di mano. (It.). The raising of the hand.

Alzando (It.). Raising.

    Alzando la mano. Raising the hand.

    Alzando la voce. Raising the voice.

Am (Ger.). Compound of *an*, at, about, for, etc., and *dem*, dat. of *der* or *das*, the.

    Am Frosch. At the nut (of the bow).

    Am Griffbrett. On the fingerboard (of the violin, etc.).

    Am Steg(e). Near the bridge (of the violin, etc.).

Amabile (It.). Sweet, agreeable, amiable.

Amarezza (It.). Bitterness, grief.

Amatore (It.). Amateur.

Amboß (Ger.). An anvil.

    18 **Amboß hinter der Scene.** 18 anvils behind the scenes.

Ame (Fr.). Soul, feeling, emotion. In violins, etc., the sound-post.

Amèrement (Fr.). Bitterly.

American organ. A key-board wind-instrument with free reeds, which are smaller and more curved than those in an harmonium; it also differs from this latter in that the wind is sucked inwards, instead of being forced outwards. It is provided with stops imitating those of the organ, another manual and pedals being occasionally added.

Amore (It.). Love.

Amorevole (It.). Tender, soft, with love.

Amorevolmente (It.). Tenderly, lovingly.

Amoroso (It.). Loving, amorous.

Amoureusement (Fr.). Lovingly, tenderly.

Amusement (Fr.). Amusement, pastime. A short composition of a pleasing nature.

An (Ger.). At, against, from, in, to.

An der großen Trommel befestigt. Attached to the bass drum.

An der Spitze. At the point (of the bow).

An jedem Pulte nur die ersten Spieler. At every desk, only the first players.

An jedem der 3 letzten Pulte. At each of the 3 last desks.

Anblasen (Ger.). To blow upon, to sound. *Stark anblasen* (to blow strongly) is used for brass instruments as the equivalent of the Fr. *cuivrev* (*q. v.*).

Anblasen ein Horn. To sound (or wind) a horn.

Anche (Fr.). A reed. *Instruments à anche*, reed instruments; *jeux à anches*, reed stops, reed-work.

Anche battante. A beating or striking reed.

Anche double. A double reed (oboe, bassoon).

Anche libre. A free reed.

Anche simple. A single reed (clarinet).

Anches de 8 et 4 P. (pieds). Reeds, 8ft and 4ft.

Anche (It.). Also, too, likewise.

Ancia (It.). A reed. (The Reedwork of an organ is called *canne a lingua*.)

Ancia battente. A beating or striking reed.

Ancia libera. A free reed.

Ancia per clarinetto. A clarinet reed.

Ancora (It.). Yet, still, again.

Ancora più mosso. Again with more animation.

Andacht (Ger.). Devotion, religious meditation.

Andächtig, *or* **mit Andacht** (Ger.). Piously, devotionally.

Andamento (It.). Literally "mode of walking, proceeding". (1) A fugue subject of considerable dimensions. (2) An episode of a fugue. (3) In the sense of the movement (tempo) of a piece, as *un andamento rapido*, a fast movement.

Andante (It.). From *andare*, to go, walk, proceed leisurely. It implies a slow tempo, but not so slow as *adagio*. The word is also used as a subs., as "an Andante" of Haydn, and has been incorporated into most languages.

Andante affettuoso. Slow and with tender emotion.

Andante cantabile. Slow and singingly.

Andante espressivo. Slow and with expression.

Andante grazioso. Slow and with grace.

Andante ma non troppo. Slow, but not too much so.

Andante maestoso. Slow and with dignity.

Andante mesto. Slow and with sadness.

Andante moderato. Moderately slow.

Andante molto. Very slow.

Andante mosso. Slow, but with animation.

Andante poco più lento della 1a volta. Somewhat slower than the 1st time.

Andante quasi adagio. Slow, almost *adagio*.

Andante tranquillo. Slow and peaceful.
Andante un poco lento. Somewhat slow.
Andantemente (It.). Fluently, without interruption.
Andantino (It.). A tempo, strictly speaking, faster than *andante*, although employed by some composers to indicate a slower movement.

Andantino con moto. Somewhat slow, but with animation.
Andantino espressivo. Somewhat slow, and with expression.
Andantino ma non troppo. Somewhat slow, but not too slow.
Andantino mosso. Somewhat slow, but with animation.
Andantino quasi allegretto. Almost as fast as *allegretto*.
Andantino quasi andante. Almost as slow as *andante*.
Andantino sostenuto e semplicemente. Somewhat slow, sustained and with simplicity.

Ander (Ger.). Other, another. Used as a subs., as *Die Anderen*, the others.

Die andere Hälfte. The other half.

And^{no}. Abbr. of *andantino*.
And^{te}. Abbr. of *andante*.
Anello (It.). A ring (on a wood-wind instrument); a thumb-ring for playing the zither. plur. both *anelli* and *anella*.
Anfang (Ger.). The beginning, commencement. *Als zu Anfang*, as at the commencement, *Tempo imo*.
Anfangs (Ger.). In the beginning, at the commencement.

Anfangs noch sehr ruhig. At the commencement, very tranquilly.
Anfangstempo. The initial (original) tempo.

Angeben (Ger.). To state, to give. *Falsch angeben*, to give a wrong note.

Angeben den Takt. To give the time.
Angeben den Ton. To give the pitch.

Angemessen (Ger.). Suitable, agreeing with.
Angenehm (Ger.). Agreeable, pleasing.
Anglais, -aise (Fr.). English. *Anglaise*, a *contredanse*, a name given by the French to the English Country Dance, Ballad or Hornpipe.
Angoscia (It.). Pain, grief.
Angosciosamente (It.). Painfully, with grief.
Angoscioso (It.). Sorrowful, anxious, grieved.
Ängstlich, Aengstlich (Ger.). Anxious, restless, troubled.
Anhalten (Ger.). To hold, sustain.
Anhaltend (Ger.). Holding, sustaining, *sostenuto*. Arresting, checking the speed. *Einen Ton anhaltend*, sustaining a note.

Anhaltende Kadenz. Organ point, pedal note.

Anhang (Ger.). Appendix; coda.
Anima (It.). Soul, mind, imagination. The sound-post of a violin, etc. *Canne d'anima*, the flue-pipes of an organ.
Animando (It.). Animating (the movement), becoming quicker.
Animato (It.). ⎱ Animated, lively, spirited.
Animé (Fr.). ⎰
Animez (Fr.). Quicken (the tempo).

Animez peu à peu. Quicken little by little.

Anim^{o}. Abbr. of *animando*.

Animo (It.). Heart, courage, energy.

Animoso (It.). Bold, spirited.

Anlage (Ger.). (1) Design, plan (of a composition). (2) Talent, capacity.

Anleitung (Ger.). Instruction, guidance.

Anmut(h) (Ger.). Agreeableness, gracefulness, suavity.

Anmut(h)ig (Ger.). Agreeable, charming, *grazioso*.

Annulaire (Fr.). The third finger.

Anreißen (Ger.). To tear. *Die Saiten stark anreißen*, the strings strongly torn, *i. e.* a pizzicato with great energy. *cf.* Arraché.

Ansatz (Ger.). (1) The cup-shaped mouthpiece of brass instruments. (2) The position of the vocal organs in singing, or the position of the player's lips, etc., in wind-instrument playing. (3) The tuning slide in wind instruments.

Anschlag (Ger.). (1) A form of turn, now obsolete. (2) Touch on a keyboard instrument. *Das Klavier hat einen guten Anschlag*, the piano has a good touch; *der Spieler hat einen harten Anschlag*, the performer has a harsh touch.

Anschlagen (Ger.). To strike, sound, touch. *Einen andern Ton anschlagen*, to sound another tone, *i. e.* to change the key; *den Ton anschlagen*, to give the pitch (key-note).

Anschläger (Ger.). The hammer in a piano.

Anschmiegend (Ger.). Insinuating, compliant, yielding.

Anschwellen (Ger.). A crescendo, a swelling on a note. *In gleicher Stärke, ohne Anschwellen*, of uniform strength, without a crescendo.

Ansia (It.). Anxiety.

Ansprache (Ger.). Sound, intonation, tone, speech (of an organ pipe).

Anspruchslos (Ger.). Unpretending, modest.

Anstatt (Ger.). Instead of, in place of.

Anstimmen (Ger.). To tune, to begin to sing, to lead (the choir). *Die Geige anstimmen*, to tune the violin; *einen andern Ton anstimmen*, to change to another key.

Anstrich (Ger.). A bow-stroke.

Antico, -a (It.). Ancient.

Antienne (Fr.). Anthem, but not exactly in the Eng. sense of the word. Originally an antiphon, *i. e.* something sung by two choirs alternately, it now means a short vocal piece set to words from the Bible, or a short instrumental one, suitable for certain portions of the Mass or Vespers.

Antifona (It.). An antiphon; an anthem. *v.* Antienne.

Antiphonie (Fr.). Singing antiphonally; two parts of the choir singing alternately.

Antropoglossa (It.). *v.* Vox humana.

Antwort (Ger.). Answer; the answer in a fugue.

Anvil. The anvil has been introduced into several operas: *Benvenuto Cellini* (Berlioz), *Il Trovatore*, *Die Königin von Saba* (Goldmark), *Das Rheingold*, etc., and is occasionally directed to be tuned to a particular note.

Anwachsend (Ger.). Increasing, swelling, *crescendo*.

Äolsharfe, Aeolsharfe (Ger.). The Æolian harp.

Aperto (It.). Open. *Le note aperte*, the open notes on a brass instru-

2*

ment; *le canne aperte*, the open pipes of an organ. An open string is *corda vuota*.

Appassionamente (It.). Passionately, ardently.

Appassionamento (It.). Ardour, passion, love.

Appassionato (It.). Passionate.

    Appassionato e molto sentimento. Passionately and with much feeling.

Appel d'anches (Fr.). A mechanism on some modern organs, by means of which certain powerful reed stops already drawn can be brought into play by pressing a pedal; by raising it, the stops again become mute.

Appell (Ger.). A trumpet or drum call, a rappel.

Appenato (It.). Afflicted, distressed

Applikatur (Ger.). Fingering.

Appoggiando (It.). "Leaning against"; laying stress upon. The term is also used for syncopated notes, and notes which are to be sung or played with *portamento*.

Appoggiato (It.). "Leant against"; accented. *v.* Appoggiando.

Appoggiatura (It.). A grace note, which may be either long or short: in the first case, it is in the nature of an auxiliary note, and occupies and subtracts from the principal note half its value; in the second case, it is usually written with a line through it, and corresponds to the modern use of the term *acciaccatura* (*q. v.*).

    Appoggiatura doppia. A double appoggiatura.

Apprestare (It.).   To prepare, to tune an instrument.
Appreti(e)ren (Ger.).

Après la parole (Fr.). "After the word". A direction signifying that though the accompaniment (as written) enters on the note with which the voice part concludes, it is to be deferred until the voice has sung that note.

Äqual, Aequal (Ger.). 8ft, as applied to organ stops.

    Äqualprinzipal. 8ft open diapason.

Arbitrario, arbitrato, arbitrio (It.). At the will (pleasure) of the performer.

Arcata (It.). Bowing, in the sense of the Fr. *coup d'archet* (Ger. *Strichart*), the particular manner in which a passage is to be bowed.

    Arcata in giù. Bowing with a down-stroke.

    Arcata in su. Bowing with an up-stroke.

Archeggiamento (It.). Bowing, in the general sense of the art of bowing.

Archeggiare (It.). To bow.

Archet (Fr.). The bow of a violin, etc.

    L'archet bien à la corde. The bow (lying) well on the string, *i. e. legato.*

Archi (It.). Plur. of *arco.*

Arco (It.). A bow.

Ardemment (Fr.). Fervently, intensely.

Ardente (It.). Ardent, fiery, amorous.

Arditamente (It.). Boldly, daringly.

Ardito (It.). Bold, daring, hardy.

Ardore (It.). Ardour, warmth, fervour.

Aria (It.). Air, song. Specifically, a piece for a solo voice with orchestral accompaniment, of a more or less set form, and which might figure in an opera or oratorio, or simply be a separate composition for concert room use. It usually consists of three parts, the last being a repetition of the first.

    Aria concertata. An aria with orchestral accompaniment.

    Aria di bravura. An aria of a florid nature.

    Aria di cantabile. An aria of a melodious flowing character.

    Aria parlante. An aria of a declamatory nature.

Arie (Ger.). Aria.

Arietta (It.). ⎫

Ariette (Fr.). ⎬ A short or diminutive aria.

Ariettina (It.). ⎭

Armonia (It.). Harmony. Also used in the sense of the Fr. *Harmonie*, a military orchestra.

Armonica (It.). (1) An harmonic. (2) The harmonica.

Armonico, -a (It.). Harmonic, musical.

Armoniosamente (It.). Harmoniously.

Armonioso (It.). Harmonious, melodious.

Armonium (It.). The harmonium.

Armure (Fr.). The number of flats or sharps in the signature.

Arpa (It.). The harp.

Arpége (Fr.). Arpeggio.

    Arpégement. Played as an arpeggio.

Arpéger (Fr.) ⎫

Arpeggiare (It.). ⎬ To arpeggio, to play an arpeggio.

Arpeggiato (It.). Played as an arpeggio.

Arpeggio (It.). The sounding of the notes of a chord in regular succession, such as is common in music for the harp (*arpa*). The word is now anglicised, and often used both as subs. and verb.

Arp⁰. Abbr. of *arpeggio*.

Arraché (Fr.). Literally "torn"; an intensified form of *pizzicato*.

Arranger (Fr.). ⎫

Arrangieren (Ger.). ⎬ To arrange, to score.

Arsis (Gk.). The up-stroke in beating time.

Arte (It.). Art.

Articolare (It.). To articulate, to pronounce.

Articolato (It.). Articulated, distinctly pronounced.

Articolazione (It.). Articulation.

Articuler (Fr.). To articulate.

Artificial Harmonics. *v.* Harmonics.

Artig (Ger.). (1) Gentle, pleasing. (2) Like, similar; in this sense often used as a suffix, as *Balladenartig*, like (in the style of) a ballad.

Artigkeit (Ger.). Gracefulness, pleasantness.

Artikulieren (Ger.). To articulate.

As (Ger.). A♭, A-flat.

    As dur. A♭ major.

    As moll. A♭ minor.

Asas (Ger.). A♭♭, A-double-flat.

Ascending piston. *v.* Valve.

Aspramente (It.). Harshly.

Asprezza (It.). Harshness, asperity.

Ass^a voce. Abbr. of *a sola voce*.

Assai (It.). Now usually meaning "very". Formerly synonymous with the Fr. *assez*.

Assemblage (Fr.). Double-tonguing or other rapid passages on a wind-instrument.

Assez (Fr.). Enough, rather, tolerably, somewhat.
    Assez animé. Somewhat animated.
    Assez lent. Rather slow.
    Assez marqué. Somewhat accentuated.
    Assez retenu. Somewhat slackened.
    Assez vif. Tolerably lively.
    Assez vite. Moderately fast.

Assieme (It.). Together, in company with, the Fr. *ensemble*. *Pezzo d'assieme*, a piece for several instruments or voices.

Assoluto, -a (It.). Absolute: free, not tied or slurred. *Prima donna assoluta*, the supreme leading lady, the "star" (female) singer.

Astuccio (It.). Case for a musical instrument.

At(h)em (Ger.). Breath.
    Atem holen. To take breath.

Attacca (It.). Attack, proceed to the next piece or movement without a break.
    Attacca subito il seguente. Immediately proceed to the following.

Attaccare (It.). To attack, to join, unite.

Attacco (It.). (1) A short phrase, used either as the subject of a fugue, or for imitation. (2) Attack (subs.). *v.* Attack.

Attack. The precise and vigorous entry of voices or instruments.

Attaque (Fr.). Attack. *Chef d'attaque*, the leader of the orchestra.
    Chaque attaque assez en dehors. Every attack somewhat prominent.

Atto (It.). Act.

Attore (It.). Actor.

Attrice (It.). Actress.

Au (Fr.). Compound of *à*, to, at, with, etc., and *le*, the (masc.).
    Au dessous. Below.
    Au dessus. Above.
    Au mouvement. In the movement (tempo).

Aubade (Fr.). Morning music; the antithesis of *serenade*.

Auch (Ger.). Also, so, but.
    Auch in Zeitmaß. But in time.

Audace (It.). Audacious, bold, rash.

Auf (Ger.). On, upon, at, near to.
    Auf das Holz der großen Trommel geschlagen. Struck on the wood (hoop) of the bass drum.
    Auf dem Griffbrett. On the fingerboard.
    Auf dem Stege. On the bridge.
    Auf dem Theater. On the stage.
    Auf der G(Saite). On the G(string).
    Auf der Mitte der Saite. At the middle of the string.
    Auf der Mitte des Bogens. In the middle of the bow.
    Auf einer Saite. On one string.
    Auf einer Seite. At one end (of a drum).

Auffassung (Ger.). Interpretation of a work; reading.

Aufführung (Ger.). Performance.

    Aufführungsrecht vorbehalten. Performing rights reserved.

Aufgeregt (Ger.). Agitated, restless.

Aufgeweckt (Ger.). Brisk, gay, lively.

Aufhalt, Aufhaltung (Ger.). Suspension.

Auflage (Ger.). Edition, impression.

Auflösen (Ger.). To resolve. *Eine Dissonanz auflösen,* to resolve a dissonance. In harp music, to restore a string to its original pitch. *b in h auflösen,* restore B♭ to B♮.

Auflösung (Ger.). Resolution. Restoration of a note to its original pitch.

    Auflösungszeichen. Restoration signs, *i. e.* ♮s, ♭s, and ♯s, introduced to contradict previous accidentals.

Aufsatz (Ger.). (1) An "ear" or "beard" of an organ pipe. (2) The stopping the string of a violin, etc., with a finger.

    Aufsatzbogen. The ordinary crook for horns, etc., placed at the mouthpiece end of the instrument, as opposed to an *Einsatzbogen,* which is fixed in the middle of the instrument.

Aufschlag (Ger.). The up-beat, *arsis.*

Aufschlagende Zunge (Ger.). A striking or beating reed.

Aufschnitt (Ger.). A cut.

Aufschreiend (Ger.). Screaming, screeching.

Aufsetzen (Ger.). To stop a string on a violin, etc.

Aufstrich (Ger.). The up-bow in violin playing.

Auftakt (Ger.). *v.* Aufschlag.

Auftretend (Ger.). Entering.

Aufzeichnung (Ger.). Notation.

Aufziehen (Ger.). (1) To string a violin, etc. (2) To draw up (the curtain at a theatre).

Aufzug (Ger.). An act of a play or opera; procession, pageant, and hence the music accompanying such pageant.

Augmenté (Fr.). Augmented. *Une quinte augmentée,* an augmented fifth.

Aumentando (It.). Augmenting.

Aumentato (It.). Augmented.

Aus (Ger.). Out of, from, by, for, in.

Ausarbeitung (Ger.). Elaboration.

Ausbilden (Ger.). To cultivate, develop. *Die Stimme ausbilden,* to develop the voice.

Ausdehnung (Ger.). Extension (of the fingers); compass.

Ausdruck (Ger.). Expression.

    Ausdrucksvoll. Full of expression, expressive.

Ausführung (Ger.). Development (of a theme). Performance, execution.

Ausfüllgeiger (Ger.). A ripieno violin-player.

Ausgehalten (Ger.). Sustained.

Ausgelassen (Ger.). Left out, omitted.

Aushalten (Ger.). To sustain. *Eine Note aushalten,* to dwell on, to sustain a note.

Aushaltung (Ger.). A sustaining, lengthening.

    Aushaltungszeichen. A pause.

Auslassen (Ger.). To leave out, omit.

Ausschlagen (Ger.). To beat. *Achtel ausschlagen,* beat quavers.

Ausser, Außer (Ger.). Out of; beside; outside.
    Außer sich. Beside himself (or herself).
Äußer (Ger.). Outward, exterior.
    Äußere Stimmen. Extreme parts.
Außerhalb (Ger.). Outside, without.
    Außerhalb des Orchesters. Outside the orchestra.
Äusserst, Äußerst (Ger.). Extremely.
    Äußerst rasch. Extremely fast.
    Äußerst ruhig. Extremely tranquil.
Aussi (Fr.). Likewise, also, too. *Aussi. . . . que,* as . . . . as.
    Aussi calme que possible. As quiet as possible.
    Aussi p. que possible. As *p.* as possible.
    Aussi tendre que possible. As tenderly as possible.
Autres (Fr.). Others.
Avanti, avante (It.). Before, forward; preceding.
Avec (Fr.). With.
    Avec abandon. With unconstraint.
    Avec ampleur. With breadth.
    Avec émotion. With emotion.
    Avec entrain. With high spirits, with enthusiasm.
    Avec la corde lâche (*or* **relâchée**). With the *corde du timbre* (*i. e.* the snare) slackened. *v.* Muffled.
    Avec les autres. With the others.
    Avec plus d'accent. With a stronger accent.
    Avec plus de mouvement. With more movement, *i. e.* faster.
    Avec (les) sourdines, avec la sourdine. With (the) mutes, with the mute.
    Avec un accent cuivré. With a brassy tone. *v.* Cuivré.
    Avec un grand sentiment recueilli et soutenu. With a deep and sustained emotion.
    Avec un peu plus de mouvement. Somewhat faster.
    Avec un sentiment de calme et de fraîcheur. With a feeling of tranquillity and freshness.
    Avec une grande tendresse. With great tenderness.
    Avec vigueur. Vigorously.
Azione sacra (It.). A sacred drama (opera).

B

B. The 7th note of the normal scale of C major, and the leading note of that key. In German it is called H, B being the English B♭; in French and Italian, it is called *si.*
    B. Abbr. of bass, and occasionally of bassoon.
    B♭ Bass. The bass saxhorn in B♭.
    BB♭ Bass. The contrabass saxhorn in B♭.
    B. C. *or* **b. c.** Abbr. of *basso continuo.*
    B. Cl. Abbr. of bass clarinet.
    B. T. Abbr. of bass tuba, or bass trombone.
B. (Ger.). B flat, B♭.
    B *or* **Be** (plur. *Been*). The flat sign (♭). *Die Be-Tonarten,* the flat keys.
    B♭. Same as B♭♭ in English.

B dur. B♭ major.
B.Kl. Abbr. of *Baßklarinette*.
B moll. B♭ minor.
B.P. Abbr. of *Baßposaune*.
Baccanale (It.). ⎰A festival in honour of Bacchus, which often de-
Bacchanale (Fr.). ⎱generated into a drunken orgy. A term some-
times used for movements (principally in ballets) of a wild orgy-
like nature.
Bacchetta (It.). A drumstick for a kettledrum, a snare-drum, or
a tenor-drum; also a conductor's bâton. plur. *bacchette*.
    Bacchette di legno. Wooden drumsticks.
    Bacchette di spugna. Sponge-headed drumsticks (for kettle-
    drums).
Bach Trumpet. A trumpet constructed for the production of the
high notes found in Bach's scores, usually of the same length and
pitch as a cornet in A. It therefore employs a lower series of
harmonics than the natural trumpet: *e. g.*, the note *a″* (actual
sound) is the 12th harmonic on the trumpet in D, and the 8th
harmonic on the Bach trumpet in A. It is provided with valves,
and is extended like a coach-horn — more for the sake of im-
pressing the eye than for any musical reason. The trumpet of
Bach's time was an entirely different instrument.
Back. That part of a stringed instrument opposed to the belly.
Badinage (Fr.). Playfulness, trifling: a term applied to pieces of
an impromptu character, and of a light playful nature.
Bagatelle (Fr.). A trifle. *cf.* Badinage.
Bagpipe, *or* Bagpipes. An instrument of ancient origin. It consists
of, (1) a leathern bag, serving as a wind-chest (the wind being
blown into it by the player, who then squeezes it under his left
arm); (2) a chanter, on which the melody is played; (3) one or
more drones, tuned in 5ths and octaves (*v.* Chanter and Drone).
In the Irish bagpipes, the leathern bag is inflated, not by the
player's breath, but by an ordinary pair of bellows, carried under
his other arm.
Baguette (Fr.). A drumstick for a kettledrum, a snare-drum or a
tenor-drum; also a conductor's bâton.
    Baguettes d'éponge. Sponge-headed drumsticks (for kettledrums).
    Baguettes de bois. Wooden drumsticks.
    Baguettes dures. Hard drumsticks.
    Baguettes ordinaires. The ordinary drumsticks.
Baisser (Fr.). To lower.
    Baissez le rideau. Lower the curtain.
    Baissez vite le mi♭ en ré♭. Lower the E♭ quickly to D♭.
Bajo (Sp.). Bass.
Balalaïka. A species of Russian guitar, with a triangular body, and
a neck of about the same length. It has three strings, which are
tuned in various keys, two being tuned to the tonic of the key
and one to the dominant.
Balancement (Fr.). An effect obtained on bowed instruments by
pressing a finger firmly on a string, and giving the finger a
tremulous motion producing a species of *vibrato*. A similar effect
was formerly obtained on the clavichord. It is called *Bebung*

in Ger., but there is no precise Eng. equivalent. *Très légèrement martelé dans un doux balancement*, very lightly *martelé* (*q. v.*) and with a gentle *vibrato*.

Balg, Bälge (Ger.). Bellows.
>**Bälgetreter.** An organ-blower. Literally "a bellows-treader", the bellows of an organ being originally worked with the feet.

Ballabile (It.). Suited to dancing. *Coro ballabile*, a chorus accompanied by dancing.

Ballad Horn. A species of tenorhorn intended to imitate the tone-quality of a French horn, but with the facility of execution of a cornet or saxhorn.

Ballade (Fr.). A ballad, in the Ger. sense.

Ballade (Ger.). (*Balladen-* in combination.) A ballad but not in the modern Eng. sense, which usually implies a simple unpretentious song. In Ger., the term is applied to a composition partaking more of the nature of a dramatic scene.
>**Balladenartig.** In the style of a ballad.
>**Balladendichter.** A ballad maker.
>**Balladenmäßig.** In ballad style.
>**Balladensänger.** A ballad singer.

Ballata (It.). (1) A song for dancing. (2) A ballad.

Ballatella, Ballatetta, Ballatina (It.). *v.* Ballata.

Ballerino, -a (It.). A dancer.

Ballet (Fr.). A ballet. (1) An artistic dance with elaborate steps, figures and postures, performed by a number of persons. (2) A pantomimic dance. (3) The persons who dance the ballet.
>**Ballet d'action.** A pantomimic dance illustrative of a story, and often in 2 or 3 acts, as the *Sylvia* and *Coppélia* of Delibes.
>**Ballet divertissement.** A ballet consisting of a number of different dances, but not illustrative of any particular story.

Ballett (Ger.). A ballet.
>**Balletttänzer.** A ballet dancer (male).
>**Balletttänzerin.** A ballet dancer (female).

Balletto (It.). A ballet.

Ballo (It.). A dance. plur. *Balli*.
>**Balli inglesi.** English dances.
>**Balli ongaresi.** Hungarian dances.

Ballonzare (It.). To dance without method; to skip about.

Band. A collection of instrumental players, usually now-a-days implying a military band, "orchestra" being as a rule the term for a band playing symphonic music. *v.* Brass Band and Orchestra.

Band (Ger.). A volume.

Banda (It.). A band. As in Eng., usually implying a military band. *cf.* Armonia.

Bande (Fr.). A band.
>**Une bande de musique militaire.** A military band. Unlike the Eng. and It. the "bande" is almost always omitted, and a military band is called *une musique militaire*, or more frequently *une Harmonie* (*q. v.*).

Bander (Fr.). To brace a drum.

Bandurria (Sp.). A species of mandoline.

Banjo. A stringed instrument consisting of: — (1) a hoop, over which parchment is stretched, acting as a sound-board; (2) a long neck serving as a finger-board. It has from 5 to 7 strings, which are plucked by the fingers of the right hand, "thimbles" being sometimes used to protect them.

Bänkelsänger (Ger.). A ballad-singer; an itinerant minstrel.

Barcarola (It.). ⎰ A barcarole, a Venetian boatman's song, usually
Barcarolle (Fr.) ⎱ in $^6/_8$ time.

Barem (Ger.). A soft stopped organ pipe, usually of 8 ft.

Bärenpfeife (Ger.). The bourdon.

Baribasso (It.). A deep bass voice.

Baritenore (It.). A deep tenor voice.

Baritonalo (It.). Baritone-like. *Strumenti baritonali*, instruments possessing a baritone register.

Baritone, Barytone. A male voice intermediate between a bass and a tenor, with a compass from A or $B\flat$ to f' or g' (or even a' for solo voices).

>**Baritone.** In military bands, the name of the baritone saxhorn.

>**Baritone clef.** The F clef on the 3rd line, now obsolete.

>**Baritone Oboe.** Sometimes called the basset oboe; an instrument an octave lower than the ordinary oboe. *cf.* Hautbois baryton and Heckelphon.

>**Baritone Sarrusophone.** A member of the sarrusophone (*q. v.*) family and practically never employed.

>**Baritone Saxhorn.** An instrument of the saxhorn (*q. v.*) family. It stands in B$\flat$, and has an effective compass from about E to $b'\flat$ or c''. Of lighter build and slenderer bore, it has less volume of tone than a bass saxhorn, or a euphonium, and lacks the low notes of these latter, although theoretically from its length of tube it should have the same compass.

>**Baritone Saxophone.** An instrument of the saxophone (*q. v.*) family, and although of use in the military band, seldom employed in the orchestra; it has however been used by Thomas (*Hamlet* and *Françoise de Rimini*), and Massenet (*Marche de Szabadi*). Its usual key is E$\flat$, but for orchestral purposes it is sometimes made in F (Strauss, *Symphonia domestica*). Its written compass is from $b\flat$ (modern instruments) to $e'''\flat$, a tone less than the alto saxophone.

Barkarole (Ger.). A barcarole (*q. v.*).

Barocco (It.). ⎫
Barock (Ger.). ⎬ Odd, bizarre; mostly applied to the whimsical artistic
Baroque (Fr.). ⎭ style of the 17th and 18th centuries.

Barra (It.). ⎰A bar-line. Also used for the low bridge of some stringed
Barre (Fr.). ⎱instruments of the lute class.

>**Barre (d'harmonie).** The bass-bar of a violin, etc.

>**Barre de luth.** The bridge of a lute.

>**Barre de répétition.** A double bar with dots, the sign of a repeat.

Barré (Fr.). In guitar playing, the stopping of two or more strings by placing the index finger of the left hand across them.

Baryton, bariton (Fr.). Baritone; the baritone voice; in military bands, the baritone saxhorn.

Baryton, Bariton (Ger.). Baritone; the baritone voice; sometimes the baritone saxhorn or *Euphonion* (euphonium).

Barytonklarinette. A name occasionally found for the *Altklarinette*.

Barytonschlüssel. The baritone clef.

Bas, basse (Fr.). Low.

    Bas à ré, sol. Low (i. e. lower) to D, G.

    Bas-dessus. The mezzo-soprano.

Basflicorno (It.). *v.* Flicorno basso.

Baskische Trommel (Ger.). The tambourine. In many Ger. scores, the name of the instrument is given as "Tambourin", a method of nomenclature which cannot but tend to confusion, since *Tambourin* (*q. v.*), the Fr. for the long drum used by Bizet in *L'Arlésienne*, is equally the Ger. name for this latter instrument.

Bass. The lowest male voice, having a range from *E* to *e'*, with a few semitones at each end for exceptional voices. In Russia are found basses trained to descend as low as $A_1\flat$.

    Bass. The violoncello; when used in the plur., the violoncellos and double-basses of the orchestra; in military bands, the bass saxhorn.

    Bass-bar. A strip of wood glued to the under side of the belly of the violin, etc., and placed under the bass or lowest string.

    Bass Clarinet. An instrument an octave below the ordinary clarinet, and thus possessing an actual compass from *D* to *f''*, when in B♭, and a semitone lower, when in A: instruments in C are rarely found. It is either written in the treble clef, when, for the B♭ instrument, the actual sounds are a minor 9th below; or, following the example of Wagner, in the bass clef (using the treble clef only for the highest register), when the sounds are only a tone lower. Originally introduced for special effects, and played by one of the ordinary clarinettists, it may now be said to form a constituent part of the orchestra (especially the operatic one) and requires a separate performer.

    Bass clef. The F clef on the 4th line.

    Bass Drum. Sometimes called the "Big Drum", an instrument of percussion made in two forms: — (1) with two heads, for military purposes, with a diameter of from 28 to 32 inches; (2) with only one head (often called a "gong" or "tambourine" drum), which is useful in orchestras, where the two-headed drum would occupy too much space, and is considered preferable by some authorities, if it be of very large diameter. Rolls are obtained on the bass drum either by a rapid movement of the ordinary drumstick, or by one having a knob at both ends, or (in modern scores) by kettle-drumsticks. The instrument has been called a double drum (*q. v.*) by some writers, but this is evidently a confusion of nomenclature.

    Bass Flute. A flute going down to *g*, and but rarely used. Bass flutes are also made descending to B♭. *cf.* Altflöte.

    Bass Horn. A keyed instrument played with a cup-shaped mouthpiece, a predecessor of the ophicleide and now obsolete, though used by Spohr and Mendelssohn.

    Bass Saxhorn. An instrument used in military bands and often

taking the "tuba" part in the orchestra. Although of the
same length as the baritone saxhorn, its larger bore, etc.
renders the production of the low notes easier. It is in B♭,
and has a compass from C to c'', the highest notes being
seldom employed. There is nothing to distinguish it from the
euphonium, which is a member of the tuba (*q. v.*) family,
and identical as regards compass. *v.* Saxhorn.

Bass Trombone. The lowest of the trombone (*q. v.*) family
used by the classic masters, and made in 3 keys: — (1) in G,
with a compass from $D♭$ to g', it is only found in Great Britain,
and is unsatisfactory since it does not give the low C found
in Mozart, Beethoven, etc.; (2) in F (a 4th lower than the
tenor trombone), extending from B_1 to f'; (3) in E♭, with
a compass a tone lower than the last. In France and Italy
the bass trombone is seldom employed; Verdi uses it in *Otello*
to form a bass to the 3 (tenor) trombones, instead of a tuba.

Bass Trumpet. An instrument pitched an octave lower than
the ordinary trumpet, in use in military (principally cavalry)
bands in several countries. Wagner uses it in his *Ring*, and
writes for it in E♭, D and C, and it has been employed by other
modern composers. It is made in E♭ for military, and in C
and B♭ for orchestral purposes.

Bass Tuba. *v.* Tuba.

Bass Viol. A now almost obsolete term for the double-bass.

Bass, Baß (Ger.). Bass. Used in combination with other words,
and often written so as to form a single word.

Baßbläser. A player on the bassoon.

Bass-Clarinette. *v.* Baßklarinette.

Baßflügelhorn. The baritone saxhorn in B♭

Baßgeige. The double-bass.

Baßklarinette. The bass clarinet.

Baßnote. A bass note.

Baßophikleid. The bass ophicleide.

Baßposaune. The bass trombone.

Baßsaite. The bass or lowest string of a stringed instrument.

Baßsänger. A bass singer.

Baßschlüssel. The bass clef.

Baßstimme. A bass voice.

Baßtrompete. The bass trumpet.

Baßtuba. The bass tuba.

Baßzeichen. The bass clef.

Bass. con. Abbr. of *basso continuo.*

Bassa (It.). Fem. of *basso,* bass, low. *Ottava bassa,* an octave lower.

Basse (Fr.). Bass. The violoncello; the bass saxhorn.

Basse chantante. A high bass voice of a flexible character.

Basse chiffrée. Figured bass.

Basse continue. *v.* Basso continuo.

Basse contrainte. Ground bass.

Basse-contre. } A deep bass voice.
Basse de Juif. }

Basse d'Harmonie. A name formerly given to the ophicleide.

Basse fondamentale. Fundamental bass.

Basse obstinée. *v.* Basso ostinato.

Basse récitante. A solo bass.

Basse tuba. The bass tuba.

Basset Horn. An alto clarinet, but with 4 extra keys, which enable it to descend to *c* (*F*, actual sound). Its name is derived from *bassetto* (a diminutive of *basso*), and "Horn", the name of the inventor, whose patronymic has been rendered literally into Fr. and It. as *Cor* and *Corno*. Although a favorite instrument of Mozart, it is now seldom used, its place being taken by the alto clarinet, which descends only to *e* (written note); and it is to be noted that some basset horns did not possess keys for producing the low *c♯* and *e♭*. The low notes were often written in the bass clef, in which case, as with the French horn, they were written an octave lower than their proper notation.

Basset Oboe. *v.* Baritone oboe.

Bassi (It.). Masc. plur. of *Basso*.

Bassin (Fr.). Basin; the cup-shaped mouthpiece of brass instruments.

Basso, -a (It.). Low; bass. A bass singer.

    Basso basso. A very deep bass.

    Basso buffo. A bass singer taking comic parts.

    Basso cantante. A "singing" bass, *i. e.* one of a lighter character, as opposed to the *basso profondo*.

    Basso cifrato. Figured bass.

    Basso continuo. A bass part, which may be figured or not, for the piano, harpsichord or organ.

    Basso costretto. Ground bass.

    Basso figurato. ⎫
    Basso numerato. ⎬ Figured bass.

    Basso ostinato. A persistent figure occurring in the bass; a ground bass.

    Basso profondo. A deep bass voice.

    Basso ripieno. A bass used only in *tutti* passages.

Basson (Fr.). The bassoon.

    Basson quinte. The tenor bassoon, — an instrument a 5th higher than the ordinary bassoon. Widor uses the term for an imaginary bassoon, which should descend a fifth *lower*: this would resemble the obsolete Ger. *Quartfagott* (*q. v.*).

    Basson russe. A species of serpent, now obsolete.

Bassone (It.). A name for the *fagotto*, bassoon.

Bassoon. A bass instrument played with a double reed, with a compass of 3 octaves from $B_1♭$. The low A_1, used by Wagner, Raff, etc., is obtained by temporarily fixing on another lower joint to the instrument. As in France all the leading orchestras possess 4 bassoons, many Fr. composers write 4 parts for the instruments; in modern Ger. scores, the usual number is three.

Bastante (It.). Sufficient, enough.

Bastoncino (It.). A conductor's bâton.

Bâton (Fr.). A stick used for conducting.

    Bâtons ronds. A method of executing a roll on the snare-drum with the drumsticks held in the manner of kettledrum-sticks, *i. e.* with the backs of the hands uppermost in both hands, and without a double (repercussive) stroke.

Batte (Fr.). The beater or stick for a bass drum, a triangle, or a gong. *cf.* Mailloche and Tampon.

Battement (Fr.). Beating, throbbing. Formerly used for a species of mordent.

Battente (It.). A beater. *cf.* Batte.

    Battente a due pomi. A bass-drumstick with two heads.

Battere (It.). To beat.

    Battere il tempo. ⎫
    Battere la misura. ⎬ To beat time.

Batterhead. That end of a snare or tenor drum, on which the performer strikes.

Batterie (Fr.). (1) The instruments of percussion, usually not including the kettledrums. (2) The rapid alternation of 2 notes, not only those a tone or semitone apart (shake), but with a greater interval between them. (3) The beating of a snare-drum; a drum call.

Battez (Fr.). From *battre*, to beat.

    Battez à 2 temps. Beat 2 to the bar.

    Battez à ³/₈. Beat in ³/₈ time.

Battimento (It.). *v.* Battement.

Battitore di musica (It.). A beater of time; a conductor.

Battre (Fr.). To beat. *Battre le tambour*, beat the snare-drum; but *blouser les timbales* (kettledrums).

Battuta (It.). (1) A beat. (2) A bar.

Batyphone. A species of double-bass clarinet, standing a 5th lower than the bass clarinet. It was employed for some little time in military bands, but without much success.

Bau (Ger.). Build, make (of a musical instrument).

Bauer (Ger.). A peasant, countryman.

    Bauerlied. A rustic song.

Baxoncello (Sp.). The open diapason.

Be (Ger.). The flat sign (♭).

Bearbeitet (Ger.). Adapted, arranged.

Bearbeitung (Ger.). Arrangement, adaptation.

Beating reed. *v.* Reed.

Beaucoup (Fr.). Much, many, a great deal. *En élargissant beaucoup*, broadening a great deal.

    Beaucoup d'archet. Much (*i. e.* many changes of) bow.

    Beaucoup de son. Much tone; sonorous.

Bebend (Ger.). Trembling, *tremolando*.

Bebung (Ger.). *v.* Balancement.

Bec (Fr.). A beak; the mouthpiece of a clarinet, or saxophone.

Bécarre (Fr.). The natural sign (♮).

Becco (It.). *v.* Bec.

Becken (Ger.). Cymbals. A single cymbal is called a *Schale*, or a *Teller*.

    Becken gewöhnlich. Cymbals played in the ordinary manner.

    Becken mit Holzschlägel. Cymbals played with a wooden beater.

    Becken nach militärischer Art an der großen Trommel befestigt. Cymbals fastened to the bass drum in military fashion.

    Beckenschläger. A cymbal-player.

Bedächtig (Ger.). Deliberate, thoughtful.

Bedeckt (Ger.). Covered.

    Bedeckte Saiten. Covered (stopped) strings, as opposed to *leere Saiten*, open strings on a violin, etc.

Bedeutend (Ger.). Significant, important, considerable.

    Bedeutend langsamer. Considerably slower.

Bedeutet (Ger.). From *bedeuten*, to signify.

    ⌣ **Bedeutet stets starkes portamento.** ⌣ Signifies always a strong *portamento*.

Bedeutungsvoll (Ger.). Full of significance, important.

Bedon (Fr.). An old name for a species of drum something like a *Tambourin* (*q. v.*).

    Bedon de Biscaye. A form of tambourine.

Bedrohlich (Ger.). Menacing, threatening.

Befestigt (Ger.). Fixed, fastened.

Beffroi (Fr.). A belfry. A name formerly given to the *Tam-tam*.

Begeisterung (Ger.). Exaltation, animation, rapture, enthusiasm.

Begleiten (Ger.). To accompany.

Begleitend (Ger.). Accompanying.

    Begleitende Stimmen. Accompanying parts.

Begleiter (Ger.). An accompanist.

Begleitung (Ger.). Accompaniment. *Ohne Begleitung*, without accompaniment.

Behaglich (Ger.). Easy, agreeable.

Behend(e) (Ger.). }
Behendig (Ger.). } Agile, nimble, dexterous.

Behendigkeit (Ger.). Nimbleness, dexterity.

Beherzt (Ger.). Resolute, determined.

Beide (Ger.). Both.

    Beide Pedale. Both pedals.

    Beide Schalen. Both cymbals, *i. e.* clashing them in the ordinary way after one has been struck by a drumstick, etc.

Beinah(e) (Ger.). Nearly, almost.

    Beinah doppelt so langsam. Almost double as slow.

    Beinah doppelt so rasch. Almost double as fast.

Beispiel (Ger.). Example.

Beißer (Ger.). A mordent.

Beizeichen (Ger.). An accidental.

Bel bello (It.). Softly, gently.

Belebend (Ger.). Becoming animated.

Belebt (Ger.). Animated. *Belebter*, more animated.

    Belebt, nicht zu rasch. Animated, not too fast.

Belieben (Ger.). Pleasure, will. *Nach Belieben*, ad libitum.

Beliebig (Ger.). Optional. *Mit beliebig starker Besetzung*, with the parts strengthened *ad libitum*.

Beliebt (Ger.). Loved, popular.

Bell. (1) A hollow metallic percussion instrument varying in shape and size from a sleigh-bell to the great bell of Moscow (yet unhung) weighing about 200 tons. The deep bells written for by composers are never by any chance heard in the octave written, on account of the practical difficulty of procuring bells weighing several tons. The effect of these low notes is produced in various ways: — a piano wire in a long wooden box, hollowed discs of bronze, tubes of metal, etc. Sets of small bells (*Carillon* or *Glockenspiel*) were used by Handel and Mozart, but now-a-days the bells are replaced by bars of steel or tuning-forks. Sleigh-bells (*q. v.*) are occasionally used for picturesque effects.

(2) The end of a wind-instrument opposed to the mouthpiece. The directions in modern scores as to the upturning of the bells for the purpose of producing a greater volume of tone, are not always well considered, since in many instances (more particularly with the horn) it is impossible to play in tune under such conditions.

Bell diapason. An open metal organ pipe with a bell mouth, of a reedy character, and generally of 8 ft pitch.

Bell gamba. An organ stop of a sweet somewhat reedy nature.

Bell metronome. A metronome (*q. v.*) so constructed that a bell is struck at the commencement of every bar.

Bellezza (It.). Beauty.

Bellicosamente (It.). In a warlike manner, bravely.

Bellicoso, -a (It.). Martial, warlike.

Bello, -a (It.). Beautiful, agreeable.

Belly. The portion of the violin, etc. on which the strings are stretched. In a harp, the soundboard into which the lower ends of the strings are fixed. In the piano, the soundboard.

Belustigend (Ger.). Rejoicing, gay, joyful.

Bémol (Fr.). The flat sign (♭). *La bémol*, A-flat, A♭.

Bémoliser (Fr.). To add a flat sign.

Bemolle (It.). The flat sign (♭). *Mi bemolle*, E flat. E♭.

Bemollizzare (It.). To add a flat sign.

Ben (It.). The most usual form of *bene*, well, very.

Ben articolato e staccato. Very distinct and detached.

Ben cantato. Well sung, *i. e.* the melody executed singingly.

Ben espressivo il canto. The melody with much expression.

Ben in tempo. In exact time.

Ben legato. Well sustained.

Ben marcata la melodia. The melody well marked.

Ben marcato il basso, ma piano. The bass distinctly marked, but softly.

Ben misurato. In exact rhythm.

Ben pronunciato. Very distinct.

Ben sostenuto. Very sustained.

Ben tenuto. Well sustained.

Bene (It.). Well, very.

Benedictus (Lat.). Part of the Mass.

Beneplacito (It.). subs. Goodwill, convenience. adv. At one's pleasure, *ad libitum*.

Bequadro (It.). The sign of the natural (♮).

Bequem (Ger.). Convenient, easy, comfortable, *comodo*.

Berceuse (Fr.). A cradle-song, lullaby.

Bereite vor (Ger.). From *vorbereiten*, to make ready, prepare.

Bereite vor, Hauptw. Flöte 8′, Rohrfl. 8′, Fugara. Prepare, Man. I, Fl. 8 ft, Rd Fl. 8 ft, Fugara.

Bereits (Ger.). Already; previously.

Bergeries (Fr.). Pastoral pieces.

Beruhigend (Ger.). Moderating, becoming more tranquil, *calando*.

Beruhigt (Ger.). Calmed.

Beruhigung (Ger.). A quieting, tranquilisation.

Bes (Ger.). B♭ flattened, *i. e.* B♭♭, usually called *bb* or *Doppel-b*.

Besaiten (Ger.). To string a violin, etc.

Beschleunigend (Ger.). Accelerating, hurrying.

Beschwingt (Ger.). Hastened, hurried.

Beseelt (Ger.). Animated, spirited.

Besetzung (Ger.). The distribution, laying-out of the parts, casting: the disposition of an organ or orchestra.

Besitzen (Ger.). To possess. *Die Kontrabässe, welche die C-Saite nicht besitzen, pausieren,* the double-basses, which do not possess the C-string, cease to play.

Besponnene Saite (Ger.). Covered strings, — as opposed to plain catgut ones.

Bestimmt (Ger.). Accentuated, with decision. A direction, like *hervortretend,* constantly found in Ger. scores, and meaning that the particular part has to be played firmly, so as to stand out from the rest. *Solo* is often found in the same connection in Fr. scores.

Betend (Ger.). Praying. *Viel betend,* prayerful.

Betonen (Ger.). To accentuate, to emphasise.

Betont (Ger.). Accentuated. *cf.* Bestimmt.

Betonung (Ger.). Accentuation, stress; intonation.

Betrübt (Ger.). Afflicted, troubled.

Bettleroper (Ger.). A "Beggars'" opera; ballad opera.

Beweglichkeit (Ger.). Agility, alertness.

Bewegt (Ger.). ⎰ With motion, movement: animated; *con*
Bewegt gehend (Ger.). ⎱ *moto.*

Bewegter (Ger.). With more motion, movement: more animated.

    Bewegter und immer mehr zu beschleunigen. With more movement, and continually faster.

    Bewegter werdend. Becoming more animated.

Bewegung (Ger.). Movement, motion, *moto. In derselben Bewegung fortfahrend,* continuing with the same movement.

Bezeichneten (Ger.). Sharply detached. *Die mit ''' bezeichneten Noten sehr kurz abgestoßen,* the notes marked ''' very sharply detached.

Bezifferter Bass (Ger.). Figured bass.

Bezifferung (Ger.). Figuring (a bass).

Bezug (Ger.). A thing furnished, *e. g.* a set of strings, hair for a bow, etc.

Bg. Abbr. of *Bogen.*

Bianca (It.). A minim. From *bianco,* white.

Bicordo (It.). A double string on a violin, etc.

Bien (Fr.). Well, very. The It. *bene.*

    Bien accusé. Well accentuated.

    Bien chanté, doux et soutenu. Well sung (*i. e.* singingly), soft and sustained.

    Bien en dehors. Very prominent. Marked against a part intended to stand out well. *cf.* Hervortretend.

    Bien rhythmé. Well rhythmed, *i. e.* the rhythm precisely marked.

Bimolle (It.). *v.* Bemolle.

Bindung (Ger.).
Bindungsbogen (Ger.). } A tie, slur.
Bindungszeichen (Ger.).
Biniou, Bignou, Binviou. A species of bagpipe found in Britany.
Biquadro (It.). The natural sign (♮).
Birn(e) (Ger.). That portion of a clarinet, in which the mouthpiece is fixed, so-called from its resemblance in ancient instruments to a "pear".
Bisbigliando (It.). Literally, "murmuring"; a term used in harp music for a species of tremolo, obtained by alternating a chord arpeggio between the two hands.

Bischero (It.). A peg of a stringed instrument.
Biscroma (It.). A semiquaver.
Biscrome (Fr.). A semiquaver; usually called *une double croche.*
Bisser (Fr.). To encore a performer, or performance.
Bittend (Ger.). Entreating, supplicating.
Biucolo (It.). A bugle.
Bizzarramente (It.). Oddly, strangely.
Bizzarria (It.). Strangeness, oddity.
Bizzarro (It.). Bizarre, extraordinary.
Bl. Abbr. of *Bläser.*
Blanche (Fr.). Fem. of *blanc,* white, blank. The name of a minim, the crotchet being called *une noire,* a black.
Blasebalg (Ger.). Bellows.
Bläser (Ger.). A performer on a wind-instrument. plur. *Bläser.*
Blasinstrument (Ger.). A wind-instrument. plur. *Blasinstrumente.*
Blasmusik (Ger.). Music for wind-instruments.
Blatt (Ger.). (1) A leaf, a sheet of paper. *Fliegende Blätter,* fly-leaves; *vom Blatte spielen,* to play from the sheet (*i. e.* at sight). (2) A clarinet reed. *cf.* Rohrblatt, Zungenblatt.
  Blattschraube. A clarinet ligature.
Blechbläser (Ger.). A player on a brass instrument.
Blechinstrument (plur. -e) (Ger.). A brass instrument.
Blitz (Ger.). A flash of lightning.
Blochflöte (Ger.). An obsolete organ stop still found in some German organs.
Blouser (Fr.). To play the kettledrums.
Bluette (Fr.). A small work full of life and wit.
Blumicht, Blumig (Ger.). Flowery.
Bn. Abbr. of bassoon, *basson.*
Bocal (Fr.). The curved metal tube, on which the reed is fixed, in a bassoon or similar instrument. The term is occasionally improperly used for *embouchure,* a cup-shaped mouthpiece.
Bocca (It.). The mouth.

3*

Bocca chiusa. (With) closed mouth; an indication that the part is to be hummed or sung with closed lips.

Bocchino (It.). A mouthpiece.

Bockpfeife (Ger.). Bagpipe.

Bockstriller (Ger.). "The bleating of a goat"; an indifferent species of shake on a single note. *Die Triller (tr) sind von den Sängern als sogenannte Bockstriller auszuführen*, the shakes (*tr*) are to be executed by the singers as so-called *Bockstriller.* (*Die Meistersinger*, Act III.)

Boden (Ger.). The back of a violin, etc.

Bogen (Ger.). (1) The bow of a violin, etc. (2) A tie, slur.

> **Bogenfrosch.** The nut of a bow.
> **Bogenführung.** Bowing (method of), as opposed to *Strichart*, the particular form of bowing.
> **Bogenhaar.** Bow-hair.
> **Bogeninstrument.** A bowed instrument.
> **Bogenstange.** A bow-stick.
> **Bogenstrich.** A bow-stroke, *coup d'archet.*
> **Bogenstrichbezeichnungen.** Signs for bowing.
> **Bogenwechsel.** Change of bow.

Bois (Fr.). Wood. *Avec le bois d'archet*, with the wood (back) of the bow, *col legno*; *baguettes de bois*, wooden kettle-drumsticks. The wood-wind instruments of the orchestra are briefly called *"les Bois".*

Boîte expressive (Fr.). The swell box of an organ.

Bolero. A Spanish dance of a lively character in $^3/_4$ time.

Bombard. (1) A family of double-reed instruments now completely obsolete. (2) A reed stop on the organ, which is also often called by one or other of the variations of Bombard found below.

Bombarda (It.). Name sometimes given to the *eufonio* (euphonium).

Bombarde (Fr.). A powerful reed stop on the organ. *Clavier de bombardes*, a manual found on some Fr. organs.

Bombardino (It.). A little *bombardo*; a baritone saxhorn.

Bombardo (It.). *v.* Bombarda.

Bombardon. The contrabass saxhorns are usually called tubas in the orchestra and bombardons in military bands. They are either in E♭, a fifth below the bass saxhorn or euphonium, or in B♭, an octave below.

Bombardone (It.). A large *bombardo*; a contrabass saxhorn, a bombardon.

Bombo (Sp.). A bass drum.

Bon temps de la mesure (Fr.). The accented note of the bar.

Bordone (It.). Bourdon (*q. v.*).

Bottoncino (It.). Pad for key of a wood-wind instrument.

Bouche fermée (Fr.). (With) closed mouth. *v.* Bocca chiusa.

Bouché (Fr.). Stopped, closed; applied to notes on the horn (*q. v.*).
> **Bouché avec un accent cuivré.** Closed, with a "brassy" tone. *v.* Cuivré.

Bourdon, Bordun. A stopped organ pipe of 16ft tone.

Bourrée (Fr.). An old dance in rapid $^4/_4$ tempo, often found in the suites of Bach and his contemporaries.

Bout de l'archet (Fr.). The point of the bow.

Boutade (Fr.). A piece, or even a short ballet, in the style of an improvisation,

Bouton (Fr.). Button. End pin of a violin; a valve top; stud of an organ.

Bow. A wooden stick with raised ends, between which are stretched a hundred or more horse-hairs, tightened by means of a screw. It is used to vibrate the strings of violins and similar instruments, after the hairs have been rubbed with rosin.

Bowing. (1) The art of using the bow. (2) The special method of manipulating the bow for particular passages; the species of bow-stroke.

Boyau (Fr.). The so-called catgut: *La corde* or *les cordes de boyau du timbre*, the snare of a side-drum, usually shortened to *timbre*.

Br. Abbr. of *Bratsche*.

Brabançonne, La. The Belgian national hymn.

Brace. (1) A bracket connecting two or more staves. (2) The leather tags round the shell of a drum (snare, tenor, or bass), through which the "ropes" or cords, which strain or relax the head, pass. In modern drums, rods and screws often take the place of the cord and braces.

Branle, Bransle (Fr.). A Brawl (*q. v.*).

Brass Band. A collection of players on brass instruments, to which are occasionally added saxophones, which although made of metal, being played with a reed, are classed amongst the "Wood-wind". The band consists mainly of saxhorns of varying pitch, cornets, and trombones, to which are added the snare-drum, bass drum and cymbals.

Brass Instruments. A convenient, if not quite correct term for metal instruments played with a cup-shaped mouthpiece (*q. v.*). The principle of all of them depends on the vibration of a column of air in a tube (*v.* Harmonics), the player's lips and breath being able (theoretically) to produce the following Harmonic Series, known on the "Brass" as *open* notes: —

The black notes are out of tune according to our modern scale, and in modern practice none are used above the *c''* (16th harmonic), Bach and Handel however writing the *d'''* and *e'''*, and Haydn, in an early symphony (*Concertante*), even venturing on the *f'''*. In practice, few instruments can produce both the very low and very high notes; and on any instrument, these extreme notes depend on the individual powers of the performer. (For this last reason, the compass of the various brass instruments must be taken as approximate.) Generally speaking, the horn employs sounds 2—16; the trumpet, 2—12; the cornet, sax-horn, trombone, etc., 2—8: and since the higher harmonics are harder to produce, it can be understood why a trumpet, for instance, is more difficult than a cornet. On a *natural* instrument (*i. e.* one without mechanism for altering the pitch), these open notes are the only ones obtainable with the lips (with one rare exception. *v.* Factitious notes), and as they always bear the same relation to the fundamental note, it is clear that if this latter be *F*, the 5th and 6th harmonics will be *a'* and *c''*, and so on for the other harmonics; if *E*, then 5 and 6 will be *g'♯* and *b'*, etc. The alteration in the length of tube necessary to produce a different fundamental note is effected by extra pieces of tubing called *crooks* (*q. v.*) or shanks added to the main tubing; and as the series is always the same, it is more convenient for the player to have his part always written in C, with an indication at the beginning as to what *crook* he is to use, this being given as: — Trumpet in F, Horn in E, etc. Obviously an instrument, which could instantly be changed into one with another crook, or, what is the same thing, instantly have the length of its tube altered, could produce all the notes of the chromatic scale. This alteration is done in three ways: — (1) By a portion of the tubing being double, one part sliding over another, and by altering the position of this *slide*, changing the length of the tube into the seven *positions* necessary for the complete chromatic scale. *Ex.* The slide trumpet, and the ordinary trombone. (2) By means of keys, which by opening holes in the tube shorten its length. *Ex.* The ophicleide and the old keyed bugle. (3) By some system of valves (*q. v.*) whereby the air can be diverted at will through additional lengths of tubing. *Ex.* All the brass instruments in use in the modern symphonic or military orchestras, with the exception of the trombones, and these too (especially in military bands) are occasionally played with valves. The number of brass instruments now-a-days is very large, and the nomenclature bewildering, for not only are manufacturers inclined to call their special makes of instruments by special names, but owing to the difficulty apparently experienced by musicians in deciding the register of an instrument (*e. g.* whether it be alto, tenor or baritone), it is difficult to identify instruments in different languages, or even in the same language, as for instance when one musician calls a form of saxhorn a *Flicorno basso*, while another denotes it a *Flicorno tenore.*

Bratsche (Ger.). The viola.

Bratschist (Ger.). A viola player.

Brautlied (Ger.). A bridal song.

Bravissimo, -a (It.). Sup. of *bravo, -a.*

Bravo, -a (It.). Bravely done! An exclamation of applause. It is to be noted, that when applied to a female performer, *brava* is used.

Bravoure (Fr.). | Literally, "bravery", and implying a style, for which
Bravura (It.). ⎰a brilliant execution and great technical skill are required.

Brawl. An old round dance.

Brechung (Ger.). A breaking.

 Brechung der Stimme. Breaking of the voice.

 Brechung eines Akkordes. An arpeggio.

Breit (Ger.). Broad, broadly.

 Breite Achtel. Broad quavers.

Breiten Strich. Broad bow-stroke.

Breit gestrichen. Broadly bowed.

Breit, ruhige Achtel. Broadly, the quavers tranquilly.

Breit stoßen. Detach broadly.

Breit und getragen. Broad and sustained (dragged).

Breit und wuchtig. Broadly and heavily, *largamente e pesante.*

Breiter (Ger.). More broadly.

Breve. A note double the length of the semibreve, ▬ or 𝅝 .

Bridge. A thin piece of wood over which are stretched the strings in stringed instruments.

Brill. Abbr. of *brillante.*

Brillant Fr.). ⎰ Brilliant; implies an execution full of fire and vir-
Brillante (It.). ⎱ tuosity.

Brillenbässe (Ger.). Literally, "spectacle basses": a familiar name

for basses such as

Brindisi (It.). A toast, a health; and hence a drinking song.

Brio (It.). Vivacity, fire, spirit.

Brioso (It.). Lively, spirited.

Brisé (Fr.). Broken. *Accord brisé*, a broken chord.

Broderies (Fr.). Embellishments.

Brummbaß (Ger.). Bourdon.

Bruscamente (It.). ⎰ Abruptly, rudely.
Brusquement (Fr.). ⎱

Bruststimme (Ger.). The chest voice.

Buccolico (It.). Rustic, bucolic.

Buch (Ger.). A book.

    Buchstabe. A letter (of the alphabet). *Die Buchstaben R. . . . und A . . . . . bedeuten geringe Ritardando und Accelerando*, the letters R. . . . . and A. . . . . indicate a slight ritardando and accelerando.

Bucolique (Fr.). Rustic, bucolic.

Buffet d'orgue (Fr.). An organ case.

Buffo, -a (It.). A comic actor or singer.

Buffonescamente (It.). In a burlesque style.

Buffonesco (It.). Droll, ludicrous.

Bügelhorn (Ger.). The keyed bugle. *cf.* Klappenhorn & Buglehorn.

Bugle. A brass instrument used in the infantry of most nations for giving calls. For practical purposes it has only 5 notes, *c′ g′ c″ e″* and *g″*. The bugle, which was at first given keys (*v.* Kenthorn), and of which the ophicleide is the bass form, was later fitted with valves, and in this guise became the parent of the saxhorn and tuba families.

Bugle (Fr.). The name is used in France for two members of the saxhorn family; the soprano saxhorn (*petit bugle mi♭*) and the contralto saxhorn (*bugle*, or *grand bugle si♭*). The term used for the infantry bugle is *Clairon.*

Buglehorn (Ger.). Also called *Signalhorn*, the bugle, *i. e.* the ordinary instrument without keys. In modern Ger., *Buglehorn* is used for a bugle, with or without keys. *cf.* Bügelhorn.

Bühne (Ger.). Scene, stage, theatre. *Posaunen auf der Bühne*, trombones on the stage.

 Bühnenweihfestspiel. The name given by Wagner to *Parsifal* and meaning, a stage sacred festival play.

Buona nota (It.). The accented note of the bar.

Burla (It.). Waggery, joke.

Burlando (It.). Quizzing, joking, ridiculing.

Burlescamente (It.). In a ludicrous style.

Burlesco (It.). Burlesque.

Burletta (It.). A farcical comedy; a burlesque operetta.

Bussando (It.). Knocking, thumping, striking with force.

C

In modern German spelling, *k* has usually been substituted for the hard *c* (*Klarinette* for *Clarinette*, *Oktave* for *Octave*, etc.), and *z* for the soft *tz* sound (*Konzert* for *Concert*). In many cases both spellings are given in the dictionary; if only one, the modern spelling has been always chosen by preference.

C. The first note of the normal scale of C major; in Fr. it is called *ut* (occasionally *do*) and in It. *do*. In stage directions C. stands for the "Centre" of the stage.

 c.a. Abbr. of *coll'arco*.

 C.angl. Abbr. of *cor anglais*.

 c.B. Abbr. of *col Basso*.

 C.barré (Fr.). ₵, the sign of *alla breve* time.

 C.Bn. Abbr. of contra-bassoon, or *contre-basson*.

 CC. (1) The note C_1. (2) In Eng. organ music, the note *C* (8 ft C).

 C clef. The clef ‖╡‖, or ‖♮‖, indicating the position of *c'* on the stave, now only used on the 3rd line (alto clef) and the 4th line (tenor clef). On the 1st line it was the soprano clef, and on the 2nd, the mezzo-soprano.

 c.d. Abbr. of *colla destra*.

 c. 8va. Abbr. of *coll' ottava*.

 c.s. Abbr. of *come sopra*.

 C string. The lowest string of the viola and violoncello.

 c.voc. Abbr. of *colla voce*.

C (Ger.). The note C.

 C dur. C major.

 C moll. C minor.

 C Saite. C string.

 C Saite nach h herunterstimmen. Lower the C string to B.

 C Schlüssel. C clef.

Cabaletta (It.). A simple air, easily impressed on the listener, and usually forming part of the It. *aria*.

Cabinet d'orgue (Fr.). A small organ case, without *montre* (*i. e.* the pipes mounted in front).

Caccia (It.). The chase, hunting.

Cachucha (Sp.). A dance in triple time of moderate tempo.

Cacofonia (It.). ⎫
Cacophonie (Fr.) ⎬ Cacophony, a discordant combination of sounds.

Cad. Abbr. of *cadenza*.

Cadence (Fr.). (1) A cadence or close. (2) A trill or shake.
    Cadence évitée. An interrupted cadence.
    Cadence imparfaite. An imperfect cadence.
    Cadence interrompue. An interrupted or deceptive cadence.
    Cadence irrégulière. An imperfect cadence.
    Cadence parfaite. A perfect cadence.
    Cadence plagale. A plagal cadence.
    Cadence rompue. An interrupted cadence.
Cadenza (It.). (1) A passage of an extempore nature introduced into a concerto or vocal piece to exhibit the powers of execution of the performer. (2) A cadence or close.
    Cadenza ad libitum. The cadenza at the discretion of the performer.
    Cadenza d'inganno. A deceptive cadence.
    Cadenza fiorita. A florid, brilliant cadenza.
    Cadenza in tempo. A passage of the extempore nature of a cadenza, but in time.
    Cadenza sfuggita. An interrupted cadence.
Cadenzato (It.). Cadenced, in good rhythm.
Cahier (Fr.). A copy book: a stitched book containing a vocal or instrumental part.
Caisse (Fr.). A chest, a box. Used also as an abbr. of *caisse à tambour*, a drum. *Grosse caisse*, the bass drum.
    Caisse à cordes. A drum braced by means of cords.
    Caisse à tringles. A drum braced by means of rods and screws.
    Caisse à vent. The wind-chest of an organ.
    Caisse claire. The *tambour militaire*, the snare or side-drum.
    Caisse plate. A side-drum of a shallow build.
    Caisse roulante. The tenor drum.
    Caisse sourde. The tenor drum, — the "dull" drum, as opposed to the *caisse claire*, the "clear" drum.
    Caisse tarolle. A flat shallow side-drum.
Caja (Sp.). *v.* Caisse. *Bombo* is a bass drum.
    Caja de guerra. The side-drum, military drum.
Cal. Abr. of *calando*.
Cala (It.). From *calare*, to lower.
    Cala la tela (*or* **il sipario**). Lower the curtain.
Calando (It.). Decreasing in volume of tone, or in speed, or in both.
Calascione (It.). A species of lute, probably of Eastern origin.
Calata (It.). A dance.
Calcando (It.). Hurrying the time.
Caldamente (It.). Warmly, with ardour.
Cal^{do} Abbr. of *calando*.
Calm. Abbr. of *calmato*.
Calma (It.). Calmness, tranquillity.
Calmato (It.). Calmed, tranquilised.
Calme et placide (Fr.). Calm and serene.
Calore (It.). Heat, ardour.
Caloroso (It.). Fiery, ardent.
Cambia (It.). Change (sing.).
    Cambia in fa. Change into F.
Cambiano (It.). Change (plur.).

Cambiano in do. Change into C.
Cambiato, -a (It.). Changed, displaced. *cf.* Nota cambiata.
Camera (It.). A room, chamber.
Camminando (It.). Literally, "travelling". Hurrying the movement.
Campana (It.). (1) A bell. (2) The bell of a wind instrument.
Campanella (It.). A little bell.
Campanetta (It.). A set of bells. *cf.* Carillon.
Can. Abbr. of *canto*.
Canaille (Fr.). subs. Rabble, mob. adj. In a coarse vulgar manner.
  (Charpentier, *Impressions d'Italie.*)
Canarder (Fr.). To "quack" on reed instruments.
Canarie (Fr.). ⎫
Canaries (Eng.). ⎬ An old dance of a lively character.
Canario (It.). ⎭
Cancellen (Ger.). *v.* Kanzellen.
Cancrizzamente (It.). Reversed.
Canna (It.). A cane, a reed; a pipe.
  Canna alingua. Reed-pipe in an organ.
  Canna aperta. An open pipe.
  Canna chiusa. A closed pipe.
  Canna d'anima. Flue-pipe.
  Canna d'organo. An organ pipe.
Canon (Gk.). A canon. The various kinds of canon are so numerous
  that a complete list would be as lengthy as it would be unnecessary;
  a selection is given below.
  Canon apertus. An open canon, one in which all the parts are
    written on a separate stave, instead of the subject alone
    being given, with signs for the entries of the other parts.
  Canon cancrizans. A "crab-like" canon, one in which the answer
    is the subject read backwards.
  Canon enigmaticus. A riddle canon, one in which the arrange-
    ment and entry of the parts have to be guessed.
  Canon finitus. A canon which is brought to a conclusion after
    all the parts have entered with an imitation of the subject.
  Canon infinitus, *or* **perpetuus.** A canon without a definite con-
    clusion, which could be performed for infinity.
  Canon per augmentationem. A canon, in which the answer is
    an augmented version of the subject.
  Canon per diminutionem. A canon, in which the answer is a
    diminished version of the subject.
  Canon per tonos. A circular canon, which on every repetition
    is in a different key, so that eventually it returns to the key
    from which it started.
  Canon polymorphus. A canon which is capable of being worked
    in a great variety of ways.
Canone (It.). A canon.
  Canone al sospiro. A canon in which the parts enter at the
    distance of a crotchet-rest from one another.
  Canone chiuso. A close canon, one not written out in full.
  Canone per moto contrario e per intervalli giusti. A canon in
    contrary motion and by exact intervals.
  Canone sciolto. A free canon.

Cantab. Abbr. of *cantabile.*

Cantabile (It.). In a singing style, singingly.

    Cantabile e molto espressivo. Singingly and with much expression.

    Cantabile e molto tranquillo. Singingly and very quietly.

    Cantabile ed espressivo. In a singing style and with expression.

Cantacchiare (It.). To sing in a low voice; to hum.

Cantamento (It.). Singing, air, tune.

Cantando (It.). Singing, singingly.

    Cantando e con espressione. Singingly and with expression.

    Cantando molto. Very singingly.

Cantante (It.). adj. Singing, that may be sung. subs. A singer.

Cantare (It.). To sing.

    Cantare a orecchio. To sing by ear.

    Cantare a prima vista. To sing at sight.

    Cantare di maniera. To sing in a florid style, with many *maniere* (ornaments).

Cantata (It.). Originally applied to something sung, as opposed to *sonata*, something sounded (an instrumental composition); generally now confined to a short oratorio, not necessarily on a sacred subject.

    Cantata da camera. A chamber cantata; one intended for a small room and requiring but small means

    Cantata da chiesa. A church cantata.

Cantatina (It.). A short cantata.

Cantato, -a (It.). Sung.

    Messa cantata. High Mass.

Cantatore (It.). A male singer.

Cantatrice (Fr. and It.). A female singer.

Canterellando (It.). Singing low, humming.

Canterino, -a (It.). A singer.

Cantico (It.). A canticle, a hymn on words taken from the Bible, and used in the service of the Church.

Cantilena (It.). ⎰ A little song; now-a-days usually a smooth flowing
Cantilène (Fr.). ⎱ melody.

Cantino (It.). The "singing" string on a bowed instrument; the E string on a violin, the A string on a violoncello.

Cantique (Fr.). *v.* Cantico.

Canto (It.). (1) A song, a melody. (2) The melodic part in vocal or instrumental music. (3) *v.* Cantino.

    Canto a cappella. Unaccompanied vocal church music.

    Canto corale. A choral song.

    Canto d'amore. A love song.

    Canto espressivo e cantabile. The melody with expression and singingly.

    Canto fermo. Plain song. *v.* Cantus firmus.

    Canto figurato. A florid melody; a melody in florid counterpoint

    Canto funebre. A funeral song, a dirge.

    Canto gregoriano. Gregorian chant, plain song.

    Canto piano. Plain song.

    Canto primo. First soprano.

    Canto recitativo. Declamatory singing.

    Canto secondo. Second soprano, mezzo-soprano

Canto solo. Unaccompanied melody.

Cantor (Lat.). A singer, especially a church singer.

Cantore (It.). A singer.

Cantoris (Lat.). The *cantoris* side in a cathedral choir is the precentor's side, as opposed to the *decani* (the dean's) side. It is usually the north side of the choir.

Cantus (Lat.). Singing, a song, a melody.

    Cantus firmus. Gregorian chant, plain song. A subject chosen for contrapuntal treatment.

    Cantus planus. Plain song. *v.* Cantus firmus.

Canzona (It.). Song, ode, ballad.

Canzoncina (It.). A short song, a canzonet.

Canzone (It.). *v.* Canzona.

    Canzone a balla. A song for dancing.

    Canzone sacra. A sacred song.

Canzonetta (It.). A little song.

Canzoniere (It.). A song book.

Capo (It.). Head, chief: beginning. *Da capo*, from the beginning.

    Capobanda. The head of a band of music, band-master.

    Capo d'opera. A masterpiece, a *chef d'œuvre*.

    Capo d'orchestra. The conductor of an orchestra, *chef d'orchestre*.

    Capo tasto, *or* **Capodastro.** (1) A sort of bridge which is fixed on the fingerboard of a guitar, whereby the strings are raised a semitone, a tone, a third, etc. (2) The thumb position on the violoncello. (3) The nut of stringed instruments.

Cappella (It.). Chapel; the musicians forming the orchestra of a church. *v.* Chapelle.

Capriccietto (It.). Diminutive of *capriccio*.

Capriccio (It.). Caprice. The term is applied to a species of fantasia. *A capriccio*, capriciously.

Capricciosamente (It.). Capriciously.

Capriccioso, -a (It.). Capricious, whimsical, fanciful.

Caprice (Fr.). *v.* Capriccio.

Caractères de musique (Fr.). The signs used in musical notation.

Carattere (It.). Character, style.

Caratteristico (It.). Characteristic.

Caressant (Fr.).⎰ Caressing, coaxing, flattering.
Carezzando (It.).⎱

Carezzevolmente (It.). Lovingly.

Caricatamente (It.). In the style of a caricature.

Caricato (It.). Overloaded with embellishments.

Carillon (Fr.). A chime, a set of bells. Also used for the *Jeu de Timbre* (*Glockenspiel*), an instrument formerly consisting of small bells and now composed of tuned plates of steel, played by small hammers or a keyboard. *Sonner un carillon*, to ring a peal.

Carilloneur (Fr.). A bell-ringer.

Carità (It.). Charity, affection.

Carmagnole (Fr.). The name of a song and dance of the Revolution.

Carola (It.). A ring or round dance accompanied by singing.

Cassa (It.). A box, chest. A drum. (A side-drum is called *tamburo*.) The swell box of an organ.

    Cassa aperta. Swell open.

Cassa grande, *or* **Gran cassa,** *or* **Cassa.** The bass drum.

Cassa rullante. A tenor drum.

Cassazione (It.). Originally a "farewell" piece, afterwards the name of a kind of serenade.

Castagnette (It.). \
Castagnettes (Fr.). } Castanets.

Castanets. Small clappers of hard wood or ivory, the rhythm of which plays a large part in Spanish dances. They were formerly made also of iron, St.-Saëns using castanets of this material in *Samson et Dalila*.

Catena di trilli (It.). A chain of shakes.

Catgut strings. More properly "gut" strings, since they have now nothing to do with a cat, but are made from a sheep. They are used for most stringed instruments, and for the *snare* of the side-drum.

Cattivo (It.). Bad, wicked.

Cattivo tempo. The unaccented part of the bar.

Cavalletto (It.). *v.* Ponticello.

Cavalquet (Fr.). A cavalry call.

Cavare il suono (It.). To produce (literally, "to dig out") the sound or tone of an instrument.

Cavatina (It.). \
Cavatine (Fr.). } A short air, or song.

Caviglia (It.). A peg of a stringed instrument. plur. *caviglie*.

Cb. Abbr. of *contra-basso*.

Cédant (Fr.). Giving way; slackening the time.

Céder (Fr.). To yield, give way, slacken.

Cédez un peu. Slacken a little.

Celeramente (It.). With speed, velocity.

Celere (It.). Swift, nimble.

Celerità (It.). \
Celerité (Fr.). } Speed, quickness.

Celesta-Mustel (Fr.). Or simply *Celesta*, a keyboard instrument usually made with a compass of 4 octaves from *c′* to *c′′′′′* (Mahler writing for it as low as *d*). As a rule the written notes are an octave below the actual sounds: Tschaïkovsky (*Casse-Noisette*) however writes the notes at their actual pitch, probably because the part is to be played by a piano, should a celesta not be available. The instrument is much like a Typophone (*q. v.*), but instead of tuning-forks, the hammers strike small plates of steel.

Céleste (Fr.). Celestial, heavenly.

Celestina. A manual 4 ft stop of delicate tone.

Celesto, -a (It.). *v.* Céleste.

Cembalista (It.). A player on the *cembalo*.

Cembalo (It.). (1) A dulcimer. *v.* Salterio tedesco. (2) An abbreviation of *Clavicembalo*, the harpsichord.

Cercar della nota (It.). Literally, to search after the note: to proceed to the next note before the proper time, and use it as a sort of grace-note to the real note.

Ces (Ger.). C flat.

Cetra (It.). The zither.

Ch. Abbr. of Choir, Choir Organ, etc.

Chaconne (Fr.). A slow dance, often founded on a ground bass.

Chaleur (Fr.). Warmth, fervour.

Chaleureusement (Fr.). Warmly, with passion.

Chaleureux, -euse (Fr.). Impassioned, glowing.

Chalumeau (Fr.). (1) A term used for the lowest register of a clarinet, and in some old scores written an octave higher, with the indication "chal." above the part. (2) *v.* Schalmei.

Changez (Fr.). Change, alter.

    Changez de jeu. Change the register (of an organ or harmonium).

    Changez la en sol. Alter A to G.

Chanson (Fr.). A song.

Chansonette (Fr.). A little song.

Chansonnier (Fr.). (1) A song-writer. (2) A song-book.

Chant (Fr.). A song, a chant; singing.

    Chant et piano. Voice-part and piano. *Partition chant et piano*, vocal score.

    Chant funèbre. A dirge.

    Chant grégorien. Plain song, chant.

Chantant, -te (Fr.). Tuneful, melodious.

Chanté (Fr.). Sung. *Bien chanté* is a direction often found in Fr. scores and means that the melody is to be played in a melodious singing style.

Chanter (Fr.). To sing.

    Chanter à livre ouvert. ⎫ To sing at sight.
    Chanter à première vue. ⎭

Chanterelle (Fr.). The 1st or "singing" string of a stringed instrument, and unless otherwise specified usually denoting the E string of a violin.

Chanteur (Fr.). A male singer.

Chanteuse (Fr.). A female singer.

Chantre (Fr.). Chanter, precentor, chorister.

Chapeau chinois (Fr.). The Turkish crescent. *v.* Crescent.

Chapelle (Fr.). (1) A chapel. (2) The musicians of a church (choir and orchestra), or those in the employment of a prince or other person of rank. *cf.* Kapelle and Cappella.

Chaque (Fr.). Each, every.

    Chaque attaque assez en dehors. Every attack (*q. v.*) somewhat prominent.

Charakter (Ger.). Character. plur. *Charakter(e)*, the characters used in music.

    Charakterstücke. Characteristic pieces.

Charivari (Fr.). Discordant music; a mock serenade with pots, pans, etc.

Chasse (Fr.). The chase, hunting.

Che (It.). Who, which.

Chef (Fr.). Head, chief.

    Chef d'attaque. The leader of the orchestra.

    Chef d'œuvre. A master-piece. plur. *chefs d'œuvre.*

    Chef d'orchestre. A conductor of an orchestra.

Chevalet (Fr.). The bridge of a violin, etc. A stand for suspending a cymbal, gong, etc.

Cheville (Fr.). A peg of a violin, etc.

Chevrotement (Fr.). The bleating of a goat. *cf.* Bockstriller.

Chevroter (Fr.). To bleat like a goat; to execute a false shake on one note. *cf.* Bockstriller.

Chiaramente (It.). Clearly, plainly.

Chiarezza (It.). Clearness; brightness, light.

Chiaro (It.). Clear, bright.

Chiaroscuro (It.). Light and shade (in painting), and like many other terms in painting occasionally applied to music.

Chiave (It.). (1) A clef. (2) A key of a wind instrument.

 Chiave di Basso. Bass clef.

 Chiave di Violino. Violin (treble) clef.

Chica (Sp.). A dance popular in South America.

Chiesa (It.). A church.

Chiffré (Fr.). Figured.

Chinese Pavilion. Usually called a Crescent (*q. v.*) or Turkish crescent.

Chirula. *v.* Galoubet.

Chitarra (It.). A guitar.

Chiudendo (It.). Closing, terminating.

Chiuso, -a (It.). Closed. *Bocca chiusa*, closed mouth; *note chiuse*, closed notes (on the horn, *q. v.*).

Chœur (Fr.). Choir, chorus. The plur. is often used in place of the Eng. sing.; *pour orchestre et chœurs*, for orchestra and chorus.

Choir. A band of singers, usually in a religious service; the portion of a church where the musicians, save the organist, as a rule, perform. *cf.* Chorus.

 Choir Organ. One of the portions of an organ, containing stops of softer character than those of the Great Organ.

Chor (Ger.). (1) Choir, chorus. (2) A rank of pipes on an organ. plur. *Chöre*.

 Choramt. Choral service.

 Chorführer. Leader of choir.

 Chorknabe. Choir-boy.

 Chorton. In old Ger. music the customary pitch of church organs, and church music. It was approximately a tone higher than the *Kammerton* (*q. v.*).

 Chorübung. Choral exercise.

Choral (Ger.). A chorale, a hymn, plain-song.

 Choralbuch. A hymn-book.

 Choralist. A chorister.

 Choralmäßig. In the style of a hymn or psalm.

Chorège (Fr.). } A leader of a choir or chorus.
Chorege (Ger.). }

Chorus. (1) A band of singers, usually applied to one singing in a secular work, or performing in a secular building. (2) A composition written for a number of voices in several parts.

Choryphée (Fr.). One of the principal members of the chorus or ballet. In concerted music a *choryphée* sometimes takes a minor part.

Chromatic Drums. *v.* Kettledrum.

Chromatique (Fr.). } Chromatic.
Chromatisch (Ger.). }

 Chromatische Tonleiter. Chromatic scale.

Ciaccona (It.). A chaconne.

Cifrato (It.). From *cifrare*, to write in figures or cyphers. *Basso cifrato*, figured bass.

Cimbal (Ger.). A name for the *Hackbrett*, dulcimer.

Cimbalo, Cimbano (It.). (1) Sometimes written for *Cembalo* (*q. v.*). (2) According to Lichtenthal, a term occasionally used for the *Tamburino* or tambourine. (3) A mixture stop on the organ.

Cimbel, *or* Zimbel (Ger.). A mixture stop on the organ. The term is sometimes used for a *Hackbrett* (*q. v.*).

Cinelli (It.). Cymbals. *Piatti* is the more ordinary term.

Cinque (It.). Five.

Ciò (It.). This, that.

Cis (Ger.). C sharp.

>**Cis dur.** C sharp major.
>**Cis moll.** C sharp minor.

Cisis (Ger.). C double-sharp.

Cit(h)ara (It.). A lute, lyre.

Cither. *v.* Zither.

Civettando (It.). Coquetting.

Civetteria (It.). Coquetry, flirtation.

Cl. Abbr. of Clarinet, *clarinette*, *clarinetto*.

>**Cl.B.** Abbr. of *clarinette basse*.
>**Cl.C.B.** Abbr. of *clarinette contre-basse*.

Clairon (Fr.). The term for an instrument corresponding to the Eng. bugle, *bugle* (Fr.) being ordinarily reserved for the acuter members of the saxhorn family. The *clairon* is made more in the shape of a trumpet than its Eng. equivalent. The name is also given to a reed-stop on the organ.

>**Clairon d'ordonnance.** The regulation bugle of the Fr. army.

Claquebois (Fr.). A name for the xylophone.

Clar. Abbr. of clarinet, etc.

Clarabella. An organ stop of fluty tone, usually of 8ft pitch.

Claribel flute. An organ stop, usually of 4ft pitch.

Clarin (Ger.). }
Clarin (Sp.). } The *clairon*.

Clarina. An instrument invented by Heckel, and resembling the saxophone. It is made in B♭ and E♭ (sounding a minor 3rd above).

Clarinet. A single reed instrument with a compass from *e* to *c''''*. Clarinets in A♭, G and F are found only in the Austrian and some few other military bands; that in E♭ is used in all military bands, and of late years in the orchestra; that in D is seldom found in bands, but has been occasionally introduced into the orchestra (*Die Walküre, Mazeppa, Symphonia domestica*, etc.); the C clarinet is now rarely employed, and where it is indicated in the scores of the older masters, the performer almost invariably transposes his part on a B♭ instrument; this last (the typical member of the family) forms the basis of the "Wood" in a military band (there being from 12 to 16 performers on the instrument), and since Mozart has always been employed in the orchestra. The A clarinet, though still constantly written for, is discarded by some players in favour of the one in B♭, and in order to obtain the $c\sharp$, the lowest (actual) note on the A, B♭ instruments are now often provided with a lengthened bell and an extra key for producing this note.

Attempts have been made to construct a clarinet of double tonality, which can be altered from a B♭ to one in A at pleasure, but hitherto without success.

Clarinete (Sp.). ⎫ Clarinet.
Clarinette (Fr.). ⎭

   Clarinette alto. The alto clarinet.

   Clarinette basse. The bass clarinet.

   Clarinette contrebasse. The double-bass or pedal clarinet.

Clarinette (Ger.). *v.* Klarinette.

Clarinettino (It.). A small clarinet. *Clarinettino in mi♭,* the clarinet in E♭ (both *Clarinetto in mi♭* and *Clarino in mi♭* are also terms used for the instrument).

Clarinettista (It.). A clarinettist.

Clarinetto (It.). A clarinet. This is the term universally used until comparatively recently, and still employed by composers who prefer to use It. names to those in their own language; It. composers more frequently use *clarino* for a clarinet.

   Clarinetto a doppia tonalità. A B♭ clarinet, which can be altered at will to one in A. *v.* Clarinet.

   Clarinetto alto. The alto clarinet.

   Clarinetto basso. A bass clarinet. *cf.* Clarone.

Clarino (It.). (1) In ancient scores, the term was given to the trumpet playing the highest parts, and afterwards to any trumpet. In scores of the first half of the 18th century, where 3 trumpets are written for, the 1st and 2nd are *clarini* and play florid passages, the 3rd which plays the lowest and simplest part being known as *principale.* (2) In modern It. scores *clarino* is a clarinet. (3) A reed-stop on the organ, usually of 4ft pitch.

   Clarino di fila. A clarinet of the rank and file, not an *obbligato* clarinet, in a military band.

   Clarino obbligato. ⎫ The principal clarinet in a military band.
   Clarino principale. ⎭

Clarion. A high pitched trumpet, the term not being now used except in a poetical sense.

Claro, -a (It.). Clear. *Clara voce,* a clear voice.

Claro. Abbr. of Clarino.

Clarone (It.). A large clarinet; the term is usually applied to a bass clarinet, but at times used for the basset horn.

Clavecin (Fr.). A harpsichord.

Claviatur (Ger.). *v.* Klaviatur.

Clavicembalo (It.). The harpsichord, and often abbreviated to *Cembalo.* As *cembalo* is the term for a dulcimer, confusion has occasionally arisen between the two instruments.

Clavichord. A precursor of the pianoforte, differing from the harpsichord in the fact that the strings were struck by hammers and not plucked.

Clavicorno (It.). *v.* Genis.

Clavier, etc. (Ger.). *v.* Klavier.

Clavier (Fr.). A keyboard, a manual (on an organ).

   Clavier d'écho. The echo organ.

   Clavier de bombardes. A manual on some Fr. organs containing some powerful reed-stops; it often corresponds to the Eng. Solo organ.

Clavier de récit. The swell organ.

Clavi-timbre (Fr.). A species of harmonica with a keyboard, but in which tubes are used instead of strips of metal.

Clé (Fr.). *v.* Clef.

Clef (Fr.). A clef. A key of a wind-instrument.

> **Clef d'ut.** C clef.
> **Clef de fa.** F clef.
> **Clef de sol.** G clef.

Cloche (Fr.). A bell.

Clochette (Fr.). A little bell.

Coda (It.). Tail, end. The concluding portion of a movement.

Closed *or* **stopped notes.** *v.* Horn.

Codetta (It.). A little *coda*. The end (often limited to a few notes) of the first part of a movement in binary form, immediately before the double bars.

Codina (It.). Diminutive of *coda*.

Cogli (It.). The usual contraction of *con* (with) and *gli* (the, masc. plur.).

> **Cogli strumenti da fiato.** With the wind-instruments.

Coi (It.). Contraction of *con* (with) and *i* (the, masc. plur.).

> **Coi fagotti.** With the bassoons.
> **Coi sordini.** With the mutes.
> **Coi violini.** With the violins.

Col (It.). Contraction of *con* (with) and *il* (the, masc. sing.).

> **Col basso.** With the bass.
> **Col c.** Abbr. of *col canto*, with the vocal part.
> **Col C.B.** Abbr. of *col contrabasso*, with the double-bass.
> **Col legno.** With the wood or back (of the bow); an effect found in modern scores (*Symphonie fantastique, Siegfried, Danse Macabre,* etc.), and only effective if there be a large body of strings.
> **Col pedale e una corda.** With the pedal and on one string, *i. e.* putting down both pedals of a piano.

Colla, coll' (It.). Contraction of *con* (with) and *la* or *l'* (the, fem. sing.).

> **Colla destra.** With the right hand.
> **Coll' ott.** Abbr. of *coll' ottava*, with the octave, *i. e.* doubling a part with the octave above or below, usually implying the former.
> **Coll' ottava bassa.** With the octave below.
> **Colla parte.** With the part, *i. e.* the accompanying parts are to wait on that of the solo voice or instrument.
> **Colla più gran forza e prestezza.** With the greatest force and rapidity.
> **Colla punta d'arco.** With the point of the bow.
> **Colla sinistra.** With the left hand.
> **Colla voce.** With the voice. *cf.* Colla parte.

Colle (It.). Contraction of *con* (with) and *le* (the, fem. plur.).

> **Colle trombe.** With the trumpets.
> **Colle viole.** With the violas.

Collo, coll' (It.). Contraction of *con* (with) and *lo* or *l'* (the, masc. sing.).

> **Coll' arco.** With the bow. An indication used to contradict a previous *col legno* or *pizzicato*.

Colofonia (It.). ⎰Colophonium or colophony, the resin used for rub-
Colophane (Fr.). ⎱bing the hair of the bows of stringed instruments.
Colorato (It.). Coloured.
Coloratur (Ger.).⎱
Coloratura (It.). ⎰A florid passage in vocal music.
Colpo (It.). Blow, stroke; the same as the Fr. *coup*.
    Colpo d'arco. A stroke of the bow, *coup d'archet*.
    Colpo di lingua. "Tonguing" on a wind-instrument, *coup de langue*.
Combinaison (Fr.). Combination.
Come (It.). As, like.
    Come il tempo del tema. Like the tempo of the theme.
    Come prima. As before, as at first.
    Come primo. Like the first (tempo).
    Come sopra. As above, as before.
    Come sta. As it stands, as it is indicated.
    Come una fantasia, ma in tempo. Like a fantasia (*i. e.* in an extempore manner), but in tempo.
Comes (Lat.). The answer of a fugue, the *dux* being the subject.
Comique (Fr.). Comic, jocular, funny. The word is often employed as the adjective of *comedy*, and therefore does not of necessity imply anything very laughable.
Comme (Fr.). As, like.
    Comme un murmure. Like a murmur, *i. e.* almost inaudible.
Com(m)odamente (It.). Conveniently, easily, leisurely.
Com(m)odo (It.). Convenient, fit, leisurely. *v.* Tempo comodo.
Compass. The complete series of sounds that can be produced on any particular voice or instrument, which is divided into registers.
Compiacevole (It.). Agreeable, pleasing.
Compiacevolmente (It.). Agreeably, pleasingly.
Componista (It.). A composer.
Composition (Fr. and Ger.). Composition.
Composition pedals. Pedals, by means of which certain combinations of stops on an organ can be brought into play at the same time, and so arranged that gradations from pp to ff can be obtained.
Composition studs, *or* **buttons.** These serve the same purpose as the composition pedals, and are placed immediately above the different manuals.
Composto (It.). Composed.
Composizione (It.). Composition.
Compound stops. *v.* Mixture stops.
Comptent (Fr.). 3rd pers. plur. of *compter*, to count. An indication found in Fr. scores when particular instruments have not a stave devoted to them for some time, *e. g. Les trombones comptent*.
Con (It.). With. *v.* Col, Collo, Colla, Coi, Cogli, Colle.
    N. B. For indications commencing with *con*, not given below, see the word to which it is prefixed.
    Con anima. With soul, feeling.
    Con animo. With spirit, animation.
    Con brio. With vivacity, fire, spirit.
    Con discrezione. With discretion, *i. e.* following the composer both in letter and spirit.

Con divisione. With division, *i. e.* making each beat of the bar separate and distinct.

Con due pedali. With both pedals.

Con espressione e semplice. With expression and in a simple manner.

Con fluidezza. With fluidity, *i. e.* flowing smoothly and evenly.

Con forza. With force.

Con garbo. With grace and lightness.

Con giustezza dell' intonazione. With true intonation.

Con gli oboi. With the oboes.

Con la punta dell' arco. With the point of the bow.

Con molto carattere. With much character.

Con molto espressione. With much expression.

Con molto passione. With great passion.

Con moto. With animation.

Con osservanza. With scrupulous care. *cf.* Con discrezione.

Con pedale. With the pedal, *i. e.* with the damper pedal.

Con precipitazione. With haste.

Con precisione. With precision. *cf.* Con discrezione.

Con replica. With repeat; repeating the same passage.

Con sdegno. With indignation, anger.

Con somma expressione. With the greatest expression.

Con sordino (plur. -ni). With the mute(s).

Con tutta la forza. With the greatest force.

Con un dito. With one finger.

Con voce. With the voice. *cf.* Colla parte.

Con voce rauca. With a hoarse voice.

Concento (It.). Concord, harmony.

Concentrato (It.). Concentrated; concealed.

Concert (Fr.). Concert.

Concert spirituel. A concert of sacred music.

Concert (Ger.). *v.* Konzert.

Concert pitch. The recognised standard pitch in any particular country.

Concertante (It.). Formerly used for compositions (with or without orchestra), in which there were parts for solo instruments. Now, usually employed to signify prominent solo parts.

Concerted music. Music for two or more performers in contradistinction from music for a solo performer (with or without accompaniment).

Concertina. A free reed instrument with keys at both ends and bellows between. The ordinary instrument (the treble) has a range from *g* to *g''''* (or even *a''''*), and in the best makes will have from 48 to 60 keys. Piccolo, baritone and bass Concertinas are also made.

Concertino (It.). A short concerto.

Concerto (It.). (1) A concert. (2) A composition for a solo instrument with orchestral accompaniment, usually in symphonic form but without a scherzo or minuet. The older form of the concerto was simply a suite with a part for a solo instrument.

Concerto da camera. A chamber concerto.

Concerto da chiesa. A church concerto.

Concerto doppio. A concerto for two solo instruments.

Concerto grosso. (1) The old name for a concerto with three or more solo instruments (*concertante*). (2) The accompanying parts in the old form of the concerto, as opposed to the solo instruments.

Concerto spirituale. A sacred concert.

Concitamento (It.). Emotion, agitation.

Concitato (It.). Moved, troubled.

Concitazione (It.). *v.* Concitamento.

Concordant (Fr.). Baritone.

Conductor. The director of the orchestra (the term, leader of the orchestra, being applied to the chief violinist), who regulates the time of the movements, sees that the various instruments and voices make their entries at the proper moment, and generally interprets the composer's ideas to the public.

Conservatoire (Fr.).
Conservatorio (It.). } A public school for music and declamation.
Conservatorium (Ger.).

Consolante (It.). Giving comfort, consoling.

Consonanz (Ger.).
Consonanza (It.). } Consonance.

Cont. Abbr. of *contano.*

Contano (It.). 3rd pers. plur. of *contare*, to count. *v.* Comptent.

Continuato (It.). Continued.

Continuo (It.). *v.* Basso continuo.

Contra. *v.* Contra (It.).

Contra-bass. *v.* Double-bass.

Contra-bass Clarinet. *v.* Pedal clarinet.

Contra-basson. *v.* Double-basson.

Contra-bass Sarrusophone. *v.* Sarrusophone.

Contra-bass Trombone. An instrument an octave lower than the tenor trombone, used by Wagner in his *Ring*, where he writes for it at its actual pitch. It has been used by d'Indy in his 2nd symphony in the place of the tuba.

Contra-bass Tuba. The bombardon in F, E♭, or B♭ (an octave below the euphonium).

Contra octave. The 16ft octave; the notes from C_1, to B_1.

Contra (Ger.). *v.* Kontra.

Contra (It.). Against, opposite to. Often used in combination with other words to express something an octave deeper. (For the sake of euphony the first consonant of the word, with which it is compounded is usually doubled.)

Contr'arco. Bowing contrary to the usual method, *i. e.* commencing the bar on the up-stroke.

Contra-basso, or **Contrabbasso.** The double-bass.

Contraddanza. A country dance, a *contre-danse.*

Contrafagotto. The double-bassoon.

Contra-gamba. An organ pipe of 16ft.

Contralto (It.). (1) The lowest female voice with a compass from *g* to *e''*, exceptional voices attaining *e* or *e♭* at the bottom, f''♯ or *g''* at the top of the compass. (2) adj. Applied to instruments, it is used in place of the Eng. or Fr. 'alto', *e. g. trombone contralto.*

Contrappuntista. A contrapuntist.
Contrappunto. Counterpoint.
Contrappunto alla duodecima. Counterpoint at the twelfth.
Contrappunto alla mente. Improvised counterpoint.
Contrappunto doppio. Double counterpoint.
Contrassoggetto. Counter-subject.
Contrattempo. Syncopation.
Contre (Fr.). Opposite to, against, contra-.
  Contre-basse. The double bass.
  Contre-basse (en cuivre). The double-bass (in brass), the contra-bass saxhorn.
  Contre-basson. The double bassoon.
  Contrepoint. Counterpoint.
  Contrepointiste. Contrapuntist.
  Contre-sujet. Counter-subject.
  Contretemps. Syncopation.
Coperto (It.). Covered, veiled. *Tamburi coperti*, muffled drums.
Copribocchino (It.). A cap for a clarinet mouthpiece.
Copricordo (It.). A wrist protector for the mandoline.
Copula (It.). The coupler of an organ.
Cor. Abbr. of *corno*.
Cor (Fr.). A horn.
  Cor à cylindres. Horn with cylinders. *v.* Valves.
  Cor allemand. German horn, equivalent to Eng. "French horn".
  Cor à pistons. Horn with pistons. *v.* Valves.
  Cor chromatique. Chromatic horn, valve horn.
  Cor d'harmonie. The ordinary horn (with or without valves), as opposed to the *cor de chasse*.
  Cor de chasse. *v.* Trompe de chasse.
  Cor de signal. The post horn.
  Cor de vaches. The cow-horn, the *Stierhorn*.
  Cor omnitonique. An instrument constructed by Sax, without crooks, but which could be pitched in any key by means of a piston moving in a graduated tube.
  Cor russe. *v.* Russian horn.
  Cor simple. The horn without valves.
Cor anglais (Fr.). The English horn, the Fr. name being usually employed. An alto oboe having a similar compass to the ordinary oboe (from *b* (*b♭*) to *f'''*), but sounding a fifth lower than the written notes. At first introduced for occasional picturesque effects and played by one of the oboists, it now forms part of the ordinary full orchestra.
Cor de Basset (Fr.). *v.* Basset horn.
Corale (It.). Plain-song, chorale.
Coranto (It.). *v.* Courante.
Corda (It.). The string of a violin, etc.; plur. *corde*.
  Corda d'acciaio. A steel string (for a piano, etc.).
  Corda di budello. Cat-gut string.
  Corda di metallo. Metal string.
  Corda di minugia. A cat-gut string, often applied to the snare of a side-drum.
  Corda doppia. Double string.

Corda fasciata. A covered string, *i. e.* cat-gut bound with wire or silk.

Corda vuota. An open string on a stringed instrument.

Corde di budello. The snare on a side-drum.

Cordage (Fr.). The rope of a drum, the cord for tightening the head.

Corde (Fr.). String of a violin, etc. In the plur. (*cordes*) it also means the snare of a side-drum, and in this sense is occasionally used in the sing. *Avec la corde lâche,* with the snare slackened.

Corde à (*or* en) **boyau.** A cat-gut string.

Corde à jour. ⎰
Corde à vide. ⎱ An open string on a stringed instrument.

Corde filée. A covered string, *i. e.* one bound with wire or silk.

Cordes du timbre. Usually abbreviated to *timbre,* the snare of a side-drum.

Cordier (Fr.). ⎰
Cordiera (It.). ⎱ The tail-piece of a violin, etc.

Corhorn (Fr.). A species of tenorhorn (*q. v.*) designed to imitate the tone of a French horn, but with the facility of execution of a cornet or saxhorn. *v.* Cornophone.

Corifeo (It.). One of the leaders of a choir.

Corista (It.). (1) A chorister. (2) A tuning-fork.

Cormorne. *v.* Cromorne.

Cornamusa (It.). The bagpipes.

Cornare (It.). To blow or wind the horn.

Cornemuse (Fr.). The bagpipes.

Cornet. (1) The obsolete *cornetto* (*q. v.*). (2) The *cornet-à-pistons,* a brass instrument with a chromatic compass from $f\sharp$ to c''' (the last 3 notes being difficult). The typical instrument is in B♭ (with a shank for changing into A), and in many brass bands a cornet in E♭ is employed (the soprano cornet, *q. v.*). Instruments are also made in C, and in some military bands are found high cornets in D and A♭. Easier to play than a trumpet (*v.* Brass instruments), the cornet lacks the nobility of the latter, but nevertheless in the hands of a skilful artist is capable of a considerable amount of expression.

Cornet (Fr.). The simple cornet, *i. e.* the cornet without valves, a brass instrument of the posthorn type, is obsolete, and the term cornet is now used for the *cornet-à-pistons,* but it is to be noted that the ordinary Fr. abbreviation is not *cornet* but *piston.* *Pistons en si♭,* cornets in B♭.

Cornet à bouquin. The ancient cornetto (*q. v.*). It has recently been revived by d'Indy in the Celtic ceremony in *Fervaal,* but is there used only to give the two notes *g* and *b♭,* as a summons.

Cornet-à-pistons. *v.* above.

Cornet de poste. The simple or natural cornet.

Cornetin (Sp.). ⎰
Cornett (Ger.). ⎱ A cornet.

Cornetta (It.). The term for the *cornet-à-pistons* in modern It. scores.

Cornettino (It.). The small cornet, in E♭, D or A♭, also called *piccolo cornetto.*

Cornetto (It.). (1) An obsolete instrument, found in scores of the

XVIth and XVIIth centuries, made originally of a goat's horn, but later of wood covered with leather. It was played with a cup-shaped mouthpiece, and had six or seven holes pierced in the side, and sometimes possessed a key. Its compass was from *a* to *a'''*. (2) The modern *cornet-à-pistons*, but unlike the French, the Italians abbreviate the name to *cornetto* or *cornetta*, reserving *"pistone"* for the cornet in E♭.

Cornetto soprano. The ordinary cornet in B♭, C or A.

Cornetto contralto. The tenorhorn.

Cornista (It.). A horn-player.

Corno (It.). The horn.

Corno alto.) Names formerly given to performers who practised
Corno basso. (the higher or lower part of the horn's compass respectively. In the scores of the classical masters, the two horn parts must be considered not as being 1st and 2nd in the modern sense, but as to be played by two instruments of equal importance, the one, the alto horn, the other, the bass horn. In fact the *corno basso* may be considered the more important, since it was the one preferred by soloists. Beethoven, it is to be noted, frequently gives a solo to the *corno basso* in preference to the *corno alto*.

Corno a macchina. A valve horn.

Corno di caccia. (1) The Fr. *Trompe de chasse.* (2) The ordinary horn.

Corno primo. First horn.

Corno secondo. Second horn.

Corno sordo. A muted horn.

Corno tenore. Usually called *Flicorno basso* (*q. v.*).

Corno di bassetto (It.). The basset-horn.

Corno inglese (It.). The cor anglais.

Cornopean. A name formerly used for the cornet-à-pistons.

Cornophone (Fr.). An alto or tenor saxhorn of somewhat narrow bore, designed to be played with a horn mouthpiece as a substitute for the Fr. horn. It is allied to the saxotrombas and the ballad horn in C, used in some Eng. wind bands.

Coro (It.). Chorus, choir.

Corona (It.). The sign ⌒.

Corpo di ricambio (It.).)
Corps de rechange (Fr.). (A crook of a horn or trumpet.

Corrente (It.). subs. Same as *coranto*, a *courante* (*q. v.*). adj. Flowing.

Corrépétiteur (Fr.).)
Corripetitore (It.). (The trainer of an operatic chorus.

Coryphée (Fr.). One of the leaders of a chorus or ballet.

Costretto (It.). Bound, constrained. *Basso costretto, v.* Basso ostinato.

Cotillon (Fr.). A dance with no particular tune attached to it, and consisting of a series of figures more resembling a game than a dance.

Couac (Fr.). An onomatopoeic word for the squeak, which the reed of an instrument gives, arising from tired lips or from some imperfection in the reed.

Coucou (Fr.). The cuckoo; an instrument for imitating the bird.

Coulé (Fr.). (1) A slur. (2) A passage included under a slur. (3) A slide in dancing.

Couler (Fr.). To slide, glide, slur.

Coulisse (Fr.). (1) The slide of a trombone or slide-trumpet. (2) In a theatrical sense, a "wing", a side scene. *Dans les coulisses*, in the wings.

Counter-tenor. A male alto voice.

Coup (Fr.). A blow, stroke.

Coup d'archet. A bow-stroke; in Eng. often to be translated as "bowing".

Coup de langue. Tonguing.

Coupler. An appliance on an organ, by which the various manuals can be connected with one another, or with the pedals.

Couplet (Fr.). A couplet, stanza.

Coupure (Fr.). A cut.

Coupure théâtrale de A à B. Theatrical (*i. e.* for stage purposes) cut from A to B.

Cour (Fr.). In a theatrical sense the *côté de la cour* is the side of the stage to the right of the spectator.

Courante (Fr.). An old spirited dance in triple time. It often formed one of the numbers of the old suite.

Couronne (Fr.). The sign ⌒.

Courroie (Fr.). A strap. *Une cymbale suspendue par sa courroie*, a cymbal suspended by its strap.

Court (Fr.). Short. *Très court le point d'orgue*, the pause very short.

Couvert (Fr.). Covered.

Couvre-bec (Fr.). A mouthpiece cap for a clarinet, or saxophone.

Cracovienne (Fr.). A Polish dance.

Cran (Fr.). A notch; a notch into which the pedal of a harp is hitched.

Crécelle (Fr.). A rattle.

Credo (Lat.). "I believe"; part of the Mass.

Cremona. A reed stop on an organ.

Cres. Cresc. Abbr. of *crescendo*.

Crescendo (It.). Increasing in loudness, becoming louder.

Crescendo al ff. Growing louder up to the *ff.*

Crescendo ed affrettando poco a poco. ⎫ Gradually growing lou-
Crescendo ed animando poco a poco. ⎭ der and quicker.

Crescendo fin al fortissimo. Becoming louder until the fortissimo.

Crescendo molto ed animato. Rapidly increasing in loudness and becoming more animated.

Crescendo pedal. A term sometimes used for the ordinary swell pedal of an organ.

Crescendo poco a poco al forte, ed un pochettino accelerando. Becoming gradually louder until the forte, and very slightly faster.

Crescendo poco a poco ed accelerando. Gradually growing louder and faster.

Crescent. Or Turkish crescent, an instrument in the form of a crescent on the top of a staff, adorned with horse tails and small bells, which jingle when the staff is struck on the ground to mark the time. It was used only in infantry bands and now is practically obsolete. It was popularly known as "Jingling Johnny".

Crin (Fr.). The horse-hair used for bows. *Une mèche de crin*, a "lock" of horse-hair for a bow.

Croche (Fr.). A quaver. *Les croches conservent toujours la même valeur*, the quavers always keep the same value.

Croisez les mains (Fr.). Cross the hands; term found in piano duets.

Croma (It.). A quaver.

Cromatico (It.). Chromatic.

Cromorne (Fr.). (1) An obsolete double reed instrument recurved at the extremity, which has given its name to (2) a soft reed stop found in Eng. organs.

Crook. (1) A length of tubing added to horns and trumpets for the purpose of altering their pitch. They are now almost always fitted on to the mouthpiece end of the instrument, but used also to be made to fit into the middle of the instrument. With the old natural instruments, the crooks required were numerous, but with modern valve instruments only a few are directed to be used, and this number is often reduced still further by the exe- cutants themselves. *v.* Brass instruments. (2) The curved metal tube of a bassoon on which the reed is fixed.

Croque-note (Fr.). An unskilled musician.

Croquer un passage (Fr.). To bungle a passage.

Cross fingering. On wood-wind instruments, closing a hole lower than that through which the sound issues.

Cross flute. The *flauto traverso*, the ordinary flute.

Crotales (Fr.). A species of clapper, usually made of wood. (From the Lat. *crotalum*.) They have been used by Massenet and other composers.

Crucifixus (Lat.). "Crucified". A portion of the *Credo* in the Mass.

Csárdás. A Hungarian dance, usually in duple time.

Cto. Abbr. of *concerto*.

Cue. A few words or notes of one part interpolated in that of another, in order to indicate to the performer of the latter, when to make his entry.

Cuivre (Fr.). Brass, copper. *Instrument de cuivre*, a brass instrument. The "Brass" of the orchestra are called "*Les cuivres*".

Cuivré (Fr.). An expression used for all the brass instruments, but more particularly for the horns. It means forcing the sound in a particular way, so that it resembles the "brassy" tone of the *Trompe de chasse* (*q. v.*) or Fr. hunting horn. *Sforzato* notes are usually played in this manner. The modern Ger. equivalent is *schmetternd* (*q. v.*). Some composers limit the term to the strident but muffled tone obtained by forcing the sound of the stopped notes.

Cuivrer (Fr.). To make brassy. The Ger. equivalent is *stark anblasen*, to blow strongly. *Cuivrez les sons*, make the sounds (tone) brassy.

Cum Sancto Spiritu (Lat.). "With the Holy Spirit"; a part of the *Gloria* of the Mass.

Cupo (It.). Deep, hollow, sombre.

Cuscinetto (It.). A pad for the key of a wood-wind instrument.

Custos (Lat.). A direct; a sign at the end of a stave to indicate the first note of the next stave.

Cylinders. A form of valve for brass instruments mostly used in Germany and Italy. It is on the principle of an ordinary brass cock.

Cylindre (Fr.). A cylinder. *Cor à cylindres*, a horn with cylindrical valves.

Cymbal (Ger.). The dulcimer; usually called the *Hackbrett*.

Cymbale (Fr.). A cymbal. Also the name of a mixture stop on the organ.

Cymbale avec la mailloche. Cymbal struck with a bass-drumstick.

Cymbale frappée avec une baguette de timbale. Cymbal struck with a kettle-drumstick.

Cymbales (Fr.). (1) Cymbals. *Une paire de cymbales*, a pair of cymbals. (2) The jingles of a tambourine.

Cymbals. Circular plates of metal, which are ordinarily clashed together, — or rather, swung together with a sliding motion. In inferior orchestras one of the cymbals is attached to the bass-drum, to the immense disadvantage of the former's tone. (That this method is not universally condemned is apparent from certain of Mahler's symphonies, where he specially directs the cymbals to be attached to the bass drum, even in places where two performers are necessary.) A species of roll (*v.* Overture to *Tannhäuser*) is obtained by rapidly rubbing the two plates together, or by agitating the beater of a triangle between the two cymbals held a short distance apart. In modern works a single suspended cymbal is often directed to be struck with a bass-drumstick, or is played upon by kettle-drumsticks or side-drumsticks.

Cymbel (Ger.). *v.* Cymbal.

Czakan. A flute with a flageolet mouthpiece, made in the form of a walking-stick, and formerly much used in Hungary.

D

D. The second note of the normal scale of C major. It is called *ré* in Fr. and *re* in It.

D. Abbr. of *destra*, or *droite*.

D. C. Abbr. of *Da capo*.

D Clarinet. A small clarinet sounding a tone above the written notes, used in *Die Walküre*, Liszt's *Mazeppa*, and several modern works.

D♭ Flute. *v.* Flute.

D (Ger.). The note D. *Des* is D flat, and *Dis* D sharp.

D dur. D major.

D moll. D minor.

D Saite. The D string.

D' (Fr.). Abbr. of *de*, of, from etc.

D'abord. At first.

D'accord. In agreement, in tune.

Da (It.). From, by, of, for, from.

Da ballo. In the style of a dance.

Da camera. For a chamber, as *sonata da camera*, a chamber sonata.

Da capo. From the beginning, meaning that the performer has to go back to the beginning of the piece and play on till *fine* is marked. The term is also used to express a desire for an encore at a theatre or concert.

Da capo al fine. From the beginning to where *fine* is marked.

Da capo al segno ✇. From the beginning to the sign ✇.

Da capo senza ripetizione, e poi la coda. From the beginning without repeats, and then the coda.

Da chiesa. For the church. *Sonata da chiesa*, church sonata.

Da destra. From the right.

Da lontano. In the distance.

Da prima. First.

Da teatro. In the theatrical style.

Dach (Ger.). A roof, covering. The belly of a violin.

Dachsweller. The swell of an organ.

Dagli, dai, dal, dall', dalla, dalle, dallo (It.). Compounds of *da* (*q. v.*) with *gli, i, il, l', la, le, lo* (all forms of the definite article).

Dal (It.). Compound of *da* (*q. v.*) and *il* (the, masc.).

Dal segno. From the sign (of repeat).

Dal segno fin al segno. From the sign (of repeat) and then to the same sign.

Damp. In a musical sense, used in two ways. (1) To check the vibrations of the string of a harp, guitar, violin, etc., or of a percussion instrument such as a gong, a suspended cymbal, etc. (2) To deaden the sound of an instrument by some mechanical contrivance, to mute. This sense is rare.

Damper. The part of the mechanism of a piano which checks the vibrations of a string as soon as the key is released.

Damper pedal. A contrivance, whereby the dampers can be kept raised from the strings of a piano, even after the fingers have left the keys. As with the inexperienced or inartistic, the effect of using this pedal is simply to increase the noise, it is vulgarly known as the "loud pedal".

Dämpfer (Ger.). A mute for a violin, etc., or for a brass instrument (horn, trumpet, trombone, etc.).

Dämpfer auf. Put on the mutes.

Dämpfer ab. ⎫

Dämpfer fort. ⎬ Take off the mutes.

Dämpfer weg. ⎭

Dämpfung (Ger.). Damping, muting; on the piano, the damper pedal.

Dann (Ger.). Then, at that time.

Dann sogleich immer langsamer. Then forthwith becoming steadily slower.

Dans (Fr.). In.

Dans les coulisses (*occasionally* **la coulisse**). In the wings, *i. e.* off the stage, from either side.

Dans une exaltation croissante. In (or with) increasing enthusiasm.

Danse Macabre (Fr.). The dance of Death.

Danza (It.). A dance.

Dare (It.). To give. (As with many other words, the final "e" is often dropped before a consonant.)

Dar la voce. To give the pitch.

Dareinfahren (Ger.). To interpose, break in.

Darmsaiten (Ger.). Cat-gut strings.

Darunter (Ger.). Under that, among, of the number.

Darunter 2 fünfsaitige. Amongst the number, 2 five-stringed (double-basses).

Das (Ger.). Neuter form of *Der*, the, which.
    Das doppelt langsamer. Twice as slow.
    Das nämliche. The same (tempo).
    Das zweite Mal. The second time.
Dasselbe (Ger.). Neuter form of *Derselbe*, the same.
    Dasselbe Zeitmaß. The same tempo.
Dauer (Ger.). The duration (of a note)
Daumen (Ger.). The thumb.
    Daumeneinsatz. The thumb position on the violoncello.
    Daumenventil. A valve operated by the thumb, found on certain
    tenor and bass trombones. *v.* Trombone.
De (Fr.). Of, from, to.
    De même que précédement. The same as before.
    De plus en plus vite. More and more quickly.
    De suite. One after another; so forth.
Debile, Debole (It.). Faint, weak.
Début (Fr.). Commencement, beginning. Of an artist, first appear-
ance. *Plus vite qu'au début*, quicker than at the commencement.
Débutant, -ante (Fr.). A performer appearing for the first time.
Dec. Abbr. of *Decani.*
Decani (Lat.). Of the Dean. Term used in cathedral music for that
part of the choir on the dean's side (usually the south side), as
opposed to the *cantoris* (*q. v.*).
Décidé (Fr.). With decision, in precise rhythm.
Decima (It.). A tenth; the interval of a tenth.
    Decima quarta. The interval of a fourteenth.
    Decima quinta. The interval of a fifteenth.
    Decima terza. The interval of a thirteenth.
Decimole (Ger.). A group of ten equal notes played in the time
of four or eight, a decuplet.
Decisissimo (It.). Sup. of *deciso*.
Deciso (It.). With decision, in precise rhythm.
Decke (Ger.). A covering. The belly of a violin, etc.
Declamando (It.). Declaiming.
Décomposé (Fr.). Incoherent, unconnected.
Décoration (Fr.). Term occasionally used for the sharps or flats in
the key signature.
Décors (Fr.). The scenery etc., of a play or opera.
Découplez (Fr.). Uncouple.
Decresc. Abbr. of *decrescendo*.
Decrescendo (It.). Decreasing in loudness.
Decresciuto (It.). Decreased, diminished in loudness.
Degré (Fr.). Degree, step; degree of the scale.
Dehnung (Ger.). A lengthening out, a prolongation.
    Dehnungsstrich. A long drawn-out stroke with a bow.
Del, dell', della, delle, dello, dei, degli. Compounds of *di* (*q. v.*) with
il, l', la, le, lo, i, gli (various forms of the definite article).
Deliberamente (It.). Deliberately.
Delicatamente (It.). Delicately, tenderly.
Delicatezza (It.). Delicacy, grace, softness.
Delicatissimo (It.). Sup. of *delicato*.
Delicato (It.). Delicate, gentle, soft.

Délié (Fr.). Loose, easy.
Delirio (It.). Raving, madness.
Deliziosamento (It.). Deliciously, sweetly.
Delizioso (It.). Delicious, sweet.
Démancher (Fr.). To "shift" on a violin, etc.
Démanchement (Fr.). "Shifting" on a violin, etc.
Demande (Fr.). A term for the subject of a fugue.
Demi (Fr.). Half.
    Demi-bâton. The sign for two bars rest.
    Demi-cadence. A half close.
    Demi-jeu. Half the power of the instrument.
    Demi-mesure. Half a bar.
    Demi-pause. A minim rest.
    Demi-quart de soupir. A demisemiquaver rest.
    Demi-soupir. A quaver rest.
    Demi-ton. A semitone.
    Demi-voix. *Mezza voce.*
Démonter (Fr.). To unstring a stringed instrument.
Demüt(h)ig (Ger.). Humble, lowly, meek.
Demüt(h)igung (Ger.). Humiliation, abasement.
Dentro (It.). Within.
    Dentro le quinte. In the "wings".
    Dentro le scene. Within (behind) the scenes.
Derb (Ger.). Firm, ponderous, vigorous. *Mit derbem Humor,* with rude humour.
Derrière (Fr.). Behind.
    Derrière la scène. Behind the scenes.
    Derrière le rideau. Behind the curtain.
Des (Ger.). D flat.
    Des dur. D flat major.
    Des moll. D flat minor.
Deses (Ger.). D double-flat.
Désespérément (Fr.). Desperately.
Desinvoltura (It.). *v.* Disinvoltura.
Désinvolture (Fr.). Freedom, ease.
Desk (Fr. *Pupitre;* Ger. *Pult;* It. *Leggio*). In the modern orchestra where the strings are often very elaborately divided, the desk (at which two performers sit) is taken as the basis of these divisions. The Fr. composers usually content themselves with dividing the desks into odd and even (*impairs et pairs*), or simply writing *à 2, à 4,* etc. The Germans, with their more elaborate string divisions, often indicate the absolute number of desks for a particular part, and thus we find such subtle directions as Desks 1, 2 and 3 playing one part, while Desks 4, 5, 6, 7 and 8 play another.
Dessin (Fr.). Plan, arrangement.
Dessous (Fr.). Under, below.
Dessus (Fr.). Above, over. As a subs., the upper part, and formerly used for the treble, both vocal and instrumental.
    Dessus de viole. The violin part (term now obsolete)
Dest. Abbr. of *destra.*
Desto (It.). Lively, brisk.
Destra (It.). The right hand. *A destra,* to the right.

Destro, -a (It.). Skilful, dexterous. Used for right, as the opposite of *sinistra*, left.

Détaché (Fr.). Detached, *staccato*. In violin playing, there are several kinds of *détaché*, the names of which somewhat vary with different authors, all however agreeing as to the *grand détaché* (*q. v.*). In piano playing, the *détaché* may be wrist *staccato*, finger *staccato*, or *mezzo staccato*

    Détaché de la pointe. Sometimes called *petit détaché*, detached notes given with the point of the bow.

    Détaché moyen. Detached notes obtained by using a third of the bow.

    Détaché sec. The same as *martelé* (*q. v.*).

Determinato (It.). Determined, resolute.

Detonieren (Ger.). } To intone falsely, to sing out of tune.
Détonner (Fr.). }

Deutlich (Ger.). Clear, distinct, conspicuous, prominent.

    Deutlicher und stets gut hervortretend. More distinctly and always well brought out.

Deutsch (Ger.). German.

    Deutsche Flöte. German flute.

    Deutsche Tänze. German dances.

Deux (Fr.). Two.

    Deux quatre. $^2/_4$ time.

Deuxième (Fr.). Second.

Devozione (It.). Devotion.

Dezimenflöte (Ger.). The piccolo in E♭.

Di (It.). Of, from, by.

    Di grado. (1) By degrees. (2) Willingly, with pleasure

    Di molto. Very much.

    Di nuovo. Anew, again, once more.

    Di petto. Of the chest, chest voice.

    Di testa. Of the head, head voice.

Diap. Abbr. of Diapason.

Diapason. A principal stop in an organ, and of two kinds: — the open diapason and the stopped diapason.

Diapason (Fr.). (1) Pitch. (2) A tuning-fork: a pitch-pipe.

    Diapason à bouche. A pitch-pipe.

    Diapason à branches. A tuning-fork.

    Diapason normal. The standard pitch decreed by the Fr. Government in 1859, *a'* being fixed at 435 vibrations at a temperature of 15° C. (59 F.).

Diatonico (It.). }
Diatonique (Fr.). } Diatonic.
Diatonisch (Ger.). }

Dicht (Ger.). Close, *serré*. Indication sometimes added to a *tremolo*, and meaning that it is to be very rapid.

Die (Ger.). The, fem. sing., and plur for all genders. (Expressions commencing with *die* will be found under the heading of the noun.)

    Die 5 ersten Pulte. The 5 first desks.

Diecetto (It.). A composition for ten instruments.

Dies irae (Lat.). "Day of wrath". The principal number of a Requiem Mass.

Diesare (It.). To sharpen, to put a sharp before a note.
Dièse (Fr.). The sharp sign (♯).
Dieselbe (Ger.). The same. (fem. and plur. form.)
    Dieselbe Bewegung. The same movement.
Diéser (Fr.). To sharpen, to place a sharp before a note.
Diesis (It.). The sharp sign (♯).
Dietro (It.). Behind.
    Dietro la scena. Behind the scene; in the wings.
Difficile (Fr. and It.) Difficult.
Digitare (It.). To finger. *Il digitare*, fingering.
Digitatura (It.). Fingering.
Dillettante (It.). An amateur; one who practises an art for pleasure and not as a profession.
Diluendo (It.). Dying away.
Dilungando (It.). Prolonging the sound.
Dim. Dimin. Abbr. of *diminuendo*.
Diminué (Fr.). Diminished. *L'accord de quinte diminuée*, the chord of the diminished fifth.
Diminuendo (It.). Diminishing (in loudness).
    Diminuendo e poco ritenuto. Diminishing in loudness and somewhat slower.
    Diminuendo e rallentando. Becoming softer and slower.
    Diminuendo poco a poco. Gradually diminishing.
Diminuer (Fr.). To diminish
Diminuito, -a (It.). Diminished.
Diminuzione (It.). Diminution.
Directeur (Fr.). A director; a conductor, usually applied to the conductor of a choir (*directeur des chœurs*).
Dirigent (Ger.). A director; conductor.
Dirigi(e)ren (Ger.). To direct; to conduct an orchestra.
Diritto, -a (It.). Direct, straight.
Dis (Ger.). D sharp.
Discretamente (It.). Discreetly. *cf.* Con discrezione.
Discreto (It.). Discreet, prudent.
Discrezione (It.). Discretion.
Disgiunto (It.). Disjunct.
Disharmonisch (Ger.). Dissonant, discordant.
Disinvolto (It.). Ease, freedom, gracefulness.
Disis (Ger.). D double-sharp.
Diskant (Ger.). Discant; soprano, treble.
    Diskantbratsche. A treble viol.
    Diskantschlüssel. The soprano clef; the C clef on the 1st line.
    Diskantstimmen, *or* **Diskantregister.** Organ stops which comprise only the treble notes.
Diskantist, *or* **Diskantsänger** (Ger.). A treble, or soprano singer.
Disperabile (It.). Hopeless.
Disperante (It.). Grievous, hopeless.
Disperatamente (It.). Desperately, madly.
Disperato (It.). Desperate, hopeless.
Disperazione (It.). Despair, desperation.
Disposition. The arrangement of the stops on an organ, or of the various instruments in an orchestra.

Dissonance (Fr.). ⎫
Dissonanz (Ger.). ⎬ Dissonance.
Dissonanza (It.). ⎭
Distanza (It.). Distance, space.
Distinto (It.). Distinct, clear.
Distonare (It.). To sing out of tune.
Diteggiatura (It.). Fingering.
Dito (It.). A finger. plur. *dita*, or (less frequently) *diti.*
    Dito annulare. The ring or third finger.
    Dito grosso. The thumb. Also *pollice.*
    Dito indice. The index or first finger.
    Dito medio. The middle or second finger.
    Dito mignolo. The little finger.
Diton (Fr.). ⎫
Ditono (It.). ⎬ An interval of two tones; a major third.
Div. Abbr. of *divisi*, or *divise.*
Divertimento (It.). A diversion, a pastime. In a musical sense, it is used (1) for a *potpourri* of tunes strung together; (2) for a composition consisting of a series of movements, much in the style of a Serenade; (3) a short ballet.
Divertissement (Fr.). *v.* Divertimento (1), (2) and (3). Also an episode in a fugue. *Une divertissement tirée de la tête du sujet*, an episode founded on the first notes of the subject.
Divided Strings. *v.* Desks.
Diviso, -a (It.). Divided. plur. *divisi, -e. Violini divisi,* divided violins; *viole divise,* divided violas.
Divotamente (It.). Devoutly, piously.
Divoto, -a (It.). Devout, devoted.
Divozione (It.). Devotion, piety.
Dixième (Fr.). Tenth; the interval of a tenth.
Do (It.). The note C. The French occasionally also use it instead of the customary *Ut.*
    Do maggiore. C major.
    Do minore. C minor.
Doch (Ger.). But, still, nevertheless.
    Doch immer noch sehr lebhaft. But still very animated.
    Doch nicht allzu sehr. But not too much.
Doglia (It.). Grief, pain.
Dogliosamente (It.). Grievously, sorrowfully.
Dogliosissimo (It.). Sup. of *doglioso.*
Doglioso (It.). Afflicted, sorrowful.
Doigt (Fr.). Finger. *L'index*, the 1st finger; *le médium*, 2nd; *l'annulaire*, 3rd; *le petit doigt*, 4th; *le pouce*, the thumb.
Doigté (Fr.). subs. Fingering. past part. Fingered.
    Doigté fourchu. Cross fingering.
Doigter (Fr.). To finger. *Le doigter*, fingering.
Dol. Abbr. of *dolce.*
Dolcan. An organ pipe of agreeable tone.
Dolce (It.). Sweet, agreeable, pleasant, soft.
    Dolce con gusto. Sweetly and with taste.
    Dolce e lusingando. Sweetly and in a caressing manner.
    Dolce e molto tranquillo. Softly and very peacefully.

Dolce e piacevolmente espressivo. Sweetly and pleasingly expressive.

Dolce grazioso ed espressivo. Softly, gracefully and expressively.

Dolce, ma marcata (la melodia). Softly, but marked (the melody).

Dolce maniera. In a pleasing style.

Dolcemente (It.). Sweetly, softly.

Dolcezza (It.). Sweetness.

Dolciano (It.). (1) A dulcian (*q. v.*). (2) An organ stop.

Dolciore (It.). *v.* Dolcezza.

Dolcis. Abbr. of *dolcissimo*.

Dolcissimo (It.). Sup. of *dolce*.

Dolcitudine (It.). *v.* Dolcezza.

Dolente (It.). Doleful, sad, plaintive.

Dolentemente (It.). Sorrowfully, sadly.

Dolentissimo (It.). Sup. of *dolente*.

Dolore (It.). Pain, anguish.

Dolorosamente (It.). Sorrowfully.

Doloroso (It.). Sad, painful.

Dolzflöte (Ger.). (1) An obsolete flute, the *flûte douce*. (2) An organ stop.

Dom (Ger.). A cathedral.

Domchor. A cathedral choir.

Dominante (Ger.). The dominant. *Dominanten-* in combination.

Dominantenakkord. The dominant chord.

Dominantendreiklang. The dominant triad.

Domine salvum fac (Lat.). "O Lord, preserve". A prayer for the reigning sovereign, sung after the Mass.

Dona nobis pacem (Lat.). "Give us peace". The last movement of the Mass.

Donner (Fr.). To give.

Donner le cor. To blow the horn.

Donner (Ger.). Thunder.

Donnermaschine. A machine for imitating thunder.

Doppel (Ger.). Double.

Doppel-B (*or* Be). The double-flat sign ($\flat\flat$).

Doppelfagott. A name for the double-bassoon (*Kontrafagott*).

Doppelflöte. A stop on the organ, the pipes of which have two mouths.

Doppelfuge. A double fugue.

Doppelgeige. A name for the *viole d'amour*.

Doppelgriff. A double-stop on a violin, etc.

Doppelkonzert. A concerto for two solo instruments.

Doppelkreuz. The double-sharp sign (×).

Doppeloktave. An interval of two octaves.

Doppelschlag. A turn.

Doppelstielige Note. A note with two stems, ♪.

Doppelstürze. A double bell; an extra joint placed on a wood-wind instrument instead of the ordinary end joint, in order to produce low notes not on the ordinary instrument, as for instance the low A_1 of the bassoon.

Doppeltriller. A double shake.

Doppelzunge. Double tonguing.

Doppelt. (Ger.). Doubled.

    Doppelt ganze Note. A breve.

    Doppelt ganze Pause. A breve-rest.

    Doppelt langsamer. }
    Doppelt so langsam. } Double as slow.

    Doppelt so schnell. Double as fast.

Doppio, -a (It.). Double.

    Doppio colpo di lingua. Double tonguing.

    Doppio movimento. A movement twice as fast as the previous one.

    Doppio pedale. In organ music, using both feet for the pedal-board.

    Doppio più lento. Double as slow.

    Doppio tempo. Double time.

Double. A term occasionally equivalent to the It. Contra (*q. v.*).

    Double bass. The lowest of the stringed instruments used in the modern orchestra, and now usually made with four strings tuned to *E. A. d. g.* (sounding an octave lower). This tuning is however not invariable, many players tuning the 4th string to *D*, and generally speaking the tuning has always been rather a matter of individual taste. The 3-stringed D. B. (tuned *A. d. g*, or *G. d. a*), though still found in many orchestras, and preferred by some on account of its greater resonance, is not written for now-a-days by composers, who on the other hand often require an instrument descending to *C*. This last is either a 5-stringed D. B., or a 4-stringed one, having a mechanical arrangement whereby the E-string can be immediately lowered to *C*, and the notes *C, C♯, D* and *E♭* obtained by means of keys. Whether the classical masters wrote for D. B. tuned down to *C*, or whether the low notes found in their scores arose from carelessness, in writing the same part for both 'cellos and D. B., is a moot point: but on the authority of Koch (*Musikalisches Lexikon*, 1802), we know that the E-string of the 4-stringed D. B. was often lowered to *E♭* and *D*.

    Double Bassoon. An instrument an octave lower than the ordinary bassoon, and formerly descending to $B_2♭$, but now only to D_1 or C_1 (Mahler writes the $B_2♮$), *e♭* or *f* being as a rule considered as its highest available note (Beethoven and Mahler however using the *a*). In most scores the notes are written an octave higher than their actual sounds, but Wagner in *Parsifal* writes them at their proper pitch. With modern instruments the D. Bn. is often made of brass, and in many orchestras it has been superseded by the contra-bass sarrusophone *v.* Sarrusophone.

    Double C, *or* **CC.** The same as C_1: in Eng. organ music, it stands for *C*, the C below the bass stave, all the notes from G_1 to *F* inclusive being called "double".

    Double diapason. An organ stop of 16 ft pitch.

    Double drum. According to some writers, a name for the bass drum, "because it is beaten on both heads", but probably this is a mistake, arising from a confused impression of the instruments given in the next paragraph.

Double drums. A term formerly used for the kettledrums, and of obvious signification, since there was always a pair of them. The term is found in almost any of the lists of the orchestras of a hundred years ago.

Double quartet. A composition for two sets of four voices or instruments.

Double reed. Two reeds bound together to form a mouthpiece, as in the oboe and bassoon.

Double stopped diapason. An organ stop of 16 ft tone on the manuals, and of 32 ft tone on the pedals, in which latter case it is often called the *Sub-bourdon.*

Double stopping. On the violin, etc., playing two notes at the same time. As a rule this is done with two fingers, but it is also possible to stop two strings with one finger, which naturally form a fifth.

Double tonguing. On the flute and brass instruments, the rapid repetition of notes made with a movement of the tongue.

Double travale. A rapid repetition of sounds on a tambourine.

Double trumpet. A reed stop of 16 ft on the organ.

Double (Fr.). Double. *Le double plus lent,* double as slow.

Double bémol. A double flat.

Double (*or* 2ble) **corde.** A double string on a stringed instrument.

Double croche. A semiquaver.

Double dièse. A double sharp.

Double mailloche. A bass drumstick with two heads, used for executing a species of roll.

Double-mains. A mechanism attached to some organs and harmoniums, whereby when a key is depressed the octave above is depressed at the same time.

Double triple. $^3/_2$ time.

Doublette (Fr.). In Fr. organs, a stop an octave above the Principal; the Fifteenth. In Eng. organs, a stop of two ranks of pipes.

Doucement (Fr.). Softly, sweetly.

Douleureusement (Fr.). Sadly, sorrowfully.

Doux, douce (Fr.). Sweet, soft.

Doux mais très soutenu. Soft but very sustained.

Douzième (Fr.). Twelfth: the interval of a twelfth.

Downbow. On a violin, etc., the drawing of the bow towards the player.

Drahtsaite (Ger.). A metal string.

Dramma (It.). Drama, play.

Dramma lirica. A lyrical drama.

Dramma musicale. ⎰ A musical drama.
Dramma per musica. ⎱

Drammaticamente (It.). Dramatically.

Drammatico (It.). Dramatic.

Drängend (Ger.). Pressing, hurrying.

Drängend und immer heftiger. Hurrying and with increasing impetuosity.

Dreher (Ger.). A species of slow waltz.

Drei (Ger.). Three.

Dreichörig. (1) Of a piano, trichord. (2) For three choirs.

Dreifach. (Often written 3fach.) Threefold. In an organ, of three ranks. The term is often found in scores indicating that one or other of the string parts is divided into three parts.

Dreiklang. A triad.

Dreisaitig. Three stringed.

Dreistimmig. In three parts; for 3 voices or instruments.

Dreitaktig (Rhythmus). In three bar (rhythm).

Dreier (Ger.). Ternary rhythm.

Dreinfahren (Ger.). *v.* Dareinfahren.

Dringender (Ger.). (The tempo) more hurried.

Dritt (Ger.). Third.

Dritte Lage. Third position.

Dritto (It.). *v.* Diritto.

Drohend (Ger.). Threatening.

Droit, droite (Fr.). Right; straight.

Drone. One of the pipes of the bagpipes, which continuously sounds the same note.

Druckknöpfe (Ger.). Drawstops (on the organ.)

Drum. In modern music, besides the kettledrums, there are three kinds of drums in general use, with the occasional addition of a fourth: — (1) the bass drum, (2) the tenor drum, (3) the side or snare-drum, (4) the *tambourin*. *v.* separate articles.

Drumsticks. For the kettledrums, drumsticks with three kinds of heads are used: — the ordinary ones, made of felt; those made of sponge covered with chamois leather, for delicate effects; those of wood, for noisy effects. For special effects, side-drumsticks, a couple of coins and the fingers have been employed by Sir Edward Elgar. The drumsticks for the side drum are of ebony; those for the tenor drum being somewhat larger, with felt or padded heads. For the bass drum a stick with a large stuffed head is used, and for producing rolls, a stick with a head at each end; occasionally a wooden-headed stick is used.

Du (Fr.). Compound of *de*, of, from, etc., and *le*, the (masc. sing.).

Du bout de l'archet. With the point of the bow.

Du talon. At the nut (of the bow).

Dudelsack (Ger.). A bagpipe.

Due (It.). Two.

Due corde. Two strings.

Due cori. Two choruses.

Due volte. Twice.

Duett (Ger.). A duet.

Duettino (It.). A short duet.

Duetto (It.). A duet.

Dugazon (Fr.). The name of a celebrated singer (Louise Rosalie Dugazon, 1753—1821), and now used to indicate a voice of the same range and quality as hers, and thus singers are described as *"jeunes Dugazon"*, *"mères Dugazon"*, etc.

Dulcian. An obsolete bassoon, an octave higher than the ordinary bassoon.

Dulciana. An 8ft organ stop.

Dulcimer. An instrument consisting of a frame and a sound-board over which are stretched wire strings. These strings are arranged in groups (2 to 5 strings forming one note), and are struck by two little hammers.

Dulzaina (Sp.). A dulcian (*q. v.*).

Dumpf (Ger.). Hollow, dull.

Duo (It.). A duet. It is also a usual term in France.

Duodecima (It.). The interval of a twelfth.

Duodecimole (Ger.). A group of 12 equal notes instead of the normal number in the beat; a dodecuplet.

Duodramma (It.). A short drama for two persons.

Duole (Ger.). A duplet.

Duolo (It.). Grief, pain, mourning.

Duplicazione (It.). Doubling.

Dur (Ger.). Major.

    Durtonart. Major key.

Duramente (It.). Harshly, cruelly.

Durch (Ger.). Through.

    Durch ein Sprachrohr. Through a speaking trumpet.

    Durch Flageolet. In harmonics.

    Durchblasen. To blow (play) through a composition on a wind-instrument.

    Durchführung. Development.

    Durchgangsnote. } A passing note.
    Durchgangston. }

    Durchgehend. Passing.

    Durchgeigen. To play through a composition on the violin.

    Durchkomponieren. To set to music: in vocal music, to set each verse to different music, according to the character of the words.

    Durchschlagende Zunge. A free reed.

    Durchspielen. To play through a composition.

Durchaus (Ger.). Throughout.

    Durchaus fantastisch und leidenschaftlich vorzutragen. To be performed fantastically and with passion throughout.

Durchweg (Ger.). Generally, usually.

    Durchweg leise zu halten. To be kept generally soft.

Dureté (Fr.). } Harshness, hardness.
Durezza (It.). }

Duro (It.). Hard, strong, firm.

Düster (Ger.). Gloomy, dark, sombre.

Dux (Lat.). The subject of a fugue.

E

E. The third note of the normal scale of C major. It is called *mi* in Fr. and It.

    E string. The highest string of the violin, called in Fr. *chanterelle*, the melody string.

E (Ger.). The note E.

    E dur. E major.

    E moll. E minor.

    E Saite. E string.

E (It.). And. Before a vowel *ed* is used.

Ebenfalls (Ger.). Again, also, likewise.

Ebenso (Ger.). In the same manner; likewise.

Ebollimento (It.). Ebullition, heat.

Écart (Fr.). Stretch of the hand in playing.

Eccedente (It.). Of intervals, augmented. *Terza eccedente*, augmented third.

Ec(c)o (It.). An echo.

Echeggiante (It.). Echoing, resounding.

Échelettes (Fr.). A name for the xylophone.

Échelle (Fr.). Scale.

   Échelle chromatique. Chromatic scale.

   Échelle diatonique. Diatonic scale.

Échelon (Fr.). The degree of a scale.

Echo. An echo effect is one in which a phrase is repeated *pianissimo*, or is sometimes merely played very softly, as though coming from a distance. With horns, the effect is produced by repeating in closed notes a phrase, which has previously been given in open notes. In the cornet, there is often a special attachment for producing the effect.

   Echo cornet. (1) A cornet with an echo attachment. (2) An organ stop, usually found on the swell.

   Echo organ, *or* **Echo-work.** One or more sets of pipes, for producing echo effects, placed at some distance from the main organ in a swell-box, and in large organs, played from a special manual.

Éclatant (Fr.). Piercing, loud, brilliant. A direction found in scores, usually against the Brass, and implying a brilliant somewhat *brassy* tone.

Éclisses (Fr.). The ribs of a violin.

Églogue (Fr.). A pastoral song, or poem.

École (Fr.). A school.

Écossais, -aise (Fr.). Scotch. *Ecossaise* (subs.), the name of a dance originally of a dignified character, but later of a lively nature.

Écouvillon (Fr.). A mop, or swab for cleaning the interior of wood-wind instruments.

Ed (It.). And (before words commencing with a vowel).

Edel (Ger.). Noble.

Éditeur (Fr.). An editor, a publisher. (The double meaning is occasionally a source of error, only the context showing which is the proper translation.)

Effect (Fr.). | Effect.
Effetto (It.). |

Effleurant. Grazing, touching lightly. *Doigt effleurant la corde,* finger lightly touching the string, as in artificial harmonics.

Effleurez (Fr.). Touch lightly, graze.

   Effleurez très légèrement. Graze (the two cymbals) very lightly.

Eguaglianza (It.). Equality, uniformity.

Eguale (It.). Equal, like, uniform.

Egualezza (It.). | Equality, uniformity.
Egualità (It.) |

Egualmente (It.). Equally, uniformly.

Eifrig (Ger.). Zealous; passionate, warm.

Eile (Ger.). Haste.

Eilen (Ger.). To hasten, hurry.

Ein (Ger.). One, a, an (masc. and neuter).

> **Ein Achtel wie ein Viertel des vorigen Taktes.** A quaver like a crotchet of the previous bar.
>
> **Ein Takt fast so schnell als eben die Viertel.** A bar almost as fast as the previous crotchets.
>
> **Ein wenig langsamer.** A little slower.
>
> **Ein wenig mäßiger als zuvor.** A little more moderate than before.
>
> **Ein wenig zurückhaltend.** Somewhat slackening.

Einchörig (Ger.). (1) One stringed. (2) For one choir.

Eine (Ger.). One, a, an (fem.).

> **Eine Oktave tiefer.** An octave lower.
>
> **Eine Saite.** One string.

Einer (Ger.). One.

> **Einer an jedem Pulte pizzicato, der andere col legno.** One at each desk pizzicato, the other *col legno*.

Einfach (Ger.). Simple; single (as opposed to *doppelt*, doubled).

Einfachheit (Ger.). Simplicity, singleness.

Einförmig (Ger.). Uniform.

Eingang (Ger.). Entrance; introduction, preamble.

Eingespielt (Ger.). Practised, exercised.

Eingestrichene Oktave. The once marked octave, *c'* to *b'*.

Eingreifen (Ger.). To cross the hands in piano-playing.

Einhaltend (Ger.). Stopping, checking.

Einheit (Ger.). Unity.

Einig (Ger.). Some. *Mit einigem Pomp*, with some pomp.

Einklang (Ger.). Unison.

Einleitung (Ger.). Introduction, prelude.

> **Einleitungssatz.** Introductory movement.
>
> **Einleitungsspiel.** Introduction, overture.

Einlenkend (Ger.). Returning. *In das Anfangs-Tempo einlenkend*, returning to the tempo of the beginning.

Einmal (Ger.). Once. *Noch einmal, da capo*, once again, da capo.

Einsatz (Ger.). An insertion.

> **Einsatzbogen.** A crook fixed into the middle of the instrument, as opposed to an *Aufsatzbogen*, a crook placed at the end of the tubing next the mouthpiece.
>
> **Einsatzzeichen.** The signs inserted in a close canon which indicate the entry of the various parts.

Einschiebebogen (Ger.). *v.* Einsatzbogen.

Einschlafen (Ger.). To slacken, abate.

Einschlagend (Ger.). Striking inwards.

> **Einschlagende Zunge.** A beating or striking reed.

Einschmeichelnd (Ger.). Coaxing, cajoling.

Einschnitt (Ger.). A phrase, section; a cut.

Einsetzen (Ger.). To enter (as with parts).

Einspielen (Ger.). To practise a piece well.

Einstimmen (Ger.). To be in accord with; to be in tune.

Einstimmig (Ger.). In unison.

Eint(h)eilung (Ger.). Division.

Eintritt (Ger.). Entrance, entry.

Einzeln (Ger.). Single, solo. *Zwei einzelne Violinen*, two solo violins. *Einzel-* in combination.

    Einzelne gestopfte Töne sind mit + bezeichnet. Single closed notes are indicated by a +.

    Einzelpartie. Solo part.

    Einzelsänger. Solo singer.

    Einzelstimme. Single voice; solo part.

    Einzeltanz. Solo dance.

Einzug (Ger.). Entrance, entry.

Eis (Ger.). E sharp.

    Eisis. E double sharp.

Élargi (Fr.). Broadened; slackened.

Élargissant (Fr.). Broadening; slackening.

Élégant, -ante (Fr.). ⎱ Elegant, fine, distinguished.
Elegante (It.). ⎰

Elegantemente (It.). Elegantly.

Eleganz (Ger.). ⎱ Elegance, refinement.
Eleganza (It.). ⎰

Elegia (It.). Elegy.

Elegiaco (It.). Elegiac; expressing grief or mourning.

Élégie (Fr.). ⎱ Elegy.
Elegie (Ger.). ⎰

Elf (Ger.). Eleven.

Elevamento, Elevatezza (It.). Elevation.

Elevato (It.). Elevated, in a sublime style.

Elevazione (It.). Elevation.

Élève (Fr.). Pupil.

Elicon (It.). *v.* Helicon.

Embellir (Fr.). To ornament, to embellish.

Embouchure. (1) The position of the lips, etc. necessary for the proper blowing of a wind-instrument. (2) The mouth-hole of a flute.

Embouchure (Fr.). (1) The position of the lips, etc. necessary for the proper blowing of a wind-instrument. (2) The mouth-hole of a flute. (3) The cup-shaped mouthpiece of a brass instrument.

Emozione (It.). Emotion, agitation.

Empâter (Fr.). "To make into a paste." Of sounds, voices, etc., to make mellow and smooth.

Empfindung (Ger.). Sentiment, sensibility.

    Empfindungsvoll. Sensitive, full of sentiment.

Emphase (Fr. and Ger.). Emphasis; stress laid on certain notes.

Emporté (Fr.). Fiery, passionate.

    Emporté et violent. Passionate and violent.

Empressé (Fr.). Ardent; ready, prompt.

Ému (Fr.). Affected, moved.

En (Fr.). In, into, on. Used with the present participle in many cases, where in Eng. the latter would stand by itself.

    En accélérant. Quickening.

    En animant un peu. Becoming somewhat animated.

    En badinant. Sporting, trifling.

    En bousculade. Going head over heels.

    En cédant. Giving way, slackening.

En cuivrant le son. Making the tone brassy. *v.* Cuivré.

En dehors. Outside, without. Indication often found against any particular part, which ought to stand out from the rest.

En diminuant. Diminishing in force or in tempo, or in both; *diminuendo*.

En élargissant. Becoming broader, slackening.

En fa, mi, etc. In F, E, etc.

En mesure. In time.

En ralentissant. Slackening.

En retenant. Holding back, *i. e.* slackening.

En s'éloignant. Becoming more distant, *i. e.* growing fainter.

En scène. On the stage.

En serrant. Becoming closer together, *i. e.* quickening.

Enarmonico (It.). Enharmonic.

Enchaînez (Fr.). Unite, connect. Indication meaning that one movement or number is to be joined on to the next without a break.

Enclume (Fr.). Anvil.

Encore (Fr.). Again; still, yet.

Encore plus vite. Still faster.

Ende (Ger.). End. *End-* in combination.

Endstück. End-piece.

Energia (It.). Energy, force, vigour.

Energicamente (It.). Energetically, vigorously.

Energico (It.). \
Energisch (Ger.). } Energetic, vigorous, forcible.

Energte. Abbr. of *energicamente*.

Enfant de chœur (Fr.). A choir-boy.

Enfasi (It.). Emphasis.

Enfaticamente (It.). Emphatically, forcibly.

Enfatico (It.). Emphatic.

Eng (Ger.). Narrow, close.

Enge Harmonie. Close harmony, *i. e.* when the tenor part lies within an octave of that of the soprano.

Enge Lage. Close position. *v.* Enge Harmonie.

Engführung. The stretto of a fugue.

Eng geschriebene Partitur. A condensed score.

Eng verbunden. Closely connected, related.

Engelstimme (Ger.). The *vox angelica* (*q. v.*).

Englisch (Ger.). English.

Englischer Tanz. An English dance.

Englisches Horn. The English horn, or cor anglais.

Enharmonique (Fr.). \
Enharmonisch (Ger.). } Enharmonic.

Enlevez (Fr.). Take off, take away.

Enlevez la pédale. Take off the pedal.

Enlevez la sourdine. Remove the mute.

Ensemble (Fr.). Together. (subs.) Whole. *Un morceau d'ensemble* is a number in an opera, oratorio etc., in which all or most of the principal characters are introduced, with or without the chorus.

Entfernung (Ger.). Distance. *In Entfernung aufgestellt*, placed at a distance.

Entr'acte (Fr.). (1) A piece of music played between the acts. (2) A "wait" or interval between the acts.
Entrain (Fr.). Animation, high spirits, "go".
Entrata (It.). ⎰(1) An introduction. (2) The entry of a part, dancer
Entrée (Fr.). ⎱or character.
Entrückung (Ger.). Rapture.
Entrüstet (Ger.). Indignant.
Entschieden (Ger.). Resolute, with decision; decidedly. *Die Viertelschläge entschieden schneller als vorhin die* ³/₈ *Schläge,* the crotchet-beats decidedly faster than the previous ³/₈ beats.
Entschlossen (Ger.). Resolute, firm, determined.
Entschlossenheit (Ger.). Firmness, determination.
Entusiasmo (It.). Enthusiasm.
Entusiastico (It.). Enthusiastic.
Entwurf (Ger.). Sketch; draft of a composition.
Eolian harp. *v.* Æolian harp.
Epicède (Fr.). ⎰Elegy; funeral oration or song.
Epicedio (It.). ⎱
Épinette (Fr.). A spinet.
Episodio (It.). Episode; a portion of a composition not based on the main subjects.
Equabile (It.). Equable, uniform.
Équisonnance (Fr.). The consonance of the unison or octave.
Ergriffen (Ger.). Moved, affected.
Ergriffenheit (Ger.). Emotion.
Erhaben (Ger.). Elevated; noble, generous; grand, magnificent.
Erheben (Ger.). To raise.
Erhöhen (Ger.). To raise; to raise the pitch, to sharpen.
Erhöht (Ger.). Raised; raised in pitch.
    Erhöht, außerhalb des Orchesters. On high, outside the orchestra.
    Erhöhtes Intervall. Augmented interval.
Erhöhung (Ger.). A raising of a note by means of a sharp. *Erhöhungs-* in combination.
    Erhöhungstritt, *or* **Erhöhtritt.** A term for a harp pedal.
    Erhöhungszeichen. The sharp sign (♯). *Doppeltes Erhöhungszeichen,* the sign of a double-sharp (×).
Erleichterung (Ger.). The simplified version of a passage.
Erlöschend (Ger.). Growing fainter, weaker.
Ermangelung (Ger.). Want, deficiency. *In Ermangelung der Harfe,* in the absence of the harp.
Ermattend (Ger.). Weakening, growing fainter.
Ermattet (Ger.). Jaded, worn out.
Erniedrigen (Ger.). To lower in pitch, to flatten.
Ernst (Ger.). Serious, solemn. (subs.) Earnestness, etc.
Ernsthaft (Ger.). Serious, solemn.
Eroico, -a (It.). Heroic, illustrious.
Erotico, -a (It.). Erotic, amatory. *Erotica,* a love song.
Ersatz (Ger.). An equivalent, substitution. *Ob. als Ersatz für E. Horn,* oboe as substitute for the English horn.
Erst (Ger.). First.
    Erste Bewegung. First movement (tempo).
    Erste Lage. First position.

Erster Satz. First movement.
Erstes Zeitmaß. First tempo, *tempo 1mo.*
Erste Violine. First violin.
Ersterbend (Ger.). Gradually dying away.
Erstickt (Ger.). Stifled, weak, faint. *Mit erstickter Stimme,* in a weak voice.
Erweitert (Ger.). Broadened, expanded.
Erweiterung (Ger.). Enlargement, expansion.
Erzürnt (Ger.). Exasperated, angered.
Es (Ger.). It.
    Es fällt schnell ein. It proceeds (to the next number).
    Es folgt.
    Es geht so fort. } It follows.
Es (Ger.). E flat.
    Es dur. E flat major.
    Es Klarinette. E flat clarinet.
    Es moll. E flat minor.
Esacordo (It.). The interval of the sixth.
Esaltato (It.). *v.* Exalté.
Esatezza (It.). Exactness, care.
Esatto (It.). Exact, precise, careful.
Esecuzione (It.). Execution, performance.
Esercizio (It.). Exercise.
Eses (Ger.). E double-flat.
Espace (Fr.). Space; space between the lines of the stave.
Espagnol, -nolle (Fr.). } Spanish.
Espagnuolo (It.).
Espansione (It.). Expansion.
Espirando (It.). *v.* Spirando.
Espress. Abbr. of *espressivo.*
Espressione (It.). Expression.
Espressivo (It.). Expressive.
Es(s)empio (It.). Example.
Estensione (It.). Compass of a voice or instrument.
Estinguendo (It.). Dying away.
Estinto (It.). Dead, extinguished. (Used for an almost imperceptible sound.)
Estravaganza (It.). *v.* Stravaganza.
Estremamente (It.). Extremely.
Estro poetico (It.). Poetic frenzy.
Esultazione (It.). Exultation.
Et (Fr.). And. *ƒ et bien soutenu,* ƒ and well sustained.
Et (Lat.). And.
    Et vitam. Part of the *Credo* in the Mass.
Éteignez le son (Fr.). Reduce the sound to almost nothing.
Éteint (Fr.). Extinguished, dull, inaudible.
    Éteint, sans expression. Dull, without expression.
Étendu (Fr.). Extended. (subs.) *Étendue,* compass.
Étouffé (Fr.). Damped.
Étouffez le son (Fr.). Damp the sound.
Étouffoirs (Fr.). The dampers of a piano.
Étude (Fr.). A study.

Etüde (Ger.). A study. plur. *Etüden.*

Étui (Fr.).
Etui (Ger.). } A case for an instrument.

Etwas (Ger.). Somewhat.

Etwas agitiert. Somewhat agitated.

Etwas belebend. Growing somewhat faster.

Etwas belebt. Somewhat animated.

Etwas belebter. Somewhat more animated.

Etwas betont, doch sehr innig. Somewhat pronounced and with much feeling.

Etwas bewegt. Somewhat agitated.

Etwas bewegter. Somewhat more agitated.

Etwas breit in Zeitmaß. Somewhat broad in tempo.

Etwas deutlicher und allmählich ausdrucksvoller. Rather more distinct and gradually with more expression.

Etwas drängend. Somewhat hurrying.

Etwas frei vorzutragen. To be played somewhat freely.

Etwas gedehnt. Somewhat drawn-out.

Etwas gehend. "Somewhat going", *i. e.* with a certain amount of movement.

Etwas gemächlicher. Somewhat more leisurely.

Etwas geschwind. Somewhat quick.

Etwas hervortretend. Somewhat prominent.

Etwas kokett. Somewhat coquettishly.

Etwas langsam. Somewhat slow.

Etwas langsamer als das Thema. Somewhat slower than the theme.

Etwas lansamer als zu Anfang. Somewhat slower than at the beginning.

Etwas langsamer und ruhig. Somewhat slower and quietly.

Etwas lebhaft und mit innigster Empfindung. Somewhat animated, and with the deepest feeling.

Etwas leichter und bewegter. Somewhat more lightly and quicker.

Etwas markiert. Somewhat accented.

Etwas mäßig, aber dennoch gehende Viertelbewegung. Somewhat moderate, but the crotchets still with a certain amount of motion.

Etwas näher als vorhin. Somewhat nearer than before.

Etwas rallent. Becoming somewhat slower.

Etwas ruhiger. Somewhat more tranquil.

Etwas schneller. Somewhat faster.

Etwas weniger breit. Somewhat less broadly.

Etwas zögernd und sehr ruhig. Somewhat slackening and very tranquil.

Etwas zurückhaltend in der Bewegung. Somewhat slackening the movement.

Eufonia (It.). Euphony.

Eufonio (It.). A euphonium.

Euphonie (Fr.).
Euphonie (Ger.). } Euphony.

Euphonion (Ger.). A euphonium.

Euphonium. A bass saxhorn with a wide bore, in contradistinction to the narrow-bored baritone (*q. v.*), which gives fulness in the lower register and enables the fundamental notes to be easily produced. It is usually made in B♭, and is often furnished with 4, rarely with 5, valves, for obtaining the complete scale down to the fundamental note. *v.* Saxhorn and Tuba.

Éveillé (Fr.). Sprightly, lively, alert.

Évocation (Fr.). Evocation; the summoning up of inferior beings (demons, evil spirits, etc.), as opposed to *Invocation*, a prayer or request to superior beings.

Exactement (Fr.). Exactly, precisely.

 Exactement rhythmé. In precise rhythm.

Exalté (Fr.). Elevated; feverish, over-excited, inspired.

Exécutant, -ante (Fr.). An executant, performer.

Exit (Lat.). He (or she) goes out, *i. e.* (in plays and operas) leaves the stage. Used in some theatrical circles as an infinitive, — to exit, and consequently, he or she exits.

Expressif, -ive (Fr.). Expressive.

 Expressif et largement chanté. Expressive, and in a broad singing style.

Expression stop. A stop on the harmonium, whereby the reeds are acted upon directly by the pedals, and therefore the various gradations of nuance are controlled by the feet.

Expressivorgel (Ger.). A term for the harmonium.

Extempore (Lat.). On the spur of the moment.

Extemporieren (Ger.). To extemporise.

Extrêmement (Fr.). Extremely.

 Extrêmement lent. Extremely slow

F

F. The fourth note of the normal scale of C major. It is called *fa* in Fr. and It.

 f. Abbr. of *forte*.

 F clef. The bass clef 𝄢, with *f* on the 4th line. Another form of F clef was the baritone clef, with *f* on the 3rd line. but this is now obsolete.

 F holes. The *f*-shaped sound-holes in the belly of a violin, etc.

 F.O. Abbr. of Full Organ.

F (Ger.). The note F.

 F dur. F major.

 F Löcher. The *f*-holes of a violin, etc.

 F moll. F minor.

 F Schlüssel. F clef; bass clef.

Fa (Fr.). The note F.

 Fa bémol. F flat.

 Fa dièse. F sharp.

 Fa majeur. F major.

 Fa mineur. F minor.

Fa (It.). The note F.

Fa bemolle. F flat.

Fa diesis. F sharp.

Fa maggiore. F major.

Fa minore. F minor.

Faces d'un accord. (Fr.). The positions of a chord.

Facezia (It.). Conceit, jest.

Fach (Ger.). Compartment, division. *-fach*, used in combination, is equivalent to the Eng. "-fold", or "-times", as *zweifach*, twofold, *vierfach*, fourfold, etc., these being often written as *2fach*, *4fach*, etc. In scores, the words mean that the instruments against which they are placed are divided into so many parts. In organs, the words are employed in the sense of ranks, as *Kornett 3fach* (or *dreifach*), Cornet 3 ranks, *Mixtur 5fach* (or *fünffach*), Mixture 5 ranks.

Facile (Fr. and It.). Easy, facile; yielding.

Facilement (Fr.). Easily, readily.

Facilità (It.). A simplified version of a passage.

Facilitato (It.). Facilitated, simplified.

Facilité (Fr.). *v.* Facilità.

Facilmente (It.). *v.* Facilement.

Fackeltanz (Ger.). A dance with torches.

Factitious notes. Certain very low notes on the horn, which form no part of the natural scale, and are produced by a modification of the embouchure. Beethoven frequently uses them, but they are no longer employed, the invention of valves having made it possible to obtain notes of the same pitch of better quality and intonation.

Facture (Fr.). The make, construction of a piece of music. The scale of organ pipes.

Fagott (Ger.). The bassoon.

Fagottino (It.). A small sized bassoon a 5th higher than the ordinary instrument; a "tenoroon". *cf.* Basson quinte.

Fagottist (Ger.). ⎫
Fagottista (It.). ⎬ A bassoon player.

Fagotto (It.). Bassoon.

Fagottone (It.). A name for the double-bassoon.

Fahnenmarsch (Ger.). March played at the lodging of the colours.

Fahre sogleich fort (Ger.). Begin the next number (or movement) immediately, *attacca*.

Faible (Fr.). Weak, faint, feeble.

Faire (Fr.). To do, make. Often combined with other verbs.

    Faire ressortir le chant. Make the melody prominent. (*v.* Rem. I.)

Faites (Fr.). Make, do.

    Faites cuivrer. Make brassy. *v.* Cuivré.

    Faites sonner. Make resound.

Falcon (Fr.). A name sometimes given to a voice resembling that of Mlle. Falcon, who was a celebrated singer in Paris in 1832 to 1837.

Fall (Ger.). Case, eventuality, instance. *Im Falle* . . . ., in case. . . .

Falsch (Ger.). Erroneous, out of tune. Of intervals, imperfect or diminished.

    Falsche Note. A wrong note.

    Falsche Quinte. A diminished fifth.

    Falsch spielen. To play out of tune, or wrongly.

Falsetto (It.). (1) The head voice. (2) A singer, who practises the head voice almost exclusively, such as a male alto.

Falsettstimme (Ger.). Falsetto.

Falso bordone (It.). *v.* Faux bourdon.

Fanatico (It.). Fanatical, enthusiastic. (subs.) A fanatic.

Fandango (Sp.). A lively dance in ternary time, usually accompanied by castanets.

Fanfare (Fr.). (1) A flourish on a horn or trumpet, corresponding to the old Eng. "tucket" and Ger. "Tusch". (2) A term used for brass instruments in general, and hence *Orchestre de fanfare* (usually abbr. to *fanfare*) is a brass band.

Fanfare (Ger.). A flourish on the horn or trumpet.

    Fanfare Supplementaire. Music for brass instruments on the stage.

Fantaisie (Fr.). ⎰ Fantasia. Fancy, imagination, caprice. The name
Fantasia (It.). ⎱ is given to pieces, in which no particular form is observed, and which may be simply founded on operatic, national airs, etc., or be an original composition having much the character of an extemporisation.

Fantasie, etc. (Ger.). *v.* Phantasie, etc.

Fantasticamente (It.). Fantastically.

Fantastico (It.). ⎱
Fantastique (Fr.). ⎰ Fantastic.

Farandola (It.). ⎰A dance of the South of France and part of Italy,
Farandole (Fr.). ⎱ in ⁶/₈ time.

Farsa (It.). A farce.

    Farsa in musica. A musical farce, a species of comic opera.

Fast (Ger.). Almost.

    Fast dasselbe Tempo. Almost the same tempo.

Fastosamente (It.). Proudly, pompously.

Fastoso (It.). Pompous, stately.

Fattura (It.). The make, construction of a piece of music.

Fausse (Fr.). Fem. of *faux*, false. Of intervals, diminished, imperfect.

    Fausse quinte. A diminished fifth.

    Fausse relation. False relation.

Fausset (Voix de) (Fr.). Falsetto.

Faux, Fausse (Fr.). False.

    Faux bourdon. A species of primitive counterpoint, originally consisting merely of a kind of drone bass.

Feathering. On the violin, etc., a form of bowing for delicate, lightly detached rapid passages.

Fébrile (Fr.). Feverish.

Feierlich (Ger.). Solemn, majestic, *maestoso*; festive.

Feierlichkeit (Ger.). Solemnity, etc.

Fein (Ger.). Fine, thin, delicate.

Feld (Ger.). Field. In combination often used in the sense of "military".

    Feldmusik. Military music.

    Feldtrompete. Military trumpet for calls and signals.

Fermamente (It.). Firmly.

Fermata (It.). A pause.

Fermate (Ger.). A pause, ⌒. *Die Fermaten sehr lang und bedeutungsvoll*, the pauses very long and significant.

Fermato, -a (It.). Fixed, firm.
Fermezza (It.). Firmness.
Fermo (It.). Firm, fast, fixed.
Ferne (Ger.). Distance. *Wie aus der Ferne*, as from a distance; *immer in der Ferne*, always at a distance.
Fernwerk (Ger.). Same as *Echowerk*, the echo-work of an organ.
Feroce (It.). Fierce, ferocious.
Ferocia, Ferocità (It.). Ferocity, cruelty.
Fertig (Ger.). Prepared, ready; skilful, dexterous.
Fertigkeit (Ger.). Skill, dexterity, facility.
Fervente (It.). Ardent, fervent.
Ferventemente, Fervidamente (It.). With ardour, vehemently.
Fervido (It.). Fervid, burning, ardent.
Fervore (It.). Warmth, ardour.
Fes (Ger.). F flat.
Feses (Ger.). F double-flat.
Fest (Ger.). adj. Firm, fast, unwavering, strictly in time.
  Festes Zeitmaß. Strict tempo.
  Festgehalten. Held fast, *ben tenuto*.
  Festhalten. To hold fast, maintain.
Fest (Ger.). subs. A festival, holiday.
  Festgesang. A festival song or hymn.
  Festmarsch. A festival march.
  Festmusik. Festival music.
  Festouverture. A festival overture.
  Festspiel. A festival play.
Festa (It.). Holiday, festival, feast.
Festevole (It.). Joyful, merry.
Festevolmente (It.). Joyfully.
Festivamente (It.). In a festive manner.
Festività (It.). Festivity, mirth.
Festivo (It.). Solemn, festival.
Festlich (Ger.). Festive, pompous, festival.
Festosissimo (It.). Sup. of *festoso*.
Festoso (It.). Lively, merry, gay.
Feu (Fr.). Fire, animation, spirit. *Feux follets*, wills-o'-the-wisp.
Feuer (Ger.). Fire, animation, vehemence.
Feu(e)rig (Ger.). Fiery, passionate.
  Feurig schwungvoll. With fiery impetuosity.
ff. Abbr. of *fortissimo*.
fff. Abbr. of *forte fortissimo*.
ffff. Abbr. of *fortissimo fortissimo*.
Fiaccamente (It.). Weakly, faintly.
Fiacchezza (It.). Lassitude, feebleness.
Fiacco (It.). subs. Ravage, ruin. adj. Weak, feeble
Fiasco (It.). Literally a "flask". A failure.
Fiata (It.). Sometimes used for *volta*, time (not in the sense of tempo). *Una fiata*, once; *due fiate*, twice.
Fiducia (It.). Confidence, trust.
Fiedel (Ger.). A fiddle.
  Fiedelbogen. A fiddle-stick.
  Fiedelmann, *or* **Fiedeler.** A fiddler.

Fier, fière (Fr.). Proud.
Fieramente (It.). | Proudly.
Fièrement (Fr.). |
Fiero (It.). Cruel, savage; proud, arrogant.
Fife. (1) A primitive species of piccolo, used in conjunction with side-drums in military Drum and Fife Bands. Its compass was from *d'* to *d'''*, sounding an 8ve above, and it was made in a variety of keys. Its modern representative in the British Army is a small flute in B♭. (2) An organ stop of 2 ft.
Fifre (Fr.). A fife.
Figur (Ger.). A figure (in music or dancing).
Figurato (It.). |
Figuré (Fr.). } Figured.
Figuriert (Ger.). |
Filare (It.). Literally "to spin".
    Filar la voce, *or* **un suono.** Gradually to augment and then diminish the sound of a note, $\prec \succ$.
Filer la voix, *or* **un son** (Fr.). *v.* Filare.
Fin (Fr.). subs. End, termination. adj. Fine, slender, delicate; fem. *fine*.
Fin (It.). Abbr. of *fino*, to, as far as, till, and *fine*.
    Fin al segno. As far as the sign.
    Fin alla meta. Until the half.
    Fin qui. Until here; until this point.
Finale (It.). The concluding number of the act of an opera. The last movement of a symphony, sonata, etc.
Fine (Fr.). Fem. of *fin*.
Fine (It.). The end, conclusion (sometimes shortened to *fin*).
Finezza (It.). Fineness, perfection.
Finger (Ger.). Finger. *Erster Finger*, or *Zeigefinger*, forefinger; *Zweiter Finger*, or *Mittelfinger*, second finger; *Dritter Finger* or *Goldfinger*, third finger; *Kleiner Finger*, little finger.
    Fingerbrett. A finger-board.
    Fingerfertig. Nimble-fingered.
    Fingerfertigkeit. Nimbleness; execution.
    Fingergelenke. The internodes, or spaces between the joints of the fingers.
    Fingerglied. Finger-joint.
    Finger liegen lassen. Let the finger remain (on the string).
    Fingersatz. Fingering.
    Fingersetzung. Fingering.
    Fingerspitze. The tip of the finger.
    Fingerstrecken. The stretching of the fingers.
    Fingerübung. Finger-exercise.
Finger-board. The strip of wood attached to the neck of instruments of the violin or guitar class, over which the strings are strained, and against which they are pressed by the fingers to form the various notes.
Finito (It.). Finished.
Fino (It.). To, as far as, until. *v.* Fin.
Finto (It.). Feigned, hid, counterfeited. *Cadenza finta*, a deceptive cadence.
Fiochetto (It.). Somewhat hoarse.

Fiochezza (It.). Hoarseness.

Fioco (It.). Hoarse, weak, faint.

Fioreggiando (It.). Ornamenting a passage with shakes, grace-notes, etc.

Fioreggiante (It.). Flowery.

Fioretto (It.). A vocal ornament of any description.

Fioriture (It.). Florid melodic ornaments.

Fis (Ger.). F sharp.

> **Fis dur.** F sharp major.
> **Fis moll.** F sharp minor.

Fisis (Ger.). F double-sharp.

Fistel (Ger.). Falsetto, head voice.

Fistulieren (Ger.). To sing falsetto.

Fl. Abbr. of flute, *flûte, Flöte, flauto.*

Flageolet. The sole survivor of the old *flûtes-à-bec*, or flutes played with a whistle-head and held vertically. The instrument is furnished with from 1 to 7 keys, and has a compass of 2 octaves and 3 semitones from *g'*. It is made in several keys (B♭, D, E♭, F, G), and is now only to be found in a few bands, which perform light music. The name is also given to an organ pipe of 2 ft.

Flageolet (Fr.). A flageolet.

Flageolett (Ger.). A flageolet.

> **Flageolett-Töne.** Harmonics on the harp and the violin, etc.

Flatter (Fr.). To caress.

> **Flatter la corde.** To bow gently and delicately.

Flatterzunge (Ger.). "Flutter-tonguing". It is used on the flute (*Don Quixote*, R. Strauss), and occasionally on the *Trompe de chasse* and other wind instruments, and consists in a rapid movement of the tongue while blowing the notes. It differs from double and triple tonguing, in that the tongue does not touch the lips at any time during its execution.

Flautando (It.). ⎰ Expressions denoting a particular form of bowing
Flautato (It.). ⎱ on the violin, etc., by means of which flute-like tones are produced. The point of the bow is used, and the string touched lightly close to the finger-board.

Flautino (It.). A small flute; a name for the *ottavino* (piccolo).

Flauto (It.). A flute.

> **Flauto a becco.** The *flûte-à-bec.*
> **Flauto amabile.** The name of an organ stop of sweet tone.
> **Flauto dolce.** Same as *flauto a becco*; also the name of a sweet toned organ stop.
> **Flauto Giorgi.** A flute held vertically, but played, not with a whistle-head, but with an embouchure like an ordinary flute.
> **Flauto piccolo.** The piccolo. This is the name found in the scores of composers (other than Italian), who employ Italian terms, but modern *Italian* composers almost invariably use *Ottavino* for the instrument.
> **Flauto principale.** An organ stop of 8 ft.
> **Flauto traverso.** The cross flute; the ordinary flute, as distinguished from the old *flauto a becco.* The *"traverso"* is now always omitted.

Flautone (It.). A large flute; the bass flute.

Flebile (It.). Mournful, sad.

Flebilmente (It.). Dejectedly, mournfully.

Flehend (Ger.). Supplicating, imploring.

Flesh-hoop. The hoop of a drum, over which the head is stretched.

Flessibile (It.). Flexible, pliable.

Flessibilità (It.). Suppleness, flexibility.

Flicorno (It.). Term corresponding to the Ger. *Flügelhorn* (*q. v.*). *Flicorni* of various sizes, all being virtually saxhorns of somewhat narrow bore, are employed in It. bands, under names which do not always accord.

> **Flicorno in Do o Si♭.** The ordinary *Flügelhorn*, corresponding in pitch with the *cornet-à-pistons*.
>
> **Flicorno in Fa o Mi♭.** The alto *Flügelhorn* or *Althorn*, called *Flicorno contralto*, or sometimes *Flicorno tenore*.
>
> **Flicorno basso in Si♭ o La.** The baritone *Flügelhorn*, called *Flicorno tenore*, or sometimes *Flicorno basso*.
>
> **Flicorno basso a tracolla.** A circular bass *Flügelhorn*.

Fließend (Ger.). Flowing, running smoothly.

> **Fließend, aber immer gemäßigt.** Flowing smoothly, but always in moderate tempo.

Flöte (Ger.). The flute.

> **Flöte blasen.** To play the flute.

Flöten (Ger.). Flutes.

> **Flötenbaß.** A bass flute.
>
> **Flötenchor.** ⎫
> **Flötenpfeifen.** ⎬ The flue or flute-work of an organ.
> **Flötenwerk.** ⎭

Flotter (Fr.). To float, to undulate. *En laissant flotter l'archet,* allowing the bow to undulate (on the strings).

Flüchtig (Ger.). Fleet, nimble.

Flüchtigkeit (Ger.). Lightness, nimbleness.

Flügel (Ger.). A grand piano.

Flügelhorn (Ger.). A valve brass instrument with a bore like that of the military bugle and corresponding to the Fr. *Bugle en si♭,* with a compass the same as the *cornet-à-pistons.* The *Altflügelhorn,* usually called the *Althorn,* is a similar instrument pitched in E♭.

Fluidezza, Fluidità (It.). Fluidity, the quality of flowing evenly and smoothly.

Fluido (It.). Fluid, fluent.

Flüssig (Ger.). Fluid, flowing evenly and smoothly. *Etwas flüssiger als zu Anfang,* somewhat more flowing than at the commencement.

Flute. The term now-a-days always implies the *flauto traverso,* or cross flute, the old *flûtes-à-bec,* of which the flageolet is the sole descendant, being obsolete. The compass of the flute is from c' to c'''', some modern instruments possessing the b and $b♭$ below. Another variety of flute is the Third Flute, an instrument sounding a minor 3rd above the ordinary flute, and in regard to this there is a confusion of nomenclature. With all other transposing instruments, the pitch is calculated from C, and thus an instrument, which produces sounds a minor 3rd above or a major 6th below the written notes is said to be in E♭, and consequently the Third Flute is correctly speaking a flute in E♭. But since the lowest note of the ordinary flute, when no keys are used, is *d'*, that flute is sometimes said to be in D, and the Third Flute to be in F. On the same principle, another flute standing a semitone above the ordinary flute is often said to be in E♭, instead of being in D♭, according to correct nomenclature. These last two varieties of flutes are now never used in the orchestra, although to be found in some military bands. For flutes sounding an octave above, *v.* Piccolo. For flutes sounding below the written notes, *v.* Bass Flute and Flûte d'amour.

Flûte (Fr.). Flute.

Flûte-à-bec. A flute with a whistle-head.

Flûte allemande. The German or cross flute.

Flûte anglaise. A species of *flûte-à-bec*.

Flûte à pavillon. An organ stop, sometimes called in Eng. bell diapason.

Flûte bouchée. A stopped diapason.

Flûte d'amour. (1) A flute sounding a minor 3rd below the written notes, and therefore standing in A, although often erroneously said to be in B♮ (*v.* Flute). The instrument is no longer in use. (2) An organ stop of 4 ft or 8 ft.

Flûte d'angleterre.
Flûte douce. ⎱ A species of *flûte-à-bec*.

Flûte harmonique. Harmonic flute, an open metal organ stop of 4 or 8 ft pitch, with pipes of double the length, but with a hole bored in them midway between the foot and the top.

Flûte ouverte. An open diapason, on the organ.

Flûte pointée. An organ stop, with the pipes smaller at the top.

Flûte traversière. The cross flute.

Flûté (Fr.). *v.* Flautato.

Foco (It.). A poetical form of *fuoco*, fire.

Focosamente (It.). Ardently, vehemently.

Focosissimo (It.). Sup. of *focoso*.

Focoso (It.). Fiery, ardent, hasty.

Foglietto (It.). Literally "a small sheet of paper". The name is given to the first violin part, when it contains the entries of the other instruments and the voices. A conductor's part.

Fois (Fr.). Time (not in the sense of tempo). *Première* (*1re*) *fois*, first time; *deuxième* (*2ième*) *fois*, second time.

Folge (Ger.). Sequence, consecution. *In einer Folge*, without interruption.

Folge der Töne. Succession of notes.

Folgend (Ger.). Following. *Der Melodie folgend*, following the melody; *dem Sänger folgend*, following the singer; *i. e.* in both cases, *col parte*.

Folgt (Ger.). Follows.

Folgt lange Pause. A long pause follows.

Folias (Sp.).
Folies d'Espagne (Fr.). ⎱ A Spanish dance.
Follia (It.).

Follemente (It.). Foolishly, extravagantly.

Fond (Fr.). Back of a violin, etc. In a theatrical sense, the back of the stage. *Au fond*, at the back of the stage.

Fonds (Fr.). Used as an abbr. of *jeux de fonds* (*q. v.*).

Fonds de 8 P. (pieds). Open diapasons 8 ft.

Forchetta (It.). A fork. *A forchetta*, cross-fingered (on a wood-wind instrument).

Forlana (It.).
Forlane (Fr.). } A lively Venetian dance, usually in 6/8 time.

Format (Fr.). Size. *Un tam-tam de petit format*, a gong of small size.

Foro (It.). A hole or ventage on a wood-wind instrument.

Fort (Fr.). Strong, loud.

Fort (Ger.). Onwards, further, constantly (when combined with *immer*). *Hervortretend immer fort*, constantly prominent.

Forte (It.). Strong, loud.

Fortement (Fr.).
Fortemente (It.). } Strongly, loudly.

Fortepiano (It.). (1) The art of increasing and softening sounds. (2) A soft nuance immediately succeeding a loud one, usually written *Fp*. (3) An old name for the pianoforte.

Fortfahrend (Ger.). Continuing, resuming. *In derselben Bewegung fortfahrend*, continuing with the same movement.

Fortissimo (It.). Sup. of *forte*: very loud, *ff*.
    Fortissimo quanto possibile. With all possible loudness.

Fortississimo (It.). An intensitive of *fortissimo*, *fff*.

Fortschreitung (Ger.). Progression.

Fortsetzung (Ger.). Continuation.

Forza (It.). Force. *Tutta forza*, as loud as possible.

Forzando (It.). Forcing (the sound); emphasising a note.

Forzare (It.). To force.
    Forzar la voce. To force the voice.

Forzato (It.). Forced, violent; emphasised, accented.

Fougueux, -euse (Fr.). Ardent, fiery, impetuous.

Fourchette (Fr.). A fork; the fork of a harp.

Fourchu (Fr.). Forked. *Doigté fourchu*, cross fingering on wood-wind instruments.

Fourniture (Fr.). One of the mixture stops on an organ.

Fp. Abbr. of *Fortepiano*.

Fra sè (It.). To himself (herself), aside.

Français, -çaise (Fr.). French. *Française* (subs.) is the name of a country dance.

Franchezza (It.).
Franchise (Fr.). } Bravery, frankness.

Frappé (Fr.). Struck.
    Frappé avec la mailloche. Struck with the bass drumstick.
    Frappé avec le bois de l'archet. Struck with the wood (back) of the bow, *col legno*.
    Frappé avec un marteau. Struck with a hammer.

Frase (It.). Phrase.
    Frase larga. A broad phrase.
    Frasi musicali. Musical phrases.

Fraseggiare (It.). To phrase. *Fraseggiando*, phrasing (exactly).

Fratzenhaft (Ger.). Grotesque, baroque.

Frauen (Ger.). Plur. of *Frau* (woman, female, lady) and used in combination.

Frauenchor. Female chorus.
Frauenstimme. Female voice.
Freddamente (It.). Coldly, without animation.
Freddezza (It.). Coldness, indifference.
Freddo (It.). Cold, frigid.
Fredonner (Fr.). To hum. *Fredonnant,* humming.
Free reeds. *v.* Reeds.
Frei (Ger.). Free.
    Freihängend. Freely suspended. (Direction found in cymbal parts, when one of the cymbals is to be struck with a drumstick.)
    Freie Nachahmung. Free imitation.
    Freie Schreibart. Free style.
French Horn. The ordinary orchestral horn. It is to be noted that the French occasionally call the instrument *un cor allemand,* a German horn.
French Hunting Horn. *v.* Trompe de chasse.

French violin clef. The G clef on the 1st line, $\text{\clef}$, now obsolete.

Frenetico (It.). Frantic, frenzied, mad.
Frescamente (It.). (1) With freshness. (2) Recently.
Fresco (It.). Coolness, freshness.
Frets. Strips of wood, metal or ivory placed across the fingerboard of instruments of the guitar class, which allow of the notes being stopped with accuracy, but without the rapidity of execution possible on a fingerboard without frets.
Fretta (It.). Haste.
Frettolosamente (It.). Hastily, quickly.
Freudig (Ger.). Joyful, glad, cheerful.
Freundlich (Ger.). Friendly, kind, gracious.
Freundschaftlich (Ger.). Friendly, amicable.
Frisch (Ger.). Fresh, cool, lusty, brisk.
    Frisch bewegt. With brisk movement.
    Frisch und fröhlich. Free and light-hearted.
    Frisch und kräftig. Lively and vigorous.
    Frisch und munter. Brisk and vivacious.
Fröhlich (Ger.). Light-hearted, joyous, merry.
Froidement (Fr.). Coldly.
Frosch (Ger.). Literally "a frog". The nut of the bow of a violin, etc. *Am Frosch,* near the nut.
    Froschschraube. The screw of the nut.
Frottola (It.). Ballad.
Früher (Ger.). Earlier, previous, foregoing. *Wie früher,* as before.
    Früheres Zeitmaß. The previous tempo.
Frühling (Ger.). Spring.
    Frühlingsgesang. A spring song.
Fuga (It.). Fugue.
    Fuga del tuono. A tonal fugue.
    Fuga in consequenza. A canon.
    Fuga ricercata. A master fugue, one introducing all the resources of counterpoint: an artificial fugue.

Fuga sciolta. A free fugue.

Fugato (It.). In the fugue style without being worked out in strict fugue form.

Fuge (Ger.). Fugue.

Fughetta (It.). A short fugue.

Fugieren (Ger.). To compose in the style of a fugue.

Fugiert (Ger.). *v.* Fugato.

Fugue (Fr.). A fugue.

Führend (Ger.). Leading. *Die führende Stimme*, the leading voice (part).

Führer der Fuge (Ger.). The *Dux*, or subject of a fugue.

Führung (Ger.). Guidance, leading, conduct.

    Führung des Bogens. *v.* Bogenführung.

Fulgente (It.). Brilliant, shining.

Full organ. Employing all, or most of the stops on an organ.

Full score. A score, in which all the parts are written on separate staves, this being somewhat modified in orchestral scores, where often two or more instruments of a kind are on one stave, not only to save space, but for convenience in reading. Formerly there were many ways of arranging the instruments, but at the present day the almost universal method is to arrange them in groups, the Wood-wind being at the top of the page, the Brass next below, then the Percussion, and the Strings at the bottom. The voices are placed between the violoncellos and violas, and the harps immediately above the violins.

Füllstimme (Ger.). Additional (*ripieno*) parts. In an organ, the mixtures.

Fulmine (It.). Lightning.

Fundamentalbass (Ger.). Fundamental bass; a bass containing the roots of the chords.

Fundamental note. The generator or foundation note of an Harmonic Series. *v.* Harmonics.

Funèbre (Fr.). } Funeral.
Funebre. Funerale (It.). } Funeral.

Fünf (Ger.). Five.

    Fünffach (5fach). Fivefold; in five parts; of organ pipes, five ranks.

    Fünfstimmig. Five-part.

Fünfte (Ger.). Fifth; the interval of a fifth.

Fuoco (It.). Fire, spirit.

Fuocoso (It.). *v.* Focoso.

Für (Ger.). For.

    Für Gesang. For voice.

    Für Klavier. For piano.

Furia (It.). Fury, rage.

Furibondo (It.). Furious, raging.

Furieusement (Fr.). } Furiously.
Furiosamente (It.). } Furiously.

Furiosissimo (It.). Sup. of *furioso.*

Furioso (It.). Furious, mad, raging.

Furlana (It.). *v.* Forlana.

Furniture. Name of one of the mixture stops on an organ.

Furore (It.). Fury, rage, passion, enthusiasm.

Fürst Pless'sches Jagdhorn (Ger.). A species of hunting horn, sometimes provided with valves.

Fusée (Fr.). A rapid series of conjunct notes before the principal note.

Fuß (Ger.). Foot.

    -füßig. Used in combination: *vierfüßig*, of four feet, *fünffüßig*,
of five feet, etc. *16füßige Stimmen*, 16 ft stops.

Fusto (It.). | The shell of a drum. The term is occasionally applied
Fût (Fr.). | to an organ case.

Fz. Abbr. of *forzando*.

G

G. The fifth note of the normal scale of C major. It is called in Fr.
and It. *sol*.

    G. Abbr. of *gauche*. Also found in violin parts to indicate the
use of the G string.

    G clef. The treble clef,

    G.O. Abbr. of Great Organ, *Grand Orgue*, *Grand' organo*.

    G string. The 4th or lowest string of the violin.

G (Ger.). The fifth note of the normal scale of C major. G flat is *Ges*.
G sharp is *Gis*.

    G dur. G major.

    G moll. G minor.

    G.P. Abbr. of *Generalpause*.

    G Saite. G string.

    G Schlüssel. G clef.

Gabel (Ger.). A fork. *Stimmgabel*, a tuning-fork.

    Gabelgriffe. Cross-fingering.

    Gabelklavier. A keyboard instrument, on which the notes are
produced by a series of tuning-forks. *v.* Typophone.

Gagliarda (It.). A dance of a vigorous character, danced by two
persons.

Gagliardo, -a (It.). Sturdy, vigorous.

Gai (Fr.). Gay, joyous.

Gaiement, *or* **Gaîment** (Fr.). Gaily, merrily.

Gaillarde (Fr.). *v.* Gagliarda.

Gaîté (Fr.). Gaiety.

Gajamente (It.). Gaily, merrily. |
Gajetto (It.). Somewhat gay. | (Sometimes Gaio, Gaiamente, etc.)
Gajezza (It.). Gaiety. |
Gajo (It.). Gay, merry, joyful. |

Galament (Fr.). Gallantly; tastefully; skilfully.

Galant, -ante (Fr.). | Gallant, agreeable.
Galante (It.). |

Galantemente (It.). Gallantly; cleverly.

Galliard (Fr.). Sturdy, vigorous.

Galop, Galipade, Galopp, Galoppade. A lively dance in ²/₄ time.

Galoubet (Fr.). The tabor-pipe. A species of *flûte-à-bec*, or flageolet,
still used in the Basque provinces. It has a chromatic scale of a

12th or more from $d'''\flat$ upwards, the notes being written two octaves lower. The instrument is held in one hand, while the other beats the *Tambourin* (*q. v.*). In Béarn, the *galoubet* or *chirula* is accompanied by the *Tambourin du Béarn* (*q. v.*). In the orchestra, the effect of the *galoubet* is obtained by the piccolo, as in Bizet's *L'Arlésienne*.

Gamba (It.). An organ stop with a tone intended to imitate the *viola da gamba* (*q. v.*).

Gambe (Ger.). The *viola da gamba*.

Gamma (It.).
Gamme (Fr.). } A gamut, a scale.

Gang (Ger.). A passage.

Ganz (Ger.). Whole, entire, quite, very.

    Ganz an der Spitze. Quite at the point (of the bow).

    Ganze Bogen. Whole bows.

    Ganze Note. A semibreve.

    Ganzer Bogen. Whole bow.

    Ganzer Takt. Whole bar.

    Ganze Stärke. Full force, strength.

    Ganze Takte schlagen. Beat whole bars.

    Ganz leise. Quite soft.

    Ganz ruhige Achtel. Very tranquil quavers.

Gänzlich (Ger.). Whole, entire, complete.

    Gänzlich verklingend. Completely dying away.

Garbatamente (It.). Gracefully.

Garbatezza (It.). Gracefulness.

Garbatino (It.). Somewhat graceful.

Garbatissimo (It.). Sup. of *garbato*

Garbato (It.). Graceful, pleasing.

Garbo (It.). Grace, elegance.

Garder (Fr.). To keep, hold. *Le 1er Vn solo garde la sourdine*, the 1st Vn solo retains the mute.

Garniture de cordes (Fr.). A set of strings.

Garrendo (It.). Chattering, rustling, twittering, purling.

Garrire (It.). To chatter, rustle, etc.

Gauche (Fr.). Left. *Main gauche*, left hand.

Gavotta (It.).
Gavotte (Fr.). } A gavotte; a moderately quick dance of a dignified character, in binary time.

Gazouillant (Fr.). Twittering (of birds), purling or babbling (of streams), rustling (of leaves), etc. *cf.* Garrendo.

Gebet (Ger.). Prayer.

Gebieterisch (Ger.). Commanding, imperative, peremptory.

Gebläse (Ger.). The bellows of an organ.

Geblümt (Ger.). Flowered, figured.

Gebrochener Akkord (Ger.). Broken chord, *arpeggio*.

Gebunden (Ger.). Slurred, tied.

    Gebundene Noten. Tied notes; notes played legato.

Ged. Abbr. of *gedämpft*.

Gedakt (Ger.). Covered.

    Gedakte Orgelpfeife. A stopped organ pipe.

Gedämpft (Ger.). Muted (Strings, horns, etc.): muffled (Drums). Of voices, *sotto voce*.

Gedeckt (Ger.). Covered. *cf.* Gedakt,
   Gedeckte Stimmen. Stops with covered pipes.
Gedehnt (Ger.). Drawn-out, protracted.
   Gedehnt und langsam. Drawn-out and slow.
Gedicht (Ger.). Poem.
Gefährte (Ger.). A companion. The answer (*comes*) to a fugue
   subject.
Gefällig (Ger.). Agreeable, pleasant.
Gefühl (Ger.). Feeling, emotion, sensibility.
   Gefühlvoll. Full of feeling, etc.
Gegen (Ger.). Towards, to; about, near; against, contrary to.
   Gegenbewegung. Contrary motion.
   Gegensatz. Countersubject.
   Gegenstrich. *v.* Contr'arco.
   Gegenthema. Countersubject.
Gehalten (Ger.). Sustained.
Gehaucht (Ger.). Breathed, whispered. *Wie gehaucht*, like a whisper.
Geheimnisvoll (Ger.). Mysterious.
Gehend (Ger.). Going. It is equivalent to *Andante*, and thus indi-
   cates a moderate speed, and like *Andante*, it is often combined
   with other words, which modify it.
Gehör (Ger.). Hearing. Usually to be translated by "ear", as *ein
   musikalisches Gehör*, a musical ear; *nach dem Gehör spielen*, to
   play by ear.
Gehörig (Ger.). Convenient, suitable.
Geige (Ger.). Violin, fiddle. plur. *Geigen*, and in combination.
   Geigenbogen. Violin-bow.
   Geigenharz. Colophony, resin for the violin.
   Geigenkasten. Violin case.
   Geigensaite. Violin string.
   Geigensattel. The nut of a violin.
   Geigensteg. The bridge of a violin.
   Geigenwirbel. A violin peg.
Geist (Ger.). Spirit, mind, intellect.
Geistlich (Ger.). Spiritual.
   Geistliche Werke. Sacred works.
Gelassen (Ger.). Calm, quiet, tranquil.
Geläufig (Ger.). Fluent, nimble.
Geltung (Ger.). Value, duration (of a note).
Gemächlich (Ger.). Convenient, leisurely, *commodo*.
Gemäßigt (Ger.). Moderate, *moderato*.
Gemebondo (It.). Plaintive, doleful.
Gemessen (Ger.). Measured, slow, precise.
Gemshorn. The chamois horn. An organ stop generally of 8 ft, of a
   conical shape and with a clear light tone.
Gemüt(h) (Ger.). Feeling, soul.
Gemüt(h)lich (Ger.). Agreeable, pleasant; full of feeling. *Im ge-
   mütlichen Menuettempo*, in easy minuet tempo.
Genannt (Ger.). Named, called (from *nennen*, to name). *Symphonie in
   C dur genannt l'Ours*, symphony in C major, called *l'Ours* (the bear).
General- (Ger.). General (used in combination).
   Generalbass. Thorough-bass.

Generalpause. A rest in all the parts.
Generalprobe. A full rehearsal.
Générateur (Fr.). The generator or fundamental note (*q. v.*) of an Harmonic Series: the root of a chord.
Genere (It.). Kind, species, sort.
Generoso (It.). Generous, noble.
Genial (Ger.). A word usually (and peculiarly) translated as "genial", which, in its customary English signification means "good-natured, jovial, etc.", while the German *genial* means "full of genius, highly gifted".
Génie (Fr.).
Genie (Ger.). } Genius.
Genio (It.).
Genis (It.). A brass instrument much the same as the tenorhorn.
Genouillère (Fr.). The knee-swell in the harmonium or American organ.
Genre (Fr.). Genus, sort, style. Term used in painting, for pictures representing everyday objects, and hence employed in the same sense in music for certain small compositions, *morceaux de genre.*
Gentil, -ille (Fr.).
Gentile (It.). } Gentle, delicate, pretty.
Gentilmente (It.).
Gentillement (Fr.). } Gracefully, gently, courteously.
Gentilezza (It.). Nobleness, courtesy.
Gerade (Ger.). Straight, even.
    Gerade Bewegung. Similar motion.
    Gerade Taktart.
    Gerader Takt. } Binary tempo.
Geraubtes Zeitmaß (Ger.). *Tempo rubato.*
Gerecht (Ger.). Fit, suitable, just.
German flute. The ordinary flute; a term seldom used at the present time.
Ges (Ger.). G flat.
Gesang (Ger.). Singing, song; vocal music. (In combination, sometimes *Gesangs-*.)
    Gesangbuch. A song-book; a hymn-book.
    Gesanglehre. Singing method; theory of singing.
    Gesanglehrer. Singing master.
    Gesanglehrerin. Singing mistress.
    Gesangsgruppe. The second subject in first movement form.
    Gesangskunst. The art of singing.
    Gesangstimme. Vocal part.
    Gesangstunde. Singing lesson.
    Gesangverein. Choral society.
    Gesangvoll. Melodious, singingly.
    Gesangweise. subs. Melody, tune. adv. In the style of a song.
Geschlecht (Ger.). Genus, species.
Geschleift (Ger.). Slurred, *legato.*
Geschlossen (Ger.). Closed, shut.
    Geschlossene Löcher. Closed holes on a wood-wind instrument.
Geschmack (Ger.). Taste.
    Geschmackvoll. In good taste, elegant; *gustoso.*

Geschmeidig (Ger.). Supple, flexible, *flessibile*.
Geschwind (Ger.). Quick, fast.
    Geschwind, doch nicht zu sehr, und mit Entschlossenheit. Fast,
      but not too much so, and with decision.
    Geschwindmarsch. } Quickstep, a quick march.
    Geschwindschritt.
Geses (Ger.). G double-flat.
Gesichtsprospektpfeife (Ger.). A "show" pipe of an organ; an organ-
pipe in front of the case.
Gesprochen (Ger.). Spoken. Direction found in opera scores, and
meaning that certain words are to be spoken instead of sung (*ge-
sungen*).
Gestopft (Ger.). Closed, stopped. (Directions to horns.) Following
Wagner's plan, single stopped notes are now usually indicated by
a +, and it is to be noted that according to the directions in the
Ring and *Meistersinger*, notes marked with a + are not only to be
stopped, but also to be *stark anblasen* (made brassy). *v.* Cuivré.
Gestoßen (Ger.). Detached, staccato.
Get(h). Abbr. of *get(h)eilt*.
Get(h)eilt (Ger.). Divided, *divisi*.
    Geteilt pultweise. Divided "desk-wise", *i. e.* that the 2 per-
      formers at the same desk are to play different parts.
Getragen (Ger.). Sustained, *legato*.
Gewichtig (Ger.). Weighty, heavy, *pesante*.
Gewidmet (Ger.). Dedicated to.
Gewöhnlich (Ger.). Usual, accustomed. Direction found in the parts
of various instruments to indicate that they are to play in the
ordinary way instead of *am Steg*, etc. (violins), *mit Holzschlägel*
(cymbals), etc.
    Gewöhnliche Schlägel. Ordinary drumsticks.
Gezogen (Ger.). Drawn; the sound drawn from one note to another,
con portamento.
Ghiribizzo (It.). Whim, fancy.
Ghiribizzoso (It.). Whimsical, capricious.
Giga (It.). A jig, *gigue*.
Gigelira (It.). A name for the *zilofone* (xylophone).
Gigue (Fr.). A jig.
Giochevole (It.). Pleasant, agreeable.
Giochevolmente (It.). In jest, jocularly.
Giocondamente (It.). Joyfully, gaily.
Giocondevole (It.). Pleasing.
Giocondezza, Giocondità (It.). Joy, mirth.
Giocondo, Giocondoso (It.). Merry, blithe.
Giocosamente (It.). Jocosely, facetiously.
Giocoso (It.). Jocose, mirthful.
Gioia, Gioja (It.). Pleasure, joy.
Gioiante, Giojante (It.). Joyful, merry.
Giojosamente (It.). Joyfully, gaily.
Giojoso, Gioioso (It.). Joyful, glad.
Gioviale (It.). Jovial.
Gis (Ger.). G sharp.
Gisis (Ger.). G double-sharp.

Gitarre (Ger.). The guitar *v.* Guitarre.
Giubilazione (It.). ⎱ Rejoicing, jubilation.
Giubilo, Giubilio (It.). ⎰
Giubiloso (It.). Overjoyed, enraptured.
Giulivamente (It.). Pleasantly, gaily.
Giulivo (It.). Joyous, mirthful. Sup. *Giulivissimo.*
Giuocante (It.). ⎱ Playful, pleasant.
Giuochevole (It.). ⎰
Giuoco (It.). Play, sport, diversion.
Giustamente (It.). Justly, precisely.
Giustezza (It.). Justness, exactness, precision.
Giusto (It.). Exact, precise.
Glänzend (Ger.). Resplendent, gorgeous, sumptuous.
Glatt (Ger.). Smooth.
Glätte (Ger.). Smoothness.
Gleich (Ger.). Equal, same.
  Gleichgültig Indifferent, unimportant.
  Gleichmäßig. Equal. *Mit gleichmäßigem Strich,* with equal stroke (of the bow).
  Gleichschwebende Temperatur. Equal temperament.
  Gleichstimmen. To tune to the same pitch.
  Gleichstimmung. A tuning to the same pitch.
  Gleichtönend. Unisonant; in unison.
  Gleichzeitig. Simultaneous.
Gleichsam (Ger.). As it were, as though; almost.
Gleiten (Ger.). To glide.
Gli (It.). Plur. of *lo*, the, (masc.).
Gliss. Abbr. of *glissando.*
Glissade (Fr.). A glissando passage.
Glissando (It.). An Italianised word from the Fr. *glisser*, to glide, slide, the more correct It. words being *sdrucciolando*, or *strisciando*. *Glissando* however is generally used, even by Italians, and means: — (1) the *portamento* of the voice; (2) the sliding of the finger between notes on the same string of a violin, etc.; (3) rapidly sliding the fingers along the strings of a harp, or the keys of a piano.
Glissato (It.). ⎱ Slid. *cf.* Glissando.
Glissé (Fr.). ⎰
Glöckchen (Ger.). A little bell.
Glocke (Ger.). A bell. plur. *Glocken.*
  Glockengeläute. A peal of bells.
  Glockenspiel. A set of bells. The *Glockenspiel* used formerly to consist of a series of small bells, which were often played with a keyboard; now it is made with steel bars struck by two little hammers. Its compass is from (*b♭*) *c′* to *b″♭* (*c‴*), the actual sounds being an octave higher. It is also the name of an organ stop.
Gloria (Lat.). One of the divisions of the Mass.
Glühend (Ger.). Glowing, ardent, fervid.
Gnaccare *or* **Gnacchere** (It.). Castanets.
Gola (It.). The throat; a throaty voice.
Goldfinger (Ger.). The third finger.
Gondellied (Ger.). A barcarole.

Gong. An Eastern instrument of percussion made in various shape. and sizes. The gong or tam-tam used in the modern orchestra is a circular shallow dish, made of metal, and with a diameter of from 15″ to 20″.

Gong drum. The bass drum with only one head, made in the shape of a gong or large tambourine.

Gorgheggiamento (It.). Trilling, warbling.

Gorgheggiare (It.). To trill, quaver, warble.

Gorgheggio (It.). A trill, shake, florid passage.

Grabgesang (Ger.). } A funeral song, a dirge.
Grablied (Ger.). }

Grâce (Fr.). Grace, charm. In the plur. it means grace-notes, and melodic ornamentation in general.

Gracieux, gracieuse (Fr.). Graceful.

Gracile (It.). Small, thin, delicate.

Grad (Ger.). Degree, step.

Gradazione (It.). Gradation.

Gradevole (It.). Agreeable.

Gradevolmente (It.). Agreeably, gracefully; willingly, with pleasure.

Graditamente (It.). In a gracious, agreeable manner.

Gradito (It.). Agreeable, grateful.

Grado (It.). Degree, step.

> **Grado ascendente.** Ascending interval.
> **Grado descendente.** Descending interval.

Graduale (Lat. and It.). Gradual (a part of the Mass). A book containing this portion.

Graduellement (Fr.). Gradually.

Gran (It.). For *Grande* (great), before a consonant.

> **Gran cassa.** The bass drum.
> **Gran gusto.** Great taste.

Grand, grande (Fr.). Great.

> **Grand barré.** In guitar playing, stopping more than three strings with the forefinger of the left hand.
> **Grand bourdon.** Great or double bourdon; an organ stop of 32ft.
> **Grand bugle.** The *saxhorn-contralto en si♭*, corresponding to the Flügelhorn of Eng. bands. The instrument is usually called simply the *bugle, grand* being employed only to distinguish it from the *petit bugle en mi♭*.
> **Grand chœur.** Full choir.
> **Grand détaché.** In the violin, etc., playing with a whole bow to every note.
> **Grand jeu.** The full power of an organ or harmonium.
> **Grand orchestre.** The full orchestra.
> **Grand orgue.** The great organ.

Grande (It.). Great.

Grandezza (It.). Grandeur, dignity.

Grandioso (It.). Grand, pompous, magnificent.

> **Grandioso e sonorissimo.** Pompous and very resonant.
> **Grandioso, ma non troppo lento.** Pompous, but not too slow.

Grandisonante (It.). Noisy, with much sound.

Grand⁻ˢᵒ. Abbr. of *grandioso*.

Grappa (It.). A brace.

Grasseyer (Fr.). To pronounce thickly.

Grausam (Ger.). Cruel.

Grave (Fr.). ⎰ Heavy, weighty, (of sound) deep. It is also used to
Grave (It.). ⎱ express a tempo, which is slower than *Adagio* and faster than *Largo*.

Gravement (Fr.). ⎰
Gravemente (It.). ⎱ Heavily, ponderously, sedately.

Gravezza (It.). Weight, heaviness, grief.

Gravità (It.). Gravity, weight, dignity.

Grazia (It.). Grace.

Graziös (Ger.). Graceful, *grazioso*.

Graziosamente (It.). Graciously, gracefully.

Graziosissimo (It.). Sup. of *grazioso*.

Grazioso (It.). Graceful.

Grazo. Abbr. of *grazioso*.

Great octave. The octave from the C below the bass stave to the B (2nd line): *C* to *B*.

Great organ. The principal portion of the organ, and that which as a rule contains the most powerful stops.

Greifen (Ger.). To strike a note on the piano, etc., or harp; to stop a note on a violin, etc.; to place the fingers for the various notes on a wood-wind instrument.

Grell (Ger.). Shrill, harsh.

 Grell lachend. Laughing shrilly.

 Grell und unrein, zur Nachahmung eines rohen Instrumentes. Harsh and out-of-tune, in imitation of a rude instrument.

Grelots (Fr.). Sleigh bells. They are occasionally used in the orchestra for picturesque effects, and Charpentier in *Impressions d'Italie* has a pair tuned to *g'* and *b'♭*.

Griff (Ger.). Literally, grasp, hold. The fingering of an instrument.

 Griffbrett. The fingerboard of a violin, guitar, etc.

 Griffloch. The key of a wood-wind instrument.

 Grifftabelle. Table of fingering of an instrument.

Grob (Ger.). Rough, coarse.

Groppetto, groppo. *v.* Gruppetto, gruppo.

Gros, grosse (Fr.). Great, large.

 Grosse caisse. The bass drum.

 Gros tambour. A name (seldom used) for the bass drum.

Gross, or Groß (Ger.). Great, large, big. Applied to intervals, major.

 Großartig. Grand, imposing.

 Große Flöte. The ordinary flute, as opposed to the *Kleine Flöte* (piccolo).

 Großer Ton. Great (much) tone. A direction indicating great resonance in the instruments.

 Großes Orchester. Full orchestra.

 Große Terz. Major third.

 Große Trommel. Bass drum.

Grosso (It.). Big, thick, coarse. *cf.* Concerto grosso.

Grösster (größter) (Ger.). Greatest. *Mit größter Energie*, with the greatest energy.

Grottesco (It.). Grotesque, ridiculous.

Grund (Ger.). Bottom, ground, foundation.

Grundbaß. Ground bass; a passage repeated again and again in the bass below the changing upper parts; *basso ostinato.*

Grundstimme. The bass or fundamental part.

Grundthema. The main or leading theme.

Grundton. Fundamental note.

Grundtonart. Fundamental key; main key of a movement.

Gruppetto (It.). A turn.

Gruppo (It.). A group of notes.

Guarnitura (It.). The fitting, mounting of an instrument.

Guerrier, guerrière (Fr.). } Warlike, brave, martial.
Guerriero, -a (It.). }

Guida (It.). A guide; subject of a fugue.

    Guida banda. A conductor's condensed score.

Guide (Fr.). Guide; subject of a fugue.

Guidon (Fr.). A direct; a sign at the end of a line showing what the next note is to be.

Guitar. An instrument with six strings (tuned *e*, *a*, *d′*, *g′*, *b′*, *e′′*, sounding an octave lower), consisting of a body, serving as a sound-board, and a neck forming a fingerboard, on which the notes are stopped by placing the fingers of the left hand between frets, the right hand plucking the strings.

Guitare (Fr.). Guitar.

Guitarra (It.). Guitar. The usual word is *Chitarra.*

Guitarre (Ger.). Guitar. Now usually written *Gitarre.*

    Guitarre-Töne. Notes played on a harp near the sound-board. and somewhat resembling those of a guitar. *cf.* Sons d'ongles.

Gusto (It.). Taste.

Gustoso (It.). Pleasant, agreeable.

Gut (Ger.). Good, well; very.

    Gut betont. Well emphasised.

    Guter Taktt(h)eil. The accented part of a bar.

    Gut gehalten. Well sustained.

    Gut gestoßen. Very staccato.

    Gut hervortretend. Well brought-out.

    Gut stimmen. To play well in tune.

H

H. In Ger. the note B natural, B being the Eng. B flat.

    h. Abbr. of *hoch.*

    H.C. Abbr. of *Haute-contre.*

    H dur (Ger.). B major.

    H moll (Ger.). B minor.

Haare (Ger.). The hair of the bow of a violin, etc.

Hack(e)brett (Ger.). A dulcimer.

Hagebüchen, *or* **Hahnbüchen** (Ger.). Coarse, clumsy.

Halb (Ger.). Half.

    Halbe Lage. Half position.

    Halbe Note. *v.* Halbnote.

    Halber Ton. *v.* Halbton.

    Halbkadenz. Half close.

    Halbmond. The Turkish crescent.

Halbnote. A minim.
Halbpause. A minim rest.
Halbprinzipal. An organ stop of 4ft pitch.
Halbschluß. Half close.
Halbsopran. Mezzo-soprano.
Halbstark. *Mezzo-forte.*
Halbtenor. A term for a baritone.
Halbton. A semitone.
Halbe (Ger.). A half.
    Halbe schlagen! $^2/_2$. Beat the half (of the bar). $^2/_2$.
Hälfte (Ger.). A half. *Die zwei Hälften der Becken schwingend gegeneinander geschlagen,* the two halves of the cymbals to be clashed against one another, *i. e.* played in the ordinary manner.
Hallen (Ger.). Resound, clang.
    Hallen lassen. Let resound, — (as a gong, for example).
Hals (Ger.). The neck of a violin, etc.
Halten (Ger.). To hold, sustain.
Hammerklavier (Ger.). The piano. *Klavier* is the term usually employed.
Hand (Ger.). The hand. plur. *Hände. Zu 2 Händen,* for 2 hands; *zu 4 Händen,* for 4 hands.
    Handgelenk. The wrist.
    Handstücke. Technical exercises.
    Handtrommel. A name for the tambourine.
Hand-Horn. *v.* Horn.
-händig (Ger.). Used as a suffix, and meaning: — having (or being arranged for) a certain number of hands, as *zweihändig,* for two hands, *vierhändig,* for four hands.
Handlung (Ger.). An action: the plot of a theatrical piece. Wagner uses the term as almost synonymous with the Eng. word 'drama'.
Hardiment (Fr.). Boldly.
Harfe (Ger.). Harp. *Harfen-* in combination. plur. *Harfen.*
    Harfe spielen. To play the harp.
    Harfenbass. An arpeggio (Alberti) bass.
    Harfenmäßig. In the style of harp music, *i. e.* playing the chords arpeggio.
    Harfenspiel, Harfenzug. Harp-playing.
    Harfenton, Harfenklang. The sound of the harp.
Harm. Abbr. of Harmonic, *Harmonique, Harmonie,* etc.
Harmonica. An instrument, in which the sounds are produced by pieces of glass (in strips or other forms) being vibrated by means of small hammers, moistened fingers, or pads. Strips of steel occasionally replace the glass strips, and the instrument sometimes possesses a key-board.
Harmonics. The secondary sounds or overtones produced by a string or column of air when vibrating in aliquot parts of its entire length: that is to say, if a string or column of air, vibrating throughout its entire length, produces the note ![note], when it vibrates in two halves the note ![note] is produced; in three thirds, the note ![note]

and so on, until the following Harmonic Series or Natural Scale is obtained, which theoretically might be extended to infinity: —

(The notes marked with a + are out of tune according to our modern scale.)

Almost every resonant body producing a musical note, at the same time produces certain of these harmonics, and the *timbre* or tone-quality of an instrument depends in a great measure on which of these are generated by the fundamental note.

On the harp, the 2nd sound of the Series is produced artificially by lightly touching with the palm of the hand the centre of the string immediately after it has been plucked.

On the violin, etc. what are termed *natural harmonics* are produced by lightly touching an open string at its $^1/_2$, $^1/_3$, etc.; *artificial harmonics*, by stopping a string with one finger (and thus altering its length), and then with another finger lightly touching the shortened string at the required distance; in both cases, the sound is usually produced by the bow on the string in the ordinary way, although solo performers have occasionally obtained the harmonics pizzicato. The Harmonic Series forms the basis of all wind-instrument playing. *v.* Brass Instruments, and Wood-Wind Instruments.

Harmonie (Fr.). (1) Harmony. (2) As an abbr. of *Musique d'harmonie*, music for wood-wind and brass instruments, and thus meaning either a military band, or the collective "Wind" of an orchestra.

    Harmonie consonante. Consonant harmony.

    Harmonie dissonante. Dissonant harmony.

Harmonie (Ger.). (1) Harmony. *Enge Harmonie*, close harmony; *weite Harmonie*, extended harmony. (2) A term for wind-instruments in general.

    Harmoniefremd. Foreign to the harmony.

    Harmoniegesetze. The rules of harmony.

    Harmonielehre. (1) Theory of harmony. (2) Treatise on harmony.

    Harmoniemusik. A wood-wind and brass band. For a military band, *Militärmusik* is the usual term.

Harmonieux, -euse (Fr.). Harmonious.

Harmonika (Ger.). The harmonica.

Harmonique (Fr.). Harmonic. *Sons harmoniques*, or simply *harmoniques*, harmonics on a harp, violin, etc.

Harmonisch (Ger.). Harmonious.

    Harmonische Töne. Harmonics. For the harmonics of a violin, etc., or harp, *Flageolettöne*, or simply *Flageolett*, is the ordinary expression.

Harmonium. A key-board free-reed instrument, in which the bellows are worked by means of pedals. Except in the smallest instruments, there are several reeds to each note, and from 6 to as many as 40 stops, large instruments often possessing two keyboards. Characteristic of the harmonium is the "Expression" stop, by means of which the air instead of entering the reservoir passes directly from the bellows to the reeds, and thus the various gradations of sound are under the immediate control of the feet.

Harp. An instrument of 47 strings, tuned diatonically from $C_1\flat$ to $g''''\flat$, and plucked by the thumb and first three fingers of each hand, — hence the chords of 5 notes for a single hand (which are found in the works even of composers who do not disdain to learn something of the instruments for which they write), are misplaced. By means of seven pedals, every note of this scale of $C\flat$ may be raised either a tone or semitone, the pedal being retained in position by being inserted in a notch in the groove, in which it works. On the ordinary harp, chromatic passages, or even passages which require a rapid alteration of many of the strings, are impossible. On the other hand, rapid glissando passages in chords of the 7th are perfectly easy by the use of what are called *homophones, i. e.* two strings tuned to the same note, as for instance $c\sharp$-$d\flat$, $a\sharp$-$b\flat$, etc. It is to be observed however that (a fact often forgotten by composers) there is no homophone of either $d\natural$, $g\natural$ or $a\natural$, and that in no case in a chord of 4 notes can all the notes be doubled by means of homophones, for the simple reason that there are only 7 notes in each octave.

> **Harp. (The Chromatic.)** An instrument like the above, but with no pedals, and with a separate string to every note of the chromatic scale. Opinions are divided as to its merits, its principal fault being a lack of resonance compared with the ordinary instrument. Naturally the use of homophones is impossible, and glissando passages, except purely chromatic ones, are equally so.

Harpe (Fr.). Harp.

> **Harpe d'Éole.** }
> **Harpe éolienne.** } Æolian harp.

Harpeggieren (Ger.). To play an arpeggio.

Harpsichord. A stringed instrument with a keyboard, one of the predecessors of the piano. The strings were plucked by quills or pieces of hard leather.

Hart (Ger.). Hard, harsh. Major.

> **Harte Tonart.** Major key.
> **Harter Dreiklang.** Major triad.

Hartnäckige Baß (Ger.). *v.* Basso ostinato.

Haupt (Ger.). Head, chief, principal.

> **Hauptgesang.** The principal melody.
> **Hauptkanal.** The principal canal (of an organ).
> **Hauptmanual.** The principal manual; the great organ.
> **Hauptmelodie.** The principal melody.
> **Hauptnote.** The principal note of a shake; an accented note.
> **Hauptorgel.** The great organ.
> **Hauptpartie.** The principal part.
> **Hauptperiode.** The principal period.
> **Hauptprobe.** Principal rehearsal; the dress rehearsal of an opera or play.

Hauptregister. A chief stop (on an organ).

Hauptsatz. Principal subject.

Hauptschluß. Full close.

Hauptstimme. Principal part or voice.

Hauptthema. Chief theme or subject.

Hauptton. *v.* Hauptnote.

Haupttonart. Principal key (of a movement).

Hauptwerk. The great organ.

Hauptzeitmaß. Principal tempo.

Hausse (Fr.). The nut of a bow.

Haut, haute (Fr.). High.

Haut-dessus. The treble part. ⎫
Haute-contre. The alto part. ⎬ These three terms are obsolete.
Haute-taille. The first tenor part. ⎭

Hautbois (Fr.). Hautboy, oboe.

Hautbois baryton. The baritone oboe; an instrument an octave lower than the ordinary oboe. It has been employed by Vidal (*La Burgonde*), and Strauss has employed a somewhat similar instrument, under the name of *Heckelphon* (*q. v.*) in *Salome*.

Hautbois d'amour. *v.* Oboe d'amore.

Hautboy. *v.* Oboe.

Heckelclarind (Ger.). An instrument invented by Heckel, and somewhat of the nature of a saxophone. It is played with a clarinet mouthpiece, and is made in B♭ and E♭ (sounding a 3rd above the written notes). It has been used to replace the cor anglais at the end of Scene I, Act III, *Tristan und Isolde*. *cf.* Tárogató.

Heckelphon (Ger.). A wood-wind instrument played with a double reed invented by Heckel, somewhat resembling the baritone oboe and standing an octave below the ordinary oboe.

Heftig (Ger.). Violent, vehement, impetuous, intense.

Heftig belebend. Becoming intensely animated.

Heftig beschleunigend. Quickening intensely.

Heftig, doch nie übereilt. Vehemently, but not over-hurried.

Heimlich (Ger.). Secret, stealthy.

Heiß (Ger.). Ardent, burning.

Heiter (Ger.). Serene, clear, bright.

Held (Ger.). A hero. *Helden-* in combination.

Heldengedicht. ⎫
Heldengesang. ⎬ An heroic poem or song, an epic.

Heldenmäßig. Heroic.

Heldentenor. *v.* Tenore robusto.

Helicon (Eng.). ⎫ The bombardon, or contra-bass tuba, when in cir-
Helikon (Ger.). ⎭ cular form.

Hell (Ger.). Clear, bright, sonorous.

Herabstrich (Ger.). The downstroke in bowing.

Herdenglocken (Ger.). Cow-bells.

Hernach (Ger.). Afterwards, hereafter, subsequently.

Heroisch (Ger.). Heroic.

Herstrich (Ger.). The downbow on a violoncello or double-bass.

Herunterstrich (Ger.). The downstroke on a violin or viola.

Hervorgehoben (Ger.). Emphasised, made prominent. *Den Rhythmus scharf hervorgehoben*, the rhythm sharply emphasised.

Hervortretend (Ger.). Stepping forward, advancing; standing in relief. A term often marked against particular instruments in a score, that are to be brought out prominently.

Herzhaft (Ger.). Brave, bold.

Hes (Ger.). A term very occasionally used for B♭.

Heses (Ger.). B double-flat.

Hier (Ger.). Here. *Von hier an Alla Breve taktieren,* from here beat two in a bar; *von hier ab fest im Zeitmaß,* from here strictly in the tempo.

   Hier geht der Vorhang auf. Here the curtain rises.

Hifthorn (Ger.). *v* Jägerhorn.

Hilfe (Ger.). Help. *Hilfs-* in combination.

   Hilfsnote. Auxiliary note.

   Hilfsstimmen. Mutation stops. *cf.* Füllstimmen and Nebenstimmen.

Hinaufstrich (Ger.). Upstroke in bowing.

Hinaufziehen (Ger.). To draw upwards. Term used to express a *portamento* from one note to a higher one.

Hinsterbend (Ger.). Dying away.

Hinstrich (Ger.). The upstroke on the violoncello and double-bass.

Hinunterziehen (Ger.). To draw down. Term used to express a *portamento* from one note to a lower one.

Hirt (Ger.). Herdsman, shepherd. *Hirten-* in combination.

   Hirtenflöte. Shepherd's pipe.

   Hirtengesang. ⎱ Shepherd's song; a pastoral.
   Hirtenlied. ⎰

   Hirtenmäßig. Shepherdlike, pastoral, rural.

His (Ger.). B sharp.

Hisis (Ger.). B double-sharp.

Hlzbl. Abbr. of *Holzbläser.*

Hoboe (Ger.). Oboe.

Hoch (Ger.). High.

   Hochamt. High Mass.

Höchst (Ger.). Sup. of *hoch.* Highest, extremely, most.

   Höchst langsam. Extremely slow.

   Höchst lebhaft. Extremely animated.

Hochzeit (Ger.). Wedding.

   Hochzeitgedicht. Wedding poem.

   Hochzeitmarsch. Wedding march.

Hof (Ger.). Court.

   Hofkapelle. Royal chapel. The royal private band.

   Hofkapellmeister. The director of the royal orchestra.

Höhe (Ger.). Height. Pitch. *Aus der höchsten Höhe,* in the highest height; *einen halben Ton in die Höhe gehen,* to raise a semitone.

   Höhepunkt. The summit; the culminating point.

Höhnend (Ger.). Scoffing, sneering.

Holz (Ger.). Wood.

   Holzbläser. (sing and plur.) A player on a wood-wind instrument. Term used for the collective "Wood-wind" of an orchestra.

   Holzblasinstrument. Wood-wind instrument.

   Holzharmonie. Music for wood-wind instruments.

   Holzharmonika. A xylophone.

Holzklapper. Wooden clapper (used by Mahler in his 5th and 6th symphonies).

Holzrand. The rope-hoop of a drum.

Holzschlägel. Wooden drumstick.

Holzstäbchen. A wooden beater. *Mit einem Holzstäbchen auf den Holzrand einer Trommel geschlagen,* struck with a wooden beater on the rope-hoop of the drum.

Holz- und Strohinstrumente. Wood and straw instrument; a xylophone.

Homophone. On the harp, two strings tuned to the same pitch.

Horae Canonicae (Lat.). The canonical hours, at which services are held in the Catholic Church.

Horn. The horn used by the classical masters is a natural instrument (*v.* Brass Instruments), on which, besides the notes of the Harmonic Series or *open* notes, the player is able to produce certain others, called *closed* or *stopped* notes. These latter are obtained by the more or less complete closing with the palm of the hand of the bell of the instrument (hence it is often known as the "Hand-horn"), which has the effect of lowering the pitch; by closing the bell from half to two-thirds of the distance usually left between the hand and the bell, any one of the open notes can be lowered a semitone, and by still further closing the bell, it is possible to lower the pitch about a tone. Naturally the more the bell is closed, the more the tone of the instrument becomes veiled and dull, and dissimilar to the tone of the open notes. The art of playing the hand-horn is in a great measure lost; judging by some of the music written for it, much of which would tax the ingenuity of a player on a valve instrument, the *virtuosi* must have assimilated the tone of the closed notes to that of the open ones in a manner now no longer attained.

The Valve-horn, which is now the form of the instrument in universal use, is the same as the above, but with the addition of valves. Naturally the use of closed notes for filling in the spaces between the open notes is unnecessary, but for special effects they are still used, and with the assistance of the valves any note of the chromatic scale can be produced as a closed note. Modern players also employ a mode of stopping the bell (apparently unknown to the old players), by means of which the pitch is *raised* a semitone, the tone then much resembling that produced by the use of the mute (*q. v.*). While the crooks (*q. v.*) for the natural horn were numerous, modern composers seldom use for the valve-horn other than those in E, E♭ and F, many exclusively writing for the last named (the most favorable for the instrument). Most players, preferring the sole use of the F crook, transpose the parts written for all lower crooks, when necessary; but they at times use shorter crooks, especially the A crook, if the music lies somewhat high.

A peculiarity of horn notation is that notes in the bass clef are written an octave lower than the note the performer is to play,

and hence is represented in the bass clef not by

𝄢 ⚬ but by 𝄢 ⚬ . Several modern composers however now employ the bass clef simply as a continuation of the treble, without the jump of an octave. The compass of the horn varies according to the crook employed (the high harmonics being easier on a low crook, and *vice versa*); for a horn in F, it may be said to be from *D* to *c''* (actual notes).

Horn (Ger.). Horn. plur. *Hörner.*

    Hornmusik. Music for brass instruments.

Hörner (Ger.). Horns.

Hosanna (Lat.). Part of the *Sanctus* of the Mass.

Hr. Abbr. of *Hörner.*

Hrn. Abbr. of Horn.

Htb. Abbr. of *Hautbois.*

Hübsch (Ger.). Charming, dainty, pretty.

    Hübsch vortragen. To be performed in a dainty manner.

Huit (Fr.). Eight.

    Huit-pieds. Eight feet.

Huitième. (Fr.). Eighth.

Hülfs- (Ger.). Used as a prefix. *v.* Hilfe.

Humor (Ger.). Humour.

Humoreske (Ger.). Humoresque.

Hüpfend (Ger.). Springing. Practically the same as *springend* (*q. v.*), although a slight distinction is made by some authors.

    Hüpfender Bogen. Springing bows, *spiccato.*

Hurtig (Ger.). Brisk, nimble, prompt.

Hymnaire (Fr.). A hymnbook.

Hymne (Fr.). Hymn, although not used in quite the sense of the Eng. "hymn", but meaning a religious song or canticle, not of necessity cut up into stanzas.

Hymne (Ger.).   ⎱ Hymn, spiritual song. *cf.* Hymne (Fr.).
Hymnus (Ger.). ⎰

I

I (It.). Plur. of *il,* the (masc.).

Idillio (It.). ⎰ An idyl or idyll; originally a short poem dealing with
Idyll (Ger.). ⎱ pastoral life; a musical composition of a quiet simple
Idylle (Fr.). ⎰ nature.

Idyllisch (Ger.). Idyllic.

Il (Fr.). He, it. *Il faut* is used in the sense of: — it is necessary.

    Il faut 3 timbaliers. 3 Kettledrummers are necessary.

    Il faut un instrumentiste pour chaque partie de la batterie. A separate player is necessary for each of the percussion instruments.

Il (It.). The (masc.).

    Il basso ben marcato. The bass very marked.

    Il canto sostenuto e legatissimo. The melody sustained and very smooth.

    Il doppio movimento. Double the tempo.

    Il più forte possibile. As loud as possible.

Im (Ger.). Combination of *in* and *dem* (in the).

   Im Anfang nicht zu rasch, nach und nach lebendiger. At the beginning not too fast, gradually more animated.

   Im Bedarfsfalle. When needed, in case of necessity. *Übernimmt im Bedarfsfalle die* 3. *große Flöte*, takes when necessary the 3rd (large) flute.

   Im gemessenen Schritt. In precise tempo.

   Im klagenden Ton. In accents of mourning.

   Im mäßigen Tempo. In moderate tempo.

   Im Notfalle. In case of need, if need be.

   Im Orchester. In the orchestra.

   Im ruhigen Tempo. In tranquil tempo.

   Im Takt. In the beat, *i. e.* in time, *a tempo*.

   Im Volkston. In the style of a Folk-song.

   Im Zeitmaß beruhigter. In the tempo, more tranquilly.

   Im Zeitmaß des Anfangs. In the tempo of the commencement.

Imboccatura (It.). (1) The cup-shaped mouthpiece of brass-instruments, or the mouth-hole of a flute. (2) The embouchure; the position of the lips, etc. for the playing of wind-instruments.

Imitando (It.). Imitating.

   Imitando il corno. Imitating the horn.

   Imitando la voce. Imitating the voice.

Imitation (Fr.). Imitation.

Imitazione (It.). Imitation.

   Imitazione all' Ottava. Imitation at the octave.

   Imitazione alla Quarta. Imitation at the fourth.

   Imitazione alla Quinta. Imitation at the fifth.

   Imitazione canonica. Strict imitation.

   Imitazione in moto eguale. Direct imitation.

   Imitazione in moto ineguale. / **Imitazione inversa.** Imitation by inversion.

   Imitazione legata. Strict imitation.

   Imitazione per augmentazione. Imitation by augmentation.

   Imitazione per diminuzione. Imitation by diminution.

   Imitazione rigorosa. / **Imitazione ristretta.** Strict imitation.

   Imitazione sciolta. Free imitation.

Immer (Ger.). Always, continually, constantly; throughout. (*Immer* often implies merely the continuance of an action and as such is almost untranslateable.)

   Immer ausgelassener und lebhafter. Always with more freedom and animation.

   Immer belebter. Always more animated.

   Immer bewegter bis zum Ende. With increasing passion until the end.

   Immer drängender. Always more hurried.

   Immer enger. Always more drawn together, *sempre più stretto*.

   Immer entfernter. Continually growing fainter.

   Immer etwas bewegter. Always somewhat more agitated.

   Immer etwas drängend. Always somewhat hurried.

   Immer etwas gedehnt. Constantly slackened a little.

   Immer G-Saite. Always (on the) G string.

Immer gleichmäßig leicht. Uniformly light throughout.
Immer langsamer. Continually slower.
Immer lebendiger. Always with more life.
Immer lebhafter. Always more animated.
Immer mit gestopften scharfen Tönen. With the notes closed and brassy throughout.
Immer noch drängend. Still hurrying.
Immer noch etwas mehr zurückhaltend. Still somewhat slackening.
Immer p, aber deutlich. Always *p*, but distinct.
Immer schwächer. Continually fainter.
Immer sehr lebhaft. Always very animated.
Immer sehr weich gebunden. Very softly sustained throughout.
Immer sehr zart. Always very sweetly.
Impair, -e (Fr.). Odd, as opposed to *pair*, even. *Les pupitres impairs*, the odd desks. *v.* Desk.
Impaziente (It.). Impatient.
Impazientemente (It.). Impatiently.
Imperioso (It.). Imperious, haughty.
Impeto (It.). Impetuosity.
Impetuosamente (It.). Impetuously, violently.
Impetuosità (It.). Impetuosity, fury.
Imponente (It.). Imposing.
Imponi(e)rend (Ger.). Imposing, majestic.
Impresario (It.). A theatrical manager; director of a concert or operatic company.
Impromptu (Fr.). An extemporised piece of music, or one written as an imitation of such a piece.
Improvisateur, -trice (Fr.). An improviser.
Improviser (Fr.). To improvise.
Improvvisamente (It.). Extemporaneously.
Improvvisamento (It.). An impromptu.
Improvvisare (It.). To improvise.
Improvvisatore, -trice (It.). An improviser.
Improvvisazione (It.). An improvisation, an impromptu.
In (Ger.). In, at, into, to.
In das mäßige Zeitmaß zurückkehrend. Returning to the moderate tempo.
In gehender Bewegung. Literally "in going movement", *i. e.* a tempo, which is not dragged.
In höchster Angst. In deepest anguish.
In lebhafter Bewegung. ⎫
In schneller Bewegung. ⎬ In quick time.
In Vierteln. In crotchets.
In zwei Abteilungen. In two parts.
In (It.). In, into, at.
In altissimo. All the notes above *g'''*.
In alto. In alt; the notes from *g''* to *f'''*.
In battere. The accented part of the bar.
In battuta. In exact time.
In disparte. Aside.
In distanza. In the distance.
In fretta. Hastily.

In giù. In bowing, drawing the bow downwards. *Arcata in giù* is the opposite of *arcata in su*.

In levare. The unaccented beat.

In lontanza, in lontananza. *v.* In distanza.

In palco. On the stage.

In partito. In score. *Canone in partito*, an open canon.

In sù. In bowing, pushing the bow upwards. *cf.* In giù.

In tempo, ma poco più lento. In time, but a little slower.

Incalcando, Incalzando (It.). Hastening, pursuing.

Incollando (It.). Striking the notes of a chord simultaneously.

Incollato (It.). Literally, "glued together". *cf.* Incollando.

Incominciando (It.). Commencing.

    Incominciando a decrescere. Commencing to decrease.

    Incominciando pianissimo per giungere al fortissimo. Commencing pianissimo and proceeding to the fortissimo.

Incordare (It.). To string an instrument.

Incrociamento, Incrocicchiamento (It.). Crossing (the hands in piano-playing).

Incrociato (It.). Crossed.

Indebolendo (It.). Growing weak, becoming faint.

Indebolito (It.). Weakened.

Indeciso (It.). Undecided.

Indicato (It.). Indicated, pointed out, prominent. *Ben indicato,* very prominent (as a particular instrument in the orchestra).

Indifferente (It.). Careless, indifferent.

Indifferentemente (It.). Indifferently, carelessly.

Indifferenza (It.). Indifference.

Infernale (It.). Infernal, hellish.

Inferno (It.). Hell.

Infiorendo (It.). Embellishing a part with grace-notes, etc.

Infra (It.). Below.

Inganno (It.). Deceit, trick; mistake. *Cadenza d'inganno*, a deceptive cadence.

Inhalt (Ger.). Contents, index.

Innig (Ger.). Heartfelt, fervent, intimate. Corresponding to the Fr. *intime*.

    Innig zu spielen. To be played with fervent expression.

Innigkeit (Ger.). Fervour, devoutness, intimacy.

Inno (It.) A hymn.

Innocente (It.). Innocent.

Innocentemente (It.). Innocently.

Innocenza (It.). Innocence.

Inquieto (It.). Restless, uneasy.

Inquietudine (It.). Inquietude, trouble.

Insegnamento (It.). Instruction.

Insensibile (It.). Imperceptible.

Insensibilmente (It.). Imperceptibly.

Insieme (It.). *v.* Ensemble. *Pezzo d'insieme, morceau d'ensemble.*

Inständig (Ger.). ⎰ Urgent, pressing.
Instante (It.). ⎱

Instantemente (It.). Pressingly, urgently, earnestly.

Instrument (Fr.). Instrument.

Instrument à archet. Bowed instrument.
Instrument à cordes. Stringed instrument.
Instrument à percussion. Percussion instrument.
Instrument à vent. Wind instrument.
Instrument de cuivre. Brass instrument.
Instrument (Ger.). Instrument. plur. *Instrumente*. *Blasinstrumente*, wind instruments; *Blechinstrumente*, brass instruments; *Holzblasinstrumente*, wood-wind instruments; *Messinginstrumente*, brass instruments; *Saiteninstrumente*, stringed instruments; *Schlaginstrumente*, percussion instruments; *Streichinstrumente*, bowed instruments (the stringed instruments of the orchestra).
Instrumental (Fr.). Instrumental.
Instrumental (Ger.). Instrumental.
  Instrumentalbegleitung. Instrumental accompaniment.
  Instrumentalmusik. Instrumental music.
Instrumentation. The art of writing for instruments, either singly or in combination. The term is often used as synonymous with "Orchestration" (the art of writing for an orchestra), but although the latter should connote a knowledge of the former, a glance at many modern scores is sufficient to reveal the fact that, whatever the general effect may be, the individual parts often display a profound ignorance on the part of the composer of the capabilities and limitations of the several instruments.
Instrumentation (Ger.). Instrumentation. In combination, *Instrumentations-*.
  Instrumentationslehre. A method (tutor) for instrumentation.
Instrumenti(e)ren (Ger.). To instrumentate.
Instrumentierung (Ger.). Instrumentation.
Instrumento (It.). Occasionally found for *Istrumento*.
Intavolare (It.). To write down music; to set to music.
Intavolatura (It.). (1) Tablature. (2) Figured bass. (3) Notation in general. (4) A diagram of fingering.
Intense (Fr.). Intense, strong. *ff mais très intense d'expression*, *ff* but with the most intense expression.
Intensità (It.). }
Intensité (Fr.). } Intensity, strength.
Intenso (It.). Intense. Sometimes applied to a sound, which vibrates strongly.
Intermède (Fr.). An interlude.
Intermedietto (It.). A small interlude.
Intermedio (It.). }
Intermezzo (It.). } An interlude.
Interrotto (It.). Interrupted.
Interruzione (It.). Interruption; pause.
Intervall (Ger.). }
Intervalle. (Fr.). } An interval.
Intervallo (It.). }
Intimamente (It.). Intimately. *cf.* Intimo.
Intime (Fr.). Intimate, inmost, heartfelt. *Avec un sentiment intime*, with deep feeling. *cf.* Innig.
Intimissimo (It.). Sup. of *intimo*.
Intimo (It.). Intimate, inmost, heartfelt. *cf.* Intime, Innig.

Intonare (It.). (1) To intone. (2) To set to music. (3) To give the key-note.

Intonation (Fr.). ⎫ Intonation. (1) The production of sounds by a
Intonation (Ger.). ⎬ voice or instrument. (2) The pitch of a note.
Intonazione (It.). ⎭ (3) In plain-song, the notes leading up to the reciting note.

Intonieren (Ger.). To intone.

Intonierung (Ger.). Intonation.

Intrade (Ger.). (1) An introduction, prelude. (2) A flourish of trumpets.

Intrepidamente (It.). Intrepidly, boldly.

Intrepidezza (It.). Intrepidity, fearlessness.

Intrepido (It.). Intrepid, dauntless.

Introduction (Fr.). ⎫ An introduction; a preparatory movement
Introduktion (Ger.). ⎬ leading up to one of the main movements of
Introduzione (It.). ⎭ the composition.

Introït (Fr.). ⎫ An introit; an antiphon, sung while the
Introito (It.). ⎬ priest approaches the altar to celebrate
Introitus (Ger. and Lat.). ⎭ Mass.

Inventionshorn (Ger.). An improved horn devised by Hampe in Dresden about 1750, furnished with a tuning slide, which could be replaced by others of different lengths, thus serving as the crooks.

Inventionstrompete (Ger.). A trumpet corresponding with the foregoing; also a trumpet (*Stopftrompete*) curved to enable closed notes to be obtained by introducing the hand into the bell.

Inverzione (It.). Inversion.

Invocation (Fr.). An invocation; a prayer or supplication addressed to a deity, saint, or some superior being, as opposed to an *Évocation* (*q. v.*), a summons addressed to inferior beings. The term is occasionally used for short pieces of a prayerful nature, as the Invocation in Massenet's *Les Erinnyes*.

Invocazione (It.). Invocation.

Ira (It.). Rage, wrath.

Iracondamente, Iratamente (It.). Angrily, passionately.

Irato (It.). Angry, irritated.

Irlandais, -aise (Fr.). ⎫ Irish.
Irländisch (Ger.). ⎭

Ironicamente (It.). Ironically.

Ironico (It.). Ironical.

Irresoluto (It.). Irresolute, undetermined.

-is (Ger.). Added to the designation of a note to signify "sharp". Thus A = A; Ais = A sharp; E = E; Eis = E sharp, etc.

-isis (Ger.). Added to the designation of a note to signify "double-sharp". Thus $Fisis$ = F double-sharp.

Islancio (It.). Glow, enthusiasm, dash. *cf.* Élan.

Istesso, -a (It.). Form of *stesso, -a*, same. *v.* L'istesso.

Istrumentazione (It.). A form of *strumentazione*, instrumentation.

Istrumento (It.). *v.* Strumento.

Italiano, -a (It.). ⎫ Italian.
Italien, -ienne (Fr.). ⎭

J

Jagd (Ger.). Chase, hunting, hunt.
  Jagdhorn. *v.* Trompe de chasse. *cf.* Waldhorn.
  Jagdstück. Hunting-piece; hunting-song.
Jäger (Ger.). A hunter.
  Jägerchor. A chorus of hunters; a hunting chorus.
  Jägerhorn. The hunting horn.
Jaleo *or* **Jallo** (Sp.). A Spanish dance.
Jämmerlich (Ger.). Deplorable, lamentable.
Jammernd (Ger.). Wailing, lamenting.
Janitscharenmusik (Ger.). Janissary music; a band composed of wind-instruments together with all the noisy instruments of percussion.
Jardin (Fr.). In theatrical terminology, the side of the stage to the left of the spectator.
Je (Ger.). At any time, ever; (with numerals) each.
  Je drei Pauken. Three drums each.
Jedoch (Ger.). However, still, yet.
Jeu (Fr.). Play, diversion, game, and hence the execution or performance of a musician or actor. The term is often used in the sense of "a set of anything", such as organ-pipes, bells, etc. *Grand jeu*, or *plein jeu*, bringing all the stops of an organ or harmonium into play (full organ).
  Jeu à bouche. A flue-stop.
  Jeu céleste. A soft stop on the harmonium; a stop of a tremulant character on the organ.
  Jeu d'anche. A reed stop on an organ.
  Jeu d'ange. The *vox angelica* stop.
  Jeu de flûte. Flute stop.
  Jeu de timbres. Set of small bells, carillon. Plates or bars of metal are now usually substituted for the bells.
  Jeu de voix humaine. The *vox humana* stop.
  Jeu d'orgue. An organ stop.
  Jeu ordinaire. The ordinary method of playing an instrument; an indication contradicting a previous one, such as: — *sur le chevalet, sons harmoniques*, etc.
Jeux (Fr.). Plur. of *jeu*.
  Jeux de fonds. The foundation stops of an organ.
  Jeux doux. Soft stops.
  Jeux forts. Loud stops.
Jingles. The little cymbals or plates, fixed in the wooden hoop of a tambourine.
Jodeln (Ger.). To yodel: to sing in the peculiar style practised in some of the Alpine districts, of which the distinguishing feature is an abrupt change into falsetto.
Jongleurs (Fr.). The old troubadours.
Jota aragonesa (Sp.). A dance.
Jouer (Fr.). To play.
  Jouer ces petites notes à defaut du saxophone. Play these small notes when there is no saxophone.

III

Joyeusement (Fr.). Joyously.
Jubelnd (Ger.). Jubilant, triumphant.
Judenbaß (Ger.). A very deep bass voice.
Jugend (Ger.). Youth.
Jusqu'à (Fr.). Until.
 Jusqu'à la fin. Until the end.
Juste (Fr.). Just, exact, accurate.
Justesse (Fr.). Exactness, accuracy.

K

K. Abbr. of *Kontra*.
 K.B. Abbr. of *Kontrabass*.
 K.F. Abbr. of *Kontrafagott*.
Kadenz (Ger.). Cadence.
Kaisermarsch (Ger.). Imperial march.
Kalamaika. A Hungarian dance.
Kalkant (Ger.). An organ blower.
Kann (Ger.). Can (from *können*, to be able).
 Kann im Notfalle von einem Piston in B übernommen werden.
 Can be undertaken if need be by a cornet in B♭.
Kammer (Ger.). Room, chamber; royal apartment.
 Kammerduett. Chamber duet.
 Kammerkantate. A chamber cantata, *i. e.* one of smaller dimen-
 sions and requiring less means for its performance than one
 intended for a concert-hall.
 Kammerkomponist. Chamber composer; a composer in the
 service of a prince.
 Kammerkonzert. A chamber concert.
 Kammermusiker, Kammermusikus. A musician in the service
 of a prince.
 Kammersänger. A singer in the service of a prince.
 Kammerstil. Style of chamber-music.
 Kammerton. In old Ger. music, the customary pitch used in
 secular music. It was approximately a tone lower than the
 Chorton (*q. v.*).
 Kammervirtuos. A virtuoso in the service of a prince.
Kanon (Ger.). Canon.
Kanzellen (Ger.). The channels or grooves of the wind-chest of an
organ.
Kapelle (Ger.). (*Kapell-* in combination.) A chapel. The musical
 establishment of a prince or nobleman, and consisting of either
 singers or instrumentalists (or of both), who not only perform in
 the church, but also take part in the secular music (operas, con-
 certs, etc.), connected with the court. The term is now used for
 any permanent body of musicians.
 Kapellist. A bandsman, member of a *Kapelle*.
 Kapellknaben. Choir-boys attached to the *Kapelle*.
 Kapellmeister. The musical director, conductor and choir master
 of a *Kapelle*.
 Kapellmeistermusik. Term of derision applied to the occasionally
 uninspired compositions of Kapellmeisters.

Kapsel (Ger.). A clarinet cap.

Kastagnetten (Ger.). Castanets.

Kasten (Ger.). Case for a stringed instrument.

Kaum (Ger.). Scarcely, hardly.

    Kaum hörbar. Scarcely audible.

    Kaum merklich bewegter. Scarcely perceptibly faster.

    Kaum vernehmbar. Scarcely audible.

Keck (Ger.). Bold, daring, audacious.

Keckheit (Ger.). Boldness, audacity.

Keifend (Ger.). Scolding, nagging, bickering.

Keineswegs (Ger.). In nowise.

    Keineswegs schnell. In nowise fast.

Kelle (Ger.). Term sometimes used for a reed of a broad spatula-like shape.

Kenner (Ger.). A connoisseur.

Kent bugle. A keyed bugle.

Kenthorn (Ger.). Same as the *Bügelhorn* or *Klappenhorn*, the keyed bugle.

Kenttrompete (Ger.). A keyed trumpet, corresponding to a keyed bugle.

Keraulophon. An organ stop of a soft reedy tone.

Kesselpauke (Ger.). The old name for a kettledrum, now always abbreviated to *Pauke*.

Kettentriller (Ger.). A chain of shakes.

Kettledrum. A percussion instrument, consisting of a hemispherical shell of metal, over which a membrane is stretched, capable of being tuned by means of screws surrounding the hoop which tightens the head. Kettledrums have always formed a part of the symphonic orchestra, the classical masters usually employing two (the larger with a compass from E to c, the smaller, from $B\flat$ to f), but in many modern works a third drum (with a compass from A to d) is necessary, and two pairs are not uncommon. Spohr uses 3 pairs in *Calvary*, Reicha (to depict the harmony of the spheres) 4 pairs, while Berlioz in his Requiem employs as many as 8 pairs.

    Chromatic drums are now required by some composers. In these, the tuning can be instantly altered by a single screw, usually turned by means of a pedal. The instruments are not entirely satisfactory, since tightening the membrane in one motion is not sufficient to ensure true intonation in delicate tunings, as the membrane does not stretch evenly, but requires to be adjusted to a different tension at different parts of its circumference.

Kicks (Ger.). Fault, blunder. Applied to the *couac* (*q. v.*) on a reed instrument.

Kind (Ger.). (*Kinder-* in combination.) A child.

    Kinderszenen. Scenes for children.

    Kindersymphonie. Toy symphony.

    Kindertrompeten. Children's trumpets; toy-trumpets.

    Kinderübungen. Exercises for children.

Kinnhalter (Ger.). Chin-rest for a violin.

Kirche (Ger.). (*Kirchen-* in combination.) A church.

    Kirchenarie. A church aria; a sacred aria.

    Kirchengesang. (1) A hymn, canticle. (2) Church-singing.

Kirchenkantate. A church (sacred) cantata.
Kirchenkonzert. A church concert.
Kirchenlied. Hymn, canticle, sacred song.
Kirchenmusik. Church music.
Kirchenstil. The church (ecclesiastical) style; *alla capella.*
Kirchentöne. The ecclesiastical modes.
Kirchenweise. A church (sacred) melody.
Kit. A small violin, formerly often used by dancing masters.
Klagend (Ger.). Complaining, wailing.
Kläglich (Ger.). Plaintive, wailing, mournful.
Klammer (Ger.). A brace, bracket, accolade.
Klang (Ger.). Tone, *timbre.*
    Klangboden. Sounding-board, sound-board.
    Klangfarbe. Tone-colour.
    Klanggeschlecht. Tone genus, which may be major, minor, diatonic, chromatic or enharmonic.
    Klanglehre. Theory of sound; acoustics.
Klappe (Ger.). A key of a flute, clarinet, etc., or of an ophicleide, keyed bugle, etc. plur. *Klappen.*
Klarinette (Ger.). (*Klarinetten-* in combination.) A clarinet. plur. *Klarinetten.*
    Klarinettenblatt. ⎱ A clarinet reed.
    Klarinettenrohr. ⎰
    Klarinettenschnabel. Clarinet mouthpiece. *cf.* Mundstück.
    Klarinettenverband. Clarinet ligature.
Klarinettist (Ger.). A clarinet-player.
Klaviatur (Ger.). Keyboard.
Klavier (Ger.). Piano.
    Klavierauszug. Piano score.
    Klavierbegleitung. Piano accompaniment.
    Klavierlehrer. Piano master.
    Klavierlehrerin. Piano mistress.
    Klavierspiel. Piano-playing.
    Klavierspieler, -in. Pianist.
    Klavierstück. Piano piece.
    Klavierübungen. Piano exercises.
    Klavier vierhändig. ⎱ Piano duet.
    Klavier zu 4 Händen. ⎰
Klein, -e (Ger.). Small. Applied to intervals, minor.
    Kleine Flöte. The piccolo.
    Kleine Terz. Minor third.
    Kleine Trommel. The side or snare-drum.
Klingen (Ger.). To sound, vibrate.
    Klingen eine Oktave höher, als notiert. To sound an octave higher than written.
    Klingen lassen. Let vibrate, *i. e.* do not damp the sound.
Klingend (Ger.). Resonant, sonorous, resounding.
Knabe (Ger.). (*Knaben-* in combination.) A boy.
    Knabenstimme. A boy's voice.
Knarre (Ger.). A rattle.
Knee-swell. A lever in the harmonium and American organ worked by the knee, and corresponding to the swell-pedal of an organ.

Kneifend (Ger.).   Plucking, *pizzicando*.
Knopf (Ger.).   A button; stud on an organ.
   Knöpfchen.   The button or tail-pin of a violin.
Komisch (Ger.).   Comic.
   Komische Oper.   Comic opera.
Komponi(e)ren (Ger.).   To compose.
Kompositionslehre (Ger.).   The theory of composition; a treatise on composition.
Kontra (Ger.).   Often used in the sense of the It. *contra*, or Eng. double.
   Kontrabass. }
   Kontrabaß. } The double bass.
   Kontrabaßposaune.   Double-bass trombone.
   Kontrabaßtuba.   Double-bass tuba.
   Kontrafagott.   Double bassoon.
   Kontrafuge.   Double fugue.
   Kontrapunkt.   Counterpoint.
Kontretanz (Ger.).   A square dance, *contre-danse*.
Konzert (Ger.).   Concert, concerto.   Until recently always spelt as *Concert*.
   Konzertflügel.   A concert grand-piano.
   Konzerthaus.   A concert-house.
   Konzertmeister.   Leader of an orchestra, the principal violin.
   Konzertsaal.   Concert-hall (room).
   Konzertsänger (masc.). }
   Konzertsängerin (fem.). } A concert singer.
   Konzertstück.   A concert-piece.
   Konzertton.   Concert-pitch.
   Konzertzither.   A zither of large size for concert use.
Kopf (Ger.).   A head.
   Kopfnote.   Head-note.
   Kopfstimme.   Head-voice.
Koppel (Ger.).   A coupler.
   Koppelzug.   The draw-stop of a coupler.
Kräftig (Ger.).   Strong, powerful, vigorous.
   Kräftig, doch nicht zu schnell.   Energetic, but not too fast.
   Kräftig gestoßen.   Forcibly detached (*staccato*).
   Kräftig und bestimmt.   Vigorous and decided.
   Kräftig und feurig.   Vigorous and spirited.
Krakowiak.   A Polish dance in $2/4$ time.
Krebs (Ger.).   A crab.
   Krebsgängig.   Retrograde.
   Krebskanon.   Canon by retrogression, *canon cancricans*.
Kreischend (Ger.).   Screeching, screaming.
Kreuz (Ger.).   The sharp sign (♯).   *Doppel-Kreuz*, the double sharp (×).
   Kreuzsaitig.   Cross-stringed (as of a piano).
Krieg (Ger.).   (*Kriegs-* in combination.)   War.
   Kriegslied.   War-song.
Kriegerisch (Ger.).   Warlike, martial.
Krone (Ger.).   Corona; the sign ⌢.
Krumm (Ger.).   Crooked.
   Krummbogen.   The crook of a horn or trumpet, now always abbreviated to *Bogen*.

Krummhorn. The same as *Cromorne* (*q. v.*).

Kuckuckinstrument (Ger.). An instrument for producing the notes of a cuckoo.

Kuhhorn (Ger.). A cow-horn; horn for calling the cattle.

Kunst (Ger.). Art. *Die schönen Künste*, the fine arts.

    Kunstfuge. A fugue exhibiting every scholastic device.

    Kunstkenner. A connoisseur.

    Kunstliebhaber. An amateur, a dilettante.

    Kunstwerk. Work of art, creation.

    Kunstwort. A technical art term.

Kurz (Ger.). Short. Used in the sense of *secco* for a sharp short chord.

    Kurze Note. An *acciaccatura*.

    Kurz und bestimmt. Short and with decision.

Kürzung (Ger.). Shortening. *Zur Kürzung des Stückes*, for the shortening of the piece.

Kustos (Ger.). A direct; a cue.

Kyrie (Gk.). The first part of the Mass, commencing *Kyrie eleison*, "Lord have mercy upon us".

L

L. Abbr. of Left, *Link*, *Links*. In stage directions, L. means in Eng. to the left of the *actor*; in Ger. to the left (*Links*) of the *spectator*.

    L.H. Abbr. of Left hand, *Linke Hand*.

L' (Fr.). Abbr. of *La* or *Le* before a word commencing with a vowel or *h* mute.

L' (It.). Abbr. of *Lo*, *La* or *Le* before a word commencing with a vowel, but its use is not invariable.

    L'accompagnamento sempre leggierissimo. The accompaniment always very light.

    L'istesso moto. ⎫
    L'istesso movimento. ⎬ The same movement.

    L'istesso tempo. The same time.

    NB. In these three expressions, the correct Italian is *lo stesso*, etc., and as such is used by all Italian composers: the *l'istesso*, etc., usually written by composers, other than Italian, are colloquialisms.

La (Fr.). (1) The (fem.). (2) The note A. *Ce La expressif*, this A with expression.

    La bémol. A flat.

    La bémol mineur. A flat minor.

    La dièse. A sharp.

    La majeur. A major.

    La 3e (troisième) Flûte prend la petite Flûte. The 3rd flute takes the piccolo.

La (It.). (1) The (fem.). (2) The note A.

    La bemolle. A flat.

    La bemolle maggiore. A flat major.

    La diesis. A sharp.

    La melodia ben marcata. The melody well emphasised.

    La minore. A minor.

La prima parte senza ripetizione. The first part without repeat.
La voce. The voice.
Labial- (Ger.). Used in combination.
    Labialpfeife. A flue-pipe of an organ.
    Labialstimme. A stop of the flue-work.
    Labialwerk. Flue-work.
Lacrimando (It.). *v.* Lagrimando.
Lade (Ger.). For *Windlade*, the wind-chest of an organ.
Lage (Ger.). Position (on a violin, etc.): register (of a voice or instrument): position of the notes of a chord, as *enge Lage*, close position, *weite Lage*, extended position.
Lagnevole (It.). Doleful, plaintive.
Lagnosamente (It.). Dolefully, mournfully.
Lagnoso, -a (It.). Plaintive, doleful.
Lagrimando (It.). Weeping, deploring.
Lagrimoso, -a (It.). Sad, full of tears.
Laisser (Fr.). To let, to allow.
    Laisser vibrer. Allow to vibrate.
Lame (Fr.). Blade; a small bar of metal.
    6 lames d'acier frappées avec 2 marteaux. 6 strips of steel, struck with 2 hammers.
Lamentabile (It.). *v.* Lamentevole.
Lamentando (It.).
Lamentandosi (It.). } Lamenting, complaining.
Lamentazione (It.). Lamentation, complaint.
Lamentevole (It.). Plaintive, sad.
Lamentevolmente (It.). Sadly.
Lamento (It.). A lament, moan.
Lamentoso (It.). Mournful.
Lampo (It.). A flash of lightning.
Lancio (It.). Spring, bound; glow, enthusiasm, *élan*.
Ländler (Ger.). A slow waltz; a "Tyrolienne".
Lang (Ger.). Long.
    Lang ausklingen lassen. Let the sound be long in dying away.
    Lange Fermata.
    Lange Pause. } Long pause.
    Langes Schweigen. Long silence.
Langsam (Ger.). Slow.
    Langsam getragen. Slowly drawn-out (sustained).
    Langsam und mit Ausdruck spielen. To be played slowly and with expression.
    Langsam und schmachtend. Slow and languishing.
    Langsam und sehnsuchtsvoll. Slow and yearning.
Langsamer (Ger.). Slower.
    Langsameres Viertel. The crotchet slower.
    Langsamer werdend. Becoming slower.
Languendo, Languente (It.). Languishing; love-sick.
Languette (Fr.). (1) The tongue of an organ reed-pipe. (2) The stem of the keys of wind-instruments.
    Languettes libres. Free reeds.
Languidissimo (It.). Sup. of *languido*.
Languido (It.). Faint, weak.

Largamente (It.). Largely, broadly.
Large (Fr.). Broad.
Largement (Fr.). Broadly; in a grand style.
 Largement chanté. Broadly sung.
Largeur (Fr.). Breadth. *Avec plus de largeur*, with more breadth.
Larghetto (It.). Diminutive of and indicating a tempo somewhat faster than *largo*. Somewhat slow and broad.
 Larghetto non troppo lento. Somewhat broad, but not too slow.
Larghezza, *or* **Largo** (It.). Breadth, slowness.
Larghissimo (It.). Sup. of *largo*.
Largo (It.). Broad. Used of a broad slow tempo, which is slower than *Adagio*.
 Largo assai. Very slow.
 Largo di molto. Very slow indeed.
 Largo ma non troppo. Slow, but not too much so.
Larigot (Fr.). An acute organ stop, sounding an octave above the 12th.
Lasciate sonare (It.). Let vibrate.
Lauda Sion (Lat.). One of the Sequences of the Catholic Church.
Lauf (Ger.). A run, roulade.
Laut (Ger.). Loud, distinct, resounding. subs. Sound, tone.
Laute (Ger.). (*Lauten-* in combination.) A lute.
 Lautenmacher. A maker of violins, etc.
 Lautenspieler, Lautenist. A lute-player.
Lavorare (It.). To work.
Le (Fr.). The (masc.).
 Le plus léger possible. As lightly as possible.
 Le Von solo avec les autres. The solo Vn with the rest.
Le (It.). The (fem. plur.).
 Le voci. The voices.
Lebendig (Ger.). Lively, animated.
Lebhaft (Ger.). Lively, vivacious, quick. Corresponds to *vivo*, *vivace*.
 Lebhaft, aber nicht zu sehr. Lively, but not oo much so.
 Lebhaft bewegt. With lively animation.
 Lebhaft doch gewichtig. Quickly but heavily.
 Lebhaft, doch kräftig und ohne eilen. Animated yet decided, and without haste.
 Lebhaft, doch nicht zu schnell. Animated yet not too fast.
 Lebhaft mit Steigerung. Animated and with exaltation.
 Lebhaft rasch. Very quickly.
Lebhafter (Ger.). More animated, more vivacious, etc.
Lebhaftigkeit (Ger.). Vivacity, animation, briskness.
Leçon (Fr.). A lesson.
Leg. Abbr. of *legato*.
Legando (It.). Slurring, tying, binding
Legatissimo (It.). Sup. of *legato*
Legare (It.). To bind, slur, tie.
Legato (It.). Tied, bound, slurred, sustained, smooth.
 Legato e con espressione. Sustained and with expression.
Legatura (It.). Ligature (of a clarinet). *Legatura di voce*, binding of the voice; singing of several notes in one breath.
Léger, légère (Fr.). Light.

Légèrement (Fr.). Lightly; slightly. *Très légèrement retenu*, very slightly slackened.

Légèreté (Fr.). Lightness.

Legg. Abbr. of *leggiero*.

Leggeramente (It.). Lightly; slightly.

Leggeranza (It.). } Lightness.
Leggerezza (It.). }

Leggermente (It.). Lightly, nimbly.

Leggero (It.). *v.* Leggiero.

Leggiadramente (It.). Gracefully, gallantly.

Leggiadretto (It.). Agreeable.

Leggiadro (It.). Nice, pretty, graceful.

Leggieramente (It.). Lightly.

Leggierezza (It.). Lightness, nimbleness.

Leggierissimo (It.). Sup. of *leggiero*.

Leggiermente (It.). *v.* Leggermente.

Leggiero (It.). Light, nimble.

Leggio (It.). A desk for holding music, etc.

Legno (It.). Wood. *Istrumenti in* (or *di*) *legno*, wood-wind instruments; *col legno*, with the wood (back) of the bow.

Leiche (Ger.). (*Leichen-* in combination.) A corpse, mortal remains.
  Leichengesang. Funeral song.
  Leichenmarsch. Funeral march.
  Leichenmusik. Funeral music.

Leicht (Ger.). (1) Easy. (2) Light, slight.
  Leicht beschwingt. Slightly quickened
  Leicht beweglich. Somewhat animated.
  Leicht bewegt. Slightly animated.
  Leicht gestoßen. Lightly detached.
  Leicht schwebend. Lightly gliding.
  Leicht und duftig. Light and vaporous
  Leicht und luftig. Light and aerial.
  Leicht und zart. Light and delicate.

Leichtfertig (Ger.). Playful, light-hearted, mischievous.

Leichtigkeit (Ger.). Ease, facility; suppleness, agility.

Leichtweg (Ger.). *v.* Leicht.

Leidenschaft (Ger.). Passion, emotion, affection.

Leidenschaftlich (Ger.). Passionate, impassioned, enthusiastic
  Leidenschaftlich bewegt. Passionately animated.

Leier (Ger.). (1) Lyre. (2) Hurdy-gurdy. (3) A hackneyed tune.

Leise (Ger.). Soft, gentle, low (not loud).
  Leise bewegt. Gently animated.
  Leise und sehr egal zu spielen. To be played softly and very equally.

Leisten (Ger.). To perform, render, accomplish.

Leistung (Ger.). A performance, rendering.

Leit (Ger.). Used in combination.
  Leitakkord. A chord leading to another, an unresolved chord, especially the chord of the dominant.
  Leitmotiv. A leading motive; a short musical phrase intended by the composer to represent some character or idea in his work.

Leitton. The leading note.
Leiter (Ger.). Usual abbreviation of *Tonleiter*, a scale.
    Leitereigen. Belonging to the scale.
    Leiterfremd. Foreign to the scale.
Leno (It.). Weak, faint.
Lent (Fr.). Slow.
    Lent et calme. Slow and tranquil.
Lentamente (It.). Slowly, gently, softly.
Lentando (It.). Slackening.
Lentato (It.). Slackened, relaxed.
Lentement (Fr.). Slowly.
Lenteur (Fr.). Slowness. *Sans lenteur*, without slowness, *i. e.* without dragging.
Lentezza (It.). Slowness.
Lentissimo (It.). Sup. of *lento*.
Lento (It.). Slow.
    Lento assai. ⎫
    Lento di molto. ⎬ Very slow.
    Lento lento. ⎭
    Lento ma non troppo. Slow, but not too much so.
Les (Fr.). The (plur.).
    Les deux Cymbales. The two cymbals, *i. e.* clashing the two halves together in the ordinary way.
    Les pp. doivent être pris brusquement. The *pp.* should be taken suddenly.
Lestamente (It.). Nimbly, quickly.
Lesto (It.). Nimble, quick.
    Lesto lesto. Very quick.
Leuto (It.). *v.* Liuto.
Levare (It.). To raise, take off.
    Levare qualche registro dell' organo per far più piano. Take off any stop to make the organ softer.
Levate (It.). Raise, take off.
    Levate i mani. Raise the hands.
    Levate i sordini (*or* **le sordine**). Take off the mutes.
Levé (Fr.). Raised. subs. The up-beat of the hand or foot.
Levez (Fr.). Raise, take away.
    Levez les mains. Raise the hands.
Levezza (It.). Lightness.
Lezione (It.). A lesson.
Liaison (Fr.). A bind, tie, slur.
Liberamente (It.). Freely.
Libertà (It.). Liberty. *Con libertà*, with freedom, freely.
Librement (Fr.). Freely.
    Librement déclamé. Freely declaimed, *i. e.* sung without paying strict attention to the tempo.
Libretto (It.). Literally,—a little book. The book of words of an opera.
Licenza (It.). Licence, freedom. *Con alcuna licenza*, with some (amount of) freedom.
Liceo (It.). Lyceum, academy.
Lié (Fr.). Tied.
Liebe (Ger.). Love. (In combination often *Liebes-*.)

Liebeglühend. Glowing with love.
Liebesflöte. *v.* Flûte d'amour.
Liebesgeige. *v.* Viola d'amore.
Liebevoll. Full of love.
Lieblich (Ger.). Pleasing, graceful, melodious.
    Lieblich gedackt. A stopped diapason of sweet tone.
Lied (Ger.). Song, ballad. (Usually *Lieder-*, in combination.)
    Liederartig. A lied or ballad style.
    Liedercyklus. A cycle of songs.
    Liederkranz. ⎰
    Liederkreis. ⎱ A garland or collection of songs.
    Liedersänger (masc.). ⎰
    Liedersängerin (fem.). ⎱ A ballad singer.
    Liederspiel. A comedietta interspersed with songs.
    Liedform. Ballad-form.
Lieder (Ger.). Plur. of *Lied*. *Lieder ohne Worte*, songs without words.
Liegend (Ger.). Lying.
    Liegender Bogen. Legato bowing, the bow lying well on the strings.
Lietezza (It.). Joyousness, light-heartedness.
Lietissimo (It.). Sup. of *lieto*.
Lieto, -a (It.). Joyous, blithe, merry.
Lieve (It.). Light, easy.
Lievemente (It.). Lightly, softly.
Lievezza (It.). *v.* Leggerezza.
Ligato (It.). *v.* Legato.
Ligatur (Ger.). ⎰ Two or more notes sung to one syllable. In the old
Ligatura (It.). ⎱ mensurable music, these notes were often absolutely
joined together.
Ligature. (1) The meaning as given above. (2) The band of metal,
with which the reed of a clarinet or saxophone is attached to the
mouthpiece.
Ligature (Fr.). Ligature, in both its meanings.
Ligne (Fr.). ⎰
Linea (It.). ⎱ A line.
    Lignes additionelles. Ledger lines.
Lingua (It.). The tongue forming the reed in an organ or harmonium
Linguetta (It.). A small reed. The reed of a clarinet, etc.
Liniensystem (Ger.). The stave.
Link (Ger.). Left.
Links (Ger.). To the left.
Lira (It.). Lyre.
Lirico, -a (It.). Lyric.
Liscio (It.). Smooth.
L'istesso (It.). *v.* under L'.
Litanei (Ger.). ⎱
Litanie (Fr.). ⎬ Litany.
Litanie (It.). ⎰
Liturgia (It.). ⎱
Liturgie (Fr.). ⎬ Liturgy.
Liturgie (Ger.). ⎰
Liturgique (Fr.). ⎰
Liturgisch (Ger.). ⎱ Liturgical.

Liuto (It.). Lute.

Lo. Abbr. of *loco*.

Lo (It.). The (masc.).

Lobgesang (Ger.). Hymn of praise.

Loch (Ger.). An opening; a hole in a wood-wind instrument, or in the belly of a stringed instrument. plur. *Löcher.*

Loco (It.). Place. Used to signify that the notes are to be played in their proper octave, instead of 8va, or 8va bassa as previously indicated.

Lointain (Fr.). Distant. In an instrumental part it signifies an echo effect.

Long Drum. A term occasionally applied to the bass-drum, but erroneously, since it is an evident translation of *tambour long* (*q. v.*), one of the Fr. names for a tenor drum.

Long, longue (Fr.). Long.

Lontano (It.). Distant. *cf.* Lointain.

Los (Ger,). Free, unfettered, *sciolto.* Also used as an exclamation: — "Play up!", "Start!"

Lourd (Fr.). Heavy.

Lourdement (Fr.). Heavily.

Loure (Fr.). (1) An ancient name for a species of bagpipe. (2) An old dance.

Louré (Fr.). A species of bowing, indicated thus: — — — — —.

Luftig (Ger.). Aerial, vaporous.

Lugubre (Fr.).
Lugubre (It.). } Mournful, sad, dreary.

Lungo, -a (It.). Long.

 Lunga pausa. Long pause.

 Longo silenzio. Long silence.

Luogo (It.). *v.* Loco.

Lusingando (It.).
Lusingante (It.). } Flattering, coaxing.
Lusinghevole. (It.).

Lusinghevolmente (It.). Flatteringly.

Lusinghiere (It.). Flattering, fawning.

Lustig (Ger.). Merry, jocund, playful.

 Lustig und immer schneller und schmetternder. Merrily, and always faster and more resonant.

Lustigkeit (Ger.). Mirth, cheerfulness.

Lute. An obsolete instrument of the guitar class.

Luth (Fr.). A lute.

Luthier (Fr.). A maker of violins, etc.

Lutto (It.). Mourning, grief, sorrow.

Luttoso, Luttuoso (It.). Mournful, sad.

Luttuosamente (It.). Mournfully, sadly.

Lyre. An ancient instrument, consisting of a hollow sound-box, from which projected two uprights joined by a yoke, from which strings (usually seven) were stretched down to the body.

Lyrique (Fr.). }
Lyrisch (Ger.). } Lyrical.

M

M. Abbr. of Manual.
 M.D. Abbr. of *Main droite, Mano destra*.
 M.G. Abbr. of *Main gauche*.
 M.M. Abbr. of Mälzel's Metronome.
 M.V. or **m.v.** Abbr. of *mezza voce*.
Ma (It.). But, however. *f ma dolce, f* but sweetly.
 Ma molto marcato. But much accentuated.
 Ma non troppo. But not too much.
 Ma poco. But not much, but little.
Macchina (It.). A machine. *Tromba a macchina*, a trumpet with valve mechanism.
Madriale (It.). *v.* Madrigale.
Madrigale (Fr.). | A madrigal.
Madrigale (It.). |
Madrigalesco (It.). In the style of a madrigal.
Maestà (It.). | Majesty.
Maestade, Maestate (It.). |
Maestevolmente, Maestosamente (It.). Majestically, with dignity.
Maestoso (It.). Majestic, noble, stately. The term is even applied to pieces in quick tempo. (*e. g.* Glazounoff, Sym. V. *Finale*.)
Maestri (It.). Plur. of *maestro*.
 Maestri cantori. Mastersingers, *Meistersinger*.
Maestria (It.). Skill, art, cleverness.
Maestro (It.). Master; one skilled in any art or science.
 Maestro del coro. Choir-master.
 Maestro di capella. *v.* Kapellmeister.
 Maestro di musica. Music master.
Maggiolata (It.). A May song.
Maggiore (It.). Major.
Magno (It.). Grand, great.
Mailloche (Fr.). A mallet. Term used for a bass-drumstick in orchestral scores since 1860/70, *tampon* having been the word in previous use. *v.* Tampon. *Double mailloche*, a bass-drumstick with two heads for the execution of rolls.
Main (Fr.). Hand. *A 4 (quatre) mains*, for 4 hands. A quire of paper.
 Main droite. Right hand.
 Main gauche. Left hand.
Mais (Fr.). But, however. *Dans la coulisse mais très près de la scene*, in the wings but very near the stage; *p. mais bien marqué, p.* but well marked.
 Mais léger et très detaché. But light and very detached (*staccato*).
 Mais sans lenteur. But without slowness, *i. e.* without dragging.
 Mais soutenu. But sustained.
Maître (Fr.). Master.
 Maître de chapelle. *v.* Kapellmeister.
 Maître de musique. Music master: a conductor, a musical director.
Maîtrise (Fr.). A school where choir boys are educated.
Majestätisch (Ger.). Majestic, stately.
Majeur (Fr.). Major.

Mal (Ger.). Time (not in the sense of *tempo*). Often employed as a suffix, as *einmal*, once, *zweimal*, twice, etc.

Malinconia (It.). Melancholy, sadness.

Malinconicamente (It.). Sorrowfully, sadly.

Malinconico (It.).
Malinconioso, Malinconoso (It.). } Melancholy, sad, dejected.

Man (Ger.). One, they, men. Corresponding to the Fr. *on*.

Mancando, Mancante (It.). Decreasing, diminishing (the sound).

Mancanza (It.). Want, lack, default. *In mancanza della fanfara*, in the absence of the brass-band.

Manche (Fr.). The neck of a violin, etc.

Mandᵒ. Abbr. of *mancando*.

Mandola (It.). A species of mandoline, used in the 17th century, and the same as the *Pandora;* at the present time the name is used for an instrument bearing the same relation to the mandoline as the viola does to the violin.

Mandoline. A stringed instrument with a neck furnished with frets, and a body somewhat the shape of a split almond. (*Mandola*, an almond.) The strings are struck by a plectrum of tortoise-shell, ivory, etc. The strings are double, usually four pairs in number, tuned g, d', a', e'', though instruments are found with five pairs. Its compass extends to e'''. It has been used by Mozart (*Don Giovanni*), Grétry (*L'amant jaloux*), and by Verdi in *Otello*, where it is combined with guitars and bagpipes.

Mandoline (Fr.).
Mandoline (Ger.). } A mandoline.

Mandolino (It.). A mandoline. *I Mandolini potranno essere sostituite da due Arpe*, the mandolines may be replaced by two harps.

Mandora (It.). *v.* Mandola.

Mani (It.). Plur. of *mano*, a hand. *A 4* (*quattro*) *mani*, for 4 hands.

Manica (It.). A shift on a violin, etc.

Manico (It.). The neck of a violin, etc.

Manier (Ger.).
Maniera (It.). } Manner, style, — either of the artist's execution, or
Manière (Fr.). } of the composition itself.

Maniéré (Fr.). Affected, mannered.

Manieren (Ger.). Grace-notes, ornaments.

Männerchor (Ger.). Male chorus.

Männergesangverein (Ger.). A society for performing compositions for male voices.

Mano (It.). Hand.
   Mano destra.
   Mano dritta. } The right hand.
   Mano manca.
   Mano sinistra. } The left hand.
   Mano sinistra sopra. Left hand above (the right).

Manritta (It.). The right hand.

Mantici (dell' organo) (It.). Bellows (of the organ).

Manual. The keyboard of an organ, which is played by the hands, as opposed to the keyboard (pedal-board), which is played by the feet.

Manual (Ger.). Manual.

Manualkoppel. A manual-coupler.
Manualtaste. A key on a manual.
Manuale (It.). Manual. plur. *Manuali.*
    Manuali accoppiati. The manuals coupled.
Manualiter (Ger.). Only for the manuals, *i. e.* organ pieces in which the pedals are not required.
Manualmente (It.). *v.* Manualiter.
Marc. Abbr. of *marcato.*
Marcando (It.). Marking, accentuating.
Marcatissimo (It.). Sup. of *marcato.*
Marcato, -a (It.). Marked, accentuated.
    Marcata la prima nota. The first note emphasised.
    Marcata la sinistra. The left hand accentuated.
    Marcato assai. Very marked.
    Marcato e legato il basso. The bass accentuated and smooth.
    Marcato il canto ma piano l'accompagnamento. The melody marked, but the accompaniment soft.
Marche (Fr.). (1) March. (2) The progression of chords or parts.
    Marche funèbre. Funeral march.
    Marches modulantes. A succession of modulatory chords.
    Marche triomphale. Triumphal march.
Marcia (It.). March.
    Marcia D. S. (dal segno) al fine senza ripetizione. The march from the sign to the end without repeat.
    Marcia marciale. Military march.
    Marcia religiosa. Religious march.
Marciale (It.). Martial, military.
Markig (Ger.). Strong, vigorous. *Immer markig gestrichen,* always vigorously bowed.
Markiert (Ger.). Marked, accentuated.
    Markiert und kräftig. Accentuated and vigorous.
Marqué (Fr.). Marked, accentuated.
Marsch (Ger.). March.
    Marschmäßig. In the style of a march.
Marteau (Fr.). A hammer.
Martelé (Fr.). Literally "hammered". A species of bowing (sometimes called *détaché sec*), in which short sharp blows are struck by the bow on the strings. The point of the bow is as a rule employed, but *martelé du talon* (with the heel, or near the nut, of the bow) is sometimes found. The term is occasionally used for other instruments than bowed ones, and signifies a sharp staccato.
Martellando (It.). "Hammering." ⎫
Martellare (It.). "To hammer." ⎬ *cf.* Martelé.
Martellato (It.). "Hammered." ⎭
Martellement (Fr.). In harp music, the repetition of a note by means of homophones (two strings tuned to the same pitch).
Martraza. A Spanish dance.
Marziale (It.). Martial, warlike.
Mascherata (It.). A masquerade.
Maschio (It.). Manly, virile.
Maß (Ger.). Measure. *Zeitmaß,* time measure, *tempo.*
Mäßig (Ger.). Moderate. *Die Hörner-, Trompeten- und Posaunen-*

Fanfaren mäßig, aber nicht roh, the flourishes on the horns, trumpets and trombones moderately loud, and not coarse. *-mäßig* as a suffix means: — (1) containing, (2) -like, suited for, as *Heldenmäßig,* hero-like, heroic.

Mäßig bewegt. With moderate animation.
Mäßiges Marsch-Tempo. Moderate march-time.
Mäßig geschwind. Moderately quick.
Mäßig im Hauptzeitmaß. Moderate, in the main tempo.
Mäßig langsam. Moderately slow.
Mäßig lebhaft. Moderately lively.
Mäßig schnell gehend. (Going) moderately fast.
Mäßig und ruhig. In moderate time and tranquilly.
Mäßigen (Ger.). To moderate (the tempo), to diminish (the loudness).
Mäßiger (Ger.). More moderate.
Massimo, -a (It.). The greatest, supreme.
Mastello (It.). The bottom of the pedestal of a harp.
Masurk, Masurek, Masurka (Ger.). A mazurka.
Matelotte (Fr.). A sailor's dance.
Mazurka, Mazurek, Mazurk. A Polish dance in triple time.
Mazza (It.). A bass-drumstick. *cf.* Mailloche.
Mazzetta (It.). Diminutive of *mazza.*
Mechanik (Ger.). The technique of a performer: the mechanism of a piano, organ or harmonium.
Mèche de crin(s) (Fr.). A "lock" of horse-hair; bow-hair.
Medesimo (It.). Same.

> **Medesimo movimento.** ⎫
> **Medesimo tempo.** ⎬ The same time.

Médiante (Fr.). ⎫
Mediante (It.). ⎬ Mediant; the third degree of the scale.

Mediator (Fr. and Ger.). The plectrum of a mandoline. It is occasionally used with a harp (Mahler, *Symphonie VI*).
Mehr (Ger.). More.

> **Mehrchörig.** For many (several) choirs.
> **Mehrfach.** Manifold.
> **Mehr langsam, oft zurückhaltend.** Slower, frequently slackening.
> **Mehrstimmig.** Polyphonic.

Meister (Ger.). Master.

> **Meisterfuge.** A master-fugue; a fugue exhibiting every possible device of counterpoint, etc.
> **Meistersinger.** A master-singer; a member of one of the musical guilds, which flourished in Germany in the 14th, 15th and 16th centuries.

Melancolia (It.). ⎫
Mélancolie (Fr.). ⎬ Melancholy.
Mélange (Fr.). A medley, a mixture.
Melodia (It.). Melody.
Melodico, -a (It.). Melodious.
Mélodie (Fr.). ⎫
Melodie (Ger.). ⎬ Melody.
Melodiosamente (It.). Melodiously.
Melodioso (It.). ⎫
Melodisch (Ger.). ⎬ Melodious.

Melodium. A species of harmonium.

Melodram (Ger.). ⎫
Mélodrame (Fr.). ⎬ Melodrama; spoken dialogue, accompanied by music.
Melodramma (It.). ⎭

Même (Fr.). Same.

    Même mouvement. The same movement (tempo).

Ménestrel (Fr.). Minstrel.

Meno (It.). Less. Sometimes abbreviated to *men*.

    Meno animato. Less animated.

    Meno forte. Less loud.

    Meno mosso. Less moved (animated).

    Meno piano. Less soft.

    Meno sonoro. Less sonorous.

    Meno tosto. Less quick.

Mensur (Ger.). The measure or scale of an organ pipe. Time, measure.

Mensuralgesang (Ger.). Mensurable music; music in measure, as opposed to the plain-song.

Mentoniera (It.). ⎫
Mentonnière (Fr.). ⎬ A chin-rest for a violin or viola.

Menuet (Fr.). ⎫
Menuet(t) (Ger.). ⎬ Minuet.

Mescolanza (It.). Medley, mixture.

Messa (It.). Mass.

Messa di voce (It.). In singing, the art of commencing and ending softly on a long note, becoming loud midway. *cf.* Filar un suono.

Messe (Fr.). ⎫
Messe (Ger.). ⎬ Mass.

Messinginstrumente (Ger.). Brass instruments.

Mestizia (It.). Sadness, melancholy.

Mesto (It.). Sad, gloomy.

Mesure (Fr.). Measure; time; a bar. La ♩= la ♪ *de mesure précédente*, the ♩ = the ♪ of the preceding bar. *Une mesure comme trois du mouvement précédent*, one bar like three of the preceding movement.

Mesuré (Fr.). Measured, in precise rhythm

Metall (Ger.). Metal.

    Metallsaite. A metal string.

    Metallstäbchen. A metal beater (for a triangle).

Metallo (It.). Metal.

    Metallo di voce. The resonant quality of a voice.

Méthode (Fr.). ⎫
Methode (Ger.). ⎬ Method.
Metodo (It.). ⎭

Metronom (Ger.). A metronome.

Metronome. An instrument for mechanically beating time. It is worked by clockwork, and consists of a pendulum, of which the vibrations are regulated by a movable weight. On the pendulum is a scale with various numbers, ranging from 40 to 208, and the metronome is correct when it beats seconds with the weight against 60. As by means of the metronome, the speed of a movement can be exactly denoted, it is a matter of regret that composers do not make more constant use of it.

Métronome (Fr.). A metronome.

Metronomisches Zeichen (Ger.). Metronomic indication.
Metronomo (It.). A metronome.
Metrum (Ger.). Metre.
Mettete (It.). Place, put.
    Mettete i sordini. Put on the mutes.
    Mettete le pedali. Put down the pedals.
Mezza (It.). Half (fem.).
    Mezza aria. Half the power of the voice or instrument, *demi-jeu.*
    Mezza battuta. A minim rest.
    Mezza manica. The half shift or second position on a violin, etc.
    Mezza orchestra. Half the orchestra.
    Mezza voce. With half the power of the voice.
Mezzo (It.). Half (masc.).
    Mezzo forte. Half loud, but nearer loud than soft; *mf.*
    Mezzo legato. Somewhat legato.
    Mezzo manico. In the middle of the fingerboard of a violin, etc.
    Mezzo piano. Half soft, but nearer soft than loud; *mp.*
    Mezzo-soprano. The female voice intermediate between the soprano and contralto.
    Mezzo staccato. Somewhat staccato.
    Mezzo tenore. A name for a baritone voice.
    Mezzo tuono. A semitone.
Mf. Abbr. of *mezzo-forte.*
Mi (Fr.). The note E.
    Mi bémol. E flat.
    Mi bémol mineur. E flat minor.
    Mi dièse. E sharp.
    Mi majeur. E major.
Mi (It.). The note E.
    Mi bemolle. E flat.
    Mi bemolle majore. E flat major.
    Mi diesis. E sharp.
    Mi minore. E minor.
Middle C. The C lying between the bass and the treble clefs, and the note indicated by the C clef.
Milieu (Fr.). Middle.
    Milieu de l'archet. Middle of the bow.
Militair (Ger.). *v.* Militär.
Militaire (Fr.). Military. *Musique militaire,* military music.
Militär (Ger.). Military.
    Militärflöte. A fife.
    Militärmusik. Military music.
    Militärtrommel. The side-drum.
Minaccevole (It.). Threatening, menacing.
Minaccevolmente (It.). Threateningly, in a menacing manner.
Minacciando (It.). *v.* Minaccevole.
Minacciosamente (It.). *v.* Minaccevolmente.
Minaccioso (It.). Full of threats.
Minder (Ger.). Less.
    Minder schnell. Less fast.
Mineur (Fr.). Minor.
Minne (Ger.). An archaic word for "love".

Minnelied. A love-song composed by a Minnesinger.

Minnesang. Love-poetry.

Minnesänger.) A minnesinger; one of the old German troubadours,
Minnesinger. (who flourished in the 12th and 13th centuries, who
were of noble birth (as opposed to the subsequent *Meistersinger*), and whose theme was mainly of love.

Minore (It.). Minor.

Minuetto (It.). A minuet; a graceful dance in ternary time, dating
from the 17th century.

Mirliton (Fr.). A mirliton; sometimes called a "speaker" or "squeaker".
A tube of wood or cardboard with the two ends covered with a
membrane, and having a triangular hole cut in the tube a short
distance from each end. By singing into one of the holes a sound
is produced not unlike that obtained by singing against a comb
enveloped in thin paper. In Tschaïkovsky's *Casse-noisette*, one of
the numbers is called *Danse des Mirlitons*, often peculiarly translated as "Reed-pipe dance". Another toy instrument on the same
principle is known as a *Kazoo*.

Mise (Fr.). Setting, putting, placing.

    Mise de voix. *v.* Messa di voce.

    Mise en scène. The setting of a stage-play or opera.

Missa (Lat.). The Mass.

    Missa pro defunctis. Mass for the dead, a requiem.

Misteriosamente (It.). Mysteriously.

Misterioso (It.). Mysterious.

Misura (It.). A measure, a bar.

Misurato (It.). Measured, in precise rhythm.

Mit (Ger.). With.

    Mit Anmut(h). With charm, grace.

    Mit anmut(h)igem Vortrage. With graceful execution.

    Mit äußerst starker Empfindung. With intensely strong emotion.

    Mit Begeisterung. With animation, inspiration, exultation.

    Mit Begleitung. With accompaniment.

    Mit beiden Händen. With both hands.

    Mit Betrübnis. With sorrow.

    Mit Bewegung. With movement (animation).

    Mit breitem Strich. With the whole bow.

    Mit Dämpfer. With the mute.

    Mit Dämpfer stark anzublasen. To be muted, and strongly
blown, *i. e.* made brassy.

    Mit Dämpfern. With mutes.

    Mit dem Basse. With the bass.

    Mit dem Bogen geschlagen. Struck with the bow.

    Mit den Fagotten. With the bassoons.

    Mit den Instrumenten. With the instruments.

    Mit den Trompeten. With the trumpets.

    Mit der ganzen Kraft. With full strength, *tutta forza*.

    Mit der Hauptstimme. With the principal part or voice.

    Mit Eifer. With warmth.

    Mit Empfindung. With feeling, emotion.

    Mit Feuer. With fire, spirit.

    Mit Fleiß. Diligently.

Mit fröhlichem Ausdruck. With cheerful expression.
Mit Gefühl. With feeling.
Mit Geist. With soul.
Mit Genauigkeit. With accuracy.
Mit Geschmack. With taste.
Mit gewöhnlichen Paukenschlägeln. With ordinary kettle-drumsticks.
Mit Gravität. With gravity, solemnity.
Mit Grazie. With grace.
Mit grossem (*or* **großem**) **Ausdruck.** With great expression.
Mit großem Schwung. With great enthusiasm.
Mit größter Energie. With the greatest vigour.
Mit gutem Humor. Good-humouredly.
Mit halber Stimme. *A mezza voce.*
Mit Holzschlägeln. With kettle-drumsticks of wood.
Mit hüpfendem Bogen. With springing bow.
Mit innigem Ausdruck. With heartfelt expression.
Mit inniger Empfindung. With deep emotion.
Mit Leben. With life.
Mit Lebhaftigkeit. With vivacity.
Mit Lebhaftigkeit und durchaus mit Empfindung und Ausdruck. With animation, and with feeling and expression throughout.
Mit Leichtigkeit. With lightness.
Mit Leidenschaft. With passion.
Mit leidenschaftlichem Vortrag. With passionate execution.
Mit mehr Affekt. With more fervour.
Mit mehr Bewegung. With more movement.
Mit Mut(h). With spirit.
Mit Paukenschlägeln. With kettle-drumsticks.
Mit Ruhe. Tranquilly.
Mit sanften Stimmen. With soft stops (of an organ).
Mit Schmerz. With pain.
Mit Schwammschlägeln. With sponge-headed (kettle-)drum-sticks.
Mit Seele. With soul.
Mit Sordin. With the mute.
Mit Sorgfalt. With care.
Mit springendem Bogen. With springing bow.
Mit springendem Daumen. With springing thumb. (Direction to tambourine-player.)
Mit starken Stimmen. With loud stops (of an organ).
Mit Steigerung. With exaltation.
Mit Tellern. With the two halves of the cymbals, *i. e.* clashing them in the ordinary manner.
Mit unruhiger Bewegung. With restlessness.
Mit voller Orgel. Full organ.
Mit Wärme. With warmth.
Mit Würde. With dignity.
Mit zartem Vortrag. With delicate execution.
Mit Zartheit. With sweetness.
Mit Zierlichkeit. With gracefulness, daintiness.
Mitleidig (Ger.). Pitiful.

Mitte (Ger.). subs. Middle, midst. *In die Mitte den Sänger zu stellen*, the singer to be placed in the midst.
Mittel (Ger.). adj. Middle, central.
    Mittelfinger. The second finger.
    Mittelkadenz. The imperfect cadence, or half close.
    Mittelsatz. Formerly the term for the second subject. *Seitensatz* is the term now usually employed.
    Mittelstimmen. The intermediate parts.
Mixtur (Ger.). A mixture stop on an organ.
Mobile (It.). Movable, fickle.
Moderatamente (It.). Moderately.
    Moderatamente allegro. Moderately fast.
    Moderatamente forte. Moderately loud.
Moderatissimo (It.). Sup. of *moderato*.
Moderato (It.). Moderate.
    Moderato assai con molto sentimento. Very moderate (in tempo) with much feeling.
    Moderato cantabile. In moderate tempo and singingly.
    Moderato e con grazia. In moderate tempo and with grace.
Modéré (Fr.). Moderate.
Modérément (Fr.). Moderately.
    Modérément animé. Moderately animated.
    Modérément lent. Moderately slow.
Modo (It.). Mode.
Modulare (It.). To modulate.
Modulazione (It.). Modulation,
Moduler (Fr.).
Moduli(e)ren (Ger.). } To modulate; to pass from one key to another.
Möglich (Ger.). Possible.
Möglichst (Ger.). Sup. of *möglich*.
    Möglichst gebunden. As smooth as possible.
    Möglichst groß, schlaff gespannt. As large as possible, slackly braced. (Indication for tenor drum.)
    Möglichst zahlreich besetzt. Laid out for as large a number as possible.
Moins (Fr.). Less.
    Moins f. Less *f*.
    Moins long. Less long.
    Moins vite. Less fast.
Moitié (Fr.). Half. *La moitié des 1ers violins*, Half the 1st violins.
Moll (Ger.). Minor.
    Mollakkord. Minor chord.
    Molleiter. Minor scale.
    Molltonart. Minor key.
Molla (It.). A spring.
Molle (It.). Gentle, tender.
Mollemente (It.). Gently, softly.
Molta (It.). Fem. of *molto*, much.
    Molta espressione. Much expression.
    Molta voce. Much voice.
Moltissimo (It.). Sup. of *molto*.
Molto (It.). Much (masc.). As an adv., much, very.

Molto allegro. Very fast.
Molto allegro con fuoco. Very fast and with spirit.
Molto cantabile. Very singingly.
Molto crescendo e animato. Increasing very much in loudness and animation.
Molto espressivo. Very expressive.
Molto largo. Very slow.
Molto lento. Very slow, not so slow as *molto largo*.
Molto marcato il basso. The bass very accentuated.
Molto meno mosso. Much less animated.
Molto più mosso quasi doppio tempo. Much more animated, almost double the time.
Molto portamento. Very smooth. *v*. Portamento.
Molto ritenuto e crescendo. Much slackened and increasing in loudness.
Molto vivace. Very quick.
Monferina (It.). A dance in $^6/_8$ time, of Piedmontese origin.
Monodrame (Fr.). ⎫
Monodramma (It.). ⎬ Monodrama; a play with only one character.
Montatura (It.). Mounting, setting.
Montatura di corde. Set of strings.
Montez (Fr.). Raise.
Montez la fa grave au la♭. Raise the low F to A♭.
Montre (Fr.). The pipes of an organ which are in front of the case; mounted diapason.
Monture (Fr.). *v*. Montatura.
Mor. Abbr. of *morendo*.
Morbidezza (It.). Softness, mellowness, delicacy.
Morbido (It.). Soft, tender.
Morceau (Fr.). Piece, movement, composition.
Morceau de fantaisie. A fantasia.
Morceau d'ensemble. *v*. Ensemble.
Morceau élégant. A drawing-room piece.
Mordant (Fr.). A mordent; the rapid alternation of a harmony note with the note above; an inverted mordent is with the note below. *adj*. In a sharp short staccato style.
Mordent (Ger.). ⎫
Mordente (It.). ⎬ A mordent.
Morendo (It.). Dying away.
Moresca (It.). A Morris dance.
Mormorante (It.). Murmuring.
Mormorevole (It.). ⎫
Mormoroso (It.). ⎬ Murmuring, purling.
Mosso (It.). Moved, impelled, stirred, animated.
Motet (Fr.). ⎫
Motette (Ger.). ⎬ A motet.
Motetto (It.). ⎭
Motif (Fr.). A motive, theme, phrase.
Motiv (Ger.). *v*. Motif. *Das Motif in den 2 Hörnern gebunden und hervorragen,* the motive in the 2 horns sustained and brought-out. *cf*. Leitmotiv.
Motivo (It.). *v*. Motif.

9*

Moto (It.). Motion, movement. *Lo stesso moto*, the same movement (tempo).

    Moto contrario. Contrary motion.

    Moto obliquo. Oblique motion.

    Moto perpetuo. Perpetual motion. Term applied to a composition, which conveys the idea that it is going on for ever.

    Moto precedente. The preceding movement

    Moto primo. The first movement (tempo).

    Moto retto. Similar motion.

Motteggiando (It.). Bantering, quizzing.

Mottetto (It.). *v.* Motetto.

Mouthpiece. The portion of a wind-instrument, which is placed in or against the performer's mouth. In the brass and in certain obsolete wood instruments, such as the serpent, the mouthpiece is cup-shaped and on the form of this depends in a great measure the tone-quality.

Mouvement (Fr.). (1) Motion, degree of speed, movement (tempo). (2) Movement (a number or portion of a suite, sonata, etc.).

    Mouvement contraire. Contrary motion.

    Mouvement de marche. March time.

    Mouvement de valse. Waltz time.

    Mouvement direct. Similar motion.

    Mouvement initial. *v.* Tempo primo.

Mouvementé (Fr.). Moved, stirred.

Movente (It.). Moving.

Movimento (It.). Movement.

Mp. Abbr. of *mezzo-piano*.

Mue de voix (Fr.). The break in a boy's voice.

Mühelos. (Ger.). Without effort.

Mundstück (Ger.). Mouthpiece.

Munter (Ger.). Brisk, sprightly, vivacious.

    Munter und straff. Lively and precise.

Murmelnd (Ger.). Murmuring, whispering, purling.

Murmurando (It.). *v.* Mormorando.

Musetta (It.). } A small species of oboe. A dance of a pastoral.
Musette (Fr.). } character on a drone bass.

Musica (It.). Music.

    Musica da camera. Chamber-music.

    Musica da chiesa. Church (sacred) music.

    Musica da teatro. Music for the theatre.

    Musica istrumentale. Instrumental music.

Musical, -e (Fr.). } Musical.
Musicale (It.). }

Musicalmente (It.). Musically.

Musicare (It.). To play, perform.

    Musicare una canzone. To set a song to music.

Musicien, -ienne (Fr.). A musician.

Musicista, Musico (It.). A musician.

Musico, -a (It.). Musical.

Musik (Ger.). Music.

    Musikdirektor. A musical director.

    Musikfest. A musical festival.

Musikkenner. A connoisseur of music.

Musikmeister. Music master.

Musikstunde. Music lesson. (Literally, "music-hour".)

Musikzeichen. Musical signs.

Musikalisch (Ger.). Musical.

Musiker, Musikus (Ger.). A musician.

Musique (Fr.). Music.

Muta (It.). Change (3rd pers. sing.). subs. A set.

    Muta di quattro ritorte. A set of four crooks.

    Muta in E. Change into E.

Mutano (It.). Change (3rd pers. plur.).

    Mutano in F. Change into F.

Mutation stops. Stops on an organ, which do not give the note corresponding to the key pressed, but the 12th, 17th or 19th above.

Mutazione (It.). Mutation.

Mute. An instrument for deadening the sound of a musical instrument, and incidentally giving it a different tone-colour. On the violin, etc., it is a kind of metal comb, which is fixed on to the bridge; in brass instruments, a cone of cardboard, wood, or metal, placed in the bell.

Mut(h)ig (Ger.). Bold, daring.

N

Nacaire (Fr.). An obsolete term for a kettledrum.

Naccare (It.). A name for the castanets. *cf.* Gnacchere.

Nach (Ger.). After, to, at, by, from. *G nach E tief,* G to low E.

    Nach Belieben. *Ad libitum.*

    Nach bestimmtem Zeitmaß. In exact time.

    Nach (Buchstaben) A, B, C, etc. To (letter) A, B, C, etc. *Rallentando nach R,* becoming slower till R.

    Nach dieser Nummer eine Pause von einigen Minuten. After this number an interval of several minutes.

    Nach Gefallen. *Ad libitum.*

    Nach Noten spielen. To play from notes.

    Nach und nach. Gradually, little by little, by degrees.

    Nach und nach belebter. Gradually more animated.

    Nach und nach immer bewegter. Gradually with increasing movement.

    Nach und nach immer langsamer werdend. Becoming gradually slower.

    Nach und nach lebendiger. Gradually more lively.

    Nach und nach mehrere Saiten. Gradually more strings, *i. e.* gradually taking off the soft pedal (*una corda*) and playing on the 3 strings of the piano.

    Nach und nach wieder geschwinder. Again becoming faster by degrees.

Nachahmung (Ger.). Imitation.

Nachdruck (Ger.). Vigour, accent, emphasis.

Nachdrücklich (Ger.). With emphasis, energetic.

Nachgehend (Ger.). Following. *Dem Cello nachgehend,* following the cello; *der Melodie nachgehend,* following the melody.

Nachlassend (Ger.). Slackening.

Nachlässig (Ger.). Careless, inaccurate.

Nachsatz (Ger.). Conclusion; concluding section.

Nachschlag (Ger.). After beat. The two grace-notes at the end of a shake. *Die Triller sind alle mit Nachschlag zu machen*, the shakes are all to be played with an after-beat.

Nachspiel (Ger.). A postlude. The concluding instrumental phrase of a song.

Nacht (Ger.). Night.

  Nachtgesang. A nocturne. A serenade.

  Nachthorn. An organ pipe of 8 ft.

  Nachtmusik. A serenade, an instrumental piece for several instruments.

  Nachtständchen. A serenade, a piece for one performer.

  Nachtstück. A nocturne.

Nachtanz (Ger.). After dance. The concluding dance of the old sets of dances.

Nachtigall (Ger.). The nightingale.

  Nachtigallpfeife. A pipe for imitating the nightingale.

Nächtlich (Ger.). Nightly, nocturnal.

Nahe (Ger.). Near.

  Nahe dem Chor. Near the chorus.

Naïf, naïve (Fr.). } Innocent, simple-minded, artless.
Naiv (Ger.). }

Naïvement (Fr.). Simply, artlessly.

Narquois (Fr.). Crafty, cunning, sly.

Narrante (It.). Relating, recording; as if narrating.

Nasard (Fr.). { An organ stop sounding a 12th above the written
Nasat (Ger.). { note.

Nasetto (It.). The nut of a bow.

Naso (It.). Nose. Occasionally used for the point of the bow.

Natur- (Ger.). Used in combination in the sense of "natural".

  Naturhorn. Natural horn.

  Naturskala. Natural scale.

  Naturtöne. Open notes on a brass instrument. *Die mit o bezeichneten Töne f sind vom 1. und 3. Horn als Naturtöne, d. h. als Ton 11 der Naturskala wiederzugeben*, the F-s marked with an o are to be played by the 1. and 3. horn as open notes, *i. e.* as the 11th of the Natural Scale.

  Naturtrompete. Natural trumpet.

Natural harmonic series. *v.* Harmonics.

Natural horn. A horn without valves. *v.* Horn.

Natural scale. *v.* Harmonics.

Natural trumpet. A trumpet without valves. *v.* Trumpet.

Naturale (It.). Natural. *Do naturale*, C natural. The sign for a natural is called *bequadro*. The term is found in scores to indicate that an instrument is to play in the ordinary manner, in contradistinction to a previous direction, such as *sul ponticello, etc.*

Naturalmente (It.). Naturally, in an unaffected manner.

Naturel, -elle (Fr.). Natural. *Ut naturel*, C natural. The sign for a natural is called *bécarre*. Natural horns and trumpets are usually called *ordinaires* or *simples*. *Son naturel*, an open note on a brass instrument.

Natürlich (Ger.). Natural. The term is found in scores to indicate that an instrument is to play in the ordinary way, and contradicting a previous *am Steg*, *Flageolett*, etc.

Natürlich drängend. Spontaneously hurrying.

Natürliche Tonleiter. The natural scale.

Ne—pas (Fr.). Two words signifying a negative, the first being put before the verb, the latter after, except with the infinitive, when both are before the verb. *Ne pas jouer* (or *Ne jouez pas*) *cette mesure, si on coupe les 4 mesures qui précèdent*, do not play this bar, if the 4 preceding bars are cut. (*v.* Remark I.)

Neben (Ger.). By, by the side of, alongside; simultaneously. *Neben-* in combination usually means "accessory", "additional", etc.

Nebenakkorde. Secondary chords.

Nebendreiklänge. Secondary triads.

Nebengedanke. An accessory thought; a new theme introduced into a movement, which has no reference to the main subjects.

Nebenlinien. Ledger lines.

Nebennote. Auxiliary note.

Nebenregister. The stops of an organ other than those which act directly on the pipes.

Nebensatz. A subsidiary phrase.

Nebenstimmen. Accessory parts. The term is applied to the mutation stops of an organ.

Nebenthema. Subsidiary theme.

Nebentonart. A relative key.

Nebenwerke. *v.* Nebenregister.

Nebenzug. An accessory draw-stop. *cf.* Nebenstimme.

Necessario (It.). Necessary.

Neck. That portion of a stringed instrument, which lies between the body and the peg-box, and on which the fingerboard is placed.

Negli (It.). Combination of *in*, in, and *gli*, the (masc. plur.).

Negligente (It.). Careless, listless.

Negligentemente (It.). Negligently, heedlessly.

Nehmen. To take.

Nehmen ebenfalls Dämpfer. Likewise take mutes.

Nehmen wieder große Flöte. Again take the (large) flute.

Nel, nell', nella, nello, nei, nelle, negli (It.). Compounds of *in*, in, and various forms of the definite article.

Nel battere. At the downbeat.

Nel medesimo. In the same time.

Nel stil' antico. In the antique style.

Nel tempo. In time.

Nella orchestra. In the orchestra.

Nelle scene lontano. In the wings, distant.

Nello stesso tempo. In the same time.

Nenia (It.). A funeral song.

Nettamente (It.). Neatly.

Netto (It.). Neat; spotless, pure.

Neun (Ger.). Nine.

Neuvième (Fr.). Ninth; interval of a ninth.

Nicht (Ger.). Not.

Nicht als Fingerübung abspielen. Not to be played as a finger exercise. (A sarcastic note of Liszt's against a harp passage in simple triplets.)

Nicht anschwellen lassen. Without swelling (on the note).

Nicht eilen. Without hurrying.

Nicht gedämpft. Not muted.

Nicht gestoßen. Not detached (staccato).

Nicht get(h)eilt. Not divided.

Nicht harpeggiert. Not played in arpeggio.

Nicht schleppen. Without dragging.

Nicht schnell. Not fast.

Nicht schnell und mit innigem Ausdruck. Not fast, and with heartfelt expression.

Nicht sehr schnell. Not very fast.

Nicht taktieren. Do not mark the beats, *i. e.* the bar or bars are to be played *senza misura*.

Nicht t(h)eilen. Do not divide, *non divisi*.

Nicht tremolieren. Not to be played as a tremolo, *i. e.* the proper number of notes to be played as written.

Nicht zu geschwind und sehr singbar vortragen. Not too fast, and to be played very singingly.

Nicht zu langsam. Not too slow.

Nicht zu rasch. ⎫
Nicht zu schnell. ⎬ Not too fast.

Nicht zu sehr. Not too much.

Nicht zu stark. Not too loud.

Nieder (Ger.). Low, nether; down.

Niederschlag. Downbeat; accented beat.

Niederstrich. Downstroke with the bow.

Niente (It.). Nothing. *Quasi niente*, almost nothing, as soft as possible.

Nimmt (Ger.). Takes (3rd pers. sing. of *nehmen*).

Nimmt 3 Fagott. Takes 3rd bassoon.

Nimmt kl. Flöte. Takes piccolo.

Nobile (It.). Noble, lofty.

Noch (Ger.). Still, yet.

♪ **noch schneller als zuvor** ♩. The ♪ still faster than the previous ♩.

Noch außen. Still without, or outside. (Of an instrument or character still in the wings, or away from the orchestra.)

Noch bewegter, sehr leidenschaftlich. Still more animated, very passionately.

Noch drängender. Hurrying still more.

Noch etwas gemessener. Still somewhat more measured, *i. e.* slower.

Noch etwas lebhafter. ⎫
Noch etwas mehr belebend. ⎬ Still somewhat more animated.

Noch langsamer. Still slower.

Noch leiser. Still more softly.

Noch mehr nachlassend. ⎫
Noch mehr zurückhaltend. ⎬ Slackening still more.

Noch schneller. Still faster.

Noch stärker. Still louder.
Noch wuchtiger. Still more heavily.
Nocturne (Fr.). A nocturne. A night-piece; a composition of a dreamy nature.
Noël (Fr.). Christmas. A Christmas carol, in which the burden is often *Noël*.
Noire (Fr.). Literally, — "a black"; a crotchet, as opposed to *une blanche*, a minim. *Une noire du Lento vaut 3 noires du Tempo 1*, a crotchet of the Lento is equal to 3 crotchets of Tempo 1.
Non (It.). Not.
   Non accoppiato. Not coupled.
   Non assai. Not very much.
   Non divisi. Not divided.
   Non legato. Not slurred.
   Non molto. Not much.
   Non rallentando. Without becoming slower.
   Non troppo. Not too much.
None (Ger.). The interval of a ninth.
Nonenflöte (Ger.). The piccolo in D♭.
Nonett (Ger.). ⎰ A nonet; a composition for nine voices or instru-
Nonetto (It.). ⎱ ments. The French use the It. term.
Nono, -a (It.). Ninth. *Nona*, the interval of the ninth.
Normal. Standard. The term is applied to standard pitch, and to the two scales of C major and A minor, since they serve as the standard for all the other scales.
Normal (Fr.). Normal. *v.* Diapason normal.
Normal (Ger.). Normal.
   Normalstimmung. Normal pitch.
   Normalton. The note to which the orchestra tunes, the A.
   Normaltonart. Normal key.
   Normaltonleiter. Normal scale.
Nota (It.). Note.
   Nota buona. An accented note.
   Nota cambiata. A changing note.
   Nota caratteristica. According to some authorities, the leading note; according to others, the minor 3rd or 6th, as being characteristic of the minor scale.
   Nota cattiva. An unaccented note.
   Nota coronata. A note with a corona (the sign ⌒) above it.
   Nota d'abbellimento. A grace-note.
   Nota di passaggio. A passing note.
   Nota di piacere. ⎱
   Nota falsa. ⎰ A grace-note, a changing note.
   Nota legata. A tied or slurred note.
   Nota martellata. A "hammered" note. *cf.* Martelé.
   Nota picchettata. A staccato note. *cf.* Piqué.
   Nota portata. A note played or sung with *portamento* (*q. v.*).
   Nota principale. The principal note, *i. e.* the harmony note in a turn or shake.
   Nota sensibile. The leading note.
Note (Fr.).
   Note bonne. An accented note.

Note caractéristique. *v.* Nota caratteristica.
Note changée. A changing note.
Note couronnée. A note with a corona (the sign ⌢) above it.
Note d'agrément. A grace-note.
Note irrégulière. A changing note.
Note liée. A tied note.
Note martelée. A "hammered" note. *cf.* Martelé.
Note piquée. A staccato note. *v.* Piqué.
Note portée. A note played or sung with *portamento* (*q. v.*).
Note sensible. The leading note.
Note syncopée. A syncopated note.
Note (Ger.). (*Noten-* in combination). A note. *Ganze Note*, a semibreve; *halbe Note*, a minim; *doppelt ganze Note*, a breve. plur. *Noten*.
    Notenbuch. A music book.
    Notenlinien. A stave.
    Notenpapier. Music paper.
    Notenpult. A music desk.
    Notenschrift. The writing of music; musical notation.
    Notensystem. A stave.
Notturno (It.). A nocturne.
Nourri (Fr.). Nourished. The French employ the term in the sense of "rich and full", as the inner parts of a score, or the quality of a voice.
Novemole (Ger.). A nonuplet. A group of 9 notes in place of 6 or 8.
Nuance (Fr.). Nuance, shade of colour, etc. The term is used generally for any one of the signs used in musical nomenclature. *La nuance bien indiquée*, the nuance (*i. e.* the shade of expression) well marked.
Nummer (Ger.). Number.
Nuovo (It.). New. *Di nuovo*, again, once more.
Nur (Ger.). Only.
    Nur die erste Hälfte der Pulte. Only the first half of the desks.
    Nur halber Frauenchor. Only half of the female chorus.
    Nur im äußersten Notfalle ad libitum. Ad libitum only in the case of the greatest necessity.
Nut. (1) The small bridge at the end of the fingerboard next the peg-box of stringed instruments. (2) The end of the bow opposed to the point; the heel of the bow.
Nutrendo (It.). "Nourishing", *i. e.* sustaining the sounds.
Nutrito (It.). Nourished. *v.* Nourri.

O

O. Abbr. of *Organo*.
    O. C. Abbr. of *organo corale*.
    O. E. Abbr. of *organo espressivo*.
Ob. Abbr. of *Oboe*.
Obb. Abbr. of *obbligato*.
Obbligato (It.). Obliged, required. Applied to an instrumental part, it implies that the part is indispensable for the performance of the piece, and may at times be as important as the solo part.

Obbliquo (It.). Oblique.

Oben (Ger.). At the top, above, on high. The term is found in piano duets, to indicate that one player has to cross his hand over that of the other player, in whose part *unten* (under) is marked.

Ober (Ger.). Upper.

    Obermanual. The upper manual, *i. e.* the one next above that of the great organ.

    Obernote. Upper note.

    Oberstimme. Upper part.

    Obertöne. Upper tones, *i. e.* harmonics.

    Oberwerk. The pipes controlled by the *Obermanual.*

Oberw. Abbr. of *Oberwerk.*

Obligat (Ger.). ⎫
Obligato (It.). ⎬ *v.* Obbligato.
Obligé (Fr.). ⎭

Oboe (It.). The hautboy, the It. term being usually employed in English. It is an instrument of conical bore played with a double reed, and has a compass from *b* (modern oboes usually possess the *b♭*) to *f'''*, or even 2 semitones higher. The term is also used for an 8 ft organ stop, slightly resembling the tone of the instrument.

    Oboe alto. The English horn.

    Oboe d'amore. An oboe with a compass from *b* to *e'''*, but sounding a minor 3rd lower. It was practically obsolete (though required for several of Bach's scores) until revived by R. Strauss in his *Symphonia domestica.*

    Oboe da caccia. One of the predecessors of the English horn.

    Oboe in Si♭. An oboe sounding a tone below the written notes, occasionally found in some continental military bands.

Oboe (Ger.). Although *Hoboe* is the ordinary term, *oboe* is also sometimes used in Ger. for the hautboy.

    Oboen in einem Klang mit den Violinen. Oboes in unison with the violins.

Oboi (It.). Plur. of *oboe.*

Oboista (It.). An oboe-player.

Occhiali (It.). Spectacles. *v.* Brillenbässe.

Octave. (1) An interval of an eighth. (2) Another name for the Principal on an organ, which is a 4ft stop on the manual, and an 8ft on the pedals.

    Octave flute. An occasional term for the piccolo.

    Octave key. A key on wood-wind instruments of the oboe and clarinet families to enable the second register to "speak" with more facility. The oboe and its allies possess two octave keys, the second being reserved for the highest notes; on many modern instruments, the two keys are worked with the same mechanism, the 1st shutting and the 2nd opening when the fingering is taken for the highest notes. The baritone oboe possesses three octave keys. The clarinet has a single key (known as the "speaker key") which vents all the natural twelfths.

Octave (Ger.). *v.* Oktave.

Octavier (Fr.). *v.* Quintoyer.

Octett (Ger.). *v.* Oktett.

Octobasse (Fr.). A large double-bass with three strings, tuned *C, G, c,* and sounding an octave lower. It is about 12ft high, and the notes are stopped by means of levers and a pedal. It has been used in festival orchestras, and Gounod wrote a part for it in his St. Cecilia Mass.

Octuor (Fr.). An octet.

Oder (Ger.). Or. *Harfe oder Piano,* harp or piano.

Oeuvre (Fr.). A work.

Offen (Ger.). Open. (1) Found in horn-parts, and meaning that the notes are no longer to be *gestopft,* closed. (2) Applied to open pipes on an organ. An open string on a violin, etc. is said to be *leere,* empty.

Offertoire (Fr.). Offertory. The music of the Mass, played during the offertory.

Oficleide (It.). The ophicleide.

Ogni (It.). Every, all.

Ohne (Ger.). Without.

    Ohne Anstrengung. Without effort, easily.

    Ohne Ausdruck. Without expression. An indication implying that merely the notes have to be played, without any nuance beyond the dynamic one (*f, p, mf,* etc.).

    Ohne Begleitung. Without accompaniment.

    Ohne Dämpfer. Without mutes.

    Ohne Eile. Without haste.

    Ohne Nachschlag. Without an after-beat, *e. g.* without the two grace-notes at the end of a shake.

    Ohne Pedal das ganze Stück. Without pedal throughout the piece.

    Ohne Sordine. Without mute.

    Ohne Wiederholung. Without repetition.

    Ohne zu schleppen. Without dragging.

Oktave (Ger.). An octave. *Oktav-* in combination.

    Oktavenfolgen. Consecutive octaves.

    Oktavflötchen. }
    Oktavflöte. } The piccolo; usually called *kleine Flöte.*

    Oktavkoppel. Octave coupler.

Olivettes (Fr.). A dance in honour of the olive harvest.

Omnitonique (Fr.). Having all the tones. *Cor omnitonique,* a horn invented by Sax which by means of a slide could be put into any pitch of the natural horn.

On (Fr.). One, men, people, as *on dit,* one says, or it is said.

    On lève la toile. The curtain is raised. (One raises the curtain.)

Ondeggiamento (It.). Undulation.

Ondeggiante (It.). }
Ondulé (Fr.). } Undulating, tremulous.

Ongarese (It.). Hungarian.

Onzième (Fr.). Eleventh; the interval of the eleventh.

Op. Abbr. of *opus,* work (Lat.), and, added to a number, giving the order of a musician's works, thus: — Op. 12, his twelfth work. Unfortunately, in practice the numbers represent the order of publication, and not that of composition.

Open. Used in the following English musical expressions.

Open diapason. The chief open foundation stop on the organ, usually of 8 ft on the manuals, and 16 ft on the pedals.

Open harmony. When the parts lie at approximately equal distances from one another, as opposed to *close* harmony, when there is a wide space between the bass and the upper parts.

Open notes. (1) On stringed instruments, the notes which are produced on the strings without their being stopped by the fingers. (2) On brass instruments, the notes produced on the tube without the assistance of the valves, *i. e.* the notes forming the Harmonic Series. (*v.* Harmonics.)

Open pipes. Pipes, of which the upper end is open.

Open score. A score, in which all the parts have a separate stave to themselves.

Open strings. The strings on a stringed instrument according to its manner of tuning; thus, on a violin, the open strings are *e''*, *a'*, *d'*, *g*.

Oper (Ger.). (*Opern-* in combination.) An opera. The term is also used for an opera-house.

Opernphantasie. A fantasia on operatic melodies.

Opernhaus. An opera-house.

Opernsänger. An opera singer (masc.).

Opernsängerin. An opera singer (fem.).

Operntext. The libretto (the words) of an opera.

Opéra (Fr.). An opera; an opera-house.

Opéra bouffe. An *opéra comique*, but with a plot of a humorous or even farcical nature.

Opéra comique. An opera, not necessarily of a comedy nature, in which dialogue takes the place of the recitative of grand opera.

Opera (It.). A work, action, deed, and as such is used by some It. composers instead of *op.* or *opus*, and thus a work is designated as *opera* 12. The specific use of the word is for a theatrical representation, in which music forms the chief part.

Operetta (It.). } A short opera, usually in one act.
Operette (Fr.). }

Ophicleide. The bass of the keyed bugle, with a compass from *B* to *c''*. As the instrument is still advertised in the catalogues of Fr. musical instrument-makers, and is still used in some Fr. churches it can hardly be said to be obsolete, although now quite superseded in the orchestra by the tuba. For many reasons this may be an advantage, since the tuba blends better with the trombones and the rest of the brass; but the tuba can never replace the ophicleide in the *Midsummer Night's Dream* overture, and the *Amen* chorus in Berlioz's *Faust* loses half its effect, when the two ophicleide-parts are played on trombones. Alto and tenor ophicleides were also formerly in use.

Ophicléide (Fr.). An ophicleide.

Opus (Lat.). A work. v. Op.

Oratorio (It.). A chapel or oratory. The term is used for a devotional composition, in which sacred subjects are treated from a contemplative rather than from a dramatic point of view, although there may be a connected story running through the work. In some oratorios however the dramatic element is so much insisted upon, that the composition is practically an opera without scenic effects or action.

Oratorium (Ger.). An oratorio.

Orchester (Ger.). Orchestra.

  Orchesterbegleitung. Orchestral accompaniment.

  Orchesterbesetzung. Orchestral disposition, *i. e.* the distribution or laying-out of the orchestra as regards the number of the instrumentalists, its strength in proportion to the size of the concert-room, etc.

  Orchester-Partitur. Full orchestral score. *cf.* Partitur.

Orchestra (It.). Orchestra. (1) A band of instrumentalists, comprising performers on (*a*) stringed (*b*) wood (*c*) brass (*d*) percussion instruments, as opposed to the military band (without *a*), and the brass band (without *a* and *b*). In a well constituted orchestra, the Strings should number at least two-thirds of the total number, although occasionally for special effects this balance may be disturbed. As regards the Wind, no rule, which would be of universal modern application, can be given as to the proportion of its constituent parts, each composer making his own additions to the classic arrangement of 2 flutes, 2 oboes, 2 clarinets, 2 bassoons, 2 trumpets, 2 (or 4) horns and 3 trombones. A piccolo (or 3rd flute), cor anglais, bass clarinet, double-bassoon (or 3rd bassoon), 3rd trumpet, and tuba in addition to the above may now be considered the rule rather than the exception, especially in operatic works, while these additional instruments added to the classic arrangement *doubled* (with the exception of the trombones), *i. e.* 4 clarinets, 8 horns, etc., are found in the later scores of R. Strauss, Mahler, etc. Generally speaking a composer now-a-days no longer looks upon the orchestra as an instrument of stereotyped range and tone-colour, but as one that can be varied according to his fancy or to the nature of the subject illustrated. (2) The place where the instrumentalists are collected.

Orchestration. The art of writing for an orchestra, and one which should include a knowledge of Instrumentation (*q. v.*). Composers too often forget that the effect of a happy experiment in orchestration will of necessity be enhanced if the instruments taking part in the combination have their parts written with due regard for their individual powers and characteristics. A composer, who writes "playable" parts, has a body of *virtuosi* to perform his work; one, who writes impossible passages or passages unsuited to the genus of the particular instrument, has merely a collection of students, willing no doubt to do their best, but who, engrossed with the difficulties of their part, have little attention to devote to the meaning of what they are playing.

Orchestre (Fr.). *v.* Orchestra.

Ordinaire (Fr.). Ordinary, usual. *Sons ordinaires*, ordinary sounds, an indication contradicting a previous direction, such as *sur le chevalet, sons harmoniques, cuivré, bouché*, etc. *Cors ordinaires*, natural horns.

Orecchio (It.). } The ear.
Oreille (Fr.). }

Org. Abbr. of Organ, *organo*.

    Org. Esp. Abbr. of *Organo espressivo*.

Organ. A wind-instrument consisting of six principal parts: — (1) A keyboard, or manual, (2) a keyboard for the feet, or pedals, (3) pipes of various sizes and tone-qualities, (4) stops or registers for bringing into play certain sets of pipes, (5) bellows, and (6) a wind-chest, in which the wind is stored. The number of the manuals may be as many as 5 in very large organs: — Great Organ, Swell, Choir, Solo and Echo; and even the smallest organs are furnished with couplers, by means of which the manuals are connected with the pedals, or with one another. The pipes are of two kinds: — flute, or flue-pipes, some being *open* pipes, whilst others are *closed* (a closed pipe sounding an octave lower than an open pipe of the same length), and reed-pipes. Characteristic of the organ are: — (1) the mutation stops, which sound a 12th, 15th, 17th or 19th above the note, of which the key is pressed; (2) the mixture stops, which sound not only the note of which the key is pressed, but many of the harmonics (often as many as 5) of that particular note.

Organetto (It.). A small organ.

Organista (It.). An organist.

Organo (It.). An organ. *Grand' organo*, Great organ.

    Organo corale. Choir organ.

    Organo di legno. The flue-work of an organ.

    Organo espressivo. The swell organ.

    Organo pieno. Full organ.

Orgel (Ger.). An organ.

    Orgelbalg. Bellows of an organ.

    Orgelbälgetreter. An organ - blower; literally, — an organ treader.

    Orgelchor. An organ loft.

    Orgelpunkt. An organ or pedal point.

    Orgelregister. An organ stop.

    Orgelspieler. An organ player.

    Orgelstimme. Organ part; an organ stop.

    Orgelzug. An organ draw-stop.

Orgue (Fr.). An organ.

    Orgue expressif. A name for the harmonium.

Oricalchi (It.). Brass instruments.

Ornamenti (It.). Ornaments, embellishments.

Ornatamente (It.). Elegantly, gracefully.

Ornato, -a (It.). Adorned. subs. An ornament.

Orné (Fr.). Adorned, embellished.

Ornements (Fr.). Ornaments.

Orphéon (Fr.). A male choral society.

Osservanza (It.). Care, attention.

Osservato (It.). With care, with attention.

Ossia (It.). Or. The indication is often found above an alternative passage.

Ostinato (It.). Obstinate, stubborn. The term is applied to a bass, in which a phrase persistently recurs, — a ground bass.

Ôtez (Fr.). Take away, take off, deprive.

    Ôtez la tirasse. Take off the pedal coupler.

Ôtez le Hautbois et mettez la Voix céleste. Take off the hautboy and put on the *Voix céleste.*

Ôtez les Jeux de Fonds au Récit et mettez le Hautbois. Take off the diapasons from the swell and put on the hautboy.

Ôtez les sourdines. Take off the mutes.

Ottava (It.). An octave. Often written *8a,* or *8va.*

  Ottava alta. The octave above.

  Ottava bassa. The octave below.

  Ottava sopra. The upper octave.

  Ottava sotta. The lower octave.

Ottavino (It.). The ordinary name for the piccolo. It is to be noted that composers of other nations, who use It. terms, invariably call the instrument "Flauto piccolo", a term seldom if ever used by It. composers.

Ottemole (Ger.). A group of eight equal notes in place of six.

Ottetto (It.). An octet.

Ottone (It.). Brass. *Strumenti d'ottone,* brass instruments.

Ouvert, -te (Fr.). Open. Applied to open organ pipes, and to the open notes of a horn, trumpet, etc.

Ouverture (Fr. and Ger.). An overture.

Overtura (It.). An overture. Until recently, *Sinfonia* was the term used by Italians for an overture, but since It. composers have written symphonies, *overtura* has come into vogue, to avoid confusion.

P

P. Abbr. of Piano, *Pied, Pult,* etc.

  P.F., Pf. Abbr. of Pianoforte.

Paar (Ger.). A pair. *Für jedes Paar ein Schläger,* for each pair one drummer.

Pacatamente (It.). Placidly, quietly, calmly.

Pacato (It.). Placid, tranquil.

Padiglione (It.). The bell of an instrument. *Il padiglione in aria,* with upturned bell. (The term for a bell is now often *campana.*)

  Padiglione chinese. The Turkish crescent.

Padovana (It.). An old It. dance, the original of the *Pavane.*

Palco (It.). The stage of a theatre.

Pallets. The valves admitting the air from the wind-chest to the pipes of an organ.

Pair, -e (Fr.). Even, as opposed to *impair,* odd. *Les pupitres pairs,* the even desks. *v.* Desk.

Pandora (It.). *v.* Mandola.

Pantalon (Fr.). The first figure of a quadrille.

Parallelbewegung (Ger.). Similar motion.

Paralleltonart (Ger.). Relative key.

Parfait, -e (Fr.). Perfect. *Cadence parfaite,* a full close.

Parlando (It.). Speaking, talking. It is found marked against phrases in an opera, which are to be spoken instead of sung; and it is occasionally used for instrumental phrases or melodies which are to be declaimed. *Il basso parlando,* the bass in a declamatory manner.

Parlante (It.). adj. Speaking. *v.* Parlando. Used substantively, it means the spoken portion of an opera with dialogue, as opposed to that which is sung.

Parlato (It.). Spoken. *cf.* Parlando.

Parodia (It.). A parody.

Parole (Fr.). Word. *cf.* Après la parole.

Part. (1) That portion of a musical or dramatic composition, which is performed by any one voice, instrument or character. (2) The book containing that portion, together with the necessary cues (*q. v.*) to ensure its entry at the proper moment.

Parte (It.). Part. *Divisi in 3 parti*, divided into 3 parts.
Parte cantante. The part having the melody.
Parte principale. The principal part.

Partial tones. *v.* Harmonics.

Partie (Fr.). An instrumental or vocal part. The part of a character in an opera or play is a *rôle. Cette partie peut être jouée par l'exécutant chargé des Timbres*, this part can be played by the performer entrusted with the carillon: but, *le rôle de Lohengrin*, Lohengrin's part.

Partimento (It.). A bass for exercises in counterpoint, and not of necessity figured. The word means "division", and implies dividing up the notes of the various chords between the different parts.

Partita (It.). (1) A species of Suite. (2) Variations. The term has not been much employed since Bach's time.

Partition (Fr.). A score.
Partition d'orchestre. Full orchestral score.
Partition piano et chant. Vocal score.

Partito (It.). Divided, shared: scored.

Partitur (Ger.). Score. Usually employed in the sense of a full score. A vocal score is *Klavierauszug mit Text*.

Partitura (It.). A score. Usually employed in the sense of a full score. A vocal score is called *Riduzione* (or *spartito*) *canto e piano*.
Partitura d'orchestra. Full orchestral score.

Partizione (It.). Sometimes used for *partitura*.

Pas (Fr.). adv. Not; with verbs, combined with *ne. v.* Ne — pas.
Pas long. Not long.
Pas trop vite. Not too fast.

Pas (Fr.). subs. A step, a pace, a march.
Pas de charge. A double quick march.
Pas de trois. A step (*i. e.* a dance) by three performers.
Pas redoublé. A quick step (march).

Passacaglia (It.). An ancient dance, constructed on a ground bass.

Passage (Fr.). } A phrase; a figure, as a scale passage; a run.
Passaggio (It.). }

Passamezzo (It.). An old dance, a species of quicker *Pavane*.

Passecaille (Fr.). *v.* Passacaglia.

Passend (Ger.). Fitting, suitable. Used in the sense of *comodo*.

Passepied (Fr.). A Paspy. An old Fr. round dance in ternary time, often introduced into suites.

Passionatamente (It.). Passionately.

Passionatissimo (It.). Sup. of *passionato*.

Passionato, -a (It.). Passionate; torn with emotions.

Passione (It.). Passion, suffering. *La passione di N. S.*, our Lord's Passion.

Passo (It.). A step in marching or dancing. *cf.* Pas (subs.).

    Passo a cinque. A dance for five performers.

    Passo di carica. A double quick march.

    Passo raddoppiato. A quick step (march).

Pasticcio (It.). Literally, a pie. A botch; a copy, bad imitation. Applied to a work composed of fragments or single numbers gleaned from various sources.

Pastiche (Fr.). A pasticcio (*q. v.*).

Pastorale (It.). Pastoral, appertaining to rural scenes. subs. A pastoral, a poem dealing with rustic characters and situations.

Pastorita (It.). A name for the *Nachthorn*, a pipe found in old organs.

Pastoso (It.). Soft, mellow.

Pastourelle (Fr.). A shepherdess; a pastoral; one of the figures of the quadrille.

Pateticamente (It.). Pathetically.

Patetico, -a (It.). Pathetic, moving.

Pathétique (Fr.). Pathetic.

Pathétiquement (Fr.). Pathetically.

Pathetisch (Ger.). Pathetic.

Patimento (It.). Suffering, pain.

Pauke (Ger.). A kettledrum. plur. *Pauken. Wenn die Pauke nicht genau auf die Höhe des oberen Fis zu bringen, dann die Stelle ganz weglassen,* if the kettledrum cannot be tuned accurately to the upper F♯, omit the entire passage.

    Paukenschlägel. Kettle-drumstick.

    Paukenschläger. A kettle-drummer.

Pausa (It.). ⎫ A pause, an organ point; specifically, a semibreve-
Pause (Fr.). ⎭ rest, and thus, since that rest is used conventionally for a bar in any time, a bar's rest.

Pause (Ger.). A pause; a rest. *Ganze Pause,* a semibreve-rest; *sechzehntel Pause,* a semiquaver-rest.

Pavana (It.). ⎫A Pavan, a stately dance in binary time, supposed
Pavane (Fr.).⎭to have originated in Padua.

Paventato, Paventoso (It.). Afraid, terrified.

Pavillon (Fr.). The bell of wind-instruments.

    Pavillons en l'air. With upturned bells. *v.* Bell.

Pavillon chinois (Fr.). The Turkish crescent.

Ped. Abbr. of Pedal, *Pedale,* etc.

Pedal. (1) A lever for the foot, either acting as a key, as on an organ or pedal-piano, or for altering the pitch of notes, as on a harp, or for controlling the mechanism concerned with the expression of an instrument, as the pedal for the swell of an organ, the soft pedal and damper pedal on a piano. On this last, where "Ped." is indicated, it always refers to the damper pedal, the soft pedal being designated by *"una corda"*. (2) In harmony, a pedal, or pedal-point, or organ-point, is a note (usually the tonic or dominant) held on in one part, while harmonies, of which it does not form a part, are played by the other parts. It is called a pedal, because originally it was always in the bass, and therefore, on an organ, was played on the pedals. (3) The fundamental note on a brass instrument, which in many cases it is impossible to produce. They are never used on the horn or trumpet, but they have been employed (principally by Berlioz) on the trombone. In instruments of the tuba family, a special feature is made of these low notes, thus giving the instruments an extended compass downwards.

Pedal-board. The keyboard of an organ, which is played by the feet; the pedals of an organ.

Pedal clarinet. An instrument an octave lower than the bass clarinet. It has been used by d'Indy with great effect in *Fervaal*, but cannot be said yet to form part of the orchestra.

Pedal coupler. A mechanism for coupling one or more of the manuals of an organ with the pedals.

Pedal piano. A piano, to which is attached a pedal-board, similar to that of an organ.

Pedal point. *v.* Pedal (2).

Pedal (Ger.). A pedal. plur. *Pedale. Pedal und Dämpfer*, both pedals.

Pedalgebrauch. The use of the pedal. *Immer mit Pedalgebrauch*, with the use of the (damper) pedal throughout.

Pedalklaviatur. The pedal-board.

Pedalpauken. Chromatic kettledrums, in which the changing of tuning is effected by means of pedals.

Pedalpfeife. A pedal pipe.

Pedaltaste. A pedal key.

Pedalton. A pedal note; a fundamental note on a brass instrument.

Pedaltritt. } A pedal stop.
Pedalzug. }

Pédale (Fr.). Pedal.

Pédale d'accouplement. A manual coupler.

Pédales de combinaison. The couplers, etc. in general.

Pedale (It.). Pedal.

Pedale accoppiato al O. E. Pedal coupled to swell.

Pedale a ogni battuta. Pedal at every beat, *i. e.* with every change of harmony.

Pédalier (Fr.). } Pedal-board.
Pedaliera (It.). }

Pelittone (It.). A bass brass instrument designed by Pelitti, of the bombardon or tuba species. It is made in C, B♭ and E♭.

Penna (It.). The plectrum of a mandoline.

Pensif, -ive (Fr.). Thoughtful.

Per (Lat.). By, through, by means of.

Per augmentationem. By augmentation, *i. e.* a theme repeated in notes of a larger value than on its first presentation.

Per diminutionem. By diminution, *i. e.* a theme repeated in notes of a smaller value than on its first presentation.

Per (It.). For, by, through, in order to.

Per augmentazione. By augmentation.

Per diminuzione. By diminution.

Per finire. In order to finish.

Per pianoforte a 4 mani. For piano duet.

Percussion Instruments. These are of two kinds: — those producing

10*

a determinate note or notes, and those which produce merely a characteristic noise. To the first class belong the kettledrums, the xylophone, celesta, glockenspiel, typophone, harmonica, bells of various sizes, etc.; to the second (and these are usually considered as the "Percussion" in the orchestra), the snare-drum, tenor drum, *tambourin*, bass drum, cymbals, gong, triangle, tambourine, *Rute* (rod), castanets and wood or metal clappers, anvil (which is occasionally tuned and then belongs to the first class), etc.

Percussione (It.). Percussion.

Perd. Abbr. of *perdendo*.

Perdendo (It.). Losing (strength or force), and hence used in the sense of dying away. Occasionally the term also implies a slackening of the speed.

Perdendosi (It.). Losing itself, *i. e.* dying away.

    Perdendosi poco a poco. Dying away by degrees.

Perfetto (It.). Perfect.

Périgourdine (Fr.). A dance in triple time, which originated in Périgord.

Periode (Fr.).   Period; a complete musical phrase.
Periodo (It.).

Perpetuo (It.). Perpetual. *cf.* Moto perpetuo.

Pesamment (Fr.). Heavily.

Pesant, -te (Fr.).   Heavy.
Pesante (It.).

Petit, petite (Fr.). Small.

    Petit détaché. A form of bowing used in rapid movements, the point of the bow being employed.

    Petit format. Small size.

    Petite bugle. The soprano saxhorn in E♭.

    Petite caisse. A term sometimes used for the snare-drum.

    Petite clarinette. A small clarinet in E♭, D, F or A♭.

    Petite flûte. The piccolo.

    Petite trompette. The small trumpet; a name given to an instrument standing in B♭ (the pitch of a B♭ cornet) or in some higher key, of which the tube is about half the length of the classic instrument.

Petto (It.). The chest. *Voce di petto*, the chest voice.

Peu à peu (Fr.). Gradually, little by little, by degrees.

Pezza (It.). *v.* Pezzo.

Pezzi (It.). Plur. of *Pezzo*, a piece.

    Pezzi concertanti. Concerted pieces.

Pezzo (It.). A piece.

    Pezzo concertato. A concerted piece.

    Pezzo d'insieme. A piece for several voices in an opera, etc. *v.* Ensemble.

Pfeife (Ger.). A whistle, pipe; an organ pipe.

Pfiffig (Ger.). Cunning, artful, sly.

Phantasie (Ger.). Imagination, fancy. A fantasia.

    Phantasiebilder. Pictures of the imagination.

    Phantasiestücke. Fantasias.

Physharmonika. An instrument with free reeds, one of the precursors of the harmonium.

Piacere (It.). To charm, please. subs. Pleasure. *A piacere*, at pleasure.

Piacevole (It.). Pleasing, agreeable.

Piacevolmente (It.). Pleasingly.

Piacimento (It.). Pleasure.

Pianamente (It.). Softly, gently.

Pianette. A small upright piano.

Piangendo (It.). Weeping, deploring.

Piangevole (It.). Deplorable, sad.

Piangevolmente (It.). Sadly.

Pianino (It.). Diminutive of *piano*; a term applied to a small pianoforte; an upright piano.

Pianissimo (It.). Sup. of *piano*, soft.

> **Pianissimo quanto possible.** As softly as possible.
>
> **Pianissimo sempre senza sordini.** Very soft and always without using the soft pedal. *v.* Sordino.

Piano -a (It.). Soft.

> **Piano ed egualmente.** Soft and evenly (equally).
>
> **Piano-forte.** Usually abbr. to *pf*. Soft-loud; commencing softly and immediately becoming loud; the reverse of *fp*.
>
> **Piano piano.** Very soft.

Piano. Abbr. of *Pianoforte* in Eng., Fr., It. It. plur. *piani*.

> **Piano à queue** (Fr.). Grand piano.
>
> **Piano droit** (Fr.). Upright piano.

Pianoforte (It.). subs. The stringed keyboard instrument, too well-known to need description.

> **Pianoforte a coda.** Grand piano.
>
> **Piano verticale.** Upright piano.

Pianto (It.). Weeping, lamentation.

Piatti (It.). Cymbals.

> **Piatti squillanti suonati con due bacchette da timpani.** Suspended cymbals played with two kettle-drumsticks.

Pibroch. A wild piece of Scotch music, played on the bagpipes, half martial, half dirge-like in character.

Picchiettando (It.). Detaching the notes. *v.* Picchiettato.

Picchiettato (It.). Detached. A species of bowing indicated by a dot over each note and a slur extending over the entire group.

Piccolino (It.). Diminutive of *piccolo*.

Piccolo. A small flute sounding an octave higher than the ordinary flute. In the orchestra the piccolo in C is the only one now used, but in military bands instruments in D♭ and E♭ (sometimes improperly designated as in E♭ and F, *v.* Flute) are still to be found.

Piccolo, -a (It.). Small. *Flauto piccolo*, though found in scores to indicate the piccolo, is seldom used by the Italians themselves, *ottavino* being the ordinary name for the instrument. *Violino piccolo*, a small violin.

> **Piccolo cornetto.** The high cornet in D, E♭ or A♭.

Piccolo (Ger.). The It. word has become Germanised for certain expressions, as

> **Piccolo Kornett.** The cornet in E♭, usually called in England the Soprano (cornet), the ordinary cornet being sometimes called in Germany *Sopranokornett*.

Pichettato (It.). Sharply detached, *spiccato*.
Pickelflöte (Ger.). A name for the piccolo.
Pièce (Fr.). Piece. Used, as in Eng. for a play (*pièce de théatre*). Piece, in the sense of a musical piece, is *morceau*.
Pieno, -a (It.). Full, complete.
    Piena orchestra. Full orchestra.
    Pieno coro. Full chorus.
Pietosamente (It.). Compassionately, piteously.
Pietoso, -a (It.). Pitiful, pitying.
Pifferare (It.). To play upon the *piffero*, fife, flageolet, etc.
Piffero (It.). A small kind of oboe, used by the It. mountaineers. For description of the *pifferari*, or players on the instrument, *v*. Berlioz, *Mémoires*, Vol. I. The term is also used for a fife.
Pincé (Fr.). Plucked; corresponding to *pizzicato*. The term was formerly used for a form of grace-note.
Pincer (Fr.). To pluck.
    Pincer la harpe. To play the harp.
Pique (Fr.). A spike; the end pin of a violoncello.
Piqué (Fr.). Sharply detached, *spiccato*.
Piquieren (Ger.). To play the notes *spiccato*.
Pirolo (It.). A peg of a violin, etc. plur. *piroli*.
Piston. A form of valve for producing the chromatic scale on brass instruments. *v*. Valve.
Piston (Fr.). A piston. The ordinary term for the *cornet-à-pistons* in C, B♭ or A.
Piston (Ger.). A *cornet-à-pistons*.
    Pistonbläser. A cornet player.
Pistone (It.). A piston. The term is often used for the high cornets (in E♭, F, etc.), the ordinary instrument being as a rule called *cornetta* or *cornetto*.
Pistonino (It.). A small cornet.
Pitch. The acuteness of a note, determined by the number of vibrations a second required to produce it. In England, there are unfortunately two standard pitches: — The new Philharmonic, which approaches, but by a serious error of judgment is not identical with, the Fr. *Diapason normal* (Ph. $a' = 439$; D.N. $a' = 435$), and the Kneller Hall pitch, which is used by military bands, and is almost a semitone higher.
Pittoresco (It.). ⎫ Picturesque.
Pittoresque (Fr.). ⎬
Più (It.). More.
    Più agitato. More agitated.
    Più allegro. Faster.
    Più animato. More animated.
    Più dolce e rall. Softer and becoming slower.
    Più f. ed espr. Louder and with expression.
    Più forte ed animato. Louder and more animated.
    Più lento e sotto voce. Slower and in an undertone.
    Più moderato. More moderately.
    Più mosso subito. Suddenly with more movement.
    Più piano. Softer.
    Più presto. Faster.

Più ritenuto. Gradually becoming slower.

Più sensibile. More perceptible, *i. e.* the part or melody becoming more prominent.

Più stretto. More closely drawn together, *i. e.* quickening the tempo.

Più tosto, (*or* **piuttosto**). More boldly; more quickly.

Piva (It.). A bagpipe.

Pizz. Abbr. of *pizzicato*.

Pizzicando (It.). Plucking (the strings of a stringed instrument).

Pizzicati (It.). Plur. of *pizzicato*.

Pizzicato (It.). Plucked. A term meaning that the fingers are to be used instead of the bow in bowed instruments. The word is also used substantively, as, the Pizzicato from *Sylvia*.

Placabile (It.). Calm, peaceable.

Placabilmente (It.). Peacefully.

Placidamente (It.). Placidly, calmly.

Placido (It.). Calm, peaceful.

Plainte (Fr.). Complaint, lamentation.

Plaisant (Fr.). Merry, sportive.

Plaisanterie (Fr.). Pleasantry, joking. A term used formerly for pieces of a cheerful jocular character.

Plaqué (Fr.). Equivalent to *acciaccato* (*q. v.*) when applied to a chord played in very rapid *arpeggio*, for the sake of greater resonance.

Plateaux (Fr.). Plates. The two halves of a pair of cymbals.

Plaudernd (Ger.). Prattling, babbling.

Plectrum. The piece of ivory or metal used for plucking the strings of a mandoline. A plectrum is occasionally used for special effects on the harp.

Plein jeu (Fr.). The full power of the organ or harmonium.

Plötzlich (Ger.). Suddenly.

Plötzlich anhaltend. Suddenly restraining (the speed of a movement).

Plötzlich etwas breiter. Suddenly somewhat broader.

Plötzlich schneller. Suddenly faster.

Plötzlich wieder im Zeitmaß. Suddenly again in the tempo.

Plus (Fr.). More.

Plus animé. More animated.

Plus de chaleur. With more warmth.

Plus de largeur. With more breadth.

Plus de mouvement. With more movement, *i. e.* faster.

Plus large. Broader.

Plus modéré. More moderate.

Plus vite qu'au début. Faster than at the commencement.

Pochette (Fr.). A kit (*q. v.*).

Pochettino (It.). ⎱ subs. A very little, a very small (quantity).
Pochetto (It.). ⎰

Pochissimo (It.). Very little, as little as possible.

Poco (It.). adj. Little, few. adv. Little, not much, somewhat, rather.

Poco agitato. Somewhat agitated.

Poco allegro. Somewhat quick.

Poco andante. Somewhat slow.

Poco animando. Becoming somewhat animated.

Poco calando. Somewhat decreasing.
Poco forte. Somewhat loud.
Poco incalzando. Somewhat hastening.
Poco lento. Somewhat slow.
Poco meno mosso. Somewhat less moved (animated).
Poco meno presto. A little less fast.
Poco più. A little more.
Poco più moderato ma non troppo. A little more moderate, but not too much so.
Poco sfz. (sforzato). Somewhat accentuated.
Poco sostenuto. Somewhat sustained.
Poco stringendo. Somewhat hurrying.
Poco a poco (It.). Little by little, gradually, by degrees.
Poco a poco accelerando. Gradually quickening.
Poco a poco animando. Gradually becoming animated.
Poco a poco crescendo, e con più di forza e di calore. Gradually increasing in loudness, and with more force and warmth.
Poco a poco crescendo e stringendo. Gradually increasing in loudness and speed.
Poco a poco diminuendo. Gradually decreasing in loudness.
Poco a poco due ed allora tutte le corde. Gradually two and then all the strings. (Direction for gradually relinquishing the soft pedal in the piano.)
Poco a poco più calando sin al fine. Gradually becoming softer until the end.
Poco a poco più di fuoco. Gradually with more spirit.
Poème symphonique (Fr.). A symphonic poem.
Poi (It.). Then, after.
Poi la coda. Then the coda.
Poi segue il rondo. Then follows the rondo.
Point (Fr.). A point, dot.
Point d'arrêt. The sign ⌒ placed over a rest.
Point de repos. A rest.
Point d'orgue. The sign ⌒ placed over a note: a cadenza.
Pointe (Fr.). A point.
Pointe d'archet. The point of the bow.
Pointé (Fr.). Dotted. *Croche pointée*, a dotted quaver.
Polacco, -a (It.). Polish. subs. *Polacca*, a polonaise.
Polifonico, -a (It.). Polyphonic.
Polka. A dance in $^2/_4$ time.
Pollice (It.). The thumb.
Polnisch (Ger.). Polish.
Polonais, -aise (Fr.). Polish. subs. *Polonaise*, a dance in $^3/_4$ time.
Polster (Ger.). Pad for key of wood-wind instrument.
Polyphonie (Fr.). Polyphony.
Polyphonique (Fr.). Polyphonic.
Pompa (It.). A double sliding tube in a brass instrument, used as a tuning-slide, and sometimes replaceable by a longer or shorter piece for the purpose of changing the pitch. It also permits the removal of the condensed breath.
Pompa di cambio. A lengthening piece.
Pompe (Fr.). *v.* Pompa.

Pomposamente (It.). Pompously.

Pomposo (It.). Pompous, majestic, lofty.

Ponderoso (It.). Heavy, ponderous.

Ponticello (It.). The bridge of a violin, violoncello, etc.

Port de voix (Fr.). (1) An obsolete grace-note. (2) The same as *portamento di voce.*

Portamento (It.). Carriage, bearing; manner, conduct. In music, the word used by itself is usually taken to be the abbr. of *p. di voce* (*v.* below).

> **Portamento della mano.** The proper use of the hands and fingers on any instrument, in order to produce the best qualities of tone, etc.
>
> **Portamento de' piedi.** The correct style of pedalling.
>
> **Portamento (di voce).** The direct contrary to *staccato*; the carrying the voice from one note to another in the strictest *legato*. The *portamento* is also employed on bowed and wind-instruments, and is sometimes indicated by a wavy line ⌒ from one note to another.

Portando la voce (It.). Carrying the voice. *cf.* Portamento di voce.

Portatif (Fr.). ⎰ Portative; applied to a small organ, which can be
Portativ (Ger.). ⎱ carried about.

Portato (It.). ⎰ Carried. *cf.* Portamento.
Portée (Fr.). ⎱

Portée (Fr.). subs. The staff or stave.

Porter la voix (Fr.). To "carry" the voice; to employ the *portamento.*

Portunal-flute. An organ stop of 4 ft and 8 ft, the pipes being of wood. It is not often found.

Pos. Abbr. of position, *Posaune.*

Posaune (Ger.). (1) The trombone. (2) A powerful reed-stop on the organ.

Posément (Fr.). Steadily; sedately.

Positif (Fr.). The choir organ.

Position. (1) On brass instruments, the various elongations of the tube (either by means of a slide or by valves), necessary for producing the several series of the Harmonic Scale, which together make up the complete chromatic scale on the instrument. (2) On stringed instruments, the various changes of the hand on the finger-board necessary for obtaining the scale, each position being one tone higher: in actual practice the violinist usually proceeds by "shifts" (*q. v.*). (3) The place on the strings touched by the bow, and thus "ordinary position" means the bow touching the strings at the accustomed place, as opposed to playing near the bridge or finger-board. (4) In harmony, the relative position of the various parts of the harmony, *close position* being when the soprano and tenor are within an octave of one another, *extended position* when they are more than an octave apart.

Position (Fr.). Position. "Shifting" is *démanchement.*

> **Position espacée.** Extended position.
>
> **Position ordinaire.** The bow in its normal position on the strings.
>
> **Position serrée.** Close position.

Positiv (Ger.). The choir organ.

Posizione (It.). Position.

Posizione naturale. *v.* Position ordinaire.

Possibile (It.). Possible.

Posthorn. In England, a straight tube from 36″ to 52″ in length, with a scale consisting of the 2nd to the 8th harmonic inclusive (*v.* Harmonics). In Germany, the *Posthorn* is a tube turned on itself into either a horn or trumpet shape. The *"Posthorn"* of Mahler's 3rd symphony is a *Flügelhorn* in B♭.

Pot-pourri (Fr.). A medley of various tunes.

Pouce (Fr.). The thumb.

Poule (Fr.). One of the figures of the quadrille.

Pour (Fr.). For.

    Pour le concert. For concert use.

Poussé (Fr.). Pushed. In violin, etc. playing, the movement of the bow from point to nut, the up-bow, designated by the sign $\vee$. *Tiré* (drawn) is the reverse movement, represented by ⊓.

pp. Abbr. of *pianissimo*. Used also as a subs., as: — *Les pp. doivent être pris brusquement*, the *pp.* should be taken suddenly.

Prächtig (Ger.). Magnificent, superb.

Präcis (Ger.). Exact, precise. *Sehr präcis im Rhythmus*, the rhythm very exact.

Pralltriller (Ger.). A mordent.

Präludi(e)ren (Ger.). To prelude.

Präludium (Ger.). A prelude.

Prästant (Ger.). The open diapason of 8 ft or 16 ft.

Préambule (Fr.). Preamble, introduction.

Precipitanto, Precipitandosi (It.). Hurrying, urging on.

Precipitato (It.). }
Précipité (Fr.). } Hurried.

Precipitosamente (It.). Hurriedly, precipitately.

Precipitoso (It.). Overhasty, precipitate.

Précision (Fr.). }
Precisione (It.). } Precision, exactness.

Preciso (It.). Precise, exact, strict.

Pregando (It.). Praying.

Preghiera (It.). A prayer.

Prélude (Fr.). }
Preludio (It.). } Prelude; introduction to a musical work.

Premier, première (Fr.). First; often abbr. to *1er* and *1ère*.

    Premier dessus. First treble.

    Première fois. First time.

Prendre (Fr.). To take. (*v.* Remark I.)

    Prendre le hautbois. Take the oboe.

    Prendre le Tam-tam. Take the gong.

Prenez (Fr.). Take.

    Prenez le doigté un $1/2$ ton au-dessus. Take the fingering a semitone above. (Direction to a horn-player, as to the production of closed notes.)

Preparare (It.). To prepare, make ready.

    Preparare sordine. Make ready the mutes.

Préparation (Fr.). }
Preparazione (It.). } Preparation. A dissonance is said to be prepared, when it has appeared in the preceding chord as a consonance.

Préparez (Fr.). Prepare.
    Préparez le ton de Mi♭. Prepare the key of E♭. (Direction in harp part.)
Près de (Fr.). Near to,
    Près de la table. Near the sound-board (of a harp).
    Près de la touche. Near the finger-board.
    Près du chevalet. Near the bridge.
Presa (It.). The *Guida*, or sign (usually §) indicating the entrance of the several parts in a closed canon.
Pressant (Fr.). Hurrying.
Pressante (It.). Pressing, urgent.
Pressez (Fr.). Hurry, quicken.
    Pressez peu à peu jusqu'à . . . . Gradually quicken till . . . .
    Pressez toujours. Continually quicken.
Prestamente (It.). Quickly, promptly.
Prestant (Fr.). The open diapason.
Prestezza (It.). Speed, haste.
Prestissimamente (It.). Very quickly.
Prestissimo (It.). Sup. of *presto*.
Prest^mo. Abbr. of *prestissimo*.
Presto (It.). Quick, nimble, prompt. Used for a tempo quicker than *allegro*.
    Presto assai. Very quick.
    Presto prestissimo. Excessively quick.
Prière (Fr.). A prayer.
Prima (It.). Fem. of *primo*, first.
    Prima donna. The leading lady in a play or opera.
    Prima parte. First part.
    Prima vista (a). At first sight.
    Prima volta. First time (not in the sense of tempo).
Primo (It.). First (masc.).
    Primo corno. First horn.
    Primo flauto. First flute.
    Primo soprano. First soprano.
    Primo tempo. First time (tempo).
    Primo uomo. The leading man in a play or opera.
    Primo violino. First violin.
Principal (Fr.). ⎫ The open diapason. In old German music, *prin-*
Principale (It.). ⎬ *cipale* is the name given to the lowest of a set of
Prinzipal (Ger.). ⎭ trumpet parts. (*v.* Clarino.)
Probe (Ger.). A rehearsal.
Procella (It.). Storm, tempest.
Professore di musica (It.). Teacher (professor) of music.
Programma (It.). Programme.
Progressivamente (It.). Progressively.
Progressivo (It.). Progressive, advancing.
Promptement (Fr.). ⎫ Quickly.
Prontamente (It.). ⎬
Pronto (It.). Ready, speedy, hasty.
Pronunziato, -a (It.). Pronounced, clearly accentuated. *Ben pronunziata la melodia*, the melody very accentuated.
Proposta (It.). The subject of a fugue

Prosa (It.).

Prose (Fr.). } A species of hymn sung in the Roman Service.

Prova (It.). A rehearsal.

Psaume (Fr.). A psalm.

Psautier (Fr.). Psalter.

Pulsatile instruments. Instruments of percussion.

Pult (Ger.). A desk. plur. *Pulte. v.* Desk.

> **Pultweise.** adv. formed from *Pult*; desk by desk. *Die C.B. nehmen pultweise allmählich sordinen,* the C.B., desk by desk, gradually put on mutes.

Punkt (Ger.). A dot.

Punkti(e)rte Noten (Ger.). Dotted notes.

Punta (It.). Point. *A punta d'arco,* with the point of the bow.

Puntando (It.). Playing the notes as though they had a dot above them.

Puntato (It.). Dotted.

Puntina (It.). A shank, or lengthening piece for a brass instrument.

Punto (It.). A point, dot.

> **Punto coronato.**
> **Punto d'organo.** } An organ point, the sign ⌢.

Pupitre (Fr.). A desk (*q. v.*).

> **Pupitres impairs.** The odd desks (1, 3, 5, etc.).
> **Pupitres pairs.** The even desks (2, 4, 6, etc.).

Putti (It.). Small boys, such as choir-boys.

Pyramidon. An organ stop of 16ft or 32ft, of which the pipes have the shape of an inverted pyramid.

Q

Quadrat (Ger.). The sign for a natural (♮).

Quadriglia (It.). } A dance in 5 or 6 parts or figures, each being a

Quadrille (Fr.). } square dance (*contre-danse*).

Quadruple croche (Fr.). A semi-demisemiquaver.

Qual (Ger.). Intense pain, agony.

> **Qualvoll.** Agonised, full of torments.

Quanto (It.). As far, as far as, as much as.

> **Quanto possible.** As much as possible.

Quart (Fr.). A fourth, a quarter. *A un quart de voix,* with a quarter of the voice, *i. e.* sung as softly as possible. *cf.* À demi-voix.

> **Quart de mesure.** A crotchet-rest.
> **Quart de soupir.** A semiquaver-rest.

Quarta (It.). A fourth, a quarter; the interval of a fourth.

> **Quarta diminuita.** A diminished fourth.
> **Quarta eccedente.** An augmented fourth.

Quarte (Fr.). The interval of a fourth.

> **Quarte augmentée.** Augmented fourth.
> **Quarte diminuée.** Diminished fourth.

Quarte (Ger.). A fourth, a quarter; the interval of a fourth. *Verminderte Quarte,* a diminished fourth; *übermäßige Quarte,* an augmented fourth. *Quart-* in combination.

> **Quartbaßposaune.** A bass trombone in F, *i. e.* a 4th below the tenor trombone.

Quartfagott. An obsolete species of bassoon, with a compass of 3 octaves from $B\flat$ but with the actual notes sounding a 4th lower. *cf.* Basson Quinte (2).

Quartett (Ger.). ⎰A quartet; a composition for 4 voices or instru-
Quartetto (It.). ⎱ments, used specifically for a composition in sonata form for 2 violins, viola and violoncello.

Quartino (It.). An $E\flat$ clarinet (a 4th above the one in $B\flat$).

Quarto (It.). A, quarter.

    Quarto d'aspetto. A crotchet-rest.

Quasi (It.). Almost, as if, like.

    Quasi allegretto. Almost allegretto.

    Quasi andante. Like an Andante.

    Quasi cadenza. In the style of a cadenza.

    Quasi chitarra. Like a guitar.

    Quasi lontana. As though from a distance.

    Quasi niente. Almost nothing.

    Quasi parlato. As if spoken, almost spoken.

    Quasi recitativo, ma in tempo. In the style of a recitative, but in strict time.

    Quasi satira. Like a satire.

    Quasi trombe. Like trumpets.

    Quasi una fantasia. In the style of a fantasia.

Quatorzième (Fr.). Fourteenth.

Quatre (Fr.). Four.

Quattricroma (It.). A semi-demisemiquaver

Quattro (It.). Four.

Quatuor (Fr.). A quartet.

Quer (Ger.). Cross, traverse.

    Querflöte. The cross or German flute, *flauto traverso*.

    Querformat. Oblong shape (in music and books).

    Querstand. False relation.

    Querstrich. A cross stroke; a traverse line drawn across (say) a minim to denote its being played as four quavers,.

Questo, -a (It.). This. plur. *questi, -e.*

    Queste note ben marcate. These notes well accentuated.

Queue (Fr.). A tail. The stem of a note. The tail-piece of a violin, etc.

Quietissimo (It.). Sup. of *quieto.*

Quieto (It.). Calm, peaceful, tranquil.

Quint- (Ger.). Used in combination in the sense of a fifth.

    Quintbaßposaune. A bass trombone in $E\flat$, *i. e.* a 5th lower than a tenor trombone.

    Quintsaite. The E string of a violin.

Quinta (It.). (1) A fifth. (2) A "wing" of a theatrical scene.

    Quinta diminuita. A diminished fifth.

Quinte (Fr.). A fifth. Term sometimes used for the E string of a violin.

    Quintes cachées. Hidden fifths.

    Quintes consécutives. Consecutive fifths.

Quinte (Ger.). (1) A fifth. (2) The E string of a violin. (3) An organ stop, in which the note sounds a 5th above the written note.

    Quinte aufsetzen. Stop the fifth, *i. e.* on the violin, stop two strings with one finger, thus forming a fifth.

Quintenfolgen. Consecutive fifths.

Quintett (Ger.).
Quintetto (It.). } A quintet: composition for 5 instruments or voices.

Quintieren (Ger.). *v.* Quintoyer.

Quintole (Ger.). A quintuplet; five equal notes in the place of 4 or 6.

Quintoyer (Fr.). When a reed wind-instrument is blown harder, it produces the octave above, if it is of conical bore, and the fifth above the octave, if it is of cylindrical bore. In the first case (oboe, saxophone, etc.), it is said to *octavier*; in the second (clarinet, etc.), it is said to *quintoyer*. On the modern cylindrical flute, on the contrary, in the usual scale the upper octave is always produced, although it is possible also to *quintoyer* on certain notes, and thus (for example) *c'''* can be produced as the 12th of *f'*.

Quintuor (Fr.). A quintet.

Quinzième (Fr.). A fifteenth.

Quodlibet (Lat.). (1) A number of different tunes sung at the same time, sometimes degenerating into what is known as a "Dutch concert", but in the hands (or throats) of a Bach family capable of a certain amount of artistic finish. (2) A *pot-pourri*; a musical work in which a number of (usually) familiar airs are combined contrapuntally.

R

R. Abbr. of Right, *recht, ripieno.* In Eng. stage-directions, it means the side of the stage to the right of the player; in Ger. to the right of the spectator.

Rabbia (It.). Rage, fury, madness.

Racler (Fr.). To scrape; to play on a violin indifferently.

Raddol. Abbr. of *raddolcendo.*

Raddolcendo, Raddolcente (It.). Becoming softer.

Raddoppiamento (It.). The doubling of the parts of a composition.

Raddoppiare le parti (It.). To double the parts.

Raddoppiato (It.). Doubled; redoubled. *Passo raddoppiato*, a quick march, *pas redoublé.*

Raffrenando (It.). Checking, moderating the speed.

Ralentir (Fr.). To slacken.

Rall., Rallen., Rall°. Abbr. of *rallentando.*

Rallentamento (It.). A slackening.

Rallentando (It.). Slackening, becoming gradually slower.
    Rallentando al fine. Slackening until the end.
    Rallentando e diminuendo. Becoming slower and softer.

Rallentato (It.). Slackened.

Rallonge (Fr.). A lengthening piece for a horn or trumpet.

Ranz des vaches (Fr.). A melody sung, or played on an Alpenhorn, by the Swiss mountaineers to call the cattle home.

Rapidamente (It.).
Rapidement (Fr.). } Rapidly.

Rapidità (It.).
Rapidité (Fr.). } Rapidity, swiftness.

Rapido (It.). Rapid, swift.
    Rapido e brillante. Rapid and brilliant.

Rapsodie (Fr.). A rhapsody.
Rasch (Ger.). Quick, fast, swift.
   Rasch bewegt. In rapid movement.
   Rasch, heftig. Quickly, hurriedly.
   Rasch, nicht zu hastig. Quick, not too much hurried.
   Rasch und wild. Quick and furious.
   Rasch wie zuvor. As quick as before.
Rascher (Ger.). Quicker.
Rasgado (Sp.). Sweeping the strings of a guitar with the thumb for full chords.
Ratsche (Ger.). A rattle.
Rattenendo (It.). Holding back the movement, becoming slower.
Rattenuto (It.). Held back.
Rauh (Ger.). Rough, harsh.
Rausch (Ger.). Rushing, uproar, rustling; the sound of wind, waves, trees, etc.
   Rauschwerk, Rauschquint, Rauschpfeife. Names of mixture stops on some old organs.
Rauschend (Ger.). Rustling, murmuring, rushing. *cf.* Rausch.
   Rauschender Beifall. Thundering applause.
   Rauschend und festlich. Dashing and festive.
Rauscher (Ger.). An old expression for the rapid alternation of two notes.
Ravvivando (It.). Becoming more animated.
Ré (Fr.). The note D.
   Ré bémol mineur. D flat minor.
   Ré dièse. D sharp.
Re (It.). The note D.
   Re bemolle. D flat.
   Re maggiore. D major.
Rechange (Fr.). Change. *Ton de rechange*, the crook of a horn or trumpet.
Recht (Ger.). Right.
   Rechte Hand. The right hand.
   Recht lustig. Right cheerfully.
Recit. Abbr. of *recitativo*.
Récit (Fr.). Recital. A vocal or instrumental solo, as opposed to a *tutti*. *Clavier de récit*, the swell manual.
Recitando (It.). Reciting; in the style of a recitative.
Récitant (Fr.). Reciting. subs. A reciter, a solo singer *cf.* Récit.
Récitatif (Fr.). Recitative.
Recitativo (It.). Recitative; musical declamation; a musical form midway between speaking and singing, somewhat free as regards tempo, and usually accompanied by simple chords. In modern music certain forms of recitative have quite died out. The term is used in instrumental music for passages, which are not to be played in strict time, and which are to be declaimed in the style of a vocal recitative.
   Recitativo accompagnato. } Accompanied recitative, *i. e.* ac-
   Recitativo obbligato. } companied by more than the usual simple chords.
   Recitativo parlante. } Unaccompanied recitative.
   Recitativo secco. }

Recitativo senza misura. A recitative, in which the tempo is even freer than in the ordinary recitative.

Recitativo strumentato. Accompanied recitative.

Réciter (Fr.). To recite, declaim.

Redend (Ger.). Speaking. *v.* Parlando.

Redoublement (Fr.). The doubling of parts.

Redowa. A Bohemian dance in triple time, something like a mazurka.

Réduire (Fr.).
Reduzieren (Ger.).} To reduce; to arrange a work for smaller means.

Reed. A thin strip of metal or of the cane-like stem of a species of reed (*Arundo donax*) set in vibration by either bellows or the breath of the player. Reeds are divided into *single* and *double* reeds. A single reed, covering the opening of a pipe, is called a *free* reed when it is smaller than the orifice and can vibrate freely in two directions, and a *striking* or *beating* reed, when it is larger than the orifice and can vibrate freely in one direction only: to the former class belong the reeds of the harmonium and some few organ pipes, to the latter class, the reeds of the ordinary reed pipes of an organ and of the clarinet and saxophone families. In the double reed, two reeds are fastened together so that the vibrating edges nearly touch; their lower ends are tied together and fit on to the staple or crook of the instrument; such are the reeds of the oboe, bassoon, sarrusophone and the chanters of instruments of the bagpipe class.

Regel (Ger.). Rule.

Regel der Oktave. Rule of the octave.

Register. (1) A portion of the compass of a voice or instrument, such as the chest register, head register, high, low or medium register. (2) An organ stop, in two senses: — the actual knob, on which the name of the pipe is written, and the set of pipes itself.

Register (Ger.). Register, stop.

Registergriff. A draw-stop.

Registerknopf. The knob of a draw-stop.

Registerpedal. A composition pedal.

Registerstimme. Register.

Registerzug. A draw-stop.

Registration, *or* **Registering.** The art of choosing the stops, singly or in combination, in organ playing.

Registri(e)ren (Ger.). To register.

Registrierung (Ger.). Registration.

Registro (It.). (1) The register of a voice or instrument. (2) An organ stop. plur. *Registri*.

Registri di ripieno. The mixture stops.

Registri dolci. Soft stops.

Règle (Fr.).
Regola (It.). } Rule.

Rein (Ger.). Pure, just, exact.

Religieusement (Fr.). Religiously.

Religieux, -euse (Fr.). Religious.

Religiosamente (It.). Religiously.

Religioso, -a (It.). Religious.

Remplissage (Fr.). The filling-in; the middle (accompanying) parts in an orchestra.

Rentrée (Fr.). Reappearance, re-entrance.

Renversement (Fr.). Inversion.

Renvoi (Fr.). The sign of repetition.

Répéter (Fr.). To repeat, to rehearse.

Répétition (Fr.). \
Repetizione (It.). } Repetition. A rehearsal.

Repetitore (It.). A rehearser; a teacher.

Replica (It.). A repeat; that portion of a composition enclosed in dotted double bars.

Replicato (It.). Repeated; doubled. *Suoni replicati*, doubled parts.

Replique (Fr.). An answer. A cue, in both a theatrical and musical sense. *Donner la replique*, to give the cue.

Répons (Fr.). A response (in the Liturgy).

Réponse (Fr.). Answer of a fugue.

Repos (Fr.). Repose, peace; rest (in music).

Reprendre (Fr.). To retake. *v.* Remark I.

　　Reprendre la grande flûte. Retake the flute.

　　Reprendre le Tamb. mil. (Tambour militaire). Resume the snare-drum.

Reprise (Fr.). (1) A repeat. (2) The revival of a work, which has been laid aside for some time.

Requiem (Lat.). The Mass for the dead, so-called from the opening words, *Requiem eternam dona eis*, give to them eternal peace.

Requinto (Sp.). The E♭ clarinet.

Résolument (Fr.). Resolutely, with decision.

Resoluto (It.). *v.* Risoluto.

Resonanz (Ger.). Resonance.

　　Resonanzboden. A sounding-board.

　　Resonanzloch. A sound hole.

Respiro (It.). Breathing, breath. Occasionally marked in a vocal part to direct the singer where to take breath; now-a-days, a comma is usually used. *v.* Signs.

Ressort (Fr.). The spring of an instrument.

Ressortir (Fr.). When combined with *faire*, to bring forward, to show off. *Faites ressortir le chant*, make the melody prominent.

Restez (Fr.). Remain. Placed above notes, it indicates that they are to be slightly dwelt upon, and prolonged.

Retardando (It.). *v.* Ritardando.

Retenu (Fr.). Retained, slackened.

Retraite (Fr.). The Tattoo, the beat of the drum recalling soldiers or sailors to their quarters or tents at night.

Retrogrado (It.). Retrograde, backward.

Retto (It.). Right, straight. *Moto retto*, direct motion.

Réunis (Fr.). Plur. of *réuni*, reunited: marked against violins, etc., after they have been *divisés*, divided.

Réveil (Fr.). The reveille, revelley; the call for soldiers to get up in the morning.

Revenez (Fr.). From *revenir*, to return.

　　Revenez peu à peu au premier mouvement. Gradually return to the first tempo.

Rezitativ (Ger.). Recitative.

Rf., Rfz. Abbr. of *Rinforzando.*

Rhapsodie (Fr. and Ger.). A rhapsody.

Rhythme (Fr.). Rhythm.

Rhythmisch (Ger.). Rhythmical.
    Rhythmisch bestimmt. Rhythmically accented.

Rhythmus (Ger.). Rhythm. *Der Rhythmus scharf markiert,* the rhythm strongly marked.

Ribattute (It.). Repeated notes.

Ricambio (It.). A crook of a brass instrument.

Ricercare, Ricercata (It.). Originally a species of prelude, but later a fugue, in which all the cleverest devices of imitation, counterpoint, etc. are freely displayed.

Richiamota (It.). The call to arms, the assembly.

Richtig (Ger.). Right, exact, accurate. *Die Hörner richtig auf 2tem Viertel des Taktes, synkopiert, einsetzen,* the horns enter exactly on the 2nd crotchet of the bar, syncopated. *Das C der Trompeten ist richtig,* the C of the trumpets is correct.

Rideau (Fr.). Curtain. *Le rideau s'ouvre,* the curtain opens.

Ridendo (It.). Laughing.

Ridotto (It.). Reduced, arranged, as a score arranged for piano, or military band.

Ridurre (It.). To reduce, arrange.

Riduzione (It.). A reduction, an arrangement.

Rifacimento (It.). A recasting of a work, a new edition.

Rifiorimenti (It.). Ornaments, embellishments.

Riga (It.). One of the lines of the stave. *cf.* Rigo.

Rigata (It.). The stave.

Rigaudon (Fr.). An animated dance in duple time.

Rigo (It.). The stave.

Rigodon. *v.* Rigaudon.

Rigore (It.). Strictness.

Rigoroso (It.). Strict, exact. *Non rigoroso in tempo,* not in strict time.

Rilasciando, Rilassando (It.). Relaxing; slackening the time.

Rilassato (It.). Slackened.

Rimettendosi (It.). Returning, restoring.
    Rimettendosi al Tempo I. Returning to Tempo I.

Rinf. Abbr. of *rinforzando.*

Rinforzamento (It.). Reinforcement. *v.* Rinforzando.

Rinforzando (It.). Reinforcing (the sound). A stress laid on a group of notes as opposed to *sforzando,* a stress laid on a single note. This distinction however is not always strictly observed.

Rinforzato, Rinforzo (It.). Reinforced; stressed, accentuated.

Ripetere (It.). To repeat; to rehearse.

Ripiane (Fr.). } A corruption of *ripieno.*
Ripiano (Eng.). }

Ripiego d'arco (It.). Recovery of the bow, *i. e.* the normal method of bowing after a *contr'arco.*

Ripieno (It.). Filling-in, auxiliary. An extra part only used in *tutti* passages. In military band scores the term (corrupted in Eng. to *ripiano*) is applied to various instruments, which are *ad libitum*;

the harmony is complete without them, but they add to the effect either by strengthening the melody or by introducing another inner part. *Registri di ripieno*, mixture stops.

Ripresa (It.). A repeat; the sign 𝄌.

Riscaldando (It.). Becoming warmer, more animated.

Risentito (It.). Resentful, spiteful.

Risolutissimo (It.). Sup. of *risoluto*.

Risoluto (It.). Decided, resolute.

Risoluzione (It.). Resolution.

Risonanza (It.). Resonance.

Risonare (It.). To resound.

Risposta (It.). The answer of a fugue.

Ristretto (It.). Compressed; the stretto in a fugue.

Ristringendo (It.). Tightening-up; quickening the tempo.

Risvegliato (It.). Roused, excited.

Rit. Abbr. of *ritardando*.

Ritardando (It.). Slackening; gradually becoming slower.

    Ritardando al fine. Becoming slower until the end.

Ritardare (It.). To retard, to keep back; to become slower.

Ritardato (It.). Slackened, held back.

Ritardo (It.). Delay, retarding.

Riten. Abbr. of *ritenuto*.

Ritenendo (It.). Becoming slower.

Ritenuto (It.). Held back; slackened, dragged.

    Ritenuto molto. Much slackened.

Ritmo (It.). Rhythm.

    Ritmo di tre battute. Rhythm of three bars.

Ritornare (It.). To return, repeat.

Ritornelle (Fr.). } (1) A repeat. (2) The instrumental introduction
Ritornello (It.). } to an air or cavatina, often in an opera musically depicting the character before his or her entrance. The term is occasionally used for similar instrumental passages in the middle of an air.

Ritorno (It.). Return.

    Ritorno al 1. tempo. Return to the first tempo.

Ritorta, *or* **Ritorto** (It.). A crook for a brass instrument.

Ritterlich (Ger.). Knightly.

    Ritterlich und galant. Knightly and courteously.

Riverso (It.). Reversed. *v.* Rovescio.

Rivolgimento (It.). The reversal of the parts in double counterpoint.

Rivoltato (It.). Inverted.

Rivolto (It.). Inversion.

Roco (It.). Hoarse, harsh.

Rococo (Fr.). Old-fashioned, quaint; properly applied to a certain style of decorative art in architecture, etc. of a florid and debased character.

Roh (Ger.). Rough, rude, coarse.

Rohr (Ger.). Cane, reed. *Spanisches Rohr*, the Spanish reed (*Arundo donax*).

    Rohrblatt. The reed of a wood-wind instrument. *Doppeltes Rohrblatt*, a double reed (oboe or bassoon); *einfaches Rohrblatt*, single reed (clarinet, etc.). A single reed is usually called *Blatt*, and a double one *Rohr*.

11*

Rohrflöte. A stop belonging to the flue-work of an organ.

Rohrquinte. An organ stop usually $5^{1}/_{3}$ft in the manual, and $10^{2}/_{3}$ft in the pedal.

Rohrwerk. The reed-work of an organ.

Rôle (Fr.). A part (character) in an opera or play.

Rollando (It.). *v.* Rullando.

Rollo (It.). (1) A roll on a drum. (2) Used in military band scores for a snare-drum.

Rolltrommel (Ger.). The tenor drum, now usually called *Rührtrommel.*

Romance (Fr.). In instrumental music, a piece of a melodious song-like nature: in vocal music, almost any short song.

Romances sans paroles. Songs without words.

Romanesca (It.). An old dance.

Romanesco, -a (It.). Romantic.

Romanza (It.).) A romance, ballad.
Romanze (Ger.).)

Rombando (It.). Humming, droning, buzzing.

Römischer Gesang (It.). Plain song.

Ronde (Fr.). A semibreve.

Rondeau (Fr.). *v.* Rondo.

Rondinetto, Rondino, Rondoletto (It.). A short rondo.

Rondo (It.). A piece, in which the principal theme recurs at least three times; it often forms the last movement of a sonata or concerto.

Rope-hoop. The hoop which tightens the head of a drum: it is so called because the rope or cord (which is tightened by means of the "braces") passes through eyelets cut in its circumference.

Rosalia (It.). The repetition of a phrase on several higher or lower degrees of the scale.

Rotondo, -a (It.). Round.

Roulade (Fr.). A series of quick notes sung on one syllable.

Roulement (Fr.). A roll on a drum or tambourine.

Roulement avec une double mailloche. Roll with a double-headed bass drumstick.

Rovesciamento, Rovescio (It.). Inversion, either of parts, or of a theme.

Rubando (It.). Robbing, stealing.

Rubato, -a (It.). Robbed. *v.* A tempo rubato.

Rückpositiv (Ger.). A choir organ, in which the pipes are placed at the back of the performer.

Rücksicht (Ger.). Consideration, regard. *Ohne Rücksicht auf den Takt,* without regard to the rhythm, *senza misura.*

Rückung (Ger.). Syncopation.

Rückweiser (Ger.). A repeat.

Rudement (Fr.). Roughly.

Rudement accentué. Roughly accented.

Ruhepunkt, Ruhezeichen (Ger.). A pause, *fermata.*

Ruhig (Ger.). Quiet, serene, tranquil.

Ruhig bewegt. Quietly animated.

Ruhige Achtel. The quavers tranquilly.

Ruhige, nicht zu langsame Bewegung. A quiet, but not too slow a movement.

Ruhig gehende Achtel. Gently moving quavers.

Ruhig gehend, nicht schleppend. With tranquil movement, but without dragging.

Ruhig, nicht schnell. Tranquil, not fast.

Ruhig und sanft. Quietly and softly.

Rührtrommel (Ger.). The tenor drum.

Rullante (It.). Rolling. *Tamburo rullante*, a tenor drum.

Russian horn. The Russian horn bands consisted of a number of performers (sometimes as many as 100), each of whom played only a single note of the scale. The horns, which are of varying length, are straight conical tubes with a mouthpiece at almost right angles.

Rustico (It.). Rustic, simple, rural.

Rut(h)e (Ger.). A rod. A kind of small broom formerly used in conjunction with an ordinary bass-drumstick, the latter striking the accented beats, and the former the unaccented. An example is to be found in Mozart's *Il Seraglio*. The *Rute* has been revived by Mahler, who has introduced it into several of his symphonies, using it as an effect apart, *i. e.* not as an accessory of the ordinary bass-drumstick. It is occasionally employed for striking a suspended cymbal, or even the rope-hoop of the bass-drum.

Rutscher (Ger.). A name for a galop.

Rythme (Fr.). Rhythm.

> **Rythme binaire.** Binary rhythm.
> **Rythme ternaire.** Ternary rhythm.

S

S. Abbr. of *segno, senza, sinistra, solo, sotto, subito.*

> **S-förmiges Mundstück.** The crook of a bassoon.
> **s. p.** Abbr. of *senza pedale.*
> **s. t.** Abbr. of *senza tempo.*
> **s. v.** Abbr. of *sotto voce.*

S' (Fr.). Abbr. of *se* or *si* before a vowel.

S' (It.). Abbr. of *si.*

> **S'alza subito il sipario.** The curtain rises suddenly.

Saccade (Fr.). A jerk; a sudden accent. In violin playing, a sudden pressure on one string for an accented note, or on three or four strings for producing the notes of a chord as simultaneously as possible.

Saccadé (Fr.). Accented in a sharp spasmodic manner.

Sackpfeife (Ger.). A bagpipe.

Sainete (Sp.). An interlude of a burlesque nature, accompanied by music and dancing.

Saite (Ger.). A string. plur. *Saiten.*

> **Saitenbezug.** A set of strings.
> **Saitenhalter.** Tail-piece of a stringed instrument.
> **Saiteninstrumente.** Stringed instruments.
> **Saite von Seide.** A silk string.
> **Saite von Stahl.** A steel string.

Salicional, Salicet, Salcional. An open organ pipe of delicate tone, of 16 ft in the pedal, and 8 ft (rarely 4 ft) in the manual.

Salmo (It.). A psalm.

Saltando (It.). Hopping, springing: a species of bowing, in which the bow hops or rebounds on the strings, used either for rapid reiterations of the same note, or for light staccato passages played with the middle of the bow.

Saltarello (It.). (1) A dance, usually in triple time, and distinguished by its "hopping" triplets. (2) A species of counterpoint, in which there are three quavers against one crotchet.

Saltato (It.). Hopped, rebounded. *cf*. Saltando.

Salteretto (It.). The figure 🎵 or 🎵.

Salterio *or* **Saltero** (It.). (1) The dulcimer. (2) A psalter, a hymn-book.

    Salterio tedesco. The dulcimer. The term, according to Lichtenthal, is the correct It. name of the instrument. Unfortunately, the Ger. term *Cymbal* has been Italianised into *cembalo*, which is also the usual It. abbr. of *clavicembalo*, and hence confusion has arisen between the two instruments.

Salto (It.). A leap, a skip from one note to another.

Salve Regina (Lat.). "Hail Queen!" The opening words of a hymn to the Virgin.

Samisen. A species of Japanese harmonica, consisting of a series of inverted bells, shaped like flattened gourds, surmounted by strips of bronze, which are struck with a felt-headed beater. Its sounds are not dissimilar to the harmonics on a harp, and the instrument has been employed in *Iris* (Mascagni) and *Madama Butterfly* (Puccini).

Sammlung (Ger.). A collection.

    Sammlung verschiedener Musikstücke. A collection of miscellaneous pieces of music, an olio.

Sampogna (It.). Bagpipe.

Sämtlich (Ger.). All, entire, the whole of.

    Sämtliche Sonaten. Complete sonatas.

Sanctus (Lat.). A part of the Mass, and of the Communion Service.

Sanft (Ger.). Gentle, delicate, sweet, soft. *Mit sanften Stimmen,* with soft stops (of an organ).

    Sanft belebt. Gently animated.

    Sanft bewegt. With gentle motion.

    Sanftflöte. Soft-toned flute (organ pipe).

    Sanft hervortretend. Softly brought out.

    Sanftgedackt. A soft-toned stopped organ pipe.

    Sanftklagend. Plaintive.

    Sanftmütig. Meek, soft-mannered.

Sänftig (Ger.). Softly, sweetly, etc.

Sänger (Ger.). A male singer.

Sängerin (Ger.). A female singer.

Sans (Fr.). Without.

    Sans accompagnement. Without accompaniment.

    Sans étouffer le son. Without damping the sound.

    Sans hâte. Without haste.

    Sans lenteur. Without slowness.

    Sans nuance. Without nuance, *i. e.* holding on a note with even strength.

    Sans pédale. Without the (damper) pedal.

Sans presser. Without hurrying.

Sans ralentir. Without slackening.

Sans reprise la 2e fois. Without repeat the 2nd time.

Sans sourdine. Without mute.

Sarabanda (It.). ⟩ A stately Spanish dance of Moorish origin, in ter-
Sarabande (Fr.). ⟩ nary time.

Sarrusophon (Ger.). ⟩ The sarrusophone. A brass instrument with
Sarrusophone (Fr.). ⟩ a conical bore, played with a double reed like
the oboe. Although made in various sizes: — Soprano, alto, tenor,
baritone, bass and contra-bass, the last named is now the only one
used in the orchestra or military band, where it takes the place of
the double-bassoon.

Sattel (Ger.). A saddle. The nut of a violin, etc.

> **Sattellage.** The half position on a violin, etc.
>
> **Sattel machen.** In violoncello music, to make a nut with the
> thumb for the highest positions.

Satz (Ger.). A composition; a movement; a period; a theme. In
hunting phraseology, a blast on a horn.

Saut (Fr.). A leap, skip from one note to another

Sautillé (Fr.). Hopped, jumped. *v* Saltato.

Saxhorn (Fr.). A saxhorn. The saxhorns constitute a family of
brass instruments with a conical bore and a bugle-like quality
of tone. They are made in the following sizes: — 1. Sopranino
B♭ (an octave above 3; this instrument sounding a 7th above the
written notes is scarcely ever used), 2. Soprano E♭ (*petit bugle*),
3. Contralto B♭ (*bugle*), 4. Alto E♭, 5. Baritone B♭, 6. Bass B♭ (of the
same length as 5, but with a wider bore and producing the lower
notes with greater facility), 7. Contrabass E♭, 8. Contrabass B♭.
The above is the Fr. nomenclature; in other countries, the adjective defining the pitch of the corresponding instrument is often
different, and this, together with the various names bestowed
by different makers, renders identification difficult. Thus, in Bel-
gium, 3. is sometimes described as a *bugle tenor*; in Italy, an instrument practically the same as 4. is called a *Flicorno basso*, whilst
in Germany 5. amongst other names is called a *Tenorbass*. The
usual English names are: — (1. and 2. unused), 3. Flügelhorn,
4. Althorn, Tenorhorn or Saxhorn, 5. Baritone, 6. Euphonium,
7. Bombardon, 8. Contrabass Bombardon; the two latter, when
built in circular form, being called Helicons. Nos 6, 7. and 8, are
constructed to reach the fundamental note, and are usually furnished with 4, sometimes 5 pistons; in the orchestra they are known
under the name of tubas (*q. v.*). In a brass band, the saxhorns
should number at least one half of the total number of instruments,
and in a military reed-band about one quarter. In the orchestra,
except 6, 7. and 8. as mentioned above, the saxhorns are but rarely
employed. 1. has been used by Berlioz (*Te Deum*) and Saint-Saëns
(*La Jeunesse d'Hercule*), while d'Indy in *Fervaal* uses 2. 3. 4. and
5, and Mahler and R. Strauss have used the Ger. equivalents of
some of these.

Saxophon (Ger.). ⟩ A saxophone. An instrument with a body of metal
Saxophone (Fr.). ⟩ (but not on that account classed amongst the
"Brass"), and played with a single reed like a clarinet. Unlike

a clarinet, it has a conical bore and therefore notes in the second register sound an octave and not a twelfth above those of the first register. There are 7 varieties: — Sopranino E♭, Soprano B♭, Alto E♭, Tenor B♭, Baritone E♭, Bass B♭ and Contrabass E♭, the first and last being seldom used. In most Fr. military bands 5 or 6 saxophones are used, and they are gradually being introduced into those of other countries. In the orchestra, Bizet, Thomas, Massenet, etc. have employed them as solo instruments with excellent effect, and Massenet and R. Strauss have each used a quartet of them.

Saxotromba (Fr.). A saxotromba. A brass instrument invented by Sax, and made in the same varieties as the saxhorns. They had a narrower bore and a quality of tone somewhat resembling that of the horn. They are no longer employed, but the instruments variously known as the Ballad Horn or Vocal Horn, the corhorn (*q. v.*), the cornophone (*q. v.*), and the Wagner tubas (*q. v.*) all more or less closely resemble them.

Saxtuba (Fr.). A saxtuba. A bass brass instrument invented by Sax. It is of powerful tone, and is found indicated in a few Fr. scores, but has been superseded by the contrabass saxhorn.

Saynète (Fr.). *v.* Sainete.

Sbalzo (It.). A leap, spring, rebound.

Sbarra (It.). A bar-line.

    Sbarria doppia. A double bar-line.

Scagnello (It.). The bridge of a violin, etc. *Ponticello* is the usual word.

Scala (It.). The scale.

    Scala cromatica. Chromatic scale.

    Scala diatonica. Diatonic scale.

Scelta (It.). Choice, selection. *A scelta del cantante*, at the choice of the singer.

Scemando (It.). Diminishing.

Scena (It.). Scene, stage, theatre; a portion of an act of an opera, during which no character makes an entrance or exit; a part of an opera for a solo voice, which is a mixture of recitative and *aria*.

Scenario (It.). The plot of a play or opera in a condensed form.

Scendete (It.). Descend. A term used in violin playing for descending towards the nut of the violin.

Scène (Fr.). Scene, stage, theatre. *v.* Scena. *Sur la scène*, on the stage.

Schäfer (Ger.). A shepherd.

    Schäferlied. A pastoral song.

    Schäfermäßig. adj. Pastoral.

    Schäferpfeife. A shepherd's pipe.

    Schäferspiel. A pastoral play.

    Schäfertanz. A shepherd's dance.

Schale (Ger.). A cymbal, *i. e.* one half of a pair of cymbals, which together are called *Becken*. *Beide Schalen*, both halves of the cymbals, *i. e.* the cymbals clashed in the ordinary way, after an indication that one of them should be struck with a drumstick.

    1 **Schale, freihängend mit Paukenschlägeln.** 1 suspended cymbal, with kettle-drumsticks.

Schalkhaft (Ger.). Roguish, waggish.
Schall (Ger.). Sound; tone; (of bells) peal, ringing.
    Schallbecher. The bell of wind-instruments.
    Schallbecken. Cymbals. Now always abbr. to *Becken.*
    Schallehre. Acoustics.
    Schallloch. Sound-hole of a violin, etc.
    Schallrohr. A speaking-trumpet: the tube of a brass instrument.
    Schalltrichter. The bell of wind-instruments.
    Schalltrichter auf. With up-turned bells. *v.* Bell.
Schalmei (Ger.). An obsolete reed instrument, which in Fr. is called a *Chalumeau,* although the true chalumeau is not the same as the *Schalmei,* which was a form of oboe, while the Fr. instrument had a cylindrical bore, and was a precursor of the clarinet. The *Schalmei,* in two sizes (*kleine* and *discant*), formed the treble of the *Pommer,* and like it had the two reeds covered over with a cap, in which was a hole through which the player blew. *Schalmei* is also the name of a reed-stop on the organ, and the term used for the chanter of a bagpipe.
Scharf (Ger.). Harsh, penetrating, sharp. The name of a mixture-stop on the organ.
    Scharf gespannt. Tightly braced. (Indication used for a tenor drum, as opposed to *tief gespannt,* slackly braced.)
    Scharf gestoßen. Sharply detached, very staccato.
    Scharf und spitzig. Sarcastic and biting.
Schattenhaft (Ger.). Shadowy, phantasmal.
Schauerig (Ger.). Gruesome. fearsome, grisly.
Schelle (Ger.). A little bell, grelot, jingle (of a tambourine). plur. *Schellen,* Sleigh-bells.
    Schellenbaum. The Turkish crescent.
    Schellengeläute. Sleigh-bells.
Schelmisch (Ger.). Knavish, roguish.
Scherz (Ger.). A joke, quip, jest.
Scherzando (It.). Trifling, dallying, jesting. Indicating a light playful execution.
Scherzante (It.). Playful, sportive.
Scherzantissimo (It.). Sup. of *scherzante.*
Scherzend (Ger.). *v.* Scherzando.
Scherzettino, Scherzetto (It.). A little scherzo.
Scherzevole (It.). Playful, facetious.
Scherzevolmente (It.). Full of playfulness.
Scherzhaft (Ger.). Playful, merry, jocular.
Scherzi (It.). Plur. of *scherzo.*
Scherzino (It.). A little scherzo.
Scherzo (It.). A joke, pleasantry, raillery. Although used for the name of a musical composition as far back as Monteverde, and employed by Bach, the true Scherzo may be said to have originated with Haydn and to have been perfected by Beethoven. Its form is founded on that of the minuet, the place of which it often takes in sonatas and symphonies.
Scherzosamente (It.). Facetiously, in jest.
Schiettamente (It.). Simply, plainly, unadorned.
Schietto (It.). Pure, honest, sincere.

Schlacht (Ger.). Battle.
    Schlachthymne. Battle hymn.
    Schlachtlied. Battle song.
    Schlachtmusik. Battle (martial) music.
Schlag (Ger.). A blow, knock.
    Schlag der Trommel. A beat of the drum.
    Schlag einer Kanone. A report of a canon.
    Schlagfeder. The plectrum of a mandoline, etc.
    Schlagfell. The batterhead, or striking end of a drum.
    Schlaginstrumente. Percussion instruments.
Schlägel (Ger.). The drumstick of a kettledrum or snare-drum, that of a bass drum being called a *Klöpfel.* plur. *Schlägel.*
Schläger (Ger.). A drummer.
Schleif- (Ger.). Used in combination. *cf.* Schleifen.
    Schleifbogen. A slur.
    Schleifnote. A slurred or tied note.
    Schleifstrich. A dash.
    Schleifzeichen. A slur.
Schleifen (Ger.). To slur. subs. The slider of an organ.
Schleifer (Ger.). A species of double appoggiatura: a rapid series of conjunct notes before the principal note. *cf.* Fusée.
Schleppen (Ger.). To drag.
Schleppend (Ger.). Dragging (the tempo). *Nicht schleppend,* without dragging.
Schluß (Ger.). Conclusion, end.
    Schlußfall. A cadence.
    Schlußsatz. Concluding movement.
    Schlußzeichen. The double bar, usually with a ⌢ above, which marks the close of a movement (such as a scherzo), in which there are repeats.
Schlüssel (Ger.). A clef.
Schmachtend (Ger.). Languishing, yearning.
Schmeichelnd (Ger.). Coaxing, flattering.
Schmelzend (Ger.). Languishing, mellow, melodious.
Schmerz (Ger.). Pain, affliction.
    Schmerzhaft. ⎰
    Schmerzlich. ⎱ Painful, dolorous.
Schmetternd (Ger.). Shrill, ringing, clanging. In modern Ger. scores it is used (against the brass) as an equivalent of the Fr. *cuivré.*
Schnabel (Ger.). A beak; the mouthpiece of a clarinet or saxophone *cf.* Bec.
    Schnabelflöte. The *flûte-à-bec.*
Schnarre (Ger.). A rattle. *Schnarr-* in combination. *cf.* Knarre.
    Schnarrpfeife. A reed-pipe in an organ.
    Schnarrsaiten. The snare of a side-drum.
    Schnarrtrommel. A snare (side) drum.
    Schnarrwerk. The reed-work of an organ.
Schnarren (Ger.). To rattle, buzz, vibrate; to sing falsetto.
Schnecke (Ger.). The scroll of a violin, etc.
Schnell (Ger.). Swift, rapid, nimble, quick.
    Schnell abdämpfen. Quickly damp (the strings of a harp, vibrating cymbal, etc.).

Schnell und drängend. Quick and hurried.
Schnell und schattenhaft. Fast and shadowy.
Schnell und stürmisch. Quick and stormy.
Schnell und zart. Quickly and delicately.
Schnell wie zuerst. As fast as at the commencement.
Schneller (Ger.). Quicker. subs. An embellishment; an inverted mordent or passing shake.
   Schneller werdend. Becoming quicker.
Schnelligkeit (Ger.). Speed, quickness, nimbleness. *Nun wieder auf die Schnelligkeit des ersten Tempo zugehend*, now returning to the speed of the first tempo.
Schottisch, -e (Ger.). Scotch. subs. An *écossaise*.
Schräge Bewegung (Ger.). Oblique motion.
Schreibart (Ger.). Style.
Schreiend (Ger.). Screaming, shrieking.
Schüchtern (Ger.). Shy, modest, retiring.
Schusterfleck (Ger.). A rosalia (*q. v.*).
Schütteln (Ger.). To shake (a tambourine).
Schwach (Ger.). Weak, feeble, delicate.
Schwächer (Ger.). Fainter, weaker.
Schwägel (Ger.). A tabor-pipe. *v.* Schwegel.
Schwankend (Ger.). Faltering, swaying, wavering.
Schwanz (Ger.). The tail or stem of a note.
Schwärmer (Ger.). The rapid repetition of a series of notes, each being repeated four or more times.
Schwebung (Ger.). A tremor, waving. In organ stops, tremulant. plur. *Schwebungen*, beats or pulsations between two notes nearly equivalent in pitch.
Schwegel (Ger.). (1) An organ pipe found in old organs. (2) The tabor-pipe or *galoubet*, a *flûte-à-bec* with 2 ventages for the fingers and 1 for the thumb. Also written *Schwiegel* or *Schwägel*.
Schweif (Ger.). Tail, *coda*.
Schweigen, Schweigezeichen (Ger.). A pause.
Schweigt (Ger.). Is silent, *tacet*.
Schweizer (Ger.). Swiss.
   Schweizerpfeife. A cross-flute, *flauto traverso*. Also the name of a pipe found in old organs.
Schwellen (Ger.). To swell, increase in loudness. Also used as a subs.
Schweller (Ger.). The swell of an organ. *Schwell-* in combination.
   Schwellkasten. Swell box.
   Schwellton. A note swelled upon.
   Schwelltritt. Swell pedal.
   Schwellwerk. Swell organ.
Schwer (Ger.). Heavy, weighty, *pesante*. Hard, difficult.
   Schwer und kräftig, nicht zu schnell. Ponderous and powerful, not too fast.
   Schwer und zurückhaltend. Ponderous and slackening.
Schwermütig (Ger.). ⎫
Schwermutsvoll (Ger.). ⎬ Melancholy, sad.
Schwindend (Ger.). Diminishing, vanishing, *smorzando*.
Schwungvoll (Ger.). Full of fire and enthusiasm.
Scialumo (It.). *v.* Chalumeau.

Scintillante (It.). Sparkling, bright.
Scioltamente (It.). With freedom, freely, fluently.
Scioltezza (It.). Freedom, liberty, nimbleness.
Sciolto, -a (It.). Free, unshackled. *Canone sciolto*, free canon; *contrappunto sciolto*, free counterpoint. In violin playing, the *grand détaché* (*q. v.*).
Scolare (It.). Scholar, pupil.
Scordato (It.). Out-of-tune, mis-tuned.
Scordatura (It.). The tuning of a violin etc., in other than its ordinary manner, *e. g.* the solo violin in the *Danse Macabre*, with the E string tuned to *e''♭*.
Score. Term usually used in the sense of a full score (*q. v.*). A *piano* score is a full score arranged for piano solo; a *vocal* score is the arrangement for piano or organ of the orchestral parts of a full score, which contains voice parts, these latter being left intact.
Scorrendo (It.). Gliding.
Scozzese (It.). Scotch.
Scucito (It.). Unconnected, discursive.
Scuola (It.). School, college.
Sdegnante (It.). Disdainful, scornful.
Sdegno (It.). Indignation, wrath, anger.
Sdegnosamente (It.). Scornfully, indignantly.
Sdegnoso, -a (It.). Scornful, angry.
Sdrucciolando (It.). Sliding, gliding.
Se (Fr.). Himself, herself, themselves.
Se (It.). conj. If, in case, provided that. pron. Oneself, himself, etc.
Sec, sèche (Fr.). ⎰ Dry, hard, plain, unornamented. Often found
Secco, -a (It.). ⎱ indicated against chords, which are to be played in a sharp staccato manner.
Sechs (Ger.). Six.
    Sechsachteltakt. Six-eight time.
    Sechsstimmig. For six voices or instruments.
    Sechsvierteltakt. Six-four time.
    Sechszehnfüssig(füßig). Of sixteen feet.
    Sechszehntelnote. A semiquaver.
    Sechszehntelpause. A semiquaver rest.
Second, -nde (Fr.). Second. *La seconde flûte prendre la petite flûte*, the second flute to take the piccolo.
    Second dessus. Second treble.
    Seconde fois. Second time.
Seconda (It.). The interval of a second.
    Seconda eccedente. Augmented second.
    Seconda maggiore. Major second.
    Seconda minore. Minor second.
Secondando (It.). Seconding, supporting. Indication to the accompanist to adapt himself to the soloist.
Seconde (Fr.). The interval of a second.
    Seconde augmentée. Augmented second.
    Seconde majeure. Major second.
    Seconde mineure. Minor second.
Secondo, -a (It.). Second. *Trombone secondo*, second trombone.
    Seconda volta. The 2nd time

Sedecima (It.). The interval of a sixteenth.

Seele (Ger.). Soul, mind, feeling. plur. and in combination, *Seelen*.

   Seelenamt. }
   Seelenmesse. } Mass for the dead.

   Seelenvoll. Full of soul, feeling.

Seg. Abbr. of *segno*.

Segno (It.). Sign. *v.* Al segno, Dal segno.

   Segno d'aspetto. Pause, rest.

Segue (It.). Follows. *E poi segue la coda*, and then follows the coda, *i. e.* one proceeds to the coda without a break. The word is sometimes used in the sense of *simile*, and means that the pattern set in the first bar as regards phrasing, bowing, etc., is to be followed in the subsequent bars.

Seguendo (It.). Following.

Seguente (It.). That which follows or comes after.

Seguidilla (Sp.). A lively dance in $3/4$ or $3/8$ time.

Seguito (It.). A suite.

Sehnsucht (Ger.). Longing, yearning.

Sehnsüchtig (Ger.). adj. Longing, yearning, anxious

Sehr (Ger.). Very, much, extremely.

   Sehr allmählich immer etwas langsamer. Becoming very gradually slower.

   Sehr allmählich immer stärker bis . . . Becoming very gradually louder till . . .

   Sehr angenehm. Very pleasing.

   Sehr ausdrucksvoll. Very expressive.

   Sehr bestimmt. Very decided.

   Sehr bewegt. Very animated.

   Sehr breit und schwer. Very broad and ponderous.

   Sehr fest und rhythmisch. Very firmly and rhythmically.

   Sehr frisch. Very brightly.

   Sehr gebunden. Very smoothly.

   Sehr gehalten aber nicht gebunden. Very sustained but not slurred.

   Sehr gehalten und betont. Very sustained and accentuated.

   Sehr gemessen, fast langsam. Very slow, almost *adagio*.

   Sehr geschwind. Very fast.

   Sehr getragen. Very sustained; very *portamento*.

   Sehr heftig. Very vehemently.

   Sehr hervortretend. Very prominent.

   Sehr innig. Very heartfelt (with great emotion).

   Sehr kräftig. Very powerfully.

   Sehr kräftig gestoßen. Very strongly detached.

   Sehr kräftig und gut zu halten, doch ohne zu binden. Very powerful and well sustained, without being legato.

   Sehr kurz gestoßen. Very shortly detached.

   Sehr langsam, frei deklamierend, sentimental im Vortrag. Very slow, freely declaimed, and played with delicate feeling

   Sehr lebhaft. Very animated.

   Sehr leichtweg. Very lightly.

   Sehr leise. Very softly.

   Sehr lieblich. Very sweetly.

Sehr markiert. Very marked.
Sehr mäßig bewegt. Very moderately animated.
Sehr mäßig und immer noch langsamer. Very moderate, and
  always becoming slower.
Sehr sanft. Very softly.
Sehr scharf und spitzig. Very sarcastic and bitter.
Sehr schnell. Very fast.
Sehr schnell und noch mehr beschleunigend. Very fast, and
  becoming still faster.
Sehr schnell und schmetternd. Very fast and resonant. *v.*
  Schmetternd.
Sehr stark. Very loud.
Sehr stark ausgehalten. Very strongly sustained.
Sehr weich. Very tenderly.
Sehr weich und klangvoll. Very soft and full (resonant)
Sehr zart. Very sweetly.
Sehr zurückhaltend. Very much retarding the tempo.
Sei (It.). Six.
Seite (Ger.). Side; end of a drum. *Auf beiden Seiten von 2 Spielern
  mit Paukenschwammschlägeln,* at both ends, by 2 players with
  kettle-drumsticks of sponge. plur. and in combination, *Seiten.*
  Seitenbewegung. Oblique motion.
  Seitensatz. A second subject.
Seizième (Fr.). Sixteenth.
  Seizième de soupir. A semi-demisemiquaver rest.
Sekunde (Ger.). The interval of a second. *Eine große Sekunde,* a
  major second; *eine übermäßige Sekunde,* an augmented second.
Sem. Abbr. of *sempre.*
Semi- (It.). Used in combination, and meaning a half, or less than
  a whole.
  Semibiscroma. A semi-demisemiquaver.
  Semibreve. A semibreve.
  Semicadenza. A half close.
  Semiditono. A minor third.
  Semiminima. A crotchet.
  Semitrillo. A shake, in which the principal note alternates only
    once with the grace-note.
  Semituono. A semitone.
Semplice (It.). Simple, pure.
Semplicemente (It.). Simply, plainly.
Semplicità (It.). Simplicity.
Sempre (It.). Always, continually. (*v.* Remark under *Immer.*)
  Sempre accelerando. Continually becoming faster.
  Sempre a mézza voce. Always with half the power of the voice
    or instrument.
  Sempre col pedale ad ogni cambiamento d'armonia. With the
    pedal at every change of harmony.
  Sempre con gran dolcezza e grazia. Always with great sweet-
    ness and grace.
  Sempre con pedale e con sordino. Always with the pedal and
    the mute, *i. e.* using both the pedals.
  Sempre diminuendo e calmato. Always becoming softer and calmer.

Sempre non divisi. Always undivided.

Sempre più affrettando il tempo. Continually hurrying the time.

Sempre più di fuoco. Always with more spirit.

Sempre pizzicato. Always pizzicato.

Sempre rinforzando. Always laying stress (on the phrases). *v.* Rinforzando.

Sensibile (It.). Sensible, perceptible. *Nota sensibile*, the leading note.

Sensibilità (It.). *⎰* Sensibility, tenderness.
Sensibilité (Fr.). *⎱*

Sensibilmente (It.). Sensibly, perceptibly.

Sensible (Fr.). Sensible, perceptible; tenderhearted *Note sensible*, the leading note.

Sentiment (Fr.). *⎰* Sentiment, feeling.
Sentimento (It.). *⎱*

Senza (It.). Without.

    Senza accompagnamento. Without accompaniment.

    Senza fiori. Without embellishments.

    Senza glissare. Without gliding.

    Senza organo. Without organ.

    Senza passione, ma espressivo. Without passion, but with expression.

    Senza replica. Without repeat.

    Senza rigore del tempo. Without strictness in the tempo.

    Senza ripetizione. Without repetition, without repeat.

    Senza ritardare. Without slackening.

    Senza sordini. Without mutes. *v.* Sordino.

    Senza tempo. Not in strict time.

Septett (Ger.). *⎰* A septet; a composition for seven voices or in-
Septetto (It.). *⎱* struments.

Septième (Fr.). Seventh; the interval of a seventh.

    Septième diminuée. Diminished seventh.

Septime (Ger.). Interval of a seventh.

    Septimenakkord. Chord of the seventh.

Septimole, Septole (Ger.). A septuplet; a group of 7 equal notes in place of 4 or 6.

Septuor (Fr.). A septet.

Sequenza (It.). A sequence. (1) The repetition of a melodic figure or harmonic progression at a different pitch. (2) A hymn sung on certain festivals at High Mass.

Sérénade (Fr.). *⎰* A serenade. (1) A composition intended to be sung
Serenata (It.). *⎱* during the evening or night under the windows of a person (often a lady), whom the singer wishes to honour. (2) A vocal composition much like a cantata, or an instrumental one in several movements. The Ger. of (1) is *Ständchen*, of (2) *Serenade*.

Sereno, -a (It.). Calm, tranquil.

Sérieux, -euse (Fr.). Serious, grave.

Serio, -a (It.). Serious, grave. *Opera seria*, a serious (tragic) opera, as opposed to *opera buffa*, a comic opera.

Serioso, -a (It.). The same as *serio*, and little used.

Serpeggiando (It.). Winding, meandering, creeping.

Serpent. An instrument in the shape of a large S made of wood covered with leather, and played with a cup-shaped mouthpiece. Its compass is from $B_1\flat$ to $b'\flat$. Although used by Mendelssohn and Wagner, the instrument is practically obsolete: it has recently (1904) been revived by Klose in *Das Leben ein Traum*. The instrument was made in two forms, *v.* below.

Serpent (Fr.). The serpent.

    Serpent d'église. The church serpent, the instrument of the shape usually found in churches.

    Serpent d'harmonie. ⎱ The military serpent, an instrument
    Serpent militaire. ⎰ differing in shape from the above, in that the arm could be passed through it, and thus it was more adapted for marching purposes, and especially for use in cavalry bands. Berlioz has indicated a serpent of this shape in his early Mass (the *Resurrexit* of which is given in the Berlioz Edition, Vol. VII, where the part is marked for a tuba) perhaps because the ordinary church serpent would be at a different pitch from that of the usual orchestral instruments.

Serpentone (It.). A serpent.

Serrando (It.). Squeezing, compressing, *i. e.* bringing the notes closer together, and thus becoming faster.

Serrant (Fr.). *En serrant*, becoming faster. *cf.* Serrando.

Serrato (It.). Compressed, tightened. *cf.* Serrando.

Serré (Fr.). *v.* Serrato.

Serrez (Fr.). Tighten, press.

    Serrez peu à peu le mouvement. Gradually quicken the movement.

Sesquialtera. An organ stop of from 3 to 6 ranks of open metal pipes, tuned in 3rds, 5ths and 8ths to the diapasons.

Sesta (It.). The interval of a sixth.

    Sesta eccedente. Augmented sixth.

    Sesta maggiore. Major sixth.

    Sesta minore. Minor sixth.

Sestetto (It.). A sextet; a composition for 6 instruments or voices

Sestina (It.). (1) A stanza of six lines. (2) A group of six notes.

Settima (It.). The interval of a seventh.

    Settima diminuita. Diminished seventh.

    Settima maggiore. Major seventh.

    Settima minore. Minor seventh.

Setzart (Ger.). The style of a composition.

Setzkunst (Ger.). The art of composing, composition.

Seufzend (Ger.). Moaning, sighing.

Seul, seule (Fr.). Alone, solo. 3 *violins seuls*, 3 solo violins.

Severamente (It.). Severely, rigidly.

Sexte (Ger.). The interval of a sixth. *Sext-* in combination; plur. *Sexten. Übermäßige Sexte*, an augmented sixth.

    Sextakkord. The chord of the 6th.

    Sextenfolgen. A sequence of sixths.

Sextett (Ger.). A sextet, a composition for six voices or instruments.

Sextole (Ger.). A sextolet; a group of six equal notes.

Sextuor (Fr.). A sextet.

Sf. Abbr. of *sforzando* or *sforzato*. Used as a subs. as *Das sf und pp nicht vernachlässigen*, pay attention to the *sf* and *pp*.

Sfoggiando (It.). Pompous, splendid, extravagant.

Sforzando (It.). Laying a stress or accent on a particular note, as opposed to *rinforzando*, laying a stress on a particular phrase, or group of notes. This distinction is however not always observed.

Sforzar la voce (It.). To force the voice.

Sforzatissimo (It.). Sup. of *sforzato*.

Sforzato (It.). Accented, marked. *cf.* Sforzando. Used as a subs. as *poco marc. gli sforzati*, the *sforzati* with only slight accentuation.

Sforzo (It.). Effort, strain; a defect of the voice, which proceeds from a violent contraction of the glottis.

Sfuggito, -a (It.). Avoided. *Cadenza sfugitta*, an interrupted cadence.

Sfz. Abbr. of *sforzando*, *sforzato*.

Sgambato (It.). Tired, weary.

Sganasciare (It.). To dislocate the jaws. To laugh or sing with wide-open jaws.

Sgrisciare (It.). To "quack" on reed instruments.

Shift. The movement of the hand on the fingerboard of a violin, etc., often used as synonymous with "position". The difference between the two is that the player proceeds by degrees of the scale in the positions, and by skips in shifts: thus, on the G (4th) string of the violin, in the 1st position the notes *a*, *b*, *c'* are stopped by the 1st, 2nd and 3rd fingers, in the 2nd, the notes *b*, *c'*, *d'*, in the 3rd, the notes *c'*, *d'*, *e'* and so on. On the other hand, one does not "shift" until the notes in the 1st position are exhausted, *e. g.* having stopped *a*, *b*, *c'*, the hand is moved sufficiently for the fingers to stop *d'*, *e'*, *f'*.

Si (Fr.). (1) If. (2) The note B.

> **Si bémol.** B flat.
> **Si bémol mineur.** B flat minor.
> **Si dièse.** B sharp.

Si (It.). (1) The note B. (2) Practically corresponding to the Fr. *on* or Ger. *man* (one, people, etc.) although strictly speaking it is the pronoun of the reflective verb. *Si dice*, one says (it is said).

> **Si accorda in fa grave colla quinta do.** One tunes (the kettle-drums) in low F with the fifth C.
> **Si bemolle.** B flat.
> **Si bemolle maggiore.** B flat major.
> **Si deve suonare tutto questo pezzo delicatissimamente, e senza sordini.** The whole of this piece must be played with the greatest delicacy and without the mutes. (For the two readings of this direction *v.* Sordino.)
> **Si leva il sordino.** Take off the mute.
> **Si levano i sordini.** Take off the mutes.
> **Si piace.** At pleasure, *ad libitum*.
> **Si possono omettere le battute tra le due A.** The bars between the two A-s can be omitted.
> **Si può, volendo, saltare le 12 battute da ✻ a ✻.** The 12 bars from ✻ to ✻ can be omitted at pleasure.
> **Si replica.** One repeats, *i. e.* the section is to be repeated.
> **Si scriva.** As written.
> **Si tace.** One is silent.
> **Si volta.** Turn over (one turns over).

Si volti subito. (Please) turn over quickly.

Sich (Ger.). Oneself; himself, herself, itself. Used with reflective verbs.

    Sich aufrichtend in höchster Demütigung. Drawing herself up in extreme humiliation. (*St. Elisabeth*, Liszt.)

    Sich verlierend. Disappearing, vanishing.

    Sich Zeit lassen. (To) allow oneself time. *v.* Remark I.

Siciliana, Siciliano (It.). } Sicilian. subs. A dance of moderate
Sicilienne (Fr.).   } movement in $^6/_8$ or $^6/_{12}$ time.

Side drum. A drum made in various shapes, but always possessing the characteristic of a "snare", *i. e.* catgut strings stretched across the lower end, or "snarehead" of the instrument, and imparting to its tone that peculiar burring rattling. The upper end, or "batterhead" is played upon by two wooden drumsticks, and must always be so tight as to allow of the drumsticks freely rebounding. The idea that this head should ever be slackly braced is erroneous, although for special effects it may be more tightly braced than ordinarily. The instrument is at times directed to be "muffled": this is usually done by placing a handkerchief between the snare and the membrane of the drum; sometimes the snare is relaxed, or unhooked at one end; and occasionally the drum is played in its linen cover. Owing to the confusion which so often arises between this instrument and the Tenor drum (*q. v.*), it would be preferable if it were always called the "Snare-drum".

Sieben (Ger.). Seven.

Sieg (Ger.). Victory, triumph in battle, conquest. *Sieges-* in combination.

    Siegesgesang. A song of victory.

    Siegeslied. A song or hymn of victory, a pæan.

    Siegesmarsch. Triumphal march.

Signalhorn (Ger.). *v.* Buglehorn.

Signaturen (Ger.). The figures and signs used in figured bass.

Signe (Fr.). A sign. *Allez au signe* ✼, go to sign ✼.

Signs. The principal signs used in modern music are the following: —

    . Above or below a note, signifies that it is to be detached, and played *staccato*, or, more strictly speaking, *spiccato*.

    ' Above or below a note, signifies that it is to be very detached. This is the true *staccato* on the piano.

    Above or below notes, signifies that they are to be detached, but not so much as in either of the above cases. With stringed instruments, this is the true *staccato*, and consists in the bow advancing by a series of small jerks without ever leaving the strings. It is only found in solo playing, since it is difficult of execution. In piano playing, it is called *mezzo staccato*.

Written.   Played.

— Above or below a note, signifies that it is to be sustained for its full value, without however being tied to the following note.

⸗ The note sustained and slightly accentuated.

⸗ ⸗ ⸗ ⸗ ⸗ The notes somewhat more sustained than with merely dots above.

‿ The slur or tie. It is called the latter, when it is placed above or below two notes of the same pitch, and indicates that they have to be played like one note equal in length to the two together. It is called a slur, when placed over or under two or more notes not of the same pitch, and then signifies that they are to be played or sung in the same bow or breath. Occasionally the length of the slur precludes this, and it must then be taken as a general indication that the whole passage must be as *legato* as possible.

➤ or ≺ *Rinforzando*, laying particular stress on a note or group of notes.

∧ or ∨ *Sforzando* or *sforzato*, laying stress on a particular note.

≺ *Crescendo*, growing louder.

➤ *Decrescendo*, growing softer.

⊓ Downbow. It is also used for *pizzicato* chords, in which the finger is drawn towards the player, *e. g.* from the 4th to the 1st string in the violin.

∨ Upbow. It is also used for *pizzicato* chords, in which the finger moves away from the player, *e. g.* from the 1st to the 4th string in the violin.

⊙ The thumb position in violoncello playing.

○ Placed above horn notes, indicates that they are to be *open* notes. In music for Strings, it signifies either an *open* string, or an harmonic. In harp music, it indicates an harmonic (the actual sound being an octave above the written note), and now-a-days is often discarded, the harp note being written with a square head instead, *i. e.*

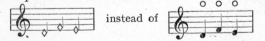

instead of

+ Usually signifies a *closed* note on the horn. Wagner however occasionally uses it to indicate a note on the horn not only closed but also made *brassy* (*cuivré*).

' Sign for taking breath, used both for voices and wind instruments. It also found in string and other parts to indicate an almost imperceptible break in the continuity of the music.

∫ & / Signs of the *portamento* in old music and modern orchestral scores.

[or (In piano music, means that two notes on different staves are to be played with the same hand: in string parts, it indicates the use of the double string.

⌢ Above a note or rest, signifies that its time-value is to be increased at the discretion of the player; above a bar-line, it denotes a break in the continuity of the music.

/ Sign of a glissando passage on a harp, the top and bottom notes being alone given.

∽ The sign for a turn (*gruppetto*).

Silence (Fr.). } Silence; a rest, pause.
Silenzio (It.). }

Sillet (Fr.). The nut of violins, guitars, etc.

Sim. Abbr. of *simile*.

Simile (It.). Like, similar. An indication showing that the pattern set in a previous bar, as regards phrasing, etc., is to be still adhered to.

Simili (It.). Plur. of *simile*, and used in the same sense.

Simple (Fr.). Simple: natural. *Contrepoint simple*, simple counterpoint; *trompette simple*, natural trumpet.

Simplement (Fr.). Simply. Indication signifying an unaffected execution.

Simplice, Simplicità (It.). *v.* Semplice, Semplicità.

Sin' (It.). Contraction of *sino* (until).
   Sin' al fine. Until the end.

Sincopa (It.). Syncopation.

Sincopato, -a (It.). Syncopated.

Sinfonia (It.). A symphony. The term used to be employed for an overture, but since symphonies have been performed and written in Italy *sinfonia* has been employed almost exclusively for a symphony, and an overture has been called *overtura*.

Sinfonico, -a (It.). Symphonic. *Poema sinfonico*, symphonic poem.

Sinfonie. A spelling of *Symphonie* occasionally found in ancient French and modern German.

Sinfonietta (It.). A little symphony, *e. g.* Raff's *sinfonietta* for 10 wind instruments.

Sing- (Ger.). Used in combination. *cf.* Singen.
   Singakademie. Singing school.
   Singbar. Singable.
   Singbaß. A vocal (as opposed to an instrumental) bass.
   Singchor. Choir; chorus of singers.
   Singfuge. A vocal fugue.
   Singkunst. The art of singing.
   Singlehrer. A singing master.
   Singlehrerin. A singing mistress.
   Singmanieren. Vocal embroideries.
   Singmeister. A master of singing; a great singer.
   Singnoten. Vocal music.
   Singoper. An opera set to music throughout, without spoken dialogue.
   Singschule. A school for singing.
   Singspiel. An operetta.
   Singstimme. (Singing) voice; vocal part. *Lied für eine Singstimme*, song for a single voice.
   Singstück. A vocal piece.
   Singstunde. Singing lesson.
   Singtanz. A dance accompanied by singing.

Singweise. (1) Way or manner of singing. (2) Air, melody, tune.

Singen (Ger.). To sing.

Singend (Ger.). Singing; singingly, *cantabile*.

Singhiozzando (It.). Sobbing.

Sinistro, -a (It.). Left. *Mano sinistra*, or simply *sinistra*, the left hand.

Sinn (Ger.). Sense; the sensitive faculties; soul, heart.

Sino, Sin' (It.). Till, until.

    Sin' al fine. 〕
    Sino alla fine. 〉Until the end.
    Sino fine. 〕

    Sino al segno. Until the sign.

Sipario (It.). The curtain of a theatre.

Sistre (Fr.). A sistrum.

Sistro (It.). Formerly a sistrum; now the term used for a *Glockenspiel*.

Sistrum (Lat.). A species of metal rattle dating back to the time of the ancient Egyptians. It has been used by Massenet and some other modern composers for picturesque effects.

Sitz (Ger.). Seat. The degree of the scale on which a chord has its lowest note, thus, the 1st inversion of the common chord of C has its *Sitz* on E.

Sixième (Fr.). Sixth; the interval of a sixth.

Sixte (Fr.). The interval of a sixth.

Skala (Ger.). Scale, gamut. *Naturskala*, the natural scale.

Skizze (Ger.). A sketch. plur. *Skizzen*.

Slancio (It.). Rush, dash, impetuosity.

Slarg. Abbr. of *slargando*.

Slargando (It.). Widening, enlarging. Slackening the time, *rallentando*.

Slargandosi (It.). The reflective form of *slargando*.

Slegato (It.). Untied, loosed. The opposite to *legato*.

Slentando (It.). Improperly used for *lentando*.

Slide. (1) A vocal or instrumental ornament consisting of two grace notes before the principal note. The term is not now much employed in English. (2) A movable piece of tubing on brass instruments used for tuning purposes, and in the Slide Trombone and Trumpet, of sufficient length to admit of the various elongations of the tube necessary for producing the chromatic scale.

    Slide trombone. *v.* Trombone.

    Slide trumpet. An instrument employed almost exclusively in England, and now little used. By means of the slide the pitch can be lowered a tone or a semitone, and thus a complete chromatic scale from *g* upwards (with the exception of *a*, *a♭*, *c'♯*) is obtained. An instrument is also made on which these missing notes are obtainable, but it is not often found.

Sliders. Part of the mechanism of an organ, whereby the draw-stop places the pipes in a condition to speak when the keys are pressed.

Smania (It.). Frenzy, rage.

Smaniante (It.). Frenzied, furious, passionate.

Smaniare (It.). To rave, to storm, to be in a fury.

Smanicare (It.). To shift on a violin, guitar, etc.

Smanioso, -a (It.). Furious, rabid, eager.
Sminuendo (It.). The same as *diminuendo*.
Sminuito (It.). The same as *diminuito*.
Smorendo (It.). Diminishing, *smorzando*.
Smorfioso (It.). Affected, prim.
Smorz. Abbr. of *smorzando*, *smorzato*.
Smorzando (It.). Extinguishing, quenching (the sound).
Snare-drum. The side-drum (*q. v.*)
Smorzato (It.). Extinguished.
Snello (It.). Nimble, agile, alert.
So (Ger.). So, in this manner, as.
　　So rasch als möglich. }
　　So schnell wie möglich. } As fast as possible.
　　So zahlreich wie möglich. As numerous as possible.
Soave (It.). Gentle, soft, suave, tranquil.
Soavemente. Gently, softly.
Soavità (It.). Sweetness, gentleness.
Società (It.). Society, club.
　　Società del Quartetto. Quartet Society.
Soffocando, Soffogando (It.). Damping the sounds of the harp with
　　the hand.
Soffocato, Soffogato (It.). Damped. *v.* above.
Sofort (Ger.). Immediately, at once.
　　Sofort abdämpfen und nicht arpeggiert. Damp immediately and
　　　　not in arpeggio. (Direction to harp.)
Soggetto (It.). Subject.
Sogleich (Ger.). The same as *sofort*.
　　Sogleich das erste Zeitmaß. Immediately the first tempo.
Sol (Fr.). The note G.
　　Sol bémol. G flat.
　　Sol dièse. G sharp.
Sol (It.). The note G.
　　Sol bemolle. G flat.
　　Sol diesis. G sharp.
Sola (It.). Fem. of *solo*. *Viola sola*, solo viola.
Solenne (It.). Solemn, grave, splendid.
Solennel, -elle (Fr.). Solemn. *Solennellement*, solemnly.
Solennemente (It.). Solemnly.
Sol(l)ennis, Sol(l)emnis (Lat.). Solemn. *Missa solemnis*, solemn Mass.
Solennità (It.). }
Solennité (Fr.). } Solemnity, celebration.
Solfa (It.). Subs. The scale or gamut in the old system of naming
　　the notes by the names *do* (*ut*), *re*, *mi*, *fa*, *sol*, *la*, *si*. The term is
　　sometimes used to express music in general. In Eng. it is used as
　　a verb, and to "solfa" is to sing the above or similar syllables.
　　Battere la solfa, to beat time.
Solfège (Fr.). A singing exercise on the syllables given in the previous
　　paragraph.
Solfeggiare (It.). To solfa.
Solfeggio (It.). *v.* Solfège.
Solfeggieren (Ger.). }
Solfier (Fr.). } To solfa.

Soli (It.). Plur. of *solo.* When used substantively, "solos" is a perfectly legitimate plural in Eng., since *solo* is now anglicised.

Solito (It.). Accustomed, habituated. *Al solito,* as usual.

Sollecitando (It.). Hastening.

Sollecito (It.). Careful, anxious: eager, prompt.

Solmizzare (It.). To solfa.

Solo, -a (It.). Alone, only, solo. The word is also used as a subs. in most languages. In orchestral scores the term is marked against a particular passage which is to be made prominent, although in modern Ger. works it is now generally replaced by *hervortretend, bestimmt,* or some such expression. In concertos, the passages where the solo instrument enters are often marked "solo" in contradistinction to the *Tutti.*

>   **Solo organ.** One of the manuals of an organ, the stops of which are mainly more or less faithful imitations of orchestral instruments, and suited rather for solo work than for combination.

Solo- (Ger.). Used in combination.

>   **Solosänger.** A solo singer (masc.).
>   **Solosängerin.** A solo singer (fem.).
>   **Solospieler.** A solo player.

Soltanto (It.). adv. Only, solely, but. *La tromba soltanto,* trumpet alone.

Sombre (Fr.). Dull, melancholy, sombre.

Sommo, -a (It.). Supreme, greatest, utmost. *Con somma passione,* with the utmost passion.

Sommesso, -a (It.). Subdued, humbled. *Con voce sommessa,* in a low voice.

Sommier (Fr.). The wind-chest of an organ.

Son (Fr.). (1) His, her, its. (2) A sound. *v.* Sons.

Sonabile (It.). Sounding, resonant.

Sonagliare (It.). To tinkle, to ring small bells.

Sonagliato, -a (It.). Tinkling.

Sonaglierà (It.). A collar of small bells such as is worn by sleigh horses.

Sonaglio (It.). A little bell.

Sonamento (It.). A sounding, playing.

Sonante (It.). Resonant.

Sonare (It.). To sound: to play upon.

>   **Sonare a raccolta.** To sound the "Assembly" (an army call).
>   **Sonare alla mente.** To play extempore.
>   **Sonare il piano-forte.** To play the piano.
>   **Sonare le campane.** To ring (peal) the bells.
>   **Sonare un corno.** To play upon (blow) a horn.

Sonata (It.). A composition *played* as opposed to one which is *sung.* The term is now used for a particular form of composition, consisting of several movements, which follow certain rules as regards their construction.

>   **Sonata da camera.** A chamber sonata. A composition of 4 or 5 movements, usually alternately quick and slow, and as a rule some form of dance music (*Bourrée, Sarabande,* etc.).
>   **Sonata da chiesa.** A church sonata. Like the above, consisting of several movements, but, as befitting their intended use, of a more dignified nature.

Neither of the above can be considered as a sonata in the modern sense, although the types are undoubtedly precursors of the later form.

Sonata per il cembalo. Sonata for the piano.

Sonate (Fr.). Sonata.

Sonate (Ger.). Sonata. plur. *Sonaten.*

Sonaten für Klavier allein. Sonatas for piano solo.

Sonatina (It.).
Sonatine (Fr. and Ger.). } A small sonata.

Sonatore (It.). The player of an instrument (masc.).

Sonatrice (It.). The player of an instrument (fem.).

Sonevole (It.). Sounding, resonant.

Songeant (Fr.). Dreaming.

Sono (It.). Sound. plur. *soni.*

Soni alterati. Chromatically altered notes.

Sonore (Fr.). Sonorous.

Sonorità (It.).
Sonorité (Fr.). } Sonority.

Sonoro, -a (It.). Sonorous, resounding.

Sonora la melodia.
Sonoro il canto. } The melody sonorous.

Sons (Fr.). Sounds; notes.

Sons bouchés. Closed notes on a horn.

Sons cuivrés. "Brassy" notes on brass instruments. *v.* Cuivré.

Sons d'écho. Sounds resembling an echo. A direction (more especially for wind-instruments) signifying a very soft distant effect. On many cornets, there is a special attachment for producing this effect.

Sons d'ongles. Literally, nail sounds. A harp effect obtained by plucking the strings close to the sound-board (belly), the result much resembling the tone of a guitar.

Sons étouffés. Damped sounds; notes on a harp produced by immediately stopping the vibrations with the palm of the hand.

Sons harmoniques. Harmonics (*q. v.*) on the harp, violin, etc.

Sons naturels. Natural sounds, *i. e.* sounds produced on an instrument in the ordinary manner; a direction contradicting some previous indication, such as *sons harmoniques, sons bouchés, sur le chevalet,* etc.

Sons ordinaires. *v.* Sons naturels.

Sons ouverts. Open notes on a brass instrument.

Sons pleins mais non stridents. The sounds full (resonant) but not blatant.

Sopra (It.). Upon, on, above. A term used to signify the crossing of hands in piano playing.

Sopra una corda. On one string (of a piano, or of a violin, etc.).

Sopran (Ger.). Soprano.

Sopransänger. Soprano singer (masc.).

Sopransängerin. Soprano singer (fem.).

Sopranschlüssel. Soprano clef.

Sopranstimme. Soprano voice.

Soprana (It.). Fem. of *soprano,* superior, upper. *Corda soprana,* the highest string on a violin, etc.

Sopranino (It.). The diminutive of *soprano*, and a term applied to an instrument of higher pitch than that defined as *soprano*.

Sopranist (Ger.). A soprano singer (masc.).

Soprano (It.). Superior, upper, highest. Used as a subs. for the highest voice in women and children, ranging from c' to g'' in the latter, and from c' to c''' (or even to e''', f''' and g''' in exceptional cases) in the former. Male sopranos are either *falsetti* or *castrati*. In Eng. brass bands, *Soprano* usually means the soprano cornet.

Soprano clef. The C clef on the 1st line, now seldom used, though found in the scores of composers as recent as Berlioz and Mendelssohn.

Soprano cornet. A high cornet in E♭, sounding a minor 3rd above the written notes.

Soprano drammatico. A dramatic soprano, a female singer possessing a voice of a full and powerful quality.

Soprano leggiero. A light soprano, one possessing a voice of a lighter quality than the above.

Soprano naturale. A male soprano, who sings in falsetto.

Soprano primo. First soprano.

Soprano sarrusophone. A member of the sarrusophone family, now never used.

Soprano saxhorn. A brass instrument much the same as the soprano cornet, but with a larger bore. Fr. *Petit bugle en mi♭*; Ger. *Piccolo Flügelhorn in Es*; It. *Flicorno soprano*.

Soprano saxophone. A member of the saxophone family, found in most large Fr. military bands. It has been used in the orchestra by Charpentier (*Impressions d'Italie*). It is in B♭.

Soprano secondo. Second soprano.

Soprano sfogato. A very high soprano.

Soprano solo. A soprano alone.

Sordamente (It.). Dully, in a veiled manner.

Sordina (It.). The modern It. for a mute. plur. *sordine*. *cf.* Sordino.

Sordin(e) (Ger.). A mute, damper.

Sordino (It.). Plur. *sordini*. (1) A mute of a violin, etc., or of a brass instrument. (2) The damper of a piano, now operated by the right hand pedal, but formerly controlled by a stop, as in the harpsichord. (3) In old pianos, a device for muting the sounds by interposing a strip of felt or leather between the hammer and the string; this was worked by a pedal and called "Céleste" or "Sordin". Afterwards this muting pedal gave place to the "shifting pedal", whereby softness was obtained by the hammer striking only one string (*una corda*) instead of three. In recent years, the muting pedal has been revived. *Senza sordini* is therefore an indication open to misconstruction in piano music of a certain date, since it may mean "without dampers", *i. e.* raising the dampers by means of the damper pedal, or it may mean "without using the mutes" (Céleste).

Sordini levati. The mutes removed.

Sordo, -a (It.). Dull, veiled. Said of an instrument with little sonority, or of a hall or theatre, badly constructed as regards its acoustical properties.

Sorgfältig (Ger.).   Careful, attentive.

Sortita (It.).   The first or entrance *aria* of a character in an opera.

Sospensione (It.).   Suspension.

Sospirando, Sospirante (It.).   Sighing, yearning.

Sospirevole (It.).   Sighing deeply, plaintive.

Sospiro (It.).   A sigh.   A crotchet rest.

Sospiroso (It.).   Sighing, plaintive.

Sost., Sosten.   Abbr. of *sostenuto*.

Sostenendo (It.).   Sustaining.

Sostenuto (It.).   Sustained.

> **Sostenuto legato.**   Sustained and slurred.

Sotto (It.).   Under, beneath, below.   Found in piano duets, where the hand of one player has to cross under that of the other.

> **Sotto dominante.**   Subdominant.
>
> **Sotto mediante.**   Submediant.
>
> **Sotto voce.**   Under the voice, softly.   Like *mezza voce*, also used for instruments.

Soubrette (Fr.).   A singer or actress of what in Eng. are known as "chambermaid's" parts; minor parts usually of a lively pert nature. The term is also used in Ger. as *Soubrettenrolle*, a soubrette's part.

Soudainement (Fr.).   Suddenly.

Soufflérie (Fr.).   The apparatus connected with the bellows of an organ.

Soufflet (Fr.).   The sign ◁ ▷.

Soufflets (Fr.).   Bellows.

Souffleur (Fr.).   A prompter.   A blower.

> **Souffleur d'orgues.**   An organ blower.

Souffleur (Ger.).   A prompter.

> **Souffleurbuch.**   A prompt-book.
>
> **Souffleurkasten.**   A prompter's box.

Sound-board *or* **Sounding-board.**   A piece of wood used for increasing the resonance of an instrument, such as the sounding-board of the piano or organ, the *belly* of the violin, harp, etc.   The term is also used for a screen placed above or behind a speaker for reflecting and regulating the direction of his voice.

Sound-holes.   *f*-shaped holes cut in the belly of a violin, etc.

Sound-post.   A small post fixed within a violin, etc., near the bridge, on the treble side.   On its position much of the tone of the instrument depends.   The Fr. term is *l'âme*, the soul.

Soupir (Fr.).   A sigh.   A crotchet-rest.

Sourdine (Fr.).   Mute, damper.

Sous (Fr.).   Under, beneath.

Soutenu (Fr.).   Sustained.

Spagnoletta (It.).   Serenade; a dance in the Spanish style.

Spagnuolo, -a (It.).   Spanish; a Spaniard, a Spanish woman.

Spalla (It.).   The shoulder.   *Viola da spalla*, a shoulder viol, as opposed to the *viola da gamba*, a leg viol.

Spandendo (It.).   Dilating, becoming louder.

Spartito (It.).   A score.   past part. Scored.

> **Spartito canto e pianoforte.**   Vocal score.

Sparto (It.). Scattered, diffuse.
Spassapensiero (It.). A Jew's harp.
Spasshaft (Ger.). Jocular.
Später (Ger.). Later.
    Später 3 große Flöten. Later 3 (large) flutes.
Spazio (It.). A space.
Spazzolino (It.). A mop, swab for cleaning the interior of wood-wind instruments.
Speaker key. A term for the key used on the clarinet, and its allies for enabling them to "speak" better in their upper register. *v.* Octave key.
Spediendo (It.). Hastening, hurrying.
Spektakel (Ger.). A great noise, hubbub, uproar.
Sperdendosi (It.). Fading away.
Spianato (It.). Even, smooth.
Spiccato (It.). Detached, separated. It is indicated by dots above the notes, and in violin-playing is played with the point of the bow. *v.* Signs.
    Spiccato assai. Very detached.
Spiegando (It.). Extending, becoming louder.
Spiel (Ger.). Play, game. Playing, performance, execution.
    Spielart.
    Spielmanier. } Mode or manner of playing; execution, touch,
    Spielweise. } rendering.
Spielen (Ger.). To play.
    Spielen vom Blatt. To play at sight.
Spielend (Ger.). Playing. adv. Easily.
Spieler (Ger.). A player, performer.
    Spielerin. A female performer.
Spinnen des Tons (Ger.). *v.* Filare la voce.
Spirito (It.). Fire, spirit. *Con spirito*, with spirit, animation.
Spiritosamente (It.). }
Spiritoso (It.). } The same as *Con spirito*.
Spitze (Ger.). Point.
    Spitze des Bogens. Point of the bow.
    Spitzflöte. Pointed flute; a soft organ stop, the pipes of which are pointed at the top.
Spitzig (Ger.). Pointed, biting, cutting.
Spöttisch (Ger.). Mocking, malicious, scoffing.
Sprachrohr (Ger.). A speaking trumpet.
Spr. Bog. Abbr. of *springender Bogen.*
Sprechend (Ger.). Speaking.
Springend (Ger.). Springing.
    Springender Bogen. In violin, etc. playing, the springing bow.
    Springender Daumen. Springing thumb. (Direction to a tambourine player.)
Springlade (Ger.). The spring-chest of an organ.
Sprung (Ger.). A skip. *Intervallensprung*, skip of an interval.
    Sprunglauf. A quick series of notes, *fusée.*
Squillo (It.). Sound, clang. A trumpet call. *Suoni a squillo*, the open notes on a brass instrument; *corno a squillo*, a natural horn.
    Squillo dietro il sipario. Trumpet-call behind the curtain.

Stabat Mater (Lat.). A Sequence of the Roman Church, sung during Passion Week.

Stabile (It.). Stable, durable, firm.

Stäbchen (Ger.). The beater of a triangle. *Mit Holzstäbchen*, with a wooden beater; *mit Metallstäbchen*, with a metal beater.

Stacc. Abbr. of *staccato*.

Staccati (It.). Plur. of *staccato*.

Staccatissimo (It.). Sup. of *staccato*.

Staccato (It.). Detached. Strictly speaking, notes with a dash above are to be played *staccato*, and with a dot above, *spiccato* (the first being sharper and shorter than the second), but this distinction is not always observed. *v.* Signs. *Staccato* is also used as a subs.

Stachel (Ger.). The spike of a violoncello or double-bass.

Stahl (Ger.). Steel.

> **Stahlharmonika.** An harmonica composed of little steel bars; the modern form of the Glockenspiel.
>
> **Stahlsaiten.** Steel strings.
>
> **Stahlstäbchen.** Steel beater (of a triangle).

Stamm (Ger.). Stem, root.

> **Stammakkord.** A fundamental chord.
>
> **Stammleiter.** Normal scale.

Stampita (It.). Air, tune.

Stance (Fr.). Stanza.

Standhaft (Ger.). Firm, steady.

Ständchen (Ger.). A serenade, but not in the sense of a composition for several instruments in many movements.

Stanghetta (It.). A bar-line.

Stark (Ger.). Strong, loud.

> **Stark anblasen.** To blow strongly; with brass instruments, the equivalent of the Fr. *cuivrer* (to make "brassy"). In modern Ger. scores, *schmettern* is the term employed.
>
> **Stark hervortretend.** Strongly brought-out, very prominent.
>
> **Stark und kräftig zu spielen.** To be played loudly and vigorously.

Stärke (Ger.). Strength, vigour, loudness.

Stärker (Ger.). Stronger, etc.

Statt (Ger.). Instead of; used in the sense of *loco* after *8va*.

> **Statt an.** In place of, instead of.

Steg (Ger.). The bridge of a violin, etc. *Am Steg*, on the bridge.

Steigernd (Ger.). Enhancing, intensifying, working-up.

Sten. Abbr. of *stendendo*.

Stendendo (It.). Delaying, holding back.

Stentato (It.). Meagre, poverty-stricken.

Sterbend (Ger.). Dying away.

Steso (It.). Extended, diffuse.

> **Steso moto.** Slow movement.

Stesso, -a (It.). The same. *Lo stesso tempo*, the same time. *v.* L'istesso.

Stets (Ger.). Always, invariably. *Die Violinen und Bratschen stets pp.*, the violins and violas always *pp*.

> **Stets das gleiche Tempo.** Always the same tempo.

Sticcato (It.). A term for a xylophone.

Stiel (Ger.). The stem of a note.

Stierhorn (Ger.). A cow horn; an instrument giving only one note. It has been used by Wagner in his *Ring*, and for the celebrated *f♯* of the Night-watchman in *Die Meistersinger*

Stil (Ger.). Style.

Stile (It.). Style.

    Stile a cappella. In the style of church music.

    Stile serio, legato, rigoroso *or* tematico. Any one of these expressions refers to a style of composition, in which all the best qualities of music are combined.

Still (Ger.). Calm, quiet, tranquil.

    Stillgedackt. A soft stopped organ pipe.

Stimme (Ger.). (1) A voice. (2) An organ stop. (3) A vocal or instrumental part. (4) The sound-post of a violin, etc. plur. *Stimmen*; in combination *Stimm-*.

    Stimmbogen. A crook of a horn or trumpet.

    Stimmenkreuzung. Crossing of parts.

    Stimmführer. Choir-master.

    Stimmführung. Progression of parts.

    Stimmgabel. A tuning-fork.

    Stimmholz. Sound-post of a violin, etc.

    Stimmschlüssel. A tuning-key.

    Stimmstock. A sound-post.

    Stimmumfang. Compass of a voice.

    Stimmwerkzeuge. Vocal organs.

    Stimmzug. A tuning-slide.

Stimmen (Ger.). To be in tune, to harmonise with: to tune. *Zum Klaviere stimmen*, to be tuned to the pitch of a piano; *ein Instrument stimmen*, to tune an instrument.

Stimmung (Ger.). Tuning; pitch, key.

Stinguendo (It.). Fading away. The same as *estinguendo*.

Stiracchiando (It.). Holding back.

Stiracchiato (It.). Held back.

Stirando (It.). Drawing-out.

Stirato (It.). Drawn-out.

Stockend (Ger.). Slackening.

Stonante (It.). Dissonant.

Stop. (1) A set of pipes in an organ, a register. (2) The knob, r draw-stop, by which the stop or register is controlled. (3) verb. To press a string of a stringed instrument against the fingerboard.

Stopfhorn (Ger.). The hand-horn. *v.* Horn.

Stopped. (1) On a stringed instrument, a note is said to be *stopped*, when it is obtained on a string pressed against the fingerboard with one of the fingers of the left hand, as opposed to an *open* note, which is obtained from the unpressed string in its natural tuning. (2) On a horn, a note is said to be *stopped* or *closed*, when in obtaining it the hand is introduced into the bell of the instrument. *v.* Horn.

Storto, -a (It.). Twisted, crooked, perverse. *Storta* (subs.) is a term for the serpent.

Stoß (Ger.). A blow, knock; a blast, a tongue-stroke (on a horn or trumpet).

Stoßen (Ger.). To push, to give a shock to. Term used for a species of staccato bowing, which consists in a series of jerks. past part. *gestoßen,* detached, *staccato.* Also, to attack a note with the tongue, hence to give a blast on a horn or trumpet.

Str. Abbr. of Strings or *Streichinstrumente.*

Stracciacalando (It.). Prattling, chattering.

Straff (Ger.). Tightly stretched (of a drum); stiff, strict.

    Straffer im Tempo, allmählich in Halbe übergehen. In stricter tempo, gradually proceeding to (beat) minims.

Strappando (It.). Plucking, snatching; playing in a violent manner.

Strascicando, Strascinando (It.). Dragging.

    Strascicando l'arco. Dragging the bow.

Strascicato, Strascinato (It.). Dragged, protracted.

Stravagante (It.). Whimsical, fantastic, extravagant.

Stravaganza (It.). Extravagance, eccentricity.

Straziante (It.). Mocking.

Streich (Ger.). A stroke (with a bow); in combination, applied to bowed instruments. *cf.* Strich.

    Streichinstrumente. Bowed instruments: the stringed instruments of the orchestra.

    Streichorchester. String-orchestra.

    Streichquartett. String-quartet.

    Streichzither. A zither played with a bow.

Streichen (Ger.). To strike (with the bow). subs. Bowing.

Streicher (Ger.). The stops in an organ, which imitate the string tone.

Streng (Ger.). Strict, rigorous.

    Streng im Takte. { Strictly in time.
    Streng im Zeitmaß. {

Strepito (It.). Noise.

Strepitosamente (It.). Noisily, loudly.

Strepitoso (It.). Noisy, obstreperous.

Stretta (It.). The final part of a musical composition, in which the time becomes more and more animated.

Stretto (It.). Drawn closer together, hurried. The *stretto* of a fugue is where the parts follow one another at a shorter interval than on their first exposition. The word is occasionally used as an equivalent to *stringendo.*

Strich (Ger.). (1) The stroke of a bow, bowing. While *Streich* simply means the striking of the strings with the bow, *Strich* means the proper use of the bow on the strings, the Fr. *coup d'archet.* (2) A bar-line.

    Strichart. Manner of bowing.

    Strichwechsel. Change of bowing.

Strident (Fr.). { Harsh, blatant, shrill.
Stridente (It.). {

Striking reed. *v.* Reed.

String. Abbr. of *stringendo.*

String. Prepared wire or catgut (often covered with silk or wire) for musical instruments. In combination, the word is used as an equivalent of the Ger. *Streich,* and is applied to instruments played with a bow. (*v.* Stringed Instruments.) It is to be noted however that "string-instrument" as a translation of *Streichinstrument* is incorrect.

String-orchestra. An orchestra composed of stringed instruments only.

String-quartet. A quartet for stringed instruments, and usually for 2 violins, viola and violoncello.

String-register. The stops in an organ, of which the tone more or less resembles that of stringed instruments.

String-trio. A trio for stringed instruments, and usually for violin, viola and violoncello.

Stringed Instruments. Although in the strictest sense, the term includes instruments of which the strings are plucked (harp, guitar, etc.), and those of which the strings are struck (piano, dulcimer, etc.), it is usually taken to mean the four kinds of bowed instruments in general orchestral use, *viz.* violin, viola, violoncello and double-bass. These are known as the "Strings", as opposed to the "Brass" and "Wood", and in a well-constituted orchestra should form at least two-thirds of the total number of performers.

Stringendo (It.). Drawing closer together; quickening the tempo.

 Stringendo poco a poco. Gradually quickening.

Stringere (It.). To bind fast together, to draw close; to quicken the tempo. past part. *stretto.*

Strisciando (It.). Gliding (from one note to another).

Strisciato (It.). Glided; slurred.

Strofa (It.). Strophe, stanza, couplet.

Strohfiedel (Ger.). The xylophone.

Strombettare (It.). To trumpet, to sound the trumpet.

Strombettiere (It.). A trumpeter.

Stromentato (It.). Instrumentated.

Stromento (It.). An instrument.

Strumentazione (It.). Instrumentation; also used in a general sense for instrumental music.

Strumento (It.). An instrument. plur. *strumenti.*

 Strumenti a corda. Stringed instruments.

 Strumenti a fiato. Wind instruments.

 Strumenti a percossa. Percussion instruments.

 Strumenti a pizzico. Plucked instruments, *i. e.* the harp, guitar, etc.

 Strumenti da arco. Bowed instruments.

 Strumenti di legno. Wood instruments.

 Strumenti d'ottone. Brass instruments.

Stück (Ger.). A piece.

Studien (Ger.). Studies.

Stufe (Ger.). Step, degree. In combination, *Stufen-.*

 Stufe der Tonleiter. Degree of the scale.

 Stufenweise absteigend. Descending by degrees (steps).

 Stufenweise aufsteigend. Ascending by degrees.

Stumm (Ger.). Dumb.

 Stummes Klavier. A dumb keyboard.

 Stummes Register. A silent stop on an organ.

Stupore (It.). Stupor, amazement.

Stürmend (Ger.). } Stormy, tempestuous.
Stürmisch (Ger.). }

Stürze (Ger.). The bell of a wind-instrument.

Stürze in die Höhe. With upturned bells. *v.* Bell.

Styl (Ger.). Style.

Sù (It.). Upon, on, above, over. Compounded with *il = sul*; with *la = sulla.*

Suabe Flute. A 4 ft organ stop of wood.

Suave (Fr.), Gentle, soft.

Suave, etc. (It.). *v.* Soave, etc.

Subitamente (It.). Suddenly.

Subito (It.). Sudden, quick.

Sudrophone (Fr.). A brass instrument invented by Sudre, in which the tone can be made to resemble that of reed instruments, and even that of strings, besides producing new species of tone-colour. The effect is obtained by means of silk membranes. The instrument is made in various sizes, corresponding to the different forms of saxhorns.

Suffocato (It.). Stifled, muffled.

Sui (It.). Compound of *su* (on, above, etc.) and *i* (the, plur.).

Suite (Fr.). A series; something which follows, a continuation; a series of instrumental movements, originally in dance measure, but now in almost any form.

Suivez (Fr.). Follow.

    Suivez le chant. Follow the melody, *colla parte.*

Sujet (Fr.). Subject.

Sul, Sull', Sulla, Sui, Sugli, Sulle. Compounds of *su* (on, over, etc.) with various forms of the indefinite article.

    Sulla mezza corda. On the half (middle of) the string.

    Sulla pedaliera. On the pedal-board.

    Sulla 4a corda. On the 4th string.

    Sulla tastiera. On the keyboard (manual).

    Sul mezzo manico. On the middle of the fingerboard.

    Sul ponticello. On (near) the bridge.

Summend (Ger.). Humming.

Sunto (It.). An extract.

    Sunto dell' atto IV. Extract from Act IV.

Suo loco (It.). In its proper place.

Suonare (It.). To sound. *v.* Sonare.

Suono (It.). A sound. plur. *suoni.*

    Suoni armonici. Harmonics.

    Suoni flautati. Flute-like tones produced on the violin, etc., by playing with the point of the bow near the fingerboard: the harmonics on a harp.

Supertonique (Fr.). The supertonic; the note above the tonic.

Supplichevole (It.). Suppliant, entreating.

Supplichevolmente (It.). Humble, in a suppliant manner.

Sur (Fr.). On, upon.

    Sur la scène. On the stage.

    Sur la touche. On the fingerboard.

    Sur le chevalet. On (near) the bridge.

Süß (Ger.). Sweet.

Susurrando (It.). Murmuring, whispering.

Svegliando (It.). Arousing, awakening.

Svegliato (It.). Lively, alert.

Svelte (Fr.). } Free, easy, nimble.
Svelto (It.). }
Symphonie (Fr. and Ger.). A symphony.
Symphonique (Fr.). Symphonic.
Symphonisch (Ger.). Symphonic.
    Symphonische Dichtung. A symphonic poem.
Syncopa (It.). }
Syncope (Fr.). } Syncopation.
Synkope (Ger.). }
Synkopieren (Ger.). To syncopate.
Synkopi(e)rt (Ger.). Syncopated.
Système (Fr.). System; a number of staves connected in one brace.

T

T. Abbr. of Tempo, Tenor, *tief*, *Tutti*, etc.
    t. c. Abbr. of *tre corde*.
    T. S. Abbr. of *Tasto solo*.
Taballo (It.). An obsolete term for *timballo*.
Tablature (Fr.). Tablature. An obsolete method of notation by means of letters, or numbers. *v.* Intavolatura.
Table (Fr.). Any smooth surface, such as the *table* of a clarinet mouth-piece, against which the reed is placed; the belly of a harp.
    Table (d'harmonie). A sound-board.
Tableau (Fr.). That portion of an act, in which there is a change of scenery.
Tabor. An obsolete species of shallow drum resembling a tambourine without jingles. Like the *tambourin (q. v.)*, it was struck by a single drumstick, and was played in conjunction with a small pipe (*cf.* Galoubet).
Taboret (Fr.). A term sometimes used for a tabor.
Tabouret (Fr.). A music stool.
Tabulatur (Ger.). } Tablature.
Tabulatura (It.). }
Tacciono (It.). 3rd pers. plur. of *tacere*, to be silent. *Violini tacciono*, the violins are silent.
Tace (It.). 3rd pers. sing. of *tacere*, to be silent. *Arpa tace*, the harp is silent.
Tacent (Lat.). *v.* Tacciono.
Tacet (Lat.). *v.* Tace.
Taci (It.). Be silent.
Tact (Ger.). *v.* Takt.
Tafelmusik (Ger.). (1) Music intended to be sung or played at meal times. (2) Music so arranged that two persons seated at opposite sides of a table can sing from the same page.
Tag(e)lied (Ger.). An aubade, a morning song.
Taille (Fr.). Tenor. A term formerly used for both voices and instruments.
    Taille de hautbois. An oboe a fifth lower than the ordinary one.
Tail-piece. In violins, etc., the part (made of ebony) into which one end of the strings is fixed.

Takt (Ger.). (1) A bar. (2) Time. *Ein Takt fast so schnell als eben die Viertel*, a bar almost as fast as the previous crotchets.

Taktart. Species of time.

Taktbezeichnung. The time indication.

Taktfest. Steady in keeping time.

Taktführer. A conductor.

Takthalten. To keep time.

Taktmäßig. Measured, well-timed; rhythmical.

Taktmesser. Metronome.

Taktnote. A semibreve.

Taktpause. A bar's rest.

Taktschlag. A beat.

Taktschlagen. To beat time.

Taktschläger. A beater of time, a conductor.

Taktstock. A stick for beating time, a baton.

Taktstrich. A bar-line.

Taktt(h)eil. Part of a bar. *Guter* or *schwerer Taktteil*, the strong accented part of the bar; *schlechter* or *leichter Taktteil*, the weak, unaccented part of the bar.

Taktwechsel. Change of time.

Taktzeichen. Time signature.

Taktig (Ger.). Pertaining to a bar. *3 taktig*, 3 bar rhythm.

Talon (Fr.). The heel, or nut of the bow of a violin, etc.

Tambour (Fr.). (1) A drum, specifically the side or snare-drum. (2) A drummer.

Tambour avec la corde lâche derrière le théatre. Side-drum with the snare loose (*i. e.* a muffled drum) behind the scenes.

Tambour de Basque. The tambourine.

Tambour long. A name for the tenor drum (*q. v.*), so called because its shell is usually deeper than that of the snare-drum. *cf.* Long Drum.

Tambour majeur. Drum-major.

Tambour militaire. The snare-drum.

Tambour roulant. *v.* Caisse roulante.

Tambourin (Fr.). A name given to two very dissimilar instruments, and a term which has given rise to confusion, since it is one of the Ger. names for a tambourine. It is also the name of a dance.

Tambourin de Provence. A long drum of small diameter, played with a single drumstick held in the right hand, while the left hand plays the *galoubet* or tabor-pipe. The instrument possesses as a rule no snare, and in the rare cases when this is present it is a single cord stretched across the *upper* end of the drum. Bizet has made effective use of this form of the *Tambourin* in *L'Arlésienne*, the *galoubet* being imitated by the piccolo. *cf.* Tabor.

Tambourin du Béarn. An instrument composed of a long rectangular sound-box, across which are stretched seven strings, tuned *c, g, c, g, c, g, c.* These are beaten with a little stick and thus form a species of drone bass to the *chirula* or *galoubet*. This form of the instrument has never been used in the orchestra.

Tambourin (Ger.). A tambourine. *cf.* Tambourin (Fr.), and Baskische Trommel.

Tambourinaire (Fr.). A player on the *tambourin* (Fr.).

Tambourine. A percussion instrument consisting of a membrane stretched over a wooden hoop, in which are fixed in pairs little cymbals or "jingles". These impart a characteristic tone to the instrument, when it is struck with the hand, or is shaken.

Tambourineur (Fr.). A player on a tambourine, or *tambour de Basque.*

Tambourstab (Ger.). A drum-major's staff.

Tamburino (It.). The tambourine.

Tamburo (It.). A drum.

    Tamburo grande. ⎱ A bass drum.
    Tamburo grosso. ⎰

    Tamburo militare. The military or snare-drum.

    Tamburo rullante. The tenor drum.

Tamburone (It.). A large drum; the bass drum.

Tampon (Fr.). (1) A bass-drumstick. This was the term used during three quarters of the last century and found in the works of Berlioz, the earlier scores of Saint-Saëns, etc.; then *mailloche* became the usual term. In modern musical catalogues, *batte* is the word generally employed. (2) A pad for a key of a wood-wind instrument, saxophone or ophicleide.

Tam-tam (Fr., Ger. and It.). The Chinese gong.

    Tam-tam (petit format) (Fr.). Gong (small size).

    Tamtamschlag (Ger.). A stroke on the gong. *Die Tamtam-schläge leise, aber vibrierend*, the strokes on the gong soft, but resonant.

Tändelnd (Ger.). Playing, toying; much the same as *scherzando.*

Tantino (It.). subs. A very little bit; moment, instant.

Tanto (It.). So much, as much; so many.

Tanz (Ger.). A dance.

    Tanzmusik. Dance music.

Tapada (Sp.). A stopped organ pipe.

Tarantella (It.). ⎱ A lively Neapolitan dance now always written in
Tarantelle (Fr.). ⎰ $^6/_8$ time.

Tardamente (It.). Slowly.

Tardando (It.). Becoming slower.

Tardantemente (It.). *v.* Tardamente.

Tardo, -a (It.). Slow, lingering.

Tárogató. An instrument which has been used in Paris and Brussels, etc., to take the cor anglais part at the end of Scene I, Act III, *Tristan und Isolde.* It is a wooden instrument of conical bore, played with a clarinet reed, and appears to be an improved form of a reed instrument of Transylvanian origin.

Tarolle Grégoire (Fr.). A species of shallow side-drum.

Tastatur (Ger.). ⎱ Keyboard.
Tastatura (It.). ⎰

Taste (Ger.). A key on a piano, organ, etc. *Schwarze Tasten*, black keys (notes); *weiße Tasten*, the white keys.

Tastiera (It.). A keyboard, manual. *Strumento a tastiera,* a keyboard instrument (piano, celesta, etc.).

    Tastiere unite. The manuals coupled.

Tasto (It.). A key on an organ, piano, etc. plur. *tasti.*

Tasto solo. A direction in figured bass, meaning that the note alone is to be played without a chord above it.

Tatto (It.). Touch.

Tattoo. The beat of the drum recalling soldiers or sailors to their quarters or tents at night.

Teatro (It.). Theatre.

Technik (Ger.). Execution.

Tedesco, -a (It.). German.

Te Deum (Lat.). An ancient hymn of the Catholic Church attributed to St. Ambrose.

Teil (Ger.). A part.

> **Teiltöne.** Partial tones; harmonics.

Teilung (Ger.). A division; subdivision of an interval.

Tela (It.). A curtain.

Teller (Ger.). Literally "a plate". Term used for one of the halves of a pair of cymbals.

Tem. Abbr. of *tempo*.

Tema (It.). Theme.

Tempérament (Fr.). ⎫
Temperamento (It.). ⎬ Temperament; the division of the octave.

Temperando (It.). Moderating.

Temperatamente (It.). Moderately.

Temperatur (Ger.). Temperament.

Tempestosamente (It.). Tempestuously.

Tempestoso, -a (It.). Tempestuous.

Tempestueux, -euse (Fr.). Tempestuous, stormy.

Tempête (Fr.). Tempest, storm. The name of a dance something like a quadrille.

Tempo (It.). Time; also used in the sense of movement, as *il 3⁰ tempo della sinfonia Patetica*, the 3rd movement of the Pathetic symphony. The word is now incorporated into most languages, as *Das Tempo bleibt immer dasselbe bei dem verschiedenen Taktwechsel*, the tempo remains always the same throughout the various changes of time. The term has been used throughout this Dictionary to denote the rate of rhythm of a musical work.

> **Tempo agitato, animato, etc., etc.** For these and other compounds of adjectives with "tempo", not given below, *v.* Agitato, Animato, etc., etc., for the meaning.
>
> **Tempo a cappella.** *v.* A cappella.
>
> **Tempo alla breve.** $^2/_2$ or $^2/_1$ time. *v.* Alla breve.
>
> **Tempo alla semibreve.** $^4/_4$ time.
>
> **Tempobezeichnung** (Ger.). Indication of movement.
>
> **Tempo binario.** Binary time.
>
> **Tempo com(m)odo.** Convenient time, *i. e.* neither too fast nor too slow.
>
> **Tempo da capo.** The same tempo as at the commencement.
>
> **Tempo debole.** The weak (unaccented) portion of a bar.
>
> **Tempo della tema.** The tempo of the theme.
>
> **Tempo di ballo.** Dance time.
>
> **Tempo di gavotta, di marcia, etc.** *v.* Gavotta, Marcia, etc.
>
> **Tempo doppio dello stesso movimento.** Double the time of the same movement.

Tempo doppio, lo stesso movimento. Double the time, the same movement.

Tempo frettoloso. Hasty time.

Tempo giusto. Appropriate (usually moderate) time.

Tempo ordinario. Ordinary time, *i. e.* a tempo in which the beats have their full value, as opposed to *alla breve.*

Tempo primo. The first (original) time.

Tempo rubato. *v.* A tempo rubato.

Tempo ternario. Ternary time; in triple measure.

Tempo wie vorher (Ger.). The tempo as before; *tempo primo.*

Temps (Fr.). Time, beat.

Temps faible. The unaccented beat of a bar.

Temps fort. The accented beat.

Ten. Abbr. of *tenuto.*

Tendrement (Fr.). Tenderly.

Tenebrae (Lat.). "Darkness". A service of the Roman Church used during Passion Week to commemorate the darkness at the Crucifixion.

Tenendo (It.). Holding, sustaining.

Tenendo il canto. Sustaining the melody.

Teneramente (It.). Tenderly.

Tenerezza (It.). Tenderness.

Tenero, -a (It.). Tender, soft, delicate.

Tenete (It.). Hold, sustain.

Tenete sino al fine del suono. Sustain the note until it dies away.

Tenir (Fr.). To hold.

Tenir la pédale. Hold on the pedal. *v.* Remark I.

Tenor. (1) The highest natural male voice, with a compass from *c* to *a'* (*b'*, *c''*). (2) A name for the viola. (3) An adjective applied to many instruments which have the same compass as a tenor voice. It is to be noted however that most instruments designated as "tenor" in Eng. are called "alto" in other languages.

Tenor Bassoon. *v.* Tenoroon.

Tenor C. The note on the 2nd space of the bass clef

Tenor Clef. The C [clef on the 4th line,

Tenor Cor. An instrument resembling the real horn in appearance, and more or less in tone, but of the saxhorn or saxotromba class. It is also called the Ballad Horn or Vocal Horn.

Tenor Drum. A drum made in various shapes and sizes and played in the same way as the ordinary side-drum, but distinguished from the latter in that it possesses no *snare,* and hence has a deeper duller tone. The Eng. Army Regulation size has a diameter of 18″. The name in Ger. was formerly *Wirbeltrommel* or *Rolltrommel* till Wagner gave it its present name of *Rührtrommel.* (In the concert room version of the *Walkürenritt* for some unknown reason the instrument is marked in the score as a *Kleine Trommel,* which is the snare-drum and naturally does not produce the same effect.) Fr. *Caisse roulante;* It. *Cassa rullante.*

Tenorhorn. The "Tenor" of military bands, the same as the Fr. *Alto en mi♭.* *v.* Saxhorn.

Tenor Sarrusophone. *v.* Sarrusophone.

Tenor Trombone. *v.* Trombone.

Tenor (Ger.). Tenor.

> **Tenorbaß.** A name for the *Tenortuba*.
>
> **Tenorbaßposaune.** A tenor trombone of the same length and compass as the ordinary tenor trombone, but with a wider bore and larger bell, and possessing increased resonance and a greater facility for producing the low notes. It is marked in many modern Ger. scores, and occasionally (*e. g.* in *Die Walküre*) is evidently intended to be furnished with the *Daumenventil* (piston for the thumb, *v.* Trombone) for the production of notes between $B_1\flat$ and E.
>
> **Tenorfagott.** The tenor bassoon. It was also called a *Quintfagott. v.* Tenoroon.
>
> **Tenorgeige.** The tenor violin, the viola.
>
> **Tenorhorn.** The tenorhorn.
>
> **Tenorposaune.** The tenor trombone.
>
> **Tenorschlüssel.** Tenor clef.
>
> **Tenortuba.** The euphonium. For the *Tenortuba* found in Wagner's scores, *v.* Wagner Tubas.
>
> **Tenorzeichen.** The tenor clef.

Tenore (It.). Tenor.

> **Tenore acuto.** A high tenor.
>
> **Tenore buffo.** A tenor, who takes comic parts.
>
> **Tenore leggiero.** A light tenor.
>
> **Tenore robusto.** A dramatic tenor with a full voice.

Tenoroon. The familiar name for the tenor bassoon, a bassoon a 5th higher than the ordinary bassoon, and now obsolete.

Tenu (Fr.). Held, sustained.

Tenuta (It.). A holding-note, a *fermata*.

> **Tenuta lunga.** A long holding-note; a *fermata* well sustained throughout its duration.

Tenuto, -a (It.). Held, sustained.

Teoria (It.). Theory.

Teorico (It.). Theoretical.

Tepidamente (It.). Coldly.

Ternaire (Fr.). } Ternary.
Ternario (It.). }

Terremoto (It.). An earthquake. A stop found in some old organs, and used for depicting the earthquake in settings of the Passion.

Terz (Ger.). A third. *Große Terz*, a major 3rd; *kleine Terz*, a minor 3rd.

> **Terzdecime.** A thirteenth.
>
> **Terzdecimole.** A group of 13 equal notes.
>
> **Terzflöte.** The Third Flute (*q. v.*).
>
> **Terzquartakkord.** The 2nd inversion of the dominant 7th, the $4/3$ chord.
>
> **Terzquintsextakkord.** The 1st inversion of the dominant 7th, the $6/5$ chord.

Terza (It.). A third.

> **Terzadecima.** A thirteenth.
>
> **Terza maggiore.** A major 3rd.
>
> **Terza minore.** A minor 3rd.

Terzett (Ger.). A trio: a composition for 3 voices or instruments.

Terzettino (It.). A short trio.

Terzetto (It.). A trio.

Terzina (It.). The Third Flute (*q. v.*).

Tessitura (It.). Web, texture. That portion of a vocal compass mostly employed in composition, *i. e.* without the extreme notes, high or low.

Tête de registre (Fr.). The initial notes of a fugue or theme.

Théâtre (Fr.). Theatre; the scenery of a theatre, as *derrière le théâtre*, behind the scenes.

Theil (Ger.). *v.* Teil.

Thema (Ger.). A theme, subject.

Thematische Arbeit (Ger.). The working-out of themes.

Thème (Fr.). Theme, subject.

Theoretiker (Ger.). } A theorist.
Théoricien (Fr.). }

Third Flute. A flute in E♭ (improperly called in F. — *v.* Flute), in which the sounds are a minor 3rd higher than the written notes. It was formerly employed in military bands, and in orchestras for parts which contained many sharps or flats in the signature. Now however, thanks to improvements in the fingering of the flute, and the skill of modern players, the Third Flute may be considered obsolete.

Tie. *v.* Signs.

Tief (Ger.). Deep, low. *E tief*, low E.

> **Tief gespannt.** Slackly braced. (Indication used for a tenor drum, as opposed to *scharf gespannt*, tightly braced.)
>
> **Tiefquart.** The lower fourth.
>
> **Tiefstimmig.** Deep-voiced.
>
> **Tieftönend.** Deep-sounding.

Tiepidamente (It.). Coldly, with indifference.

Tiepidità (It.). Coldness, indifference.

Tierce (Fr.). (1) A third. (2) An organ stop sounding a 17th above the diapasons.

> **Tierce de Picardie.** In old music, the major chord which often ends a composition in a minor key.

Timb. Abbr. of *Timbales*.

Timbales (Fr.). Kettle-drums.

> **Timbales chromatiques.** Kettle-drums, which can be instantly altered in pitch by means of a master screw, usually worked by a pedal.

Timbalier (Fr.). A kettle-drummer.

Timballo (It.). A name formerly used for the kettle-drum.

Timbre (Fr.). (1) Tone-colour, clang-colour. (2) The snare of a side-drum, in which case it is an abbreviation of *les cordes* (or *la corde*) *du timbre*, the catgut strings on the lower end of the instrument, which give it its peculiar tone. *Sans timbre*, without the snare. *v.* Side-drum.

Timore (It.). Fear, apprehension.

Timorosamente (It.). Fearfully, timorously.

Timoroso, -a (It.). Timorous.

Timpani (It.). Kettle-drums.

Timpani coperti.
Timpani sordi. } Muffled kettle-drums.

Tintamarre (Fr.). Hubbub, great noise.

Tintement (Fr.). Tinkling; tolling of bells.

Tintinnabulo (It.). A small bell.

Tintinnando (It.). Tinkling.

Tintinto (It.). Ding-dong, a term expressive of the sound of bells.

Tira tutto (It.). A pedal acting on all the stops of an organ.

Tirade (Fr. and Ger.). A run; a succession of rapid notes between the two notes of an interval.

Tirando (It.). Drawing (the bow of a violin, etc., to oneself).

Tirant (Fr.). A tag or strap, which braces the cords round the shell of a side, tenor or bass drum.

Tirarsi (It.). *v.* Da tirarsi.

Tirasse (Fr.). A pedal coupler.

Tirato (It.). Drawn. (1) The down-bow. (2) Using the whole or greater part of the bow on the strings.

Tiré (Fr.). Drawn. The down-bow, ⊓. *cf.* Poussé.

Tirolese (It.). Tyrolese.

Toccata (It.). "Touched", used substantively for a prelude-like composition, which usually has a persistent flowing figure.

Toccatina (It.). A short toccata.

Toccato, -a (It.). Touched.

　Toccato appena. Scarcely touched (as for instance a gong).

Tocsin (Fr.). Tocsin, alarm-bell; warning beat of a drum.

Todten-, etc. *v.* Toten-.

Togli (It.). Take, take away.

　Togli l'accoppiamento. Take off the coupler.

　Togli Ripieno e Tromba al G. O. Take off Mix. and Trpt. from Gt.

Toile (Fr.). Curtain. *Derrière la toile,* behind the curtain.

Tombeau (Fr.). A tomb. A lament over a tomb; an elegiac song.

Ton (Fr.). (1) Tone, pitch, key. (2) A crook, or a shank on a brass instrument.

　Ton de rechange. A crook.

　Ton générateur. The fundamental tone.

　Ton majeur. A major key.

　Ton mineur. A minor key.

Ton (Ger.). A tone; note; pitch; *timbre.* plur. *Töne. Ganzer Ton* or *Ganzton,* a whole tone; *halber Ton* or *Halbton,* a semitone.

　Tonabstand. An interval.

　Tonart. Key.

　Tonausweichung. Modulation.

　Tonbild. Tone-picture.

　Tonbildung. Tone-formation.

　Tondichter. Tone-poet, composer.

　Tondichtung. A tone-poem.

　Tonfall. Cadence.

　Tonfarbe. Tone-colour, *timbre,* clang-colour.

　Tonfigur. Tone-figure; group of notes.

　Tonfolge. A succession of notes.

　Tonführung. Modulation.

　Tonfülle. Volume of sound; melodiousness.

Tonfuß. Musical foot.

Tonfüßig. Term used in describing the tonal pitch of organ pipes, as 8 *Tonfüßig*, of 8 ft tone.

Tongebung. Tonality.

Tongeschlecht. Musical genus. The character of a mode, *e. g.* major or minor in modern music.

Tonhöhe. Pitch. *Die gleiche Tonhöhe*, the same pitch, *i. e.* in unison.

Tonkunst. The musical art; music.

Tonkünstler. A musician.

Tonlage. Compass.

Tonleiter. Scale.

Tonmalerei. Tone-painting.

Tonmaß. Time, measure.

Tonreich. Rich and full in tone.

Tonsatz. Musical composition; a musical composition.

Tonschluß. A cadence.

Tonsetzen. To compose.

Tonsetzer. A composer.

Tonsetzkunst. Musical composition.

Tonsinn. Musical talent.

Tonstück. A piece of music, a composition.

Tonstufe. Degree of the scale. Pitch of a note.

Tonumfang. ⎱ Compass.
Tonweite. ⎰

Tonwissenschaft. Science of music.

Tonzeichen. Signs used in music.

Tonada (Sp.). Air, melody, song.

Tonalità (It.). ⎫
Tonalität (Ger.). ⎬ Tonality.
Tonalité (Fr.). ⎭

Töne (Ger.). Plur. of *Ton*.

Tönend (Ger.). Resounding, sonorous.

Tonguing. On wind instruments, the action of the tongue necessary to produce the notes. On the reed instruments, single tonguing is alone possible, but on the flute, and on the acuter brass instruments, double and triple tonguing are frequently employed.

Tonica (It.). ⎫
Tonika (Ger.). ⎬ The tonic.
Tonique (Fr.). ⎭

Tonisch (Ger.). Tonic.

Tonnerre (Fr.) Thunder.

Tons (Fr.). Plur. of *ton*.

  Tons d'église. Church modes.

  Tons de la trompette. Crooks of the trumpet.

  Tons du cor. Crooks of the horn.

Tornando (It.). Returning.

Tosto (It.). Quick, prompt.

Toten- (Ger.). Used in combination, and usually signifying something connected with a funeral.

  Totenamt. Burial service; mass for the dead.

  Totenmarsch. A funeral march.

Totenmesse. Mass for the dead, requiem.

Totenmusik. Funeral music.

Touche (Fr.). The fingerboard of a violin, etc. The fret of a guitar, etc. The key of a piano, organ, etc.

Toucher (Fr.). To touch; to play upon a keyboard instrument. In Fr. the verb "to play" varies greatly according to the instrument: *Jouer le violin, pincer* (or *toucher*) *la harpe, toucher le piano* or *l'orgue, donner le cor, sonner la trompette, blouser les timbales, battre le tambour.* As a subs., *toucher* means touch.

Toujours (Fr.). Always.

> **Toujours plus animé.** Always more animated.
>
> **Toujours unis.** Always united, *i. e.* not divided.

Tous, toutes (Fr.). Plur. of *tout, toute.*

Tout, toute (Fr.). All.

> **Tout à coup.** Suddenly.
>
> **Tout à fait.** Completely.
>
> **Toute la force.** As loud as possible.

Tpt. Abbr. of trumpet.

Tr. Abbr. of *trillo,* and used to indicate a shake, or a roll on a drum, tambourine, etc. In long shakes or rolls the *tr.* is usually followed by a wavy line 〰〰.

Tradotto (It.). **Traduit** (Fr.). Translated.

Traîné (Fr.). Dragged.

Trait (Fr.). A series of quick notes; a run, rapid passage.

> **Trait de chant.** A melodic phrase.
>
> **Trait d'harmonie.** A succession of chords.

Traité (Fr.). A treatise.

> **Traité d'instrumentation.** A treatise on instrumentation.

Tranché (Fr.). Cut off. *Note tranchée,* a note instantly damped.

Tranquillamente (It.). Tranquilly.

Tranquillità (It.). Tranquillity, quiet.

Tranquillo, -a (It.). Tranquil, calm, peaceful.

Transponieren (Ger.). To transpose.

Transponierende Instrumente (Ger.). Transposing instruments.

Transposing instruments. Instruments in which the written notes do not correspond to the actual sounds. Although for convenience of notation the piccolo is written an octave below the actual sounds, and the double-bass and double-bassoon an octave above, and they are therefore strictly speaking transposing instruments, the term is usually taken to mean those instruments which play in a different key from that of the piece, *e. g.* the cor anglais, of which the written part is a fifth higher than the actual notes, and therefore plays in A when the orchestra is in D, and so on.

Trascinando (It.). Dragging.

Trasporto (It.). Transport, passion.

Trasposto (It.). Transposed.

Trattato (It.). A treatise.

Trattenuto (It.). Held back, detained; sustained.

Trattimento (It.). A treatise.

Tratto (It.). Dragged.

Trauer (Ger.). Sorrow, grief.

Trauermarsch. Funeral march.
Trauermusik. Funeral music.
Trauern (Ger.). To grieve, mourn. subs. Mourning, lamentation.
Träumend (Ger.). Dreaming.
Träumerei (Ger.). Reverie.
Träumerisch (Ger.). Dreamy.
Traurig (Ger.). Sad, dejected.
Traversière (Fr.). Oblique, cross. Term applied to the ordinary
Traverso (It.). flute to distinguish it from the old *flûte-à-bec*, which was held upright.
Tre (It.). Three.
> **Tre corde.** Three strings. Term used in piano music to contradict a previous *una corda*.
Treble. The highest voice, soprano; the highest part in a musical composition. In defining the pitch of instruments, *soprano* is nearly always used in preference to "treble".
> **Treble C.** The C above middle C; c″.
> **Treble clef.** The G clef on the 2nd line, often called the violin clef,

Treibend (Ger.). Hurrying.
Trem. Abbr. of *tremolo*.
Tremando (It.).
Tremante (It.). Trembling.
Tremblant (Fr.). Trembling.
Tremblement (Fr.). A shake.
Tremendissimo (It.). Sup. of *tremenao*.
Tremendo (It.). Dreadful, horrible.
Tremolando (It.). Trembling.
Tremolante (It.). *v.* Tremolo.
Tremolieren (Ger.). To produce a tremolo. *Nicht tremolieren, genau 16tel*, do not make a tremolo, strictly semiquavers.
Tremolo (It.). A rapid reiteration of one or more notes. On a bowed instrument this is obtained by a rapid motion of the bow; on a piano, by the alternation of two or more notes; on a harp, either by the rapid alternation of the two hands, or the alternation of two or more notes by means of homophones. (*v.* Bisbigliando.) On wind instruments a tremolo effect can be obtained as on the piano, or (on the flute and certain of the acuter brass) it can be imitated by double or triple tonguing. The term is used for a stop on the organ and harmonium which produces a tremulous effect.
> **Tremolo brisé.** A tremolo on two notes (on a violin, etc.),
> **Tremolo legato.** either on two strings or on the same string.
> **Tremolo ondulé.** A species of tremolo, now obsolete, produced
> **Tremolo vibrato.** by an undulating movement of the bow.
Trénise (Fr.). One of the figures of a quadrille.
Très (Fr.). Very; very much.
> **Très accentué.** Very accentuated.
> **Très attaqué.** Vigorously attacked. *v.* Attack.
> **Très déclamé.** Very much declaimed.
> **Très éclatant.** Very brilliant.

Très élargi. Very much broadened.
Très expressif. Very expressive.
Très fort. Very loud.
Très fortement accentué. Very strongly accented.
Très léger. Very light.
Très long. Very long.
Très marqué. Very marked, *ben marcato.*
Très modéré. Very moderate, *molto moderato.*
Très ralenti. Very much slackened.
Très rhythmé. The rhythm well marked.
Très saccadé. Very jerkily. *v.* Saccade.
Très sec. Very abrupt.
Très simplement. Very simply.
Très sonore. Very sonorous.
Très soutenu et expressif. Very much sustained and with expression.
Très vif. Very lively.
Très vite. Very quickly.
Triangel (Ger.). ⎫ A triangle.
Triangle (Fr.). ⎬
Triangle. An instrument formed of a steel bar bent into the shape of an isosceles triangle and giving a clear indeterminate sound when struck by a "beater". This latter is usually also of steel, but Weingartner in *Das Gefilde der Seligen* has for a special effect used one of wood.
Triangolo (It.). A triangle.
Trichter (Ger.). The bell of a wind-instrument; abbr. of *Schalltrichter.*
Trille (Fr.). A trill, shake.
Triller (Ger.). A trill, shake. *Die Triller in den ersten Flöten lang, mit wenigstens 7 Noten,* the shakes in the 1st flute long, and containing at least 7 notes.
Trillo (It.). A trill, shake.
　　Trillo caprino. A bad shake on a single note, resembling the bleat of a goat. *cf.* Bockstriller.
　　Trillo in maggiore. A major shake, *i. e.* with the note a tone above.
　　Trillo in minore. A minor shake, *i. e.* with the note a semitone above.
Trinklied (Ger.). A drinking song.
Trio (It.). (1) A composition for 3 voices or instruments. (2) The middle portion of a minuet, scherzo, march, etc., so called from its having been originally written in three parts.
Triole (Ger.). A group of 3 equal notes in place of 2, a triplet. *Die Triolen rhythmisch markiert,* the triplets rhythmically marked.
Triomphal (Fr.). ⎫
Trionfale (It.). ⎬ Triumphal.
Trionfante. (It.). ⎭
Tripel- (Ger.). Word used in combination and meaning "triple": as a simple word, *dreifach* = triple.
　　Tripelconcert. *v.* Tripelkonzert.
　　Tripelfuge. A triple fugue.
　　Tripelkonzert. A concerto for three solo instruments.
　　Tripeltakt. Triple time.

Tripelzunge. Triple tonguing.

Triple (Fr.). Triple.

Triple croche. A note with three hooks, a demi-semiquaver.

Tristesse (Fr.). } Sadness, melancholy.
Tristezza (It.). }

Triton (Fr.). } A tritone, an interval composed of 3 tones, forming
Tritono (It.). } an augmented 4th.

Tritt (Ger.). A pedal, treadle.

Trittbrett. The pedal of an organ; treadle for blowing the organ.

Trittharfe. Pedal harp.

Triumphmarsch (Ger.). A triumphal march.

Trois (Fr.). Three.

Tromba (It.). Trumpet.

Tromba a chiavi. A keyed trumpet (keyed bugle).

Tromba a macchina. A valve-trumpet.

Tromba a pistoni. A piston-trumpet.

Tromba bassa. Bass trumpet.

Tromba cromatica. Chromatic or valve-trumpet.

Tromba marina. *v.* Trompette marine.

Trombe (It.). Plur. of *tromba.*

Trombetta (It.). A small trumpet.

Trombettatore (It.). A trumpeter.

Trombettino (It.). A very small trumpet.

Trombone. A brass instrument, in which the chromatic scale is obtained either by means of a slide or by valves, the latter form being principally found in foreign military bands though used in many Fr. and It. orchestras. The instrument is made in various sizes: (a) The Soprano, now quite obsolete; (b) the Alto, in E♭, now seldom found in orchestras; (c) the Tenor, in B♭, with a compass from *E* to *b'♭* (*c''*, *d''*) and 4 pedal notes descending chromatically from *B₁♭*; this form occasionally possesses a single piston worked by the thumb, which enables the player to bridge over the missing notes between the highest pedal, and the *E* (*v.* Tenorbaßposaune); (d) the Bass, which is made in 3 keys (*v.* Bass Trombone); (e) the Contra-bass, an octave below the Tenor, but although found in Wagner's *Ring*, seldom used. In France, 3 tenor trombones are the rule; in England and Germany, 2 tenor and 1 bass.

Trombone (Fr.). A trombone.

Trombone à coulisse. Slide trombone.

Trombone à pistons. Piston-trombone.

Trombone basse. Bass trombone.

Trombone (It.). A trombone.

Trombone a cilindri. Trombone with cylinders.

Trombone a tiro. } A slide trombone.
Trombone duttile. }

Trombonino (It.). A small trombone; the alto trombone.

Trommel (Ger.). A drum, the term being applied to any drum other than a kettledrum.

Trommelfell. A drum-head.

Trommelklöppel. A drumstick for a bass-drum.

Trommelleine. The cord of a drum for tightening the head.

Trommelreifen. The hoops of a drum.
Trommelruf. A drum-call.
Trommelsaiten. The snare of a side-drum.
Trommelschläger. A drummer.
Trommelschleife. A snare.
Trommelstock. A drumstick for a side-drum.
Trommelwirbel. A roll on a drum.
Trommler (Ger.). A drummer.
Trompe de chasse (Fr.). The Fr. hunting horn, and the immediate precursor of the orchestral horn. It has a somewhat larger mouthpiece tapering to a narrow throat, but otherwise does not differ in any essential particular. It is usually pitched in D, and possesses no crooks, and since *closed* notes are not proper to it, its scale is merely the natural harmonic one. It is occasionally called *cor de chasse*, and is the *Jagdhorn* of the Germans.
Trompete (Ger.). A trumpet. In plur. and in combination, *Trompeten.*
  Trompete blasen. To blow the trumpet.
  Trompetenbläser. A trumpeter.
  Trompetentusch. A flourish on a trumpet.
  Trompetenzug. The slide of a slide-trumpet.
Trompeter (Ger.). A trumpeter.
Trompette (Fr.). A trumpet.
  Trompette à clefs. A keyed bugle.
  Trompette à pistons. Piston-trumpet.
  Trompette chromatique. Valve-trumpet.
  Trompette marine. A stringed instrument, whose tone was supposed to bear a certain resemblance to that of the trumpet. It was composed of a triangular body with a neck, and had one string stretched over a bridge supported on feet, one of which did not touch the body, but was free to vibrate, and thus imparted a peculiar tremulous burring effect to the notes. It was played with a bow, the left hand producing the notes in harmonics, thus giving precisely the same series of notes as a trumpet.
Tronco, -a (It.). Cut off. *Nota tronca*, a note suddenly damped. *cf.* Tranchée.
Troppo (It.). Excess, more than enough (subs.). Too much (adj.).
Trou (Fr.). A hole. A ventage on a wood-wind instrument.
  Trou fermé. A closed hole.
  Trou ouvert. An open hole.
Troublé (Fr.). Troubled.
Trugkadenz, Trugschluß (Ger.). An interrupted cadence.
Trumpet. The modern orchestral trumpet is a valve instrument (piston or cylinder), the natural trumpet being now used only for cavalry calls, and the slide-trumpet being but seldom found, even in England, where alone it ever had any vogue. Unfortunately an instrument, of the length of a natural trumpet in D or C is unsatisfactory when furnished with valves; and for this reason and also for the easier production of the high notes, the valve-trumpet is often constructed in B♭, or C, with a tube not much more than half the length of the trumpet employed by Beethoven,

Mozart, etc.; it is easier to play, but the tone, especially in the lower notes, loses much of its virility, and approaches that of the cornet. In some of the best orchestras of England and the Continent, a valve-trumpet in F is now used, and this is as good a substitute for the natural instrument as can be reasonably desired. As early as 1829, Berlioz (8 *Scenes from Faust*) used mutes for trumpets, but Wagner was the first to employ them systematically, to imitate the effect of toy-trumpets in *Die Meistersinger* and for comic effects in *Siegfried*; since then they have been freely employed for a variety of effects. The compass of the modern trumpet may be said to be from $f\sharp$ to c'', the Fr. composers usually writing them in C, and the Germans as a rule in B♭.

Trunscheit (Ger.). The Marine Trumpet.

Tschung (Ger.). A name for a Chinese gong.

Tuba. A generic name for bass brass instruments usually of the saxhorn type, with a wide bore, so that the fundamental note can be obtained, and the lowest register is full and resonant. The orchestral tuba in England and France is usually the Bombardon (bass saxhorn in F), and in Germany the corresponding instrument (with a somewhat smaller bore) originally designed by Wieprecht. The Euphonium in C or B♭, and the Contrabass Bombardon (an octave lower) are sometimes employed in the orchestra. In fact the "Tuba" or "Bass Tuba" marked in modern scores may almost be considered to be more the name of a part rather than signifying any particular instrument, since the part is taken in different countries and at different times by almost any variety of deep brass instrument. The "Wagner tubas" (*q. v.*) are somewhat different instruments.

Tumultuoso (It.). Tumultuous, riotous.

Tuning. Adjusting an instrument to a particular pitch.

> **Tuning cone.** An instrument used for tuning the metal pipes of an organ.
>
> **Tuning fork.** A steel instrument with two prongs, which being put into vibration produces a note almost entirely free from harmonics, and thus is useful for serving as a standard of pitch. For orchestral purposes or for tuning a piano, it is tuned to a', for military bands, to $b'♭$, and for vocal music to c'.
>
> **Tuning-key.** A key used for turning the pegs to which the strings of a harp or piano are attached.
>
> **Tuning wire.** A wire in a reed-pipe of an organ, by means of which it can be tuned.

Tuoni (It.). Tones, modes, sounds. Plur. of *tuono*.

> **Tuoni aperti.** Open notes.
>
> **Tuoni chiusi.** Closed notes.
>
> **Tuoni ecclesiastici.** Church modes.

Tuono (It.). A tone. Thunder.

Turba (Lat.). A crowd.

Turca (It.). } Turkish.
Türkisch (Ger.). }

Tusch (Ger.). A flourish of trumpets.

Tutta (It.). Fem. of *tutto*, all, every.

Tutta (la) forza. With full force, as loud as possible.

Tutte (It.). Fem. plur. of *tutto*.

> **Tutte (le) corde.** All the strings. In piano-music, the opposite to *una corda*, one string.
>
> **Tutte viole.** All the violas.

Tutti (It.). Masc. plur. of *tutto*. Used in concertos for the passages played by the orchestra alone, in contradistinction to the *solo* passages. Used in scores to signify that all the instruments playing a particular part are to play.

Tutto, -a (It.). All, every. adv. Wholly, entirely.

> **Tutto arco.** With the whole bow.
>
> **Tutto legato.** Entirely (very) legato.
>
> **Tutto leggiero.** Light throughout.

Tuyau (Fr.). An organ pipe.

> **Tuyau à anche.** A reed-pipe.
>
> **Tuyau bouché.** A stopped pipe.
>
> **Tuyau ouvert.** Open pipe.

Tympanist (Ger.). A kettledrum player.

Typophone (Fr.). A keyboard instrument much the same as the Celesta, but in which the hammers strike tuning forks instead of steel bars. D'Indy has made an effective use of it in *Le Chant de la Cloche*.

Tyrolien, -enne (Fr.). Tyrolese. *Tyrolienne*, a Tyrolese song, usually including the *Jodel*.

U

u. (Ger.). Abbr. of *und*.

> **U. C.** Abbr. of *una corda*.
>
> **u.s.f.** Abbr. of *und so fort.* } and so on, and so forth, etc.
> **u.s.w.** Abbr. of *und so weiter.* }

Üben, Ueben (Ger.). To practise.

Über, Ueber (Ger.). Above, over.

> **Überall.** Everywhere.
>
> **Überblasen.** (1) To blow or sound a horn, trumpet, etc. (2) To overblow.
>
> **Übereilt.** Over-hurried.
>
> **Übereinstimmend.** Consonant, harmonious.
>
> **Übergang.** A passing-over: transition passage, modulation.
>
> **Übergang zum Vorspiel des zweiten Bildes.** Transition passage to the prelude of the second tableau.
>
> **Übergehen.** To proceed.
>
> **Übergehend.** Proceeding to, blending into. *Allmählich bewegter, ins Tempo I. übergehend....*, gradually more animated, merging into Tempo I. ...
>
> **Überlegen.** In piano playing, to pass the finger over the thumb.
>
> **Überleitung.** An intermediate passage; the bridge passage connecting the subjects in a musical composition.
>
> **Übermäßig.** Excessive. Of intervals, augmented. *Eine übermäßige Sekunde*, an augmented second.
>
> **Übermäßiger Sechstakkord.** The Italian sixth.
>
> **Übermütig.** Merry, gay.

Überschlagen. In piano playing, to cross the hands.
Übersetzen. (1) To translate. (2) *v.* Überlegen.
Übersetzung. A translation.
Überspringen. To skip a note or interval.
Überstimmen. To tune too high.
Überstürzt. Hurried. *Die Triole immer schnell, aber nicht überstürzt,* the triplets always fast, but not hurried.
Übertönend. Sounding above the rest, — an intensive form of *hervortretend.*
Übrigen (Die). (Ger.). The rest.
Übung, Uebung (Ger.). An exercise. plur. *Übungen.*
Übungsstück. An exercise-piece, an exercise.
Uguaglianza (It.). Equality, uniformity.
Uguale (It.). Equal.
Ugualità (It.). *v.* Uguaglianza.
Ultimo, -a (It.). Last, farthest, greatest.
Ultima volta. The last time.
Umfang (Ger.). Compass of a voice or instrument. *cf.* Tonumfang.
Umkehrung (Ger.). Inversion. *Kanon in der Umkehrung,* canon in inversion, one in which the answer is the subject inverted.
Umore (It.). Humour.
Umoristico (It.). Humorous.
Umstellen (Ger.). To invert.
Umstellung (Ger.). Inversion.
Umstimmen (Ger.). To alter the pitch, to retune. *A in As umstimmen,* change A into A♭. *Es nach F umstimmen,* tune the E♭ to F.
Un, une (Fr.). A, one.
Un, un', uno, una (It.). A, one.
Un peu (Fr.). A little, somewhat.
Un peu élargi. Somewhat broadened.
Un peu en dehors. Somewhat prominent.
Un peu largement. Somewhat broadly.
Un peu marqué. Somewhat accentuated.
Un peu modéré. Somewhat slackened.
Un peu moins lent. A little less slow.
Un peu moins vite. A little less fast.
Un peu plus calme. Somewhat more tranquil.
Un peu plus large. Somewhat broader.
Un peu plus librement. Somewhat more freely.
Un peu retenu. Somewhat restrained (slackened).
Un peu vif et gaîment. Somewhat quickly and gaily.
Un pochettino (It.). }
Un pochissimo (It.). } A very little.
Un poco (It.). A little, somewhat. Sometimes written *un po',* as *un po' largamente,* somewhat broadly.
Un poco allargando. Somewhat broadening.
Un poco animando. Somewhat quickening.
Un poco crescendo. Somewhat increasing in loudness.
Un poco animato. Somewhat quickened.
Un poco decrescendo. Somewhat decreasing in loudness.
Un poco diminuendo. Somewhat diminishing in loudness.
Un poco lento. Somewhat slow.

Un poco meno. A little less.

Un poco meno moto. Somewhat less motion, *i. e.* somewhat slower than before.

Un poco meno presto. A little less fast.

Un poco più animato. Somewhat more animated.

Un poco più forte. Somewhat louder.

Un poco più lento. Somewhat slower.

Un poco più piano. A little softer.

Un poco rallentando. Gradually slackening a little.

Un poco ritenuto. Somewhat held back (slackened).

Una (It.). Fem. of *uno*, a, one.

Una corda col pedale. One string, with pedal. Direction implying use of both the pedals of a piano.

Una sola. One only, a single one.

Unbedeckt (Ger.). Uncovered.

Unbedeutend (Ger.). Insignificant, unimportant.

Und (Ger.). And.

Unda maris (Lat.). An open 8 ft organ stop of an undulating character.

Undecima (It.). Eleventh; the interval of an eleventh.

Undecimenakkord (Ger.). Chord of the eleventh.

Undecimole (Ger.). A group of 11 equal notes.

Ungarisch (Ger.). Hungarian.

Ungebunden (Ger.). Free.

Ungeduldig (Ger.). Impatient.

Ungefähr (Ger.). About, nearly. $\quad \downarrow = 54$ *ungefähr,* $\downarrow = $ about 54.

Ungerader Takt (Ger.). Ternary time.

Ungestüm (Ger.). Impetuous, wild.

Ungleiche Taktart (Ger.). Ternary time.

Ungleichschwebende Temperatur (Ger.). Unequal temperament.

Unharmonischer Querstand (Ger.). False relation.

Uni (Fr.). United; past part. of *unir.*

Unione (It.). Union, connection; coupler.

Unione al G. Org. Coupled to Gt.

Unione del G. Org. coll' Esp. Gt. coupled to Sw.

Unis. (1) Abbr. of *Unisoni.* (2) Plur. of *uni.*

Unis. 8a. Abbr. of *unisoni ottava,* in unison with the octave.

Unisono, -a (It.). In unison, unisonous. plur. *unisoni, -e.*

Unisono al primo flauto. In unison with the first flute.

Unisson (Fr.). Unison.

Unitamente (It.). Conjointly with, together with.

Unito, -a (It.). United, joined. *Arpe unite,* harps united.

Unito all' Esp. Coupled to Sw.

Unmerklich (Ger.). adj. Imperceptible. adv. Insensibly.

Unmerklich belebend. }
Unmerklich drängend. } Insensibly quickening.

Unmerklich etwas bewegter. Very slightly more animated.

Unmerklich zu Tempo I. Insensibly (returning) to Tempo I.

Uno, -a (It.). One.

Uno ad uno. One by one.

Uno solo. Only one, a single one (masc.). *Una sola* (fem.).

Unregelmäßige Bewegung (Ger.). Irregular motion.

Unrein (Ger.). Impure; out of tune.

Unreiner Ton. A false note.
Unruhig (Ger.). Restless.
Unschuldig (Ger.). Innocent, pure.
Unter (Ger.). Under, beneath, among, between. Sometimes marked in piano duets, where the hand of one player crosses *under* that of the other, *oben* (above) being indicated in the other part.
    Unter der Stimme. Under the voice, *sotto voce*.
    Unterbrochene Kadenz. Interrupted cadence.
    Unterdecke. The back of a stringed instrument.
    Unterdominante. Sub-dominant.
    Untermediante. Sub-mediant.
    Untersatz, *or* **Unterbaß.** Sub-bass.
    Untersetzen. In piano playing, to pass the thumb under.
    Untersetzung. In piano playing, the passing-under of the thumb.
    Unterstimme. The lowest part.
    Untertasten. The lower (*i. e.* the white) keys on a keyboard.
    Unterwerk. The lowest manual on an organ.
Unverziert (Ger.). Unadorned, unembellished.
Unvollkommen (Ger.). Imperfect.
    Unvollkommene Kadenz. Imperfect cadence.
Uomo (It.). A man. plur. *Uomini.*
Upbeat. The unaccented part of the bar.
Upbow. The movement of the bow from the point to the nut.
Upper partials. *v.* Harmonics.
Ut (Fr.). The note C. *Cors en Ut,* horns in C.
    Ut bémol majeur. C flat major.
    Ut dièse mineur. C sharp minor.

V

V. Abbr. of *violino, voce, volti,* etc.
    V. S. Abbr. of *volti subito,* turn over quickly.
    V. V. (Occasionally written as "W") Abbr. of *violini.*
Va. Abbr. of *Viola.*
Vacillando (It.). Vacillating, wavering. On stringed instruments, meaning the same as the Ger. *Bebung,* or Fr. *Balancement* (*q. v.*).
Vacillant (Fr.). Wavering.
Vaghezza (It.). Charm, grace.
Vago (It.). Undefined, ambiguous.
Valeur (Fr.). ⎱ (1) Valour, bravery. (2) Value (of notes, etc.).
Valore (It.). ⎰
Valse (Fr.). Waltz.
Valves. A mechanism applied to brass instruments with a cup-shaped mouthpiece, which changes the length of the tube by diverting the air current through supplementary tubes of varying lengths, thus instantly altering the pitch. The two forms of valves now in general use are the piston and the cylinder, the former being found usually in England and France, the latter in Germany and Italy. There are usually three valves, the first lowering the pitch 2 semitones; the second 1, and the third 3, occasionally 4. In some bass instruments a 4th valve is added, lowering the pitch 5 semitones. Since the Harmonic Series (*q. v.*) can be obtained

with every difference of pitch, it follows that by means of the valves (either singly or in combination) every note of the chromatic scale can be obtained. For the easier production of the high notes, instruments are also made in which the third valve *raises* the pitch 2 semitones, the complete chromatic scale being obtained as before with the exception of *d♯*. Sax invented instruments with 6 valves, each acting independently of one another: these, though giving truer intonation, have disadvantages, and have been never much employed; an example of their use may be found in d'Indy's *Le chant de la Cloche.*

Vaporeux, -euse (Fr.). Vapoury, vaporous. Indication implying a very light delicate execution.

Var. Abbr. of variation.

Variamente (It.). Variously.

Variantemente (It.). Differently; with variety.

Variationen (Ger.). ⎫ Variations.
Variations (Fr.). ⎭

Variato (It.). Varied.

Variazioni (It.). Variations.

Varié (Fr.). Varied.

Vaterländisches Lied (Ger.). A patriotic song.

Vaut (Fr.). Is worth, is equal to. From *valoir*, to be worth. *La ♩ vaut la ♩ de la mesure précédente*, the ♪ equals the ♩ of the preceding bar.

Vc. Vcllo. Abbr. of *Violoncello.*

Veemente (It.). Vehement, impetuous.

Veemenza (It.). Vehemence, passionate fervour.

Vehemenz (Ger.). *v.* Veemenza, Heftigkeit.

Velato (It.). Veiled, muffled. The term is applied to voices, and is used in the sense of *coperto (q. v.)* for drums

Vellutato (It.). Velvety.

Velo (It.). A cloth or veil; the cloth used for muffling a drum.

Veloce (It.). Quick, rapid.

Velocemente (It.). Quickly, rapidly.

Velocissimamente (It.). Sup. of *velocemente.*

Velocissimo (It.). Sup. of *veloce.*

Velocità (It.). ⎫ Velocity, rapidity.
Velocité (Fr.). ⎭

Velouté (Fr.). Velvety.

Ventil (Ger.). A valve.

    Ventilhorn. A valve horn.

    Ventilposaune. A valve trombone.

    Ventiltrompete. A valve trumpet.

Venusto (It.). Graceful, charming.

Vêpres (Fr.). Vespers.

Veränderungen (Ger.). Variations, alterations.

Verbindung (Ger.). Connection, combination, union.

    Verbindungsakkord. Connecting chord.

    Verbindungszeichen. A tie, slur. *Bogen* is often used in the same sense.

Verdeckt (Ger.). Covered, hidden.

    Verdeckte Quinten. Hidden fifths.

Verdoppelt (Ger.). Doubled.
Verdoppelung (Ger.). Doubling.
Vergrößern (Ger.). To increase.
Vergrößerung (Ger.). Augmentation.
Verhallend (Ger.). Dying away.
Verhältnis (Ger.). Relation (of intervals, etc.).
Verkehrung (Ger.). Inversion. *cf.* Umkehrung.
Verkleinern (Ger.). To diminish.
Verkleinerung (Ger.). Diminution.
Verklingend (Ger.). Dying away.
Verkürzend (Ger.). Drawing closer together, *stringendo.*
Verkürzung (Ger.). A drawing closer together, *stretto.*
Verlag (Ger.). Publication.
   Verlagsrecht. Copyright.
Verlauf (Ger.). Course, progress. *Im Anfang ruhiges, im Verlauf bewegtes Tempo,* at the commencement, tranquil, in the course (of the movement) animated tempo.
Verliebt (Ger.). Loving, tender.
Verlöschend (Ger.). Dying away.
Vermindert (Ger.). Diminished. *Eine verminderte Quinte,* a diminished fifth.
Verminderung (Ger.). Diminution.
Vernehmlich (Ger.). Distinct, clear.
Vers (Fr.). A verse, usually used in the strict sense of a line of a poem.
Verschiebung (Ger.). A shifting. In piano music, "the shifting" or soft pedal. *Mit Verschiebung,* with the soft pedal; *ohne Verschiebung,* without the soft pedal.
Verschieden (Ger.). Several, various. *Die verschiedenen Stimmen abwechselnd,* various voices alternating.
Verschmelzen (Ger.). To blend. *Die Töne verschmelzen,* to blend the notes. *cf.* Empâter.
Verschwindend (Ger.). Dying away.
Versetzen (Ger.). To transpose.
Versetzungszeichen (Ger.). Accidentals.
Verstärkend (Ger.). Strengthening (the sound); *rinforzando.*
Verstärkt (Ger.). Strengthened.
Verstärkung (Ger.). A strengthening.
Vertauschen (Ger.). To exchange.
Vert(h)eilt (Ger.). Divided.
Vertonen (Ger.). To compose.
Vertonung (Ger.). Composition.
Verträumt (Ger.). Dreamy.
Verwandte Tonarten (Ger.). Relative keys.
Verwechs(e)lung (Ger.). Change, inversion.
Verzierend (Ger.). Ornamental. *Der verzierende Vorschlag,* the ornamental appoggiatura.
Verzierter Kontrapunkt (Ger.). Figurate counterpoint.
Verzierung (Ger.). An ornament, embellishment. plur. *Verzierungen.*
   Verzierungsnote. A grace note.
Verzögerungen (Ger.). Retardation.
Verzweifelt (Ger.). Broken-hearted, despairing.
Verzweiflungsvoll (Ger.). Despairingly, full of despair.

Vezzosamente (It.). Gracefully, prettily.
Via (It.). Away, off.
 Via l'unione. The coupler off.
 Via sordine. The mutes off.
Vibrante (It.). Vibrating, resounding.
Vibratissimo (It.). Sup. of *vibrato.*
Vibrato (It.). Vibrated. Term applied to both voices and instruments,
 and signifying attacking the notes vigorously with a certain ringing
 tremulousness. *cf.* Balancement.
Vibrazione (It.). Vibration.
Vibrer (Fr.). To vibrate. *Laisser vibrer,* let vibrate.
Vibrieren (Ger.). To vibrate. *In dem Streichquartett mehr vibrieren
 lassen als tremolieren,* in the string-quartet more a vibrato than a
 tremolo.
Vibrierend (Ger.). Vibrating.
Vicendevolmente (It.). Alternately, reciprocally.
Vicino (It.). Near.
Vide (Fr.). Empty. *Corde à vide,* an open string.
Viel (Ger.). Much, many.
 Viel bewegter. Much more animated.
 Viel Bogen (wechselnd). Many changes of bow.
 Viel gemessenere Bewegung als zu Anfang. Much more measured
  movement than at the commencement.
 Viel langsamer. Much more slowly.
 Viel ruhiger. Much more tranquil.
 Viel Ton! Much tone! Indication denoting a resonant vigorous
  execution.
Vielle (Fr.). A hurdy-gurdy.
Vielstimmig (Ger.). Polyphonic.
Vier (Ger.). Four. *Die vier Taktschläge bedeutend schneller als vorher
 die Viertel,* the four beats of the bar considerably faster than
 the previous crotchets.
 Vierfach. Fourfold. Often written *4fach.*
 Vierhändig. For four hands.
 Vierklang. A chord of four notes, specifically a chord of the 7th.
 Vierstimmig. In four parts.
 Viertaktig. Four bar rhythm.
Viertel (Ger.). A quarter. A crotchet. *Das 3te Viertel immer kurz
 abgestoßen,* the 3rd crotchet always shortly detached; *die Viertel
 langsamer als vorher die Achtel,* the crotchets slower than the
 previous quavers.
 Viertel schlagen. Beat crotchets.
 Viertelnote. A crotchet, — usually abbreviated to *Viertel.*
 Viertelpause. A crotchet rest.
 Viertelschlag. A crotchet-beat. *Die Viertelschläge etwas ruhiger
  als vorher,* the crotchet-beats somewhat more tranquil than
  before.
Viervierteltakt (Ger.). $4/4$ time.
Vierzweiteltakt (Ger.). $4/2$ time.
Vif, vive (Fr.). Quick, lively.
Vigore (It.). Vigour.
Vigorosamente (It.). Vigorously.

Vigoroso, -a (It.). Vigorous.

Vigueur (Fr.). Vigour.

Villanella (It.). ⎰ A pastoral poem or song.
Villanelle (Fr.). ⎱

Villareccio, Villereccio, Villesco (It.). Rustic, pastoral.

Villota (It.). A Venetian folksong.

Vinata (It.). A vintage song.

Viola (It.). A bowed instrument with 4 strings tuned to *c, g, d', a',* and with an orchestral compass to about *c'''*. It is written in the alto clef, the treble clef being used for the highest register. The tuning may be said to be invariable, although instances are found in *Le Pré aux Clercs* (Hérold) and *Don Quixote* (R. Strauss) where the 4th string (*c*) is lowered a semitone. In some modern Ger. scores the term *Viola* is now used instead of *Bratsche*, the plur. being *Violen* instead of the It. *viole.*

Viola alta (It.). A viola designed by Hermann Ritter, who aimed at producing one, in which the length of the strings should bear the same proportion to the body as it does in a violin. It is larger than the ordinary viola, possesses a fuller and more resonant tone, and has a 5th string tuned to *e''*, to enable the player to execute the high passages of modern scores with greater facility. Wagner introduced some of them into his Bayreuth orchestra, but, in spite of advantages, they are not in general use, since they require a performer endowed with exceptionally large hands.

Viola d'amore (It.). An obsolete instrument of the viola type, with seven strings (*d, f♯, a, d', f'♯, a', d''*), and with seven others tuned sympathetically, and running beneath the bridge. The obbligato to Raoul's Romance (*Les Huguenots*, Act I) is intended for this instrument, and illustrates its facility in producing harmonics. In the score the part is merely indicated as *"Un Alto solo"*; it was originally written as a violoncello solo, and is now usually played on an ordinary viola. The instrument has been recently revived.

Viola da gamba (It.). Practically an obsolete instrument, although now being cultivated in some quarters. It resembles a violoncello, and has 6 strings, *D, G, c, e, a, d'*. The instrument was made in different sizes, and occasionally with 7 strings.

Viola-Streichzither (Ger.). An instrument of the zither type, but played with a bow. It has 4 strings tuned *c, g, d', a'*.

Viole d'amour (Fr.). *v.* Viola d'amore.

Violen (Ger.). Plur. of *Viola*, which is now the term found in modern Ger. scores instead of *Bratsche*.

Violent (Fr.). Violent, impetuous.

Violentamente (It.). Violently.

Violento (It.). Violent, impetuous.

Violin. A bowed instrument with 4 strings tuned *g, d', a', e''*. In orchestral music the compass extends to *d''''*, or *e''''*, and by the use of harmonics several notes higher. When it is used as a solo instrument, Paganini and others have altered the tuning for the sake of greater brilliancy, and Saint-Saëns in his *Danse Macabre* directs the solo violin to tune the 1st string to *e''♭*; in the orchestra, the tuning may be said to be invariable, although R. Strauss has on occasion altered the 4th string to *g♭* (*f♯*).

Violin clef. Now, the G clef on the 2nd line, the ordinary treble clef; the old French violin clef had the G clef on the 1st line.
Violin diapason. An organ stop of 8 ft.
Violine (Ger.). A violin. *Violin-* in combination. plur. *Violinen*.
  Violinboden. The back of a violin.
  Violinbogen. A violin bow.
  Violinconcert. *v.* Violinkonzert.
  Violindecke. The belly of a violin.
  Violinhaare. Hair for a violin bow.
  Violinkasten. A violin case.
  Violinkonzert. A violin concerto.
  Violinschlüssel. The violin clef.
Violino (It.). A violin. plur. *Violini*.
  Violino primo. First violin.
  Violino principale. The leader of an orchestra; the solo violinist in a concerto.
Violon (Fr.). Violin.
Violoncell (Ger.). A violoncello. plur. *Violoncellen*.
Violoncelle (Fr.). A violoncello.
Violoncello (It.). A bowed instrument with 4 strings tuned C, G, d, a, the 4th string (C) being very occasionally lowered a semitone, as at the commencement of *Samson et Dalila* (Saint-Saëns) and *Also sprach Zarathustra* (R. Strauss). In the orchestra its compass may be said to extend to e'', although modern composers do not fear even the a'' (5th symphony, Mahler). For the lower register the bass clef is used; for the upper both the tenor and the treble, the latter often with the signification that the notes are an octave higher than the actual sounds. This peculiarity however is seldom found in modern music (and never unless the G clef immediately follows the F clef), yet Mahler is careful to add a note to the passage cited above: — *NB. Nicht eine Oktave tiefer.* (Not an octave lower.)
Virtuos (Ger.). A virtuoso, a clever artist, great master. Used in compounds, *e. g. Hornvirtuos, Violinvirtuos*, etc.
Virtuosità (It.).
Virtuosität (Ger.). } Virtuosity, consummate skill, artistic perfection.
Virtuosité (Fr.).
Virtuoso (Fr. and It.). A virtuoso.
Vis (Fr.). A screw.
Vista (It.). Sight. *A prima vista*, at first sight.
Vistamente (It.). Quickly.
Vite (Fr.). Quick.
Vite (It.). A screw (such as one for the nut of a bow).
Vitement (Fr.). Quickly.
Vitesse (Fr.). Quickness, celerity.
Vivace (It.). Lively, brisk, gay, vivacious. A term implying an execution faster than *allegro*.
  Vivace con grazia. With vivacity and grace.
  Vivace ma non troppo. Quick, but not too fast.
  Vivace scherzoso. Lively and playful.
Vivacemente (It.). Hastily, with vivacity.
Vivacetto (It.). Diminutive of *vivace*; lively, animated, gracious.
Vivacissimo (It.). Sup. of *vivace*; very quick, brisk, etc.

Vivacità (It.). ⎫
Vivacité (Fr.). ⎬ Vivacity, ardour, fire.

Vivamente (It.). Briskly, gaily.

Vive (Fr.). Fem. of *vif*; quick, lively.

Vivement (Fr.). With animation, quickly, with spirit.

Vivido (It.). *v.* Vivace, Vivo.

Vivissimo (It.). Sup. of *vivo*.

Vivo (It.). Full of life, animated; term indicating a performance faster than *allegro*.

Vllo. Abbr. of *violoncello*.

V°. Abbr. of *violino*.

Vocale (It.). Vocal.

Vocalisation (Fr.). Vocalisation; the art of singing on vowels.

Vocalise (Fr.). *v.* Vocalizzo.

Vocalisieren (Ger.). ⎫
Vocalizzare (It.). ⎬ To vocalise.

Vocalizzazione (It.). Vocalisation.

Vocalizzo (It.). A singing exercise on vowels.

Voce (It.). Voice.

    Voce buona. A good voice, which according to Lichtenthal may be *chiara* (clear), *sonora o di metallo* (sonorous or ringing), *piena* (full), *intuonata* (singing), *agile* (agile), *flessibile* (flexible), *robusta* (powerful), *forte* (strong), *grata* (pleasing), *dolce* (sweet), *pastosa* (mellow), *ricca d'estensione* (of an extensive compass),etc.

    Voce cattiva. A bad voice, which according to the same authority may be *debole* (weak), *sottile* (thin), *strillante* (screeching), *gagliarda* (stubborn), *nasale* (nasal), *di gola* (throaty), *appannata* (worn), *velata* (veiled), etc.

    Voce di media. The medium register of a voice.

    Voce di petto. The chest voice.

    Voce di testa. The head voice.

    Voce umana. At one time a name for the cor anglais. An 8 ft reed stop on the organ.

Voci (It.). Plur. of *voce*.

    Voci miste. Mixed voices.

Voicing. Regulating the tone of an organ pipe.

Voilé (Fr.). Veiled, muffled. Term applied to voices of a veiled quality of tone, or to drums when covered with a cloth or otherwise muffled. Charpentier in *Impressions d'Italie* directs his horns to be at times *voilés*.

Voile (Fr.). A veil or cloth; the cloth placed over drums for the purpose of muffling them. *Une voile sur le peau de la Timbale*, a cloth on the skin (head) of the kettledrum.

Voix (Fr.). Voice.

    Voix célestes. A stop of an undulating character in an organ, each note being sounded by two pipes, one of which is tuned a little sharper than the other.

    Voix de poitrine. The chest voice.

    Voix de tête. The head voice.

    Voix humaine. *v.* Vox humana.

    Voix voilée. A veiled voice.

Vokalisieren (Ger.). To vocalise.

Vokalmusik (Ger.). Vocal music.
Vokalquartett (Ger.). Vocal quartet.
Volante (It.). Flying. Term indicating a light, rapid, delicate execution.
Volata (It.). A flight; a roulade.
Volk (Ger.). The people, the populace, the lower classes. *Volks-* in combination.
    Volkslied. A song of the people.
    Volkst(h)ümlich. Popular, national.
    Volkston. The fashion of the people.
    Volksweise. A melody of the people, a popular air.
Voll (Ger.). Full, whole, complete. ⌢ 5 *volle Takte lang,* ⌢ 5 complete bars long. *Voll* is also used as a suffix, like "-ful" in English; *Gefühlvoll,* full of feeling, *Klangvoll,* full of sound (resonant).
    Volles Orchester. Full orchestra.
    Volles Werk. Full organ.
    Volles Zeitmaß. The full time (of the movement).
    Vollkommen. Perfect. *Vollkommene Kadenz,* perfect cadence.
    Voll Rührung. Full of emotion.
    Voll Sehnsucht. Full of yearning.
    Vollstimmig. Full-voiced, full-toned. *Vollstimmiger Akkord,* full chord; *Vollstimmiger Chor,* full-voiced choir.
    Vollstimmigkeit. Full tone; complete harmony.
    Volltönig. Full-toned, sonorous. *Dieser Akkord sehr kurz und volltönig abgestoßen,* this chord very sharply staccato and sonorous.
Völlig (Ger.). Complete, perfect. *In völliger Entrückung,* in perfect rapture.
Volonté (Fr.). Will, wish. *À volonté,* at will, *ad libitum.*
Volta (It.). Time (not in the sense of *tempo*). *Prima* (1*a*) *volta,* first time; *seconda* (2*a*) *volta,* second time.
Voltare (It.). To turn.
Volteggiando (It.). Flying. Term implying a very light and rapid execution.
Volti (It.). Turn over, P. T. O.
    Volti presto. ⎱
    Volti subito. ⎰ Turn over quickly.
Volubilmente (It.). Lightly, flippantly.
Vom (Ger.). Compound of *von* and *dem*; of the, by the, from the, etc.
    Vom Anfang ohne Wiederholung bis zum Schluß. From the beginning to the end without repetition.
    Vom Blatte spielen. To play at sight.
    Vom Frosch. By the nut (of the bow).
    Vom Zeichen. From the sign.
Von (Ger.). From, by, of, etc.
    Von Anfang. From the commencement.
    Von einem geschlagen. Struck by one (performer).
    Von hier ab im Zeitmaß. Henceforward in tempo.
    Von hier an nicht mehr schleppen! Do not slacken from here onwards.
    Von zwei Paukenschlägern auf beiden Seiten. By two kettle-drummers on both ends (of the bass drum).

Vorangehend (Ger.). Preceding.
Vorausnahme (Ger.). Anticipation.
Vorbereiten (Ger.). To prepare. *Ces und Fes vorbereiten*, prepare C♭ and F♭. (Direction in harp part.)
Vorbereitet (Ger.). Prepared.
 Vorbereitete Dissonanz. A prepared discord.
Vorbereitung (Ger.). Preparation.
Vorgeiger (Ger.). Leader of an orchestra.
Vorgreifung, Vorgriff (Ger.). Anticipation.
Vorhalt (Ger.). Suspension, retardation.
Vorhanden (Ger.). Existing, present, at one's disposal. *Wenn vorhanden doppelt besetzt*, when possible the parts to be doubled.
Vorhang (Ger.). Curtain.
 Vorhang (geht) auf. The curtain rises.
 Vorhang fällt. The curtain falls.
Vorher (Ger.). Previously, formerly.
Vorhergehend (Ger.). Preceding, previous.
Vorherig (Ger.). Previous, preceding.
 Vorheriges Zeitmaß. The preceding tempo.
Vorig (Ger.). Preceding, previous. ♩ = ♩ *des vorigen Zeitmaß*, ♩ = ♩ of the preceding tempo.
Vorsänger (Ger.). Leader of a choir, a precentor.
Vorschlag (Ger.). Grace-note, *appoggiatura*. *Die Vorschläge kurz und sehr deutlich*, the grace-notes short and very distinct.
 Vorschläge so schnell als möglich. The grace-notes as quick as possible.
Vorspiel (Ger.). A prelude. The opening symphony of a song.
Vorspieler (Ger.). Leader, principal performer. *Die Vorspieler an den 3 ersten Pulten*, the leaders of the first 3 desks.
Vortanz (Ger.). The "fore-dance"; the first dance in a series of dance movements.
Vortrag (Ger.). Execution. *Vortrags-* in combination.
 Vortragsbezeichnungen. Signs of execution; marks of expression.
 Vortragsstück. Executive piece, a "show piece", *morceau de concert.*
Vorwärts (Ger.). Forwards, onwards. Term corresponding to *stringendo.*
Vorzeichnung (Ger.). Key signature.
Voto (It.). *v.* Vuoto.
Vox humana (Lat.). A soft 8 ft stop on the Swell or Choir organ, more or less resembling the tone of the human voice.
Vuoto, -a (It.). Empty. *Corda vuota*, an open string. *Vuota* is sometimes marked when there is a rest for all the parts. *cf.* G. P.

W

W. Abbr. of *Violini.* Sometimes written "VV".
Wachsend (Ger.). Increasing the sound, *crescendo.*
Wachtel (Ger.). A quail. The indication is found in the Pastoral Symphony, where the oboe imitates the cry of the bird.
 Wachtelpfeife. An instrument used for imitating the note of the quail. The bird's call can also be imitated by chipping two clear-sounding pebbles together.

Wagner Tubas. These instruments are practically saxhorns (alto in E♭ and bass in B♭), or more strictly speaking saxotrombas (*q. v.*), with certain modifications. As originally devised they were intended to be played by horn-players, the pistons (3 or 4) being controlled by the *left* hand, as in a horn, and the bell, instead of being directed vertically upwards, being bent to the right of the player; and, unlike the ordinary saxhorns, they were to be played with a horn mouthpiece. In practice, the original intentions have been departed from, and the parts are now usually played by a trombone or euphonium-player, with a trombone mouthpiece. In *Das Rheingold* and the Prologue to *Götterdämmerung*, the 2 tenor tubas are written in B♭, and the 2 bass in F; for the remainder of the *Ring*, they are in E♭ and B♭ respectively, and in this latter case Wagner has used the bass clef with the same signification as in horn music, the notes being written an octave lower than their proper notation. It is to be observed that this alteration in the pitch of the tubas is only apparent, and affects merely the parts as given in the scores; in the *separate* parts, the instruments are *Tenortuben in B* (B♭) and *Baßtuben in F* throughout the whole of the *Ring*. Wagner altered their notation in the scores of *Die Walküre, Siegfried* and the three acts of *Götterdämmerung* under the impression that he thereby made the parts easier to read. Bruckner, Nicodé, etc. have also employed these instruments.

Während (Ger.). While.

    Während der 3te Flötist die kleine Flöte nimmt. While the 3rd flute takes the piccolo.

Wald (Ger.). Wood, forest.

    Waldflöte. A Ger. organ stop of tin, metal or wood, of 2 ft.

    Waldflute. An Eng. organ stop of wood of 4 ft.

    Waldhorn. Originally a term for the hunting horn (*trompe de chase*), it then became the name of the orchestral natural horn. To prevent confusion of nomenclature, it is preferable to confine the term to the latter instrument, calling the hunting horn by its other name of *Jagdhorn*.

    Waldpfeife. *v.* Waldflöte.

    Waldteufel. A "Wood-devil"; an instrument of tin or cardboard used in comic fantasias to imitate the whistling of the wind.

Wankend (Ger.). Undecided, wavering.

Wärme (Ger.). Warmth.

Wechseln (Ger.). To change, alter.

    Wechseln in F. Change into F.

    Wechseln mit Klarinetten in A. Change to clarinets in A.

Wechselnote (Ger.). A changing note.

Weglassen (Ger.). Omit, leave out.

Wehmüt(h)ig (Ger.). Woeful, sorrowful.

Weich (Ger.). Soft, tender, delicate, gentle. *Mit einem weichen Klöppel geschlagen*, struck with a soft bass-drumstick.

    Weiche Tonart. The minor key.

    Weich gestoßen. Lightly detached; light staccato.

    Weich gestrichen. Gently bowed.

    Weich und bewegt. Soft and animated.

    Weich und getragen. Soft and sustained.

Weichheit (Ger.). Tenderness.
Weichherzig (Ger.). Kind-hearted, compassionate.
Weinend (Ger.). Crying, weeping, lachrymose.
Weite (Ger.). Wide, dispersed.
   Weite Harmonie. Extended harmony.
   Weite Lage. Extended position.
Wenig, weniger, am wenigsten (Ger.). Little, less, least.
   Weniger abgemessen. Less measured (faster).
   Weniger breit. Less broad.
   Weniger lebhaft. Less animated.
   Weniger stark. Less powerfully.
Wenn (Ger.). If, in case.
   Wenn ein Harmonium vorhanden ist. If an harmonium be
     procurable.
Werden (Ger.). To become. *Etwas breiter werden*, become somewhat
   broader.
Werk (Ger.). Work. plur. *Werke.*
Wesentlich (Ger.). Essential, real.
Wie (Ger.). As, like.
   Wie am Anfang. As at the commencement.
   Wie ein Kondukt. Like a funeral procession.
   Wie früher. As before.
   Wie gepeitscht. Like the crack of a whip.
   Wie oben. As above.
   Wie Orgeltöne. Like organ tones.
   Wie träumend. Dreamily.
   Wie vorher. As previously.
   Wie vorhin. As before.
   Wie wütend dreinfahren. As though angrily interposing.
   Wie zuvor. As before.
Wieder (Ger.). Again, once more.
   Wieder belebend. Again becoming animated.
   Wieder belebter, wie zuvor. Again more animated, as before.
   Wieder beschleunigend. Again quickening.
   Wieder bewegter. Again more animated.
   Wieder das vorhergehende Hauptzeitmaß. Again the previous
     principal tempo.
   Wieder etwas gedehnter. Again somewhat more drawn-out.
   Wieder etwas ruhigeres Tempo. Again a somewhat more tranquil
     tempo.
   Wieder etwas zurückhaltend. Again somewhat slackening.
   Wieder früheres Zeitmaß. Again the previous time.
   Wieder gedehnter. Again more drawn-out.
   Wieder gemessener. Again more measured.
   Wieder lebhafter werdend. Again becoming more animated.
   Wieder mäßig. Again moderate.
   Wieder nachlassend. Again slackening.
   Wieder noch einmal so langsam. Once more as slow again
     (twice as slow).
   Wieder ruhiger, wie zuvor. Again more tranquilly, as before.
   Wieder schnell. Again fast.
   Wieder sehr lebhaft. Again very animated.

Wieder sehr mäßig. Again very moderate.
Wieder zögernd. Again lingering (slackening).
Wieder zurückhaltend. Again slackening.
Wiederholen (Ger.). To repeat.
Wiederholung (Ger.). Repetition.
    Wiederholungsstrich. The sign for the repetition of a phrase.
    Wiederholungszeichen. The sign for a repeat.
Wiederkehr (Ger.). The re-entry of a part.
Wiederschlag (Ger.). Repercussion; the reappearance of a subject in a fugue.
Wiederum (Ger.). Again.
    Wiederum kläglich. Again mournfully.
Wiegenlied (Ger.). A cradle song.
Wild (Ger.). Furious, ferocious, *feroce*.
Wind (Ger.). The wind.
    Windharfe. The Æolian harp.
    Windkasten. Wind-trunk.
    Windlade. Wind-chest.
    Windmaschine. A wind-machine. An instrument which is used in theatres to imitate the rising and falling of the wind; R. Strauss has employed one in *Don Quixote*.
Wind-band. (1) A military band, a band composed of wind-instruments. (2) The wind-instruments (the "Wind") of a symphonic orchestra, as opposed to the "Strings".
Wind-chest. That portion of an organ in which is collected compressed air ready to be admitted into the pipes. Each manual possesses a separate wind-chest, and occasionally even a single stop may have one of its own.
Wind-instruments. These, while strictly speaking including such instruments as the organ, harmonium, concertina, etc., are usually taken to be those in which the wind is supplied by the human lungs. They are divided into "Wood" and "Brass", — convenient, though inexact definitions. Whether the material, out of which a wind-instrument is constructed, affects the tone is a subject fiercely debated: some declaring that a trumpet of *papiermaché* produces a tone indistinguishable from that of the ordinary trumpet; others being equally emphatic that an instrument of (say) aluminium produces an indifferent tone. But in any case, the tone depends mainly on the shape and proportions of the instrument, and on the form and material of its mouthpiece. This in the Brass, is cup-shaped, while in the Wood, it may be merely an orifice, as in the flutes, a single reed (clarinet family), or a double reed (oboe and bassoon families). In the Brass, the lips of the performer may be said to act as reeds.
Wind-trunk. That portion of an organ which conveys the wind from the bellows to the wind-chest.
Wirbel (Ger.). (1) A peg of a stringed instrument. (2) A roll on a drum. *Einen Wirbel schlagen*, to give a roll.
    Wirbeltrommel. The tenor drum, now generally called *Rührtrommel*.
Wirbeln (Ger.). To roll on a drum.
Wischer (Ger.). A swab or mop for cleaning wood-wind instruments.

Wohl (Ger.). Well. Word used in combination with many words.
    Wohlgefällig. Pleasing, agreeable.
    Wohlklang. Concord; harmony; melodiousness.
    Wohlklingend. Melodious, harmonious.
    Wohllaut. A concord.
Wood-wind, *or merely* **Wood.** The instruments in a symphonic orchestra forming a group opposed to the "Strings" and "Brass". The tone of the horn being, except for special effects, more nearly allied to the Wood than the Brass, the instrument is frequently associated with the former, and is often placed between the clarinets and bassoons in the score.
Wort (Ger.). A word. plur. *Worte & Wörter.*
Wuchtig (Ger.). Weighty, heavy, *pesante.*
    Wuchtig, jedoch nicht schleppend. Heavily, but not dragging.
Würde (Ger.). Dignity, noble bearing.
    Würdevoll. Full of dignity, dignified.
Wüt(h)end (Ger.). }
Wüt(h)ig (Ger.). } Raging, furious.

X

Xylophon (Ger.). Xylophone.
Xylophone. A species of harmonica composed of strips or cylinders of wood, played upon by two little wooden hammers. It is made of various sizes, and possesses a compass of about 3 octaves from *e* or *g*, its effective notes lying between *c'* and *c'''.* The notes are sometimes written an octave lower than the actual sounds. It has been used by Saint-Saëns (*Danse Macabre*), Humperdinck (*Hänsel und Gretel*), Holbrooke (*Queen Mab*), Mahler (*6th Symphony*), etc.

Z

Zampogna (It.). A bagpipe.
Zänkisch (Ger.). Quarrelsome, cantankerous.
Zapateado. A wild Spanish dance, in which the performers strike their shoes with their hands.
Zapfenstreich (Ger.). The tattoo, *la retraite*: in a wider sense, the public performance of a military band.
Zart (Ger.). Tender, delicate, soft.
    Zart gesteigert. Gently worked-up.
    Zart gesungen. Delicately sung.
    Zart hervortretend. Softly prominent.
    Zart und liebevoll. Tender and affectionate.
Zartflöte (Ger.). A 4 ft stop on the organ, the *flauto dolce.*
Zärtlich (Ger.). Sweetly, tenderly.
    Zärtlich bewegt. Gently stirred, with gentle movement.
    Zärtlichkeit. Tenderness, affection.
Zarzuela (Sp.). An opera with spoken dialogue; an operetta.
Zeffiroso (It.). Like a zephyr. Term indicating a very light delicate execution.

Zehn (Ger.). Ten.

Zeichen (Ger.). Sign, indication.

Zeigefinger (Ger.). The index or first finger.

Zeit (Ger.). Time.

    Zeitdauer der Noten. The time-duration (value) of notes.

    Zeiteinteilung. The division of the time (movement).

    Zeit lassen. Allow time, do not hurry.

    Zeitmass, Zeitmaß. (Spelt in Wagner's works as "Zeitmaass".) Measure, time, tempo. *Das Zeitmaß sehr allmählich beschleunigen*, very gradually quicken the tempo.

    Zeitmass des ersten Stückes. Time of the first piece.

    Zeitmesser. A metronome.

Zelante (It.). Zealous, fervent, ardent.

Zèle (Fr.).
Zelo (It.). } Zeal, ardour.

Zelosamente (It.). Zealously, ardently.

Zeloso, -a (It.). Zealous, full of affection.

Zerfließend (Ger.). Melting away, dying away.

Zergliederung (Ger.). Analysis, dissection (of a chord, etc.).

Zerstreut (Ger.). Dispersed, scattered.

    Zerstreute Harmonie. Extended harmony.

Ziehen (Ger.). To draw; to string a violin; to draw-out, sustain.

Ziehharmonika (Ger.). The accordion.

Ziemlich (Ger.). Moderately.

    Ziemlich bewegt. Moderately stirred, with moderate movement.

    Ziemlich geschwind, doch kräftig. Moderately quick, but powerfully.

    Ziemlich langsam. Moderately slow.

    Ziemlich lebendig. Moderately animated.

    Ziemlich lebhaft. Moderately fast.

    Ziemlich rasch. Moderately rapid.

    Ziemlich schnell. Moderately fast.

Zierlich (Ger.). Graceful, elegant, dainty.

    Zierlichkeit. Gracefulness, prettiness, daintiness.

Zierat(h)en (Ger.). Ornaments.

Zigeuner (Ger.). A gipsy.

    Zigeunerartig. In the gipsy style.

    Zigeunermarsch. A gipsy march.

    Zigeunermusik. Gipsy music.

Zilafone (It.). A xylophone.

Zingano, -a (It.). A gipsy. *Zingana*, a gipsy song or ballad.

Zingara (It.). A gipsy (fem.). plur. *Zingare*.

Zingaresca (It.). A gipsy song.

Zingaro (It.). A gipsy (masc.). plur. *Zingari*.

Zinke (Ger.). (1) A *cornet à bouquin* (*q. v.*). (2) A reed organ stop. Both now obsolete.

Zither. An instrument possessing some 30 or 40 strings, of which 5 or 6 are used for the melody and plucked by a plectrum fastened on to the thumb, while the remainder are employed to form an accompaniment and are played by the four fingers. The melody strings are placed above a fingerboard with frets as in a guitar. For instruments with 36 strings the compass is from B_1 to f''.

Zittern (Ger.). To quiver, tremble. When used as a noun, it is equivalent to *Bebung* (*q. v.*).

    Zittern der Stimme. Faltering.

Zitternd (Ger.). Quivering, tremulous, *tremolando*.

Zögernd (Ger.). Lingering, hesitating, *ritardando*.

Zoppo, -a (It.). Lame, halting: syncopated.

Zornig (Ger.). Incensed, irate.

Zu (Ger.). To, at, by, for, in.

    Zu sehr. Too much, *troppo*.

    Zu zwei Händen. For two hands.

    Zu vier Händen. For four hands.

    Zu 2. Used in the sense of *a* 2, and meaning either that 2 instruments play the same part, or, less frequently, that a number of instruments playing one part divide into two.

Zufällig (Ger.). Accidental, casual.

    Zufälligkeitszeichen. Accidentals. (Flats, sharps, naturals.)

Zuf(f)olare (It.). To whistle; to play on a whistle or flute.

Zuf(f)olino (It.). Whistling; a small flute or fife.

Zuf(f)olo (It.). A whistle, pipe, flageolet.

Zug (Ger.). (1) A draw-stop on an organ or harmonium. (2) The slide of a trombone or trumpet. (3) The pedal of a piano.

    Zugknöpfe. Composition studs or buttons.

    Zugposaune. Slide trombone.

    Zugtrompete. Slide trumpet.

    Zugwerk. The mechanism in general of the draw-stops.

Zum (Ger.). Combination of *zu* and *dem*, to the, for the, etc.

    Zum Privatgebrauch. For private use. Term often found on full scores, and meaning that the copy must not be used for public performance.

Zunehmend (Ger.). Increasing, *crescendo*.

    Zunehmende Bewegung. Increasing movement, becoming faster.

Zunge (Ger.). A tongue. Of instruments, a reed. plur. and in combination, *Zungen*.

    Zungenblatt. The reed of a clarinet.

    Zungenpfeife. A reed pipe on an organ.

    Zungenschlag. On wind-instruments, tonguing. *Alle in den Bläsern als ♪ notierten Stellen sind mit Zungenschlag auszuführen*, all passages in the Wind marked ♪ are to be tongued.

    Zungenstimmen. Reed pipes in an organ.

    Zungenstoß. The attack with the tongue (on a brass instrument).

Zungenwerk. Reed-work in an organ.

Zupfend (Ger.). Plucking, *pizzicato*.

Zurück (Ger.). Back, backwards, behind. A word often used in combination.

    Zurückführend. Leading back.

    Zurückgehend. Going back, returning.

    Zurückhaltend. Holding back, restraining, slackening.

    Zurückhaltung. A holding back.

    Zurückkehrend. Returning. *Wieder zurückkehrend in das Hauptzeitmaß*, again returning to the main tempo.

Zurückstimmen. To tune back, to retune. *C nach H zurück-stimmen,* tune C back to B.

Zus. Abbr. of *Zusammen.*

Zusammen (Ger.). Together, at the same time, in all.

    Zusammen 3 Schläger. 3 drummers in all.

    Zusammengesetzt. Composed, made up of.

    Zusammensetzung. Something put together; a composition.

    Zusammenklang. Harmony, concord.

    Zusammenziehend. Drawing together, *stringendo.*

Zwei (Ger.). Two.

    Zwei Bratschen allein (1tes Pult). Two violas alone (1st desk).

    Zweichörig. For two choirs: on a piano, two strings to one note.

    Zweifach, 2fach. Two-fold.

    Zweifüßig. Two foot (adj.). A term applied to 2ft organ pipes.

    Zweigesang. A duet.

    Zweigestrichene Oktave. Twice accented octave, c'' to b''.

    Zweihalbe Takt. $^2/_2$ time.

    Zweihändig. For two hands.

    Zweimal. Twice.

    Zweistimmig. For two voices or parts.

    Zweitaktig. Two-bar rhythm.

    Zweiunddreißigstel. A demisemiquaver.

    Zweivierteltakt. $^2/_4$ time.

Zweite, Zweites (Ger.). Second.

    Zweite Lage. Second position.

    Zweites Paar. Second pair.

Zwischen (Ger.). Between.

    Zwischenakt. Between the acts, *entr'acte.*

    Zwischenaktmusik. Music played between the acts.

    Zwischenraum. Space between the lines of the stave.

    Zwischensatz. An episode.

    Zwischenschlag. The two grace notes at the end of a shake. *v.* Nachschlag.

    Zwischenspiel. Interlude. The symphony between the verses of a song.

    Zwischenton. An intermediate note.

Zwölf (Ger.). Twelve.

    Zwölfachteltakt. $^{12}/_8$ time.

Printed by Breitkopf & Härtel in Leipzig.